THE ENDURING ENTERPRISE

HOW FAMILY BUSINESSES THRIVE IN TURBULENT CONDITIONS

DEVIN DeCIANTIS AND IVAN LANSBERG

PUBLICAFFAIRS
New York

PublicAffairs
Hachette Book Group
1290 Avenue of the Americas, New York, NY 10104
www.publicaffairsbooks.com
@Public_Affairs

Printed in the United States of America

First Edition: November 2024

Published by PublicAffairs, an imprint of Hachette Book Group, Inc. The PublicAffairs name and logo is a registered trademark of the Hachette Book Group.

Library of Congress Cataloging-in-Publication Data

Names: DeCiantis, Devin, author. | Lansberg, Ivan, 1954- author.
Title: The enduring enterprise : how family businesses thrive in turbulent conditions / Devin DeCiantis and Ivan Lansberg.
Description: First edition. | New York : PublicAffairs, 2024. | Includes bibliographical references and index.
Identifiers: LCCN 2024034854 | ISBN 9781541703650 (hardcover) | ISBN 9781541703674 (epub)
Subjects: LCSH: Family-owned business enterprises.
Classification: LCC HD62.25 .D38 2024 | DDC 658/.045—dc23/eng/20240814
LC record available at https://lccn.loc.gov/2024034854

ISBNs: 9781541703650 (hardcover), 9781541703674 (ebook)

LSC-C

Printing 1, 2024

To Nathalie and Margarita, our greatest sources of stability,
and to Oskar, Zara, Michelle, Claudia, and Dario,
our inspiration and urgency for the enduring work that lies ahead

CONTENTS

PART 1
THE NEW AGE OF UNCERTAINTY

Doubt is not a pleasant condition, but certainty is absurd.
—Voltaire

Uncertainty is rarely the first topic to arise at a cocktail party, or the breakfast table, or even the boardroom. If anything, the modern world has been designed to reinforce a sense of perpetual predictability. Those of us fortunate enough to live in affluent societies have learned to expect that light will brighten a dark room at the flip of a switch, clean water will flow with a twist of a faucet, and a few taps on our phones will bring fresh groceries to our doorstep, or an Uber to shuttle us safely to dinner. With so much convenience and certainty, it's easy to take for granted the many invisible institutions and infrastructures—both private and public—that enable such an effortless, on-demand lifestyle, 24/7/365.

It is only once we step outside of the comfort and safety of these so-called advanced economies that we begin to understand how control is just an illusion: a superficial layer of stability masking much deeper structural volatility. In these less predictable environments, we are reminded that uncertainty is the rule rather than the exception. Blackouts are pervasive, potable water is a luxury, grocery shelves are often bare, and it's best to avoid getting into cars with strangers.

This book is about how enterprising families have managed to thrive for generations under precisely these conditions, and what their survival and success have to teach business leaders everywhere. Why, you might wonder, would operating in New Delhi or Lagos have any relevance to some of the world's most sophisticated businesses in New York or London? The answer is simple: stability within these privileged environments is evaporating before our very eyes. Polarization is increasing and trust in institutions is declining, a sharp reversal of a global trend that has supported economic development and commercial activity for nearly a century. Consequently, success will require a fundamentally different approach to governance, organizational design, and business strategy.

As you'll learn in the chapters ahead, family enterprises operating in frontier economies have developed a unique form of resilience[1] to help them thrive in turbulent times. In fact, some of the most incredible examples of resilience and innovation in modern corporate history were forged during protracted crises. The stories of DuPont and Cargill during the American Civil War and Marriott during the Great Depression remind us that uncertainty is as inescapable as gravity—a natural force that has guided human affairs for thousands of years, and one requiring a special form of strategic vigilance and foresight.

What then should we make of the past half-century of unprecedented economic, political, and social progress? Though we may not have reached the "end of history" that some thought possible after the Cold War, haven't we at least achieved an "end of uncertainty"? In many ways, the decades since the end of World War II have been a golden age of stability and prosperity—certainly for those living and working in the West.[2]

In the most affluent societies, the rise of sophisticated public and private institutions spawned technologies, networks, and infrastructure that improved countless lives and generated vast fortunes. They incubated some of the largest and most valuable companies in history, from Microsoft and Apple to Tesla and Walmart. But they also unleashed powerful economic, ideological, and environmental forces that are increasingly shrinking corporate lifespans, destabilizing entire industries, and threatening the modern world order.[3]

For the handful of countries that created, sustained, and benefited most directly from these oases of stability, the coming storm will be most disruptive. Like immune systems that haven't been exposed to diseases in years, their governments, companies, and citizens have no living memory of what it's like to navigate tumultuous waters, and they are ill-prepared for the greater volatility that lies ahead. Over the past several decades of relative peace and prosperity, they have become less resistant to new threats, and are now more fragile and prone to collapse.

However, outside this privileged club of advanced nations, instability and scarcity are endemic, as they have been for most of human existence. Consequently, those living and working in emerging and frontier economies are naturally better prepared for the New Age of Uncertainty that lies ahead, and their experience provides us with extraordinary lessons about resilience[4] and longevity.

Rising Uncertainty Is a Global Phenomenon

World Uncertainty Index paints an ominous picture

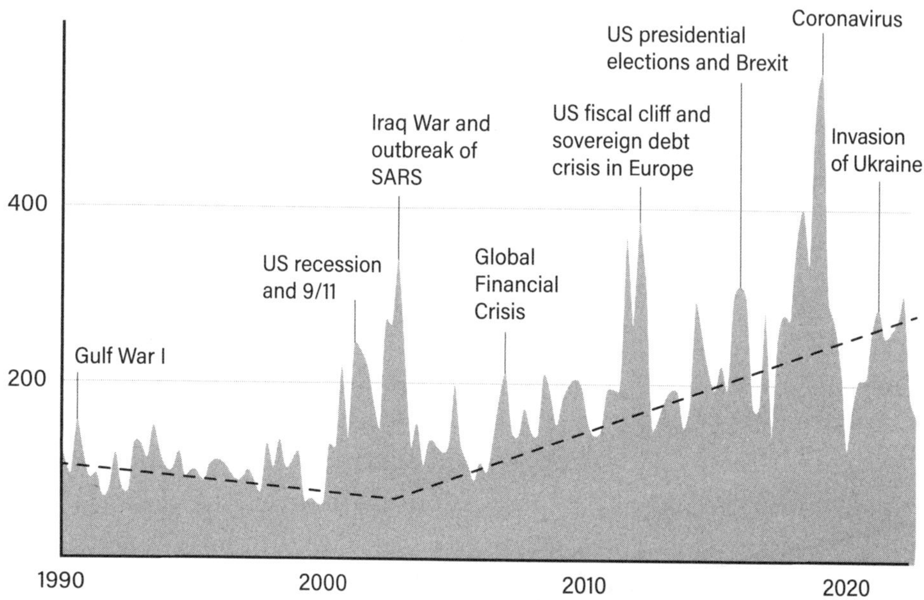

Source: Ahir, H, N Bloom, and D Furceri (2022), "World Uncertainty Index", NBER Working Paper.

RISKY BUSINESS

Both as scholars and practitioners, we've always been deeply interested in economic development, inspired by our diverse ethnicities (including Lebanese, Italian, Venezuelan, and Dutch). That said, we first became interested in writing about risk in the wake of a crisis—a literary tradition that goes back to the dawn of recorded history.[5] From ancient battles through the middle and modern ages, many curious minds have sought to understand how the world's great empires—both political and economic—were so prone to rise and fall.

The initial catalyst to develop and share our own perspectives on risk was the onset of the Global Financial Crisis in 2007. At the time, many business leaders, policymakers, academics, and citizens were just beginning to understand that a complex modern society—one that had previously seemed so powerful and resilient—could in fact be quite fragile and prone to systemic collapse. However, it was only years later, on June 18, 2014, that our early research took an unexpected turn, changing our understanding of organizational resilience in the face of chronically elevated uncertainty.

That morning, we received an article from a close friend about a shooting at a hotel in downtown Caracas. A German businessman had arrived at Simon Bolivar International Airport and gotten into an armored car with his security detail. Together they drove into the heart of the city and up the long winding driveway of the Eurobuilding Hotel, one of the few luxury properties remaining in Venezuela's capital. As he stepped out of the car and into the gilded foyer, he was promptly gunned down by two armed assailants, who snatched his briefcase and sped away on their motorcycle into the chaotic downtown traffic.

While this was clearly a dramatic event, the story isn't particularly remarkable for anyone who has been tracking the slow-motion train wreck that is modern Venezuela. After all, in that same year there were an estimated 24,000 murders in the city of Caracas—more than Baghdad at the height of the US occupation—making it the murder capital of the world. That's over 65 murders every single day. To put this in context, in major American cities of a similar size (such as Los Angeles, Chicago, or Houston), there were between 100 and 600 murders that year, or less than two per day.

But the most intriguing detail from that particular story was the scene of the crime. We often stayed at the very same hotel when visiting our clients in Venezuela, including once only weeks before the shooting. What's more, we followed the exact same sequence from the airport into the city. That article could easily have been written about us.

As you can imagine, these parallels elicited a predictable range of reactions from the mundane to the sublime. For instance, we prioritized finding a more secure hotel for future visits and doubled down on personal security. We also began meeting in neighboring countries where our client had built a network of offshore distributors, and took comfort in the protected status of health-care companies within the otherwise anti-capitalist Chavista regime. Most importantly, we gained a deeper and more visceral understanding of what it means to operate daily under conditions of elevated uncertainty and diminished trust, and how this is categorically different from what gets taught in most Western business schools.

This incident prompted a broader reflection that now seems obvious in hindsight, though at the time it was hiding in plain view. There are many parts of the world where external stability is elusive, and existential crises are not acute but chronic. To survive and thrive in these environments, leaders need to focus on building internal stability before investing in growth. For instance, when supply chain disruptions are pervasive, many organizations build redundancy and diversity directly into their core operating model. Despite the added cost and inefficiency, their mantra is "just in case," not "just in time." This focus on resilience may fly in the face of Western "best practices," but it is also necessary for survival and success.

As we dug deeper into these structural differences, we also observed another unique characteristic—the extremely high prevalence and influence of enterprising families in volatile environments. Early in the book, we'll examine how family businesses are the dominant organizational form in these economies, representing up to 90 percent of all economic activity, employment, and R&D. Many of these businesses are so-called mom-and-pop shops—local restaurants, convenience stores, retailers. But some are among the largest and most systemically important private enterprises on the planet, global brands that many of us would easily recognize (though often not as family-controlled), and they each overcame significant odds on their path to success.

Interestingly, we found that these families are more inclined to invest in, and care for, the communities they serve. Some even take it upon themselves to build critical public infrastructures that are often overlooked by local governments, yet which enable commercial and social life to flourish. In both our research and our work, we've seen countless examples of family firms investing in roads, bridges, hospitals, schools, community centers, housing, and even telecommunications grids to help fill these institutional voids. The willingness to take on this role naturally fosters loyal and trustworthy partners, customers, and employees, generating another unique source of resilience while also driving economic development.

To be clear, our families can be sources of both organizational stability and instability, as Ivan knows only too well. He grew up in Venezuela, where his father founded Segurosca, which evolved into Grupo Lansberg, among the largest insurance brokerages in Latin America. While he never held a managerial role, Ivan was in graduate school when the succession planning exercise began, and he sat in on many of the meetings. In the end, Ivan's older brother and a non-family executive took control of the business, committing to a fast growth strategy fueled by debt financing at a time when the country was about to enter into an economic tailspin. Shortly after the transition, interest rates shot up, the new leaders were unable to keep servicing the debt, and the business eventually failed. It left Ivan with a strong sense of the complexity of managing a business at a time of acute crisis, as well as the ancient truth that through adversity, lessons can be learned and a deeper understanding can emerge. A more nuanced view, therefore, requires us to understand families as both a feature and a bug of modern capitalism.

WHY UNCERTAINTY MATTERS

This book is a product of our own experiences and our curiosity about what it takes to succeed in turbulent times. It reflects an eclectic combination of academic and intellectual interests inspired by our different backgrounds. One of us grew up in Canada—among the safest places on Earth, though not without its own extremes. The other was born amid the lush beauty of Venezuela during the golden age of Latin American development—then observed with sadness and frustration the country's descent into economic and political chaos. One of us is naturally inclined to an "outside-in," systems-level view—particularly through the lens of macroeconomics, geopolitics, and ecology. The other is more inclined to an "inside-out" view—particularly the dynamic family enterprise systems that shape our understanding of the world and form the building blocks of modern civilization.

These diverse perspectives have enriched our friendship, partnership, and scholarship for years. Consequently, writing this book together was a great joy, and an opportunity to capture our latest thinking on what it takes to achieve enduring intergenerational success. It was informed by decades of research and teaching at the Kellogg School of Management and Harvard University, and especially through our work advising leading families around the world over the past thirty years. After all, as Kurt Lewin, the father of social psychology, once observed, "If you want truly to understand something, try to change it."

We quickly realized that popular business school case studies about the Waltons and Arnaults didn't reflect the complex realities our clients and students were facing in places like São Paulo and Mumbai, where operating conditions would make a Fortune 500 CEO blush. Nor were they well suited to prepare leaders for moments of crisis and turmoil, as many now expect virtually everywhere in the years ahead. So we studied both G7 countries like the United States and Canada (where predictability has been the norm for most of our living memory), and, importantly, those less-well-understood family businesses operating fearlessly in frontier economies like Venezuela and Ukraine (where disruption is a daily ritual).

In some cases, we discovered that entrepreneurial endurance was an intentional goal, emerging from proactive planning and the anticipation of adversity. For others, it was the gift of good fortune: being in the right place at the right time. Still others learned the hard way from catastrophic failure, and found the strength and stamina to pivot and rebuild. Importantly, in every case featured throughout the book, we found that the owning families themselves played a critical role in helping their enterprises to adapt and grow.

Building on these insights, we begin the book in Part 1 by laying out both the familiar and the unfamiliar contours of the "frontiers of capitalism"—that is, the unique challenges and opportunities that come with leading a private enterprise under conditions of chronic scarcity and turmoil. We then explore the origins of stability, and how social systems invest with intention to exert greater control over their environment. This includes an introduction to external stabilizers, such as private contracts and public markets, which operate like lighthouses in a storm, encouraging individuals to venture out in search of commercial opportunity. We also include a thorough examination of internal stabilizers, such as a family's core values and risk management systems, which act like the ballasts on a ship and help organizations remain on course. Such stabilizing investments are not random, but fall into seven distinct and replicable patterns, which, as we'll show, can be strategically deployed before, during, and after a crisis to enhance performance.

Then in Part 2 we dive into the heart of our framework and examine these stabilizing strategies one at a time. In each chapter we introduce an iconic case study that exemplifies a particular strategy, which we'll then explore in greater detail. These will include:

- A Peruvian family that built a soft drink company from the ground up during an active terrorist conflict, whose company has since become an international giant challenging first-world multinationals.
- A Korean family best known for exporting dried fish, before being tapped by a visionary government to help modernize the country, eventually becoming a global titan of technology and industry.
- A Syrian family whose entrepreneurial successes were unceremoniously seized after a military coup, forcing them to migrate into a neighboring country to start from scratch, where they rebuilt an international empire.

- A Haitian family whose iconic hotel business has been tested by every form of disaster imaginable, from earthquakes to coups to rampant crime and economic collapse, yet has endured against the odds.
- An Indian family that started its business in cotton exports under the British Raj, pioneering some of the most progressive worker benefits and social programs in history, before growing into one of the largest and most successful global conglomerates.

These cases, and many others throughout the book, will demonstrate how seven stabilizing strategies have helped enduring enterprises for centuries in the face of constant adversity, and that it's always best to be prepared.

Finally, Part 3 brings us back "up to the balcony" to explore how we can apply these inspiring stories and fresh insights to our own families, organizations, and communities. We introduce a comprehensive framework for navigating crises with confidence, managing risk in an age of uncertainty, and building an enduring enterprise that can stand the tests of time. These lessons from the frontiers of capitalism will be helpful for anyone unexpectedly confronted with risks, whether conventional ones like economic recessions, or "fat tail" disruptions such as 9/11, major pandemics like COVID-19, or international conflicts like those in Ukraine and the Middle East.

By the end of the book, you will have a new inventory of tools and inspirational case studies to leverage in good times and bad, a greater appreciation for the unique role of enterprising families in the global economy, and an achievable path to building greater resilience and long-term success wherever you live, work, and play.

1

INTRODUCING THE FRONTIERS OF CAPITALISM

Trust is like the air we breathe. When it's present, nobody really notices; when it's absent, everybody notices.

—Warren Buffett

Trust is the great accelerant of modern civilization. It encourages bankers to lend and merchants to trade with confidence. It allows consumers to enjoy high-quality goods and trains to run on time. It helps us treat strangers like friends, and friends like family.

Leading thinkers from Confucius to Adam Smith to Francis Fukuyama have recognized that all social order begins in families, where kinship is naturally hardwired into our ancient brains.[1] Step beyond our kin, however, and trusting strangers requires specific cultural and environmental conditions—external stabilizers that encourage us to venture out into the world with confidence.

For those of us who live and work in advanced postindustrial societies, consider how seamlessly we hop into an Uber and trust a complete stranger to deliver us promptly and safely to our destination—without a dollar physically changing hands. Then consider that for most of human history, trusting strangers with our lives and livelihoods was a reckless fantasy.

The German sociologist Georg Simmel was an early observer of this phenomenon, drawing from his experience migrating from the German countryside into Berlin during the frenzied urbanization of the late nineteenth century. Unlike many of his contemporaries, who saw humanity's future in sprawling new cities, Simmel argued that we would be better off living in smaller communities, where family could provide an intrinsic source of stability and support. In these socially fragmented environments, trust is nurtured within extended networks of relatives, rather than manufactured "synthetically" through commercial contracts. But in the growing industrial cities of Western Europe, for the first time in history, new urban denizens were more likely to trade with strangers than with family, rarely with the same stranger twice, and increasingly via common currencies rather than personal favors or credit.[2]

These economic and organizational developments prompted a shift away from the foundational constructs of Confucius and Aristotle that celebrated our natural trust in family—what Simmel's colleague Ferdinand Tönnies called *Gemeinschaft*, or informal "communities." In its place, various structures and incentives emerged to induce broader trust in "the system"—what Tönnies called *Gesellschaft*, or formal "societies."

Prior to this mass urban migration, we were more likely to visit our town baker to purchase bread on credit (*Gemeinschaft*) than shop at Walmart with a tap of our phone (*Gesellschaft*). Though it may seem trivial to modern observers, such change is more than just a shift in habits. This more transactional form of exchange also requires additional stabilizing infrastructures like reliable banks, courts, and regulators, which help us to build trust in the quality of the bread, and in the value of the currency changing hands. It also requires reliable power grids, telecommunications networks, supply chains, and public markets to ensure that growing populations can access these basic resources whenever and wherever they want.

Over centuries, the scale, scope, and sophistication of these public institutions became one of the distinguishing features of the most *advanced economies*—market democracies such as the United States, Japan, and Germany, with high incomes and sophisticated social welfare programs. These high-trust, high-growth environments naturally accelerate the pace of investment and innovation. After all, when stability and abundance are underwritten by governments, businesses and households can focus almost exclusively on their private aspirations.

Contrast this with *emerging economies* like China, Brazil, and India, which have experienced rapid economic growth and development in recent decades but still face endemic challenges, including poverty, inequality, and corruption that limit their full economic potential and global influence. Success in these environments requires a mix of growth and resilience—because periods of rapid economic development are still punctuated by intermittent currency crises, political turmoil, natural disasters, and social unrest. With fewer external stabilizers available to enhance trust in the system, businesses and households can only afford to keep one eye on the future, with the other focused with vigilance on the present.

Now consider what it's like to operate in *frontier economies*—countries such as Nigeria, Vietnam, and Venezuela, where political instability, social unrest, and economic volatility are rampant. Success in these environments is a Darwinian tournament of the fittest. Only the most resilient are able to cope with these primordial economic conditions and overcome the endemic lack of trust in all but their closest relatives.[3] The prime directive here is collective survival, and any planning for the future beyond the next year or two is a willful act of fantasy.

THE GREAT ACCELERANT

Nobel Prize–winning economist Kenneth Arrow was among the first to study these structural differences in the early 1970s. In his classic work "Gifts and Exchanges," he observed that "virtually every commercial transaction has within itself an element of trust, certainly any transaction conducted over a period of time." He argued that "much of the economic backwardness in the world can be explained by the lack of mutual confidence."[4] In advanced economies, trust is truly like the air we breathe—an abundant resource we barely notice, but that enables commercial life to proliferate. In frontier economies, trust is elusive, and economic activity is consequently stifled.

Consider what it takes for us to feel comfortable buying from, selling to, investing in, or borrowing from a stranger. Above all else, we need a reasonable expectation that if we come to some agreement, the baker, the banker, or the broker with whom we're transacting will honor their end of the bargain. Additionally, if for some reason they don't, we need mechanisms such as contracts and courts to seek justice.

Without these external stabilizers, strangers will struggle to engage in mutually beneficial exchange, as they have throughout history. Humanity will remain locked in a primeval *bellum omnium contra omnes*, or "war of all against all," as Thomas Hobbes warned in the mid-seventeenth century. Such institutions influence how individuals, families, organizations, and nations build and sustain trust over time, and are a key driver of social order, economic growth, and business strategy. In short, they enable the more predictable conditions within which economies can flourish.[5]

Throughout this book, we'll use the term "institutions" to refer to the norms, laws, processes, organizations, and infrastructures that establish and enforce the "rules of the game" in social and economic affairs. By reducing the uncertainty that comes with trading goods and services with strangers, they exponentially increase the breadth and depth of commercial activity. Compounded over time, these institutions are powerful drivers of development. They represent one of the most important structural advantages of advanced economies over their less affluent peers.

In their 2012 best-selling book *Why Nations Fail*, professors Daron Acemoglu from the Massachusetts Institute of Technology and James A. Robinson from Harvard University make a compelling case that such institutions are the primary determinants of whether a society provides stability and generates welfare for all, or concentrates power and resources in the hands of the elite, leaving the rest vulnerable to shocks and collapse. These institutions come in two distinct flavors—inclusive and extractive—each of which profoundly affects economic and political outcomes over time.

Inclusive institutions help to accelerate economic development, much like fertilizing a growing garden, by protecting basic rights and freedoms and encouraging broad participation in economic affairs. When property rights are respected, businesses and citizens are more inclined to invest and innovate. When justice systems are fair and impartial, contracts can be easily enforced and disputes can be resolved without fear or favor. When public services are reliable, more people can access opportunities and participate in commercial and social life. Perhaps most importantly, when political power is broadly distributed, governments become more accountable and responsive to citizens.

Most popular business and management literature is focused precisely on how to operate effectively within these well-regulated environments, where trust and stability are ubiquitous. Today's largest and most successful corporations are precisely engineered to capitalize on systemic predictability and abundance.

Yet the vast majority of humanity lives outside of these privileged bubbles. In these environments, extractive institutions are more pervasive, exploiting political and economic systems for the benefit of dynastic elites. As a result, citizens are less likely to engage in commerce and trade, since they are less likely to trust "the system" and feel the rules are rigged against them. Acemoglu and Robinson make a compelling case that "a businessman who expects his output to be stolen, expropriated, or entirely taxed away will have little incentive to work, let alone any incentive to undertake investments and innovations."[6]

Counterintuitively, we found that trust still abounds in these exotic environments, as does economic activity. It's simply focused on areas that receive far less attention than they deserve in the management literature, in boardrooms, and in the halls of government.

On these exotic frontiers of commercial activity, enterprising families help to bring safety and stability to the otherwise turbulent rhythms of daily life, and they do so in some remarkably counterintuitive ways. Unlike their peers in the "Global North," these enduring families have navigated uncertainty for most of their history, and are much less fazed by "black swan" events—those unexpected, highly impactful shocks that challenge our deepest assumptions and biases. Under these conditions, families are prepared to wake up one morning and discover that their companies have been nationalized, their access to foreign currency has been restricted, a shareholder or executive has been kidnapped, or their employees are facing sniper fire on the way to work.

In the absence of reliable institutional stabilizers, enterprising families are forced to invest in stability privately, deploying a unique portfolio of strategies such as redundancy and simplification, which we'll introduce in Chapter 4 and explore in detail in Part 2. To be clear, we're not arguing that these private investments are a durable replacement for public stabilizers. Nor are we ignoring the fact that the relative "stability" achieved by some dynastic families can inhibit broader economic development. But as we'll argue throughout the book, we believe these investments are essential for surviving and thriving in turbulent times.

In contrast, for those born and raised in advanced economies, sudden expropriation, currency devaluation, and social unrest remain the stuff of history or science fiction—dramatic events for binge watching, not the daily grind of corporate governance or firm management. Such existential crises are inconceivable to many leaders operating exclusively in Western capitals. Moreover, when shocks occasionally do emerge, businesses and citizens can rely on progressive public institutions, such as disaster management agencies, corporate bailouts, and stimulus checks, to deliver them safely from harm.

These more generous and sophisticated institutional stabilizers are among the most distinguishing features of advanced economies. They also don't emerge overnight. Gordon Brown, the former British prime minister, captured this challenge artfully, saying, "In establishing the rule of law, the first five centuries are always the hardest."[7]

Without the benefit of a "Magna Carta Moment" in the distant past, businesses and citizens in frontier economies must endure what Western sociologists call "institutional voids"—gaps in public systems and infrastructures that persist wherever public governance is weak, inefficient, and unscrupulous. Under these conditions, there is a natural scarcity of capital, resources, and talent, and consequently more limited economic activity. After all, when the goods and services we purchase are faulty or dangerous, the incentive to consume them declines. Similarly, when the companies we build are taken by force and our ideas copied without our permission, the incentive to invest is suppressed.

Such institutional failures are endemic to frontier economies and clearly make commercial success more difficult. But they are not a death sentence. Thriving under these conditions simply requires a fundamentally different approach to strategic planning—one that balances resilience with growth and that harnesses the unique advantages of family capitalism.

THE FAMILY FACTOR

Two colleagues at the Harvard Business School, Tarun Khanna and Krishna G. Palepu, significantly advanced our understanding of how businesses need to adapt their strategies to compete effectively outside of the world's few advanced economies. We first came across their work on the Creating Emerging Markets (CEM) project at Harvard several years ago while interviewing family business leaders who also participated directly in their study.[8]

Their focus, like ours, was on how businesses survive and thrive both in growth and through turbulence, and the interviews they published reinforced many of the themes we explore throughout this book. Drawing on candid interviews with leaders from over 180 companies—spanning Africa, Asia, Latin America, and the Middle East—the authors identified a chronic lack of institutional trust as the biggest structural difference between advanced and emerging economies. They also demonstrated how these distinct institutional contexts drive organizational structures and operational strategies—a perspective that is entirely consistent with our own research and experience.

However, while they highlighted "reputation" as a key driver of long-run survival, we found it odd that *family* was mostly overlooked.[9] Though nearly half of the businesses featured in the CEM study were owned and operated by families, in a seminal paper by Khanna and his colleagues summarizing their latest research, the term "family" was used only once in over 14,000 words.[10]

Yet in Georg Simmel's idyllic *Gemeinschaft*, and in frontier environments more generally, it is families—rather than governments or markets—that are uniquely capable of fostering microclimates of trust. Their multigenerational networks lower the frictional costs of doing business with organizations big and small, providing an essential lubricant for commercial activity that is often overlooked and underappreciated.

In the face of chronic uncertainty, it is families who invest in creating oases of stability, both for themselves and for their key stakeholders. Like the gated communities that line the sandy coastlines of virtually every country in the Global South, families often take stability into their own hands, deploying their own capital—physical, human, social, and

Emerging and Frontier Economies Are Driving Global Growth...

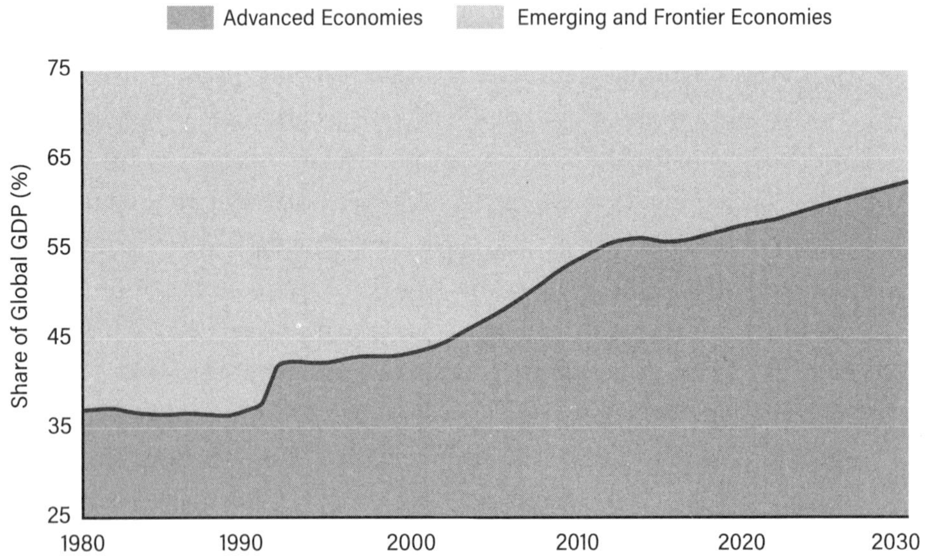

...Precisely Where Family Business Influence Is Greatest

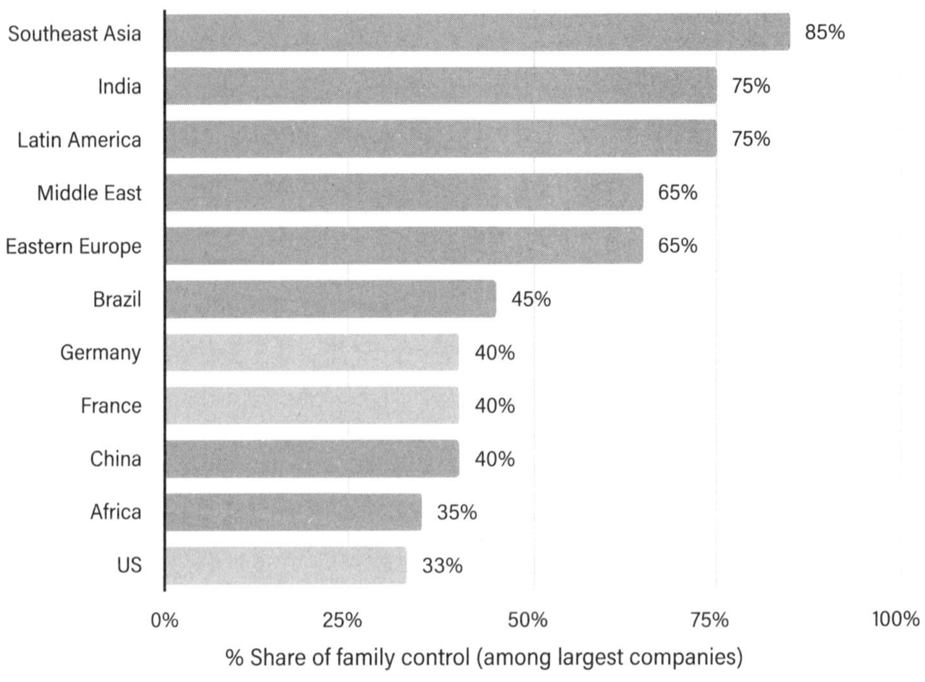

Source: IMF, McKinsey, *The Economist*

financial—to fill the institutional voids left by dysfunctional markets, incoherent regulations, ineffective security, and unreliable infrastructure.

"Family capitalism" consequently becomes embedded, both informally and formally, in the institutional frameworks that support every emerging and frontier economy. This helps to explain why family businesses represent such a disproportionate share of activity and influence in these exotic locales.

While it may not seem obvious to the uninitiated, family enterprises are, in fact, the dominant organizational form in modern capitalism.[11] Though only one-fifth of Fortune 500 companies are family-controlled, outside the United States that number can rise to as high as 90 percent of all business activity and employment. Western business schools and market commentators mainly focus on blue chips, tech titans, and big banks, but the real drivers of our modern global economy are enterprising families. This is especially so in unstable emerging and frontier economies, where much of the world's wealth and development will be generated in the decades ahead, and where success often requires flipping organizational designs and strategic plans on their head.[12]

DANCING LANDSCAPES

Navigating crises, particularly when life is at stake, has a way of focusing our attention on the essentials. From droughts and recessions to wars and depressions, extreme conditions squeeze every ounce of ingenuity out of all dynamic systems. In that way, all frontiers of survival are similar and have much to teach each other. During our early research, we were particularly inspired by the structural similarities between organizational and biological systems. As Nobel laureate August Krogh argued nearly a century ago: "For a large number of problems there will be some animal of choice, or a few such animals, on which it can be most conveniently studied."[13]

Over billions of years, survival has been hardwired into nature's deepest operating systems. As a result, even the most treacherous corners of our home planet are teeming with life forms most of us have never seen or even imagined—from heat-resistant bacteria thriving in active volcanoes, to bioluminescent fish lurking deep in the oceans, to slimy biofilms coating the walls of radioactive mines.[14]

Prior to the mid-1970s, there was little interest in business and science to study each other for clues into resilience under adverse conditions. But that all changed when a new class of ultra-resilient microbial organisms was discovered, upending centuries of conventional wisdom about the conditions necessary for sustaining organic life.[15]

It turns out that nature is replete with so-called *extremophiles*—species that not only survive but actually thrive in extremely hostile conditions. Their existence shouldn't surprise us. As Andreas Weber, a philosopher of biology, once wrote, "Everything that lives wants more of life."[16] That said, these hearty organisms take survival to the next level. Some are capable of coping with extreme temperatures and pressures, while others are unfazed by extreme radiation and acidity that would kill most other forms of life.[17] As scientists have unlocked the secrets of their invincibility, their discoveries have prompted major breakthroughs in biotechnologies (such as cold-active enzymes), material sciences (biopolymers), pharmaceuticals (antibiotics), and agriculture (biofertilizers), to name just a few.

These hearty creatures remind us how much our external context frames the structural and behavioral conditions necessary for enduring success. Such "systems thinking" goes back to Georg Simmel, Émile Durkheim, and their pioneering community of early sociologists. But it significantly expanded in the 1940s and 1950s through the efforts of physicists, biologists, and engineers who recognized that all systems—from individual organisms to complex organizations to entire societies—are powerfully influenced by their dynamic external environments. Concluding that nature's secrets weren't isolated to any one domain of knowledge or experience, they developed a more holistic perspective of the forces shaping biological and organizational fitness.

Many of these groundbreaking ideas were incubated at the Santa Fe Institute (SFI), a nonprofit research center that emerged in the 1980s in direct response to the siloed thinking among hard scientists and humanists. Ever since, the SFI has been at the forefront of interdisciplinary research on complex systems, bringing together insights from physics, biology, economics, sociology, computer science, and even astronomy to "search for order in the complexity of evolving worlds."[18]

One of the faculty members at SFI, Dr. Scott Page, developed a visual metaphor to explain systems-level complexity that aligns intuitively with our research on thriving in the face of uncertainty. He describes a landscape where organizational performance is like an elevation, where peaks mean business successes while valleys mean failures or collapse. Building on this logic, Page argues that all environments fall into one of three distinct categories: simple, rugged, or dancing, each with its own unique topography.

Think of *simple landscapes* as representing "Mount Fuji" problems, named after the symmetrical topography of Japan's iconic, solitary, white-capped peak. Under these relatively straightforward conditions, performance functions can be solved relatively easily, since there is a single optimal outcome (the peak of the mountain) that can be reached by following some

Context Matters for Strategic Planning and Organizational Design

Hiking Mount Fuji is very different from sailing the open seas

Simple landscapes (Advanced Economies) | **Rugged landscapes (Emerging Economies)** | **Dancing landscapes (Frontier Economies)**

Source: Images generated by Microsoft Copilot

formula or rule. Mathematics and engineering are the weapons of choice for optimization within these single apex systems.[19]

In contrast, *rugged landscapes* contain multiple peaks separated by valleys. Think of the Rocky Mountains—where a variety of paths point upward to a variety of summits, all at different elevations. The premise is the same as for simple landscapes—higher is better. However, unlike Mount Fuji problems, sometimes in a rugged landscape we must first descend one peak (that is, move further away from efficiency) in order to reach an even higher elevation. Scenario planning, which we will explore in the next chapter, is an extremely effective tool whenever we need a nudge to embrace greater loss or uncertainty in the short run on the path to greater long-term success.

Finally, Page introduces us to the most exotic variant of them all: *dancing landscapes*. These environments are just as complex as rugged landscapes, but they're also inescapably dynamic. One day you may be standing on the summit, basking in the warm glow of a benevolent sunset. Then the next morning, you wake up to find yourself in a deep valley, far from food and shelter. The same basic logic holds for all complex systems, from hurricanes and stock markets to cities and political parties. In these contexts, scenario planning is useful, but insufficient on its own. We also need robust risk management systems to anticipate and brace for unexpected shocks and turbulence—and additional mechanisms to help us navigate through protracted crises when they inevitably occur.

In many ways, the stabilizing strategies we will explore throughout the book are purpose-built for dancing landscapes—volatile environments where enduring success is hard, and operating conditions are constantly in flux. One day a business can generate billions of dollars in profits, and the next its primary technology might be obsolete, or expropriated, or ravaged by disaster. One day the king is your savior, and the next your head is on the chopping block. One day you're an apex predator, and the next you're extinct.

In more volatile environments, failing to prepare is preparing to fail. Consequently, the most successful leaders plan multiple paths to every summit and are ready to pivot at a moment's notice. In frontier economies, redundancy is not wasteful, but an essential form of stability. Diversity is not a buzzword, but a critical source of insurance.

To be clear, in advanced economies, volatility is still pervasive. But the landscapes dance with far less frequency and intensity. In fact, most of the time they operate like rugged landscapes—suspended by powerful public institutions in a form of punctuated equilibrium. Only during shocks and crises do Western leaders even notice that their landscapes also dance. But by the time greater uncertainty spikes, it's often too late. The resilience of their business models, which previously seemed unassailable, has already been compromised.

PLAY IN THE GRAY

Such dancing landscapes have a way of disorienting even the most sure-footed of leaders. Not only are the strategic goalposts constantly moving, but the moral ones also sway back and forth, leaving amorphous gray markets within which the shared rules of engagement aren't entirely clear.

Business leaders must learn to navigate these environments with diplomacy and discretion. Enduring success requires regular contact with multiple layers of authority, from national to local to informal. Each of these is also prone to its own pageantry around corruption and graft. As a result, successful leaders must learn how to assess when "shared interests" cross the line into bribery and extortion, and whether the benefits of proceeding are worth the risk.

The most successful leaders on the frontiers of capitalism have learned to play in the gray.[20] Grounded by a core set of values and an unwavering commitment to long-term success, they begin to dance with the landscape rather than fighting against it.[21] This dynamic style may seem daunting or unfamiliar to Western audiences. But remember that a lot of business takes place in these environments every day. Countries like Equador, Yemen, and South Sudan may languish at the bottom of the World Bank's rankings for "ease of doing business," yet commercial activity still abounds at the base of the economic pyramid.[22] Under these conditions, however, ethical considerations are often secondary to survival.

When faced with this dilemma, how can businesses operate with both strategic and moral integrity? Moisés Naím, a leading Venezuelan journalist and former minister of trade and industry, offers a compelling answer. Drawing from his vast experience leading a frontier economy, he argues that ethical dilemmas are inevitable whenever power is shifting and fragmenting. In his book *Illicit: How Smugglers, Traffickers, and Copycats Are Hijacking the Global Economy*, he suggests that all companies will need to constantly adjust their strategies to survive in a world where no consistent moral standard has emerged.[23] Even the most sophisticated organizations can easily make a wrong move whenever the market shifts, compromising their core values and winding up on the wrong side of history.

Consider Google's entry into the Chinese market in the early 2000s. The future tech giant was eager to expand globally and to defend its early market dominance against emerging rivals, including Baidu and Alibaba. To comply with Beijing's increasingly stringent demands, Google eventually began censoring its search results. This move sparked controversy among Western activists, who quickly accused Google of betraying its foundational motto: "Don't be evil." The company made a utilitarian argument that it was better to provide some information than none at all. But many observers were appalled by the company's choice to put profits above ethics.

Google's approach contrasted sharply with that of the New York Times, whose controlling owners—the Ochs-Sulzberger family—responded by refusing to launch a censored Chinese-language edition of its website, forgoing considerable subscription and advertising revenue. The newspaper also continued to publish uncensored news and opinions about China's politics, economy, and human rights record in both English and Mandarin. In the face of this moral dilemma, the family chose to apply its core values and moral compass worldwide. It was a risky maneuver, but quickly generated a much larger readership—albeit outside the massive Chinese market. As Arthur Sulzberger Jr., a fourth-generation family member and publisher of the *Times*, has argued, "*The Times* serves the cause of the truth. An informed public, we believe, is the most important ingredient in a healthy democracy."[24]

Like each of us, every business has the right to define its own moral compass, then to live with the reputational consequences. But in frontier conditions, survival often requires bending the prevailing rules, and occasionally even breaking them. This is especially true when operating under corrupt and extractive regimes, whose rules are designed to inhibit freedom and progress. Within these environments, even the most basic business activities—procuring supplies, paying taxes, hiring talent, and securing permits—can involve brown envelopes filled with cash, and favors granted to influential politicians. Some companies will, like the New York Times, take a principled stance. But not everyone has the privilege of choosing where they operate, or the resources to invest in a moral crusade.

Perhaps most concerningly, advanced economies appear less immune to these moral ambiguities than ever. As we'll see in the chapters ahead, trust in our most sacred institutions is collapsing everywhere—from governments and businesses to nonprofits and the media. Inclusive markets for goods, capital, justice, and information that took centuries of investment and goodwill to build are now looking grayer than ever.

Yet all hope is not lost. As we'll show in the chapters ahead, not only is success possible under conditions of greater uncertainty, but it also follows a replicable formula. The enduring enterprises you will meet have developed innovative playbooks for navigating turbulent times. We believe their insights can help any organization achieve greater resilience and performance, whether they operate in Toronto or Taipei.

KEY INSIGHTS

- This chapter introduces the concept of trust as the fundamental building block for all economic activity—one which we often take for granted.
- Advanced economies have strong institutions (e.g., rule of law, infrastructure, markets, social security) that promote trust and predictability, while emerging and frontier economies lack strong institutions, making trust more difficult to establish.
- Family businesses play a crucial role in emerging and frontier economies by creating "microclimates of trust"—providing stability in the absence of strong public institutions.
- Enduring enterprises need to be adaptable and resilient in these environments, deploying strategies designed for "dancing

landscapes" (or turbulent operating conditions), which are more prevalent on the frontiers of capitalism.

- Ethical dilemmas become more frequent in these environments as well, given weaker institutions and unclear rules, so businesses need to navigate these complexities carefully while maintaining some level of moral integrity.

2
NAVIGATING THE HIERARCHY OF STABILITY

Who is the happier man, he who has braved the storm of life and lived or he who has stayed securely on shore and merely existed?

—Hunter S. Thompson, "Security," 1955

Long before writing his most famous book, *Fear and Loathing in Las Vegas*, Hunter S. Thompson was among the earliest in a new wave of journalists to challenge prevailing wisdom about the value of stability and affluence. Like a modern Huckleberry Finn, Thompson left his hometown of Louisville, Kentucky, at an early age to pursue a life of adventure, free from societal norms and filled with provocative exploits.

In 1955, as a seventeen-year-old high school student—and over a dozen years before he embraced the "gonzo" style for which he later became famous—he submitted an essay titled "Security" to a literary magazine called *The Spectator*. The essay provided a surprisingly insightful teenage critique of postwar America. In a few short paragraphs, he put forth a compelling argument that security is a delusion, one which stifles creativity and happiness. Risk-taking, he proposed, was essential for living a meaningful and fulfilling life.

At the time, America's influence was ascendant, and the dividends from global peace were both abundant and unquestioned. The country's new status as one of the world's first advanced economies enabled, and even encouraged, massive infrastructure spending, funded by windfall taxes and budgets that were no longer needed to support a global war machine. Reliable transportation, energy, and communication networks proliferated, supporting growing global demand for American goods and services. In a few short years, this new infrastructure crisscrossed the country, dramatically altering the fabric of American society.

Families that could afford to left behind crowded cities and moved in droves to the suburbs in search of a better life. These suburbs were seen as safe havens, where families could raise their children away from the dangers of urban living, and be comforted by the promise of the American Dream—that hard work would pave a secure and predictable path to happiness.

This is where Thompson's essay on "Security" is at its most provocative, and for our purposes, most insightful. He argues that the stability sought by these migrating families was not a blessing but rather a curse. If anything, suburbs don't breed happiness but rather a fear of losing material possessions and status. When humans are hypnotized by safety and stability, they lose their innate capacity for creativity and resilience:

> Let us visualize the secure man; and by this term, I mean a man who has settled for financial and personal security for his goal in life. In general, he is a man who has pushed ambition and initiative aside and settled down, so to speak, in a boring, but safe and comfortable rut for the rest of his life. His future is but an extension of his present, and he accepts it as such with a complacent shrug of his shoulders. . . .
>
> Turn back the pages of history and see the men who have shaped the destiny of the world. Security was never theirs, but they lived rather than existed. Where would the world be if all men had sought security and not taken risks or gambled with their lives on the chance that, if they won, life would be different and richer?[1]

We're not suggesting that stability *requires* "wasting one's life in mediocrity," or that risk-seeking behavior is inherently more rewarding or productive. But Thompson provides a helpful reminder that exposure to uncertainty generates a special form of resilience, and that many of us who live and work in advanced economies have become dangerously complacent after decades of stability and abundance.

As a result, we've forgotten how disorienting it can be to lose access to key resources and markets, as we learned during the COVID-19 pandemic. We've forgotten how disruptive it can be when price stability is elusive, and inflation threatens both the financial system and the broader economy. Perhaps most concerningly, we've forgotten how fragile the global political order can be when we take civility and peace for granted, and when polarization and armed conflict threaten to burn the whole system to the ground.

EVERYTHING, EVERYWHERE, ALL AT ONCE

Such evolutionary changes are a defining characteristic of a universe in constant motion—whether we seek it out like Thompson or avoid it like the plague. Some scientists call this force *entropy*, which, in layman's terms, is one way of measuring how much uncertainty or randomness there is in a system. Entropy is what happens to your house if you don't do any maintenance to it. As time goes by, the light bulbs burn out, the roof and plumbing will leak, and the termites will move in. The bigger the house, the quicker entropy sets in. It is like nature's tax, one that breaks down complex systems over time. Entropy explains why ice melts, why food spoils, why buildings decay, and why stars die. It also helps to expose the natural vulnerabilities of our modern global civilization, and the many businesses operating in advanced economies who take enduring stability for granted.

Consider Canada, one of the world's most prosperous and predictable places to live, work, and play. Just a century ago, survival in most of the country was far from certain, particularly as winter temperatures can be colder than the surface of Mars. But over time, these chaotic frontiers were tamed by generations of public and private investment—in power systems, transportation systems, medical systems, educational systems, and financial systems—all of which now enable more than 40 million people to safely inhabit one of the largest and most untamed landmasses on Earth.

Modern Canadians have grown comfortable—and even complacent, as Thompson warned—having mostly forgotten how dangerous and unforgiving life was in this part of the planet only a few generations ago. We can barely survive a typical winter storm without broadband internet and home delivery, let alone without basic heat and shelter. Now consider how people will cope as extreme weather events, such as wildfires, droughts, and violent storms, become commonplace in the years and decades to come.

Canadian authorities are relatively good at managing adverse climate events—it would be irresponsible not to build up these capabilities, considering the persistent threat to commercial and social life. But many countries have neither the experience, nor the resources, nor the will to confront such challenges head-on. Mitigating the impact of climate change in Lower Manhattan, coastal Florida, or rural France will take years and cost billions, and these budgets and timelines are neither well aligned with election cycles nor hedge-fund investment horizons.

Now consider that the environment is just one of a variety of systemic risks that will increasingly require the attention of business leaders everywhere. After all, humanity is perfectly capable of self-destruction without nature's help. The conflict between Russia and Ukraine, which arguably began in 2014 and has been smoldering for more than a decade, is just one example of how geopolitical tensions can permanently disrupt the flow of critical raw materials, energy, and people. A much larger conflict between the United States and China over Taiwan would have even more destabilizing repercussions, not to mention a nuclear stand-off in the Middle East.

So far, these rising geopolitical tensions haven't materially affected economic outcomes, with global growth and asset prices continuing their steady upward ascent. But as policymakers begin to unwind decades of unprecedented fiscal and monetary stimulus, financial systems from the United States and China to Europe and Japan are flashing warning signs. Some now speculate that we're approaching a major inflection point in the global monetary system unlike anything since the Great Depression. Paired with a sharp slowdown in global growth and a rise in distressed debt, an imminent popping of "the everything bubble" seems virtually inevitable.[2]

The Everything Bubble

Asset prices have been inflated by massive borrowing at all levels

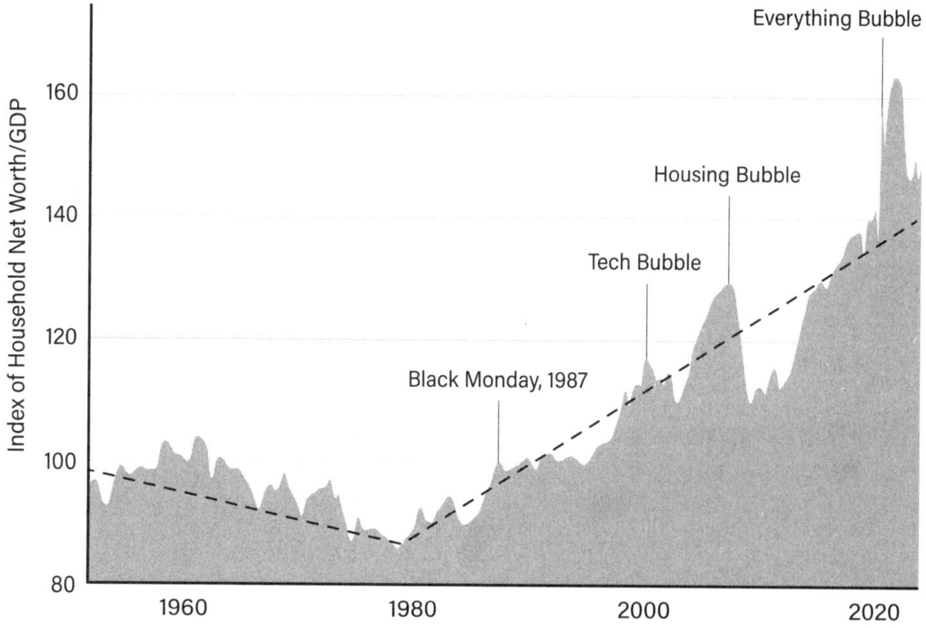

Source: Federal Reserve Bank of St. Louis

Now layer in the dawn of a new AI-led Technological Revolution, which could be every bit as disruptive and transformational as the Industrial Revolution. The daily news cycle in 2023 was flooded with reports about groundbreaking advances, leading various investment banks and think tanks to estimate that artificial intelligence technologies had the potential to disrupt hundreds of millions of jobs in the coming years, transforming entire economies as many basic clerical tasks become fully automated.

At another time in history, any one of these structural shifts alone would be enough to mobilize action from citizens, businesses, and governments. Today, all of them are flashing red simultaneously in a pattern ominously resembling the 1930s at the precipice of World War II. Even still, policymakers and business leaders can't seem to organize a coherent and systematic response.

The term *polycrisis* was coined in 1999 by French philosopher Edgar Morin to describe precisely this web of complex and interactive risks. Since then, scholars, politicians, and pundits have adopted it to capture the state of global affairs in the early twenty-first century. The World Economic Forum presciently highlighted this dangerous trend back in 2018: "Humanity has become remarkably adept at understanding how to mitigate conventional risks that can be relatively easily isolated and managed with standard risk-management approaches. But we are much less competent when it comes to dealing with complex risks in the interconnected systems that underpin our world, such as organizations, economies, societies and the environment."[3]

Navigating a polycrisis requires a different playbook than managing conventional risks—one that comes naturally in frontier economies but is foreign to those who have only ever operated in the most advanced economies. Leaders in New York, London, and Berlin often struggle to orient themselves within these dancing landscapes. Their strategic intuition isn't particularly helpful—and can even be harmful—without careful adaptation.[4]

Contrast this with life in modern Ukraine, for those living under the shadow of polycrisis. Igor Mazepa, director general of the investment bank Concorde Capital, captured the dynamics in chilling simplicity: "When you're constantly thinking about invading Russians, you're not going to go buy a new phone, or a car, or a house." His fellow Ukrainian entrepreneur Iryna Chechotkina, CEO of the online retailer Rozetka, has a more sanguine perspective. She and her husband launched their family business in 2005 and now provide same-day delivery in Kyiv and next-day delivery throughout Ukraine from over 300 locations, employing over 8,000 workers—despite the ongoing conflict with Russia. "Born during a time of change," she said, "our business was baptized from the start to be fast and flexible."[5]

Unburdened by the false sense of stability, frontier capitalists not only manage the typical risks associated with doing business in any competitive environment, but also the extreme uncertainty that comes with the daily threat of missile strikes, power outages, fuel shortages, sequestered materials, and aging equipment. This lack of predictability is precisely what makes these environments more challenging to navigate, especially for those who are out of practice. It's the difference between anticipating the daily rise and fall of coastal tides in Long Island Sound versus forecasting the rare but devastating effects of a Japanese tsunami. In short, uncertainty and stability each require their own unique approach to decision-making. As Hunter S. Thompson keenly observed, "When the going gets weird, the weird turn pro."[6]

RISK VS. UNCERTAINTY

Decision-makers often use the terms "risk" and "uncertainty" interchangeably, but in fact they're quite distinct. In its simplest definition, first framed by the University of Chicago economist Frank Knight, *risk* refers to any situation in which the outcome is known or can be estimated with some probability.[7] For example, leaders can decide to invest in a new product line based on market research, customer feedback, and comprehensive financial projections. However, there is always a chance that the products will fail to meet expectations or face intense competition from substitutes. Leaders can estimate the probability and impact of these adverse outcomes, and use that information to make more informed decisions about whether to proceed with the investment or reallocate capital elsewhere. Such risks typify the simple and rugged landscapes most common among advanced economies.

Uncertainty, on the other hand, refers to situations in which the potential outcomes aren't known, or can't be estimated with confidence. This dynamism is the hallmark of dancing landscapes, and consequently it is pervasive among frontier and emerging economies. For instance, when businesses operate in countries experiencing political turmoil and social unrest, there are too many interacting variables at play—such as rising inequality, radicalization, market failures, and foreign interference—most of which we can't anticipate or measure accurately, let alone forecast with precision.[8]

Under conditions of elevated uncertainty, probabilistic models and statistical methods inevitably break down, and "unknown unknowns" become pervasive. As a result, decision-makers need to rely much more on strategic scenario planning to make better decisions about the future. Yet scenario planning as a decision-making tool for business is a fairly recent phenomenon. In fact, it was a direct response to the last era of sustained polycrisis nearly a century ago.

One of the earliest proponents was the British military strategist Basil Liddell Hart, who developed a form of structured planning during the chaos of World War II. The concept is simple: while the content of any specific plan may become obsolete or irrelevant under constantly changing conditions, the process of planning is indispensable. It forces us to examine the underlying dynamics shaping our environment, and then to imagine multiple scenarios and contingencies that could unfold, in an effort to help us anticipate and plan for inevitable change.

This exercise naturally expands our perceptions about the future and prepares us to act with greater agility and confidence under more ambiguous and uncertain conditions. To be clear, such planning is not an end in itself, but rather a means to an end. As President Dwight D. Eisenhower argued, plans are worthless, but planning is everything. It's a cognitive vaccine, one that primes us to respond to future threats more effectively because it minimizes the element of surprise.[9]

In the decades since it crossed over from military to civilian applications—most notably in the 1970s through the Anglo-Dutch energy company Shell, and its landmark study on the future of the energy industry—the world has only grown more complex and interconnected. Mathematical simulations are now a fundamental part of all macroeconomic analysis, but even our most powerful computational systems and sophisticated machine learning algorithms struggle to predict the weather just a few hours in advance, let alone forecast dynamic pricing for capital, goods, and labor years in the future. If anything, these models are a form of statistical alchemy, creating a false sense of confidence in our understanding of the modern global economy.

In short, risks can be priced effectively by financial markets but uncertainty cannot, despite our best efforts. Investors can use historical data and models to estimate default risk for a single company, and consequently demand higher returns. But investors cannot easily price the uncertainty of a geopolitical conflict, a pandemic, or a financial crisis, because these events are rare, unpredictable, and have complex and nonlinear effects on the economy. Consequently, they defy conventional statistical modeling and can easily disorient leaders, investors, and consumers, leading to a range of adverse and unexpected outcomes.[10]

Given how frequently adverse events unfold within frontier economies, those born and raised under these conditions are naturally better at adapting to disruption and change. Those who don't share these same instincts and experiences need to be much more intentional about how they navigate uncertainty, and invest with intention in new strategies that generate greater agility and endurance. Perhaps they can be forgiven for not doing this instinctively. After all, these activities can consume significant time and resources, and in relatively stable environments, this can feel wasteful or even counterproductive. But like any good vaccine, testing our defenses isn't a waste of time—it prepares us for the day when crisis inevitably strikes.

RESISTANCE BREEDS RESILIENCE

One of the most inspiring speeches of the twentieth century was delivered by President John F. Kennedy at Rice University on September 12, 1962. In front of thousands of students under the warm Texas sun, JFK announced his bold vision to land a man on the moon before the end of the decade—*and* to return him home safely. Kennedy explained that going to the moon was not only a scientific and technological achievement, but also a moral and ideological one. It was a way of expressing the human spirit of exploration and discovery, proving that democracy can lead the world in advancing the frontiers of knowledge and prosperity.

JFK argued compellingly that we do these things not because they are easy, but precisely because they are hard.[11] We take on risk and push ourselves beyond the frontiers of our comfort zone because we understand that it's the surest path to a better future. We overcome the destabilizing forces of uncertainty and entropy because we want to endure. Like athletes lifting weights, we recognize that it is only by intentionally tearing our muscles that we can induce them to heal and grow stronger, and that the amount of resistance we absorb through training is directly proportional to our gains in strength and endurance.

Historians will remind us that the initial response to JFK's speech wasn't universally enthusiastic. The National Aeronautics and Space Administration would be competing directly with other key domestic and foreign priorities for funding, and Congress was understandably skeptical. But this massive moonshot investment also triggered an explosion of scientific progress in a vast array of fields, including advanced semiconductors, telecommunications, polymer fabrics, water purification, power storage, cordless tools, and even freeze-dried foods. These advances may have never been possible without the will to overcome the odds and achieve something many thought was impossible.

Resilience is thus born from adversity—whether by choice or by force. It comes from challenging the boundaries of our comfort zone. As Hunter S. Thompson once quipped, "Anything that gets your blood racing is probably worth doing."[12] This advice is particularly relevant for the affluent leaders operating in advanced economies, who have been coddled by long stretches of economic and geopolitical stability, and up until the COVID-19 pandemic, had little experience managing sustained disruptions to their businesses. Their decision-making systems need to be deliberately stressed by challenges that act something like the stimulating effects of an ice-cold shower.

Contrast these leaders with those operating under conditions of chronic and elevated stress. As the Roman philosopher Seneca noted, "Difficulties strengthen the mind, as labor does the body."[13] Individuals and organizations that are constantly provoked by the uncertainty and volatility intrinsic to this Darwinian contest of survival naturally develop both the hardware (e.g., "thicker skin") and the software (e.g., "agile thinking") to survive and thrive.

At the same time, pushing ourselves too far past the frontiers of our current abilities can also be counterproductive, resulting in greater stress and even systems-level failure. Excessive tolerance for stress can easily leave us complacent and vulnerable, like the proverbial frog failing to react to a slowly boiling pot of water, and being cooked alive.

The Goldilocks scenario involves exposure to an optimal level of uncertainty—one which keeps us on our toes without stressing us out. Think of a spectrum that begins in the reassuring comfort of Manhattan's

Resistance Breeds Resilience

But too much of a good thing is just as dangerous as too little

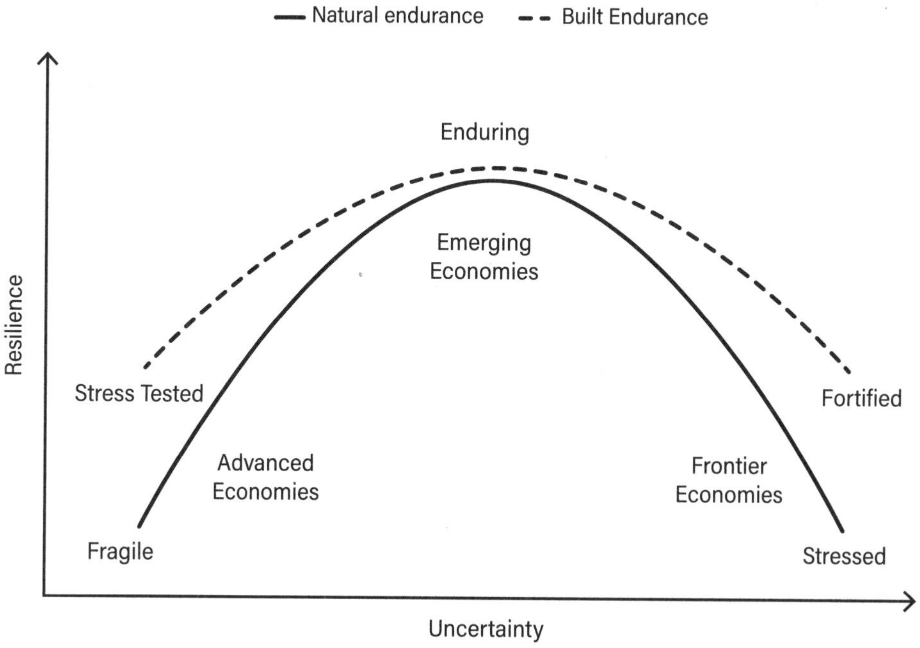

Upper East Side and ends in the chaotic slums of Manila. So Singapore and Dubai would be in the sweet spot.[14] This parabolic curve helps to explain why emerging economies have been engines of growth and development since the early seventeenth century, and reinforces Thompson's thesis that too much stability can be just as dangerous as too little.

THE HIERARCHY OF STABILITY

In the late 1990s, Hugh Courtney, a mid-level manager at the consultancy McKinsey & Company, assembled a model of how companies make big bets under varying conditions of uncertainty. He eventually captured these theories in a best-selling book, *20/20 Foresight: Crafting Strategy in an Uncertain World*, which challenged the prevailing wisdom of a binary view of uncertainty—that it is an "all-or-nothing phenomenon."[15] When leaders trust in the stability of their environment, the best predictor of tomorrow's customer needs and market conditions is, in fact, yesterday. But when the world is uncertain, basing future strategy on past performance can be dangerous, like driving down the highway by looking in the rear-view mirror.

In these unfamiliar contexts, many leaders often rely too much on intuition. Instead, Courtney proposed a four-level framework for diagnosing the level of residual uncertainty that managers face "after the best possible analysis to separate the knowable from the unknowable."[16] He challenged leaders not to confuse the two—arguing that "even the most uncertain business environments contain a lot of strategically relevant information," such as demographics, elasticities of demand, and competitors' publicly announced plans: "Underestimating uncertainty can lead to strategies that neither defend against the threats nor take advantage of the opportunities that higher levels of uncertainty may provide.... At the other extreme, assuming that the world is entirely unpredictable can lead managers to abandon the analytical rigor of their traditional planning processes altogether, and base their strategic decisions primarily on gut instinct."[17]

To help provide some categorical guidance, he laid out a framework including four distinct levels of residual uncertainty to help leaders understand the relative value of strategic analysis. Not coincidentally, these levels map naturally to the spectrum from stability to uncertainty that we've used to differentiate between advanced, emerging, and frontier economies. The main difference between Courtney's framework and ours is that, within his research, fully half of the strategy problems fell into Level 1, with the remaining half split between Levels 2 and 3. In contrast, among the cases we studied in emerging and frontier economies, the vast majority operated within Levels 3 and 4. Even still, this idea of a "spectrum" is essential for helping us escape the false binary of stability vs. uncertainty.

For instance, under Level 1 and 2 conditions, most common among advanced economies, planning is naturally more linear and straightforward—a series of familiar scenarios where the outcomes are relatively certain. Forecasting future sales and profits is mostly a simple mathematical exercise. However, under Level 3 and 4 conditions, the future is rarely a linear extension of the present. Forecasting accurately even a few years ahead becomes virtually impossible. Instead, we need to plan for a wider array of potential outcomes or risk significant losses and even failure.

Given that many of us will be spending more time under Level 3 and 4 conditions in the years ahead, we need to broaden our strategic planning toolkit. Courtney uses the example of companies considering major investments in post-communist Russia in 1992 to drive the point home:

> They could not outline the potential laws or regulations that would govern property rights and transactions. That central uncertainty was compounded by additional uncertainty about the viability of supply chains and the demand for previously unavailable consumer goods and services. And shocks such as a political assassination or a currency default could have spun the whole system toward completely unforeseen outcomes. . . .
>
> Still, it is critical to avoid the urge to throw one's hands up and act purely on gut instinct. . . . Managers can also identify patterns indicating possible ways the market may evolve by studying how analogous markets developed in other level 4 situations, determining the key attributes of the winners and losers in those situations and identifying the strategies they employed.[18]

While this advice was first crafted a quarter century ago, it is even more relevant today. We use it here to help frame a new strategic planning tool we call the "Hierarchy of Stability." Leaders can leverage it to identify better benchmarks for survival and success, seeking fresh insights from other places and times where uncertainty has been higher or lower than usual.[19]

At the base of the pyramid (what Courtney called "Level 4 conditions"), life and business are clearly still viable, though subject to the greater uncertainty that make black swan events, such as epidemics and wars, more likely to happen several times in a leader's career. In contrast, these events happen so infrequently in advanced economies at the top of the pyramid that they are almost mythical, and therefore rarely built into strategic plans and organizational designs.

Introducing the Hierarchy of Stability

Our context powerfully shapes the conditions necessary for survival and success

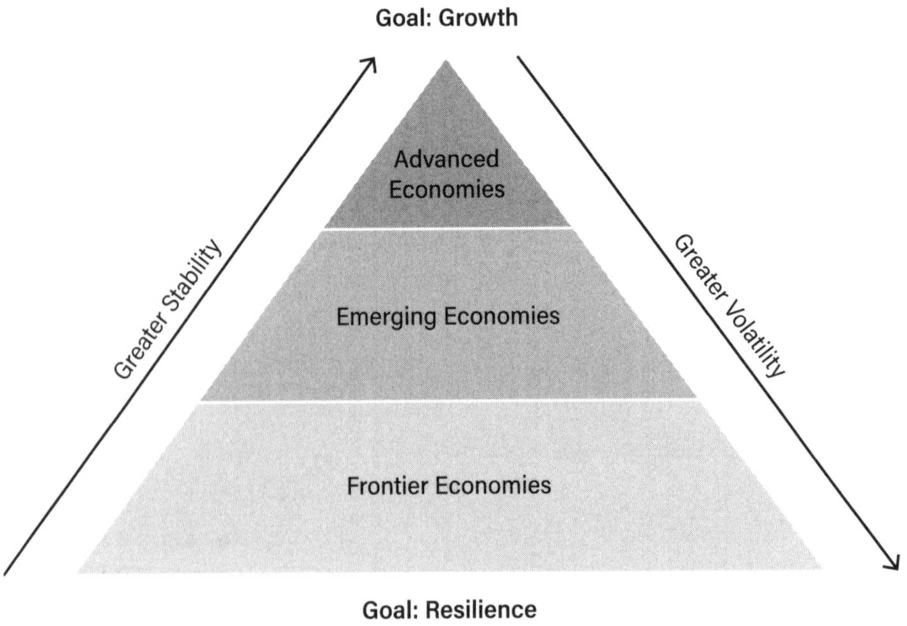

At the peak of the hierarchy, leaders tend to prioritize efficiency and growth, constantly tweaking production and distribution in a relentless drive for greater profitability. Their business models can only tolerate modest deviations from macroeconomic plans—for instance, inflation must remain between 1 and 2 percent, prime rates between 3 and 7 percent, population growth between 0 and 1 percent, unemployment between 4 and 6 percent, real growth in gross domestic product (GDP) of 2 to 4 percent, and so on. Risks need to be easy to identify, and probabilities easy to model. Any small deviations can be anticipated and managed by coordinated teams, informed by reams of data, and supported by abundant resources and powerful central governments.

Under these more stable conditions, the recent past becomes a reliable predictor of the near future, and growth is mostly a function of access to capital and appetite for risk. The paradox, of course, is that chronic stability also leaves us easily disoriented when conditions unexpectedly change and the prevailing wisdom no longer applies. Organizations are more fragile and prone to collapse precisely because they are over-optimized for stability and ill-prepared for the unexpected.

Contrast this with the greater volatility endemic to life in emerging and frontier economies, where risks are challenging to identify, let alone to model accurately and mitigate effectively. Material deviations from strategic plans are inevitable when resource security is interrupted by protesting civilians, corrupt officials, failures of infrastructure, and climate catastrophes. The recent past is rarely a reliable predictor of the near future, let alone the longer term, forcing leaders to invest in contingency plans and stabilizing systems that can limit efficiency and profitability. The baseline goal in these environments is survival. Only then can we build oases of trust and predictability within which economic life can flourish.

Without confidence in the stability of the most critical drivers of economic performance, it's much harder to deploy billions of dollars in capital for infrastructure projects that may take decades to build and operate, or to invest millions in new training facilities if there aren't enough skilled workers to hire, or to borrow to make these investments when interest rates and currencies are constantly in flux. That said, it's clearly not impossible. Emerging and frontier economies are among the fastest growing in the world, and as we'll demonstrate throughout this book, the enduring enterprises that operate in them are a source of strategic inspiration for those who want to learn how to thrive in turbulent times.

We'll close this chapter by acknowledging that not all of us will have the temperament of Hunter S. Thompson to grab life by the proverbial horns and seek our fortunes in environments that we know will test our resilience.[20] But in the years ahead, we firmly believe that all leaders and organizations will need to strike a better balance between safety and adventure, between comfort and stress, and between prosperity and endurance. As we enter this New Age of Uncertainty, the ultimate goal may be less about "getting to Denmark," as Francis Fukuyama once argued, and more about "getting to Doha."

KEY INSIGHTS

- Stability can be a double-edged sword—while it fosters prosperity, it can also lead to complacency and a lack of preparedness for change.
- Advanced economies have enjoyed a period of stability that has led to immense prosperity, but also a lack of resilience.
- Those operating in frontier economies understand that building resilience is essential for survival and enduring success, and that it grows through experience with adversity.
- Polycrisis, arising from the interconnected web of complex risks facing the world today, such as climate change, geopolitical tensions, and technological disruption, is perhaps the defining characteristic of the early twenty-first century.
- Leaders everywhere need to be prepared for a future characterized by greater uncertainty than they encountered in the past, where outcomes are more difficult to predict, decision-making presents a more significant challenge, and greater investments in organizational resilience are required.
- The Hierarchy of Stability is a framework we will use throughout the book to help leaders understand their unique context for strategic planning, which looks quite different at the peak than it does at the base.

Structural Differences Across the Hierarchy of Stability

	Factors	Advanced Economies (e.g., Denmark)	Emerging Economies (e.g., India)	Frontier Economies (e.g., Nigeria)
Economic	Property Rights	Respected, high ownership society	Respected by elites, skeptical otherwise	Ignored, low ownership society
	Capital Markets	Large, liquid, global	Growing, regional	Small, illiquid, provincial
	Product Markets	Reliable, extensive	Mostly reliable, extensive	Mostly reliable, limited, expensive
	Information Markets	Diverse, uncontrolled	Diverse, controlled	Limited, controlled
	Infrastructure	Reliable, extensive, public goods	Reliable, limited, mix of public and private	Unreliable, limited, often private
	Regulations	Protect public interests	Often varies by industry and region	Protect captive interests
Political	Governance	Network (modular, transparent, inclusive)	Market (general principles and independent agents)	Hierarchical (opaque, extractive, autocratic)
	Accountability/ Enforcement	Consistent, inclusive, respected	Consistent, limited	Inconsistent, exclusive, ignored
	Corruption	Limited by transparency, ethics	Greater in regulated industries	Pervasive, cost of doing business
	Public Data	Diverse and reliable	Diverse and unreliable	Limited and unreliable
Social	Talent Markets	Well-funded public schools, higher participation	Basic public schools with well-funded private schools	Well-funded private schools, lower participation
	Internal/External Conflict	Conflict resolved politically	Mix of hard and soft power	Conflict resolved with military
	Ethnic Tensions	Collaborative multicultural relations	Moderate	Adversarial multicultural relations
	Social Mobility	High	Moderate	Low
	Trust	High	Moderate	Low
	Importance of Family	Moderate	High	High

3

UNDERSTANDING THE ORIGINS OF STABILITY

The only way to have a stable state is to have a good army and good friends.

—Niccolò Machiavelli

In late 2019, just before the COVID-19 pandemic threw the entire world into a tailspin, we landed in Tokyo on a mission. The ideas that culminated in this book were still percolating, and we were in the midst of gathering case histories from family business leaders on their extraordinary resilience, often across centuries of opportunity, adversity, and revolutionary change. We chose Japan because it is a prolific incubator of these ancient dynasties—the Imperial House alone recognizes 126 lineal descendants over thousands of years. In particular, we wanted to understand how these enduring enterprises navigate both the external and the internal dimensions of stability and how this context influences business strategy and organizational design.

We define *external* forces as those imposed on us by higher powers—monarchs and governments whose ideologies and actions determine the predictability of the environments in which we live, work, and play. In contrast, *internal* forces—such as the unique values and customs we inherit from our ancestors, and the seven stabilizing strategies we'll introduce in the next chapter—emerge naturally within family enterprises, and they can both reinforce and undermine organizational endurance.

Our central thesis throughout the book is the intrinsic tension between these two opposing forces—how the strength of a society's public institutions influences the extent to which businesses must rely on their own internal stabilizers to manage through turbulent times. In advanced economies, where credible central banks, transparent electoral processes, and sophisticated educational and social welfare programs have existed for nearly a century, stability is more pervasive than in frontier economies, and greater trust in "the system" provides a natural incentive for individual entrepreneurial experimentation and investment. In frontier economies, where stability is the exception to the rule, trust must be developed from the inside out—with the family operating as the primary catalyst for social and commercial activity. In this chapter we will examine both variants of these powerful forces, with a particular focus on how they evolve and interact over time.

Such longer-term patterns are precisely what made Japan such a fascinating environment to test out our earliest hypotheses. Our plan was to meet with representatives from five of the country's most ancient family businesses,

Sources of Stability Are Determined by Context

Internal investments fill the institutional voids further down the Hierarchy of Stability

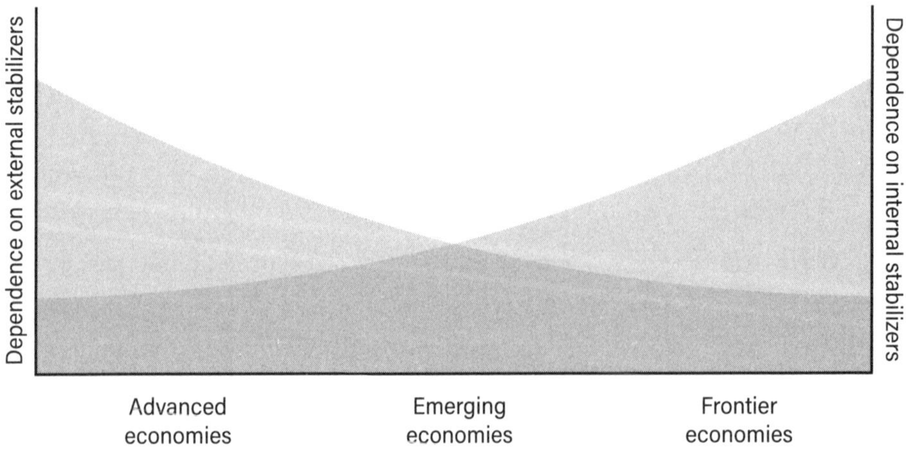

precisely to understand how they navigated across key event horizons in the evolution of the Japanese economy—from its feudal origins centuries ago to its status today as one of the most advanced economies.[1] With a combined age of over 2,500 years, their fascinating histories validated and inspired many of the ideas in this book, because they have each successfully operated across all three levels on the Hierarchy of Stability.

That said, in terms of longevity, Kongō Gumi was truly in a league of its own. For nearly 1,500 years, the Kongō family built and maintained temples for Japan's royal family. They are truly the ultra-marathoners of entrepreneurial endurance—and by some accounts, the world's oldest company.

At a nondescript hotel in downtown Tokyo, we met over lunch with a leading historian of the Kongō family, Professor Hidekazu Sone of Shizuoka University. Sitting cross-legged on the floor of a private dining room, we conversed through our Japanese colleagues about the history of this remarkable family business.

Professor Sone began the meeting by pulling a scroll out of his briefcase that nearly extended right out of the room when fully unfurled. It had been produced in the seventeenth century during Japan's long experiment with feudalism (think shogun and samurai) and traced the ancestral lineage of the Kongō family back to its founders over a thousand years before.

Since before the rise of Islam, this family-owned business had built and restored some of Japan's most iconic and sacred structures, from the majestic Osaka Castle to the ancient Hōryū-ji temple. The family and the business have survived through centuries of volatility, including countless wars, economic crises, urban fires, natural disasters, and political attempts to eradicate Buddhism. They managed to thrive by strategically adapting to these changing external contexts and by preserving a core set of internal family values, beliefs, and customs that were passed down across forty generations of Kongō sons and daughters.

Their story begins when Prince Shōtoku, modernizer of the sixth-century Japanese government, and a regional champion for Buddhism, summoned three Korean temple builders to construct Shitennō-ji, or the Temple of the Four Heavenly Kings. They were skilled *miyadaiku*, traditional Japanese carpenters, who engineered and built the most impressive Buddhist temple of the era—all without using a single nail. This design ensured that each individual piece of timber could be replaced countless times over the temple's infinite lifetime, using lumber cut and preserved from local forests, which the Kongō family also managed. As a result, it was one of the earliest and most sustainable human structures ever built.

Kongō Gumi's highly specialized building, maintenance, and restoration business became a reliable source of wealth and power for the family. Given the generational time horizons required for success, the Kongōs became skilled at transferring their artisanal skills, natural resources, and treasured relationships with the Imperial Court across generations. In this way, the family itself became a critical source of internal stability for their collective enterprise. In fact, their core strategies and values were considered so essential to their enduring success that the family's thirty-second successor, Yoshisada Kongō, drafted a creed his heirs later called *Shokoku kokoro no koto*, or "family knowledge of the trade."

This collection of sixteen principles documented centuries of the family's accumulated wisdom for building an enduring enterprise. They include time-tested business strategies such as managing reputational risk, as well as personal guidelines for the family, including how to dress, drink in moderation, and treat others with the utmost respect. Passed with devotion from generation to generation, these principles were the company's strategic north star, helping to guide each Kongō heir in service of the family's enduring entrepreneurial mission.

It's no coincidence that these guidelines were formally codified in the mid-nineteenth century during the Meiji Restoration, a time of revolutionary change for Japanese society. In an effort to drag the country away from feudal isolation, pro-Shinto governments systematically burned tens of thousands of Buddhist temples to the ground as they ushered in a new age of rapid industrialization. In the face of this existential threat to Kongō Gumi's core business model, the family recognized that its values and conduct were just as important to sustaining generational success as their commitment to fine carpentry, fair pricing, and customer service.[2] Staying true to their artisanal heritage helped to sustain the company's reputation and commercial viability for another 150 years.

Yet despite over fourteen centuries of entrepreneurial success, perhaps the most remarkable aspect of Kongō Gumi's long and storied history is that it's also a cautionary tale. Like many industrializing economies springing up around the turn of the twentieth century, as Japan migrated further up the Hierarchy of Stability, its political and commercial systems quickly transformed. Urban lifestyles became more common, interest in Buddhism began to wane, capital markets supported greater competition and trade, customers demanded more modern materials and techniques, government institutions grew more influential, and close familial relationships with the Imperial House became less valuable for securing new projects.

Disoriented by these shifting conditions, Kongō Gumi deployed a variety of strategies, such as diversifying beyond traditional construction methods and even moving away from temple building. At the time, these strategies appeared sensible, but they ultimately weakened the company's focus and diminished its competitive edge. Later, in the 1980s, during Japan's massive economic bubble, Masakazu Kongō, the family member then leading the firm, took on sizable loans, hoping to expand the company's portfolio and compete with larger and more sophisticated peers. When the bubble finally burst, Kongō Gumi was left with massive debts it could not repay. It was unceremoniously acquired in 2006 by the more innovative and agile Takamatsu Construction Group.[3]

The Kongō family's incredible entrepreneurial legacy reminds us that even the most enduring enterprises can't rest on their laurels. As the structural stability of our external environment waxes and wanes, our focus on internal stability—like a hydraulic system—quickly needs to recalibrate.

Consequently, as the whole world now seems destined to slide at least a few notches down the Hierarchy of Stability in the years ahead, we all need to dust off our strategic playbooks—along with our history books and family albums—and use them as inspiration for how to respond.

THE ORIGINS OF EXTERNAL STABILITY

Over a long enough time horizon, every society is prone to structural change. Sometimes these developments can usher in eras of greater peace and prosperity. Other times they can plunge entire regions into prolonged periods of chaos. Enduring enterprises like Kongō Gumi learn to anticipate and adjust to these revolutionary event horizons, sometimes by dumb luck, though more often by leveraging lessons from the past.

Following their lead, we found it deeply illuminating to revisit the revolutionary contexts within which frontier, emerging, and advanced economies first developed. Tracing their origins and evolutions helped us to better understand how organizations at all levels of the Hierarchy of Stability must adapt to significant structural changes—whether by choice or by force.

Reading this book from the modern comforts of your home or office—or perhaps cruising mid-flight above the clouds—it's easy to forget that prior to the sixteenth century, living conditions for most humans were "solitary, poor, nasty, brutish, and short," as the philosopher Thomas Hobbes famously observed.[4] Beyond Roman roads and organized religions, few public institutions existed or persisted long enough to hold large and diverse human societies together in sustained peace and prosperity.[5] Instead, existential threats, including wars, droughts, and plagues,

A Brief History of Stability

The Hierarchy of Stability captures six centuries of economic development

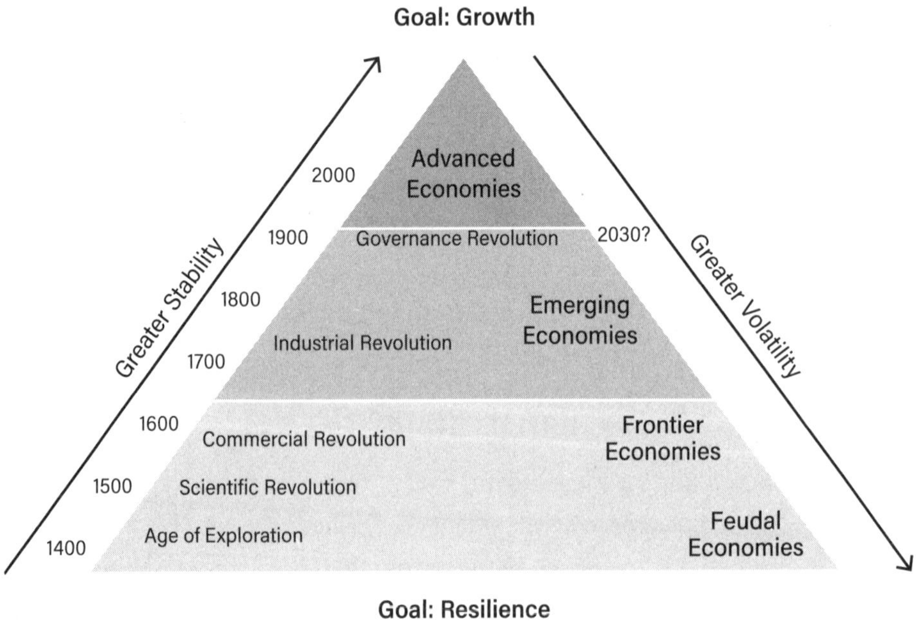

remained both frequent and unpredictable, providing little incentive to venture out and risk starvation or death in search of a better life.

Most peasant families were basically subsistence farmers, toiling from dawn to dusk on feudal manors, paying agricultural rents, and serving at the whims of privileged lords—knights and shogun more interested in jousting and banquets than inclusive governance and economic development. Women and children worked alongside men, each contributing to the productivity of the household. Families rarely traveled far from their manorial villages and had limited access to wealth or opportunity. Entrepreneurship was not incentivized; nor were there infrastructures such as property rights, corporations, and retail banks to enable this type of enduring commercial enterprise. Instead, echoing the tightly bound *Gemeinschaft* described by Georg Simmel, these intimate networks of families banded together to provide the basic necessities for survival—putting food on the table, offering rudimentary shelter, and tending to health needs through informal medicinal traditions. Stability during this era was essentially achieved through inertia rather than through deliberate attempts to foster sustained growth and shared prosperity.

It would take the emergence of a general system of "commercial law"—a concept first coined by the sociologist Max Weber—to finally jolt the medieval world out of protracted stagnation.[6] Over centuries of trial and error, merchants and traders eventually standardized a framework for commercial contracts that promoted joint risk-taking, along with trustworthy courts and jurists to help these partnerships resolve disputes peacefully. Their greatest novelty was allowing strangers to more easily collaborate like friends and even family, bound by mutual trust in common rules of engagement and reliable means of enforcement. Ever since, these simple but powerful commercial principles have formed the basis for every public market, from medieval fairs in Champagne to modern derivatives on Wall Street.

As commercial speculation became more accessible, and the risks and rewards more predictable, there were naturally greater incentives for families to save up their agricultural surpluses, then engage in microentrepreneurship in search of a better life. A growing community of merchants and craftsmen began to congregate in market towns and urban centers, which over time became bustling hubs of barter and trade in textiles, pottery, tools, spices, and entertainment.

Some of the oldest businesses in the world were founded in these early frontier economies, including the many family-run hotels, wineries, breweries, and restaurants that sprang up to service growing communities of urban denizens. Leaving behind their agrarian lifestyles and manorial obligations, these enterprising families sought their fortunes in free towns that embraced the "Commercial Revolution," where goods and ideas from faraway places would mix and mingle and greater opportunities abounded.

To be clear, stability in these early frontier economies wasn't provided by governments, but rather by private guilds and cartels, often dominated by families, that ensured product quality, provided capital, and regulated competition—conditions and traditions still present in many frontier economies today. As we'll learn in Chapter 6, these familial networks can sustain extended islands of trust that allow for much greater commercial activity and capital accumulation.[7] The integrity, honesty, and reputation of these families would allow them to attract customers, and then to sustain their loyalty across generations, despite frequent wars, plagues, and famine. However, much like feudal lords, these guilds were also resistant to innovation and competition, and their rigid structures ultimately inhibited broader economic growth.

The young Dutch Republic was among the earliest European states to develop an alternative structural solution, beyond contracts and guilds, to promote greater entrepreneurship, commerce, and trade. Their "killer app" was pioneered in Amsterdam at the turn of the seventeenth century and would quickly catapult the small trading nation ahead of its continental peers in terms of economic growth and political influence.

The invention of the joint-stock company was the critical turning point in the evolution of emerging economies. Not only did it allow complete strangers to co-invest in enduring entrepreneurial ventures, but for the first time in history, it also allowed them to sell their "shares" to complete strangers without affecting the continuity of the enterprise. This modular form of ownership was truly revolutionary, allowing companies to remain permanently capitalized—not merely for a single maritime voyage, but theoretically to operate in perpetuity.[8]

Now, hundreds and even thousands of independent speculators could invest in a common enterprise like the Dutch East India Company (or VOC, for Vereenigde Oostindische Compagnie) without necessarily knowing their fellow investors personally, and trust that the company's directors would be responsible fiduciaries. As the VOC built out a vast and lucrative trade network in the Far East, often by force, shareholders received regular dividends based on their proportionate ownership while continuing to own the underlying equity. They could also choose to sell their stock at a moment's notice, at a fair market value in a public exchange, and receive their capital within a few short days.

Contemporary "investors" (as commercial gamblers and wealthy merchants first became known around that time) were quick to take note.[9] These new regulated investment vehicles made speculating inherently more predictable and profitable than it had been in the past while diminishing reliance on extended families as a primary source of information, capital, and support. As a result, vast riches migrated into companies listed on the Amsterdam Stock Exchange, and into the coffers of the city's new fractional reserve banks, giving rise to the Dutch Golden Age. For nearly a century after the launch of the VOC, the Dutch had become one of the most dominant empires in the world, leading in trade, shipping, finance, culture, scholarship, and even scientific discovery.

By the early nineteenth century, other early adopters of these new regulated capital markets, including the British, French, and Americans, eventually joined the Dutch among the ranks of the first emerging economies. Migrating together up the Hierarchy of Stability, each of these societies was rapidly industrializing, which dramatically changed what people made and bought, where they lived and worked, what they ate and drank, who set the rules, and how they enforced them.

The joint-stock companies operating within these more stable and sophisticated economies were no longer managing single ships cruising around the Mediterranean, but fleets of hundreds sailing halfway around the planet. Their governments were no longer simply responsible for waging war, but also for managing peace and enabling prosperity. Their private companies were no longer isolated households making textiles or bread, but now included massive rail and telegraph trusts that gathered humans in the tens of thousands, requiring entirely new management systems and even ways of telling the time.

Importantly, while these early emerging economies incubated some iconic family businesses—from the Rothschilds in Prussia to the Cargills in the United States and the Hermès in France—these public investments in stability also diminished the traditional role of family, which for millennia had formed the cornerstone of all commercial and social life. Households were quickly being replaced by factories as the basic units of economic output, making individuals more dependent on strangers for employment, food, shelter, and access to health care, and thus reducing the inherent benefits of family membership. The importance of this shift cannot be overstated. The rise of emerging economies, and eventually of advanced economies, has profoundly affected the role and impact of the family ever since.

THE EVOLUTION OF MODERN ECONOMIES

In many ways, the Industrial Revolution was like a test rocket blasting off, launching a small group of pioneering nations toward an exciting but unknown future, at a pace both powerful and perilous, and with implications for society and the family that were yet unknown. New joint-stock companies, central banks, steam-powered factories, telegraphs, railroads, and global supply chains all helped these few vanguard economies achieve developmental "escape velocity"—breaking free from the inertia of the Middle Ages while racing toward the dynamism and abundance of the modern world. However, such immense commercial energy also unleashed greater complexity and volatility, requiring ever more sophisticated approaches to governance, business strategy, and organizational design, along with greater trust in "the system" to stabilize and regulate public affairs.

The scale and scope of these new institutional stabilizers has remained one of the greatest structural distinctions between emerging and advanced economies ever since. Governments in the United Kingdom, the United States, and Germany, which were early to invest in this sophisticated infrastructure, were able to generate a sustained abundance of

Economic Development Doesn't Happen Overnight

It took centuries for external stabilizers to enable humanity's exponential growth

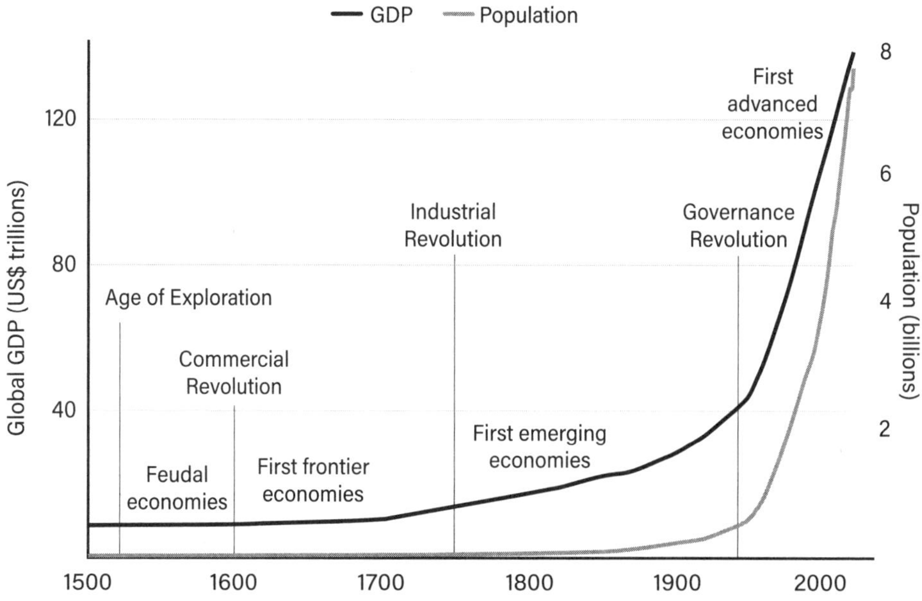

Source: Our World in Data, Authors

goods, services, and infrastructures. Though that abundance wasn't evenly distributed, the rising tide was so significant that it managed to lift most ships—if not directly through entrepreneurship and employment, then indirectly through taxes and public investment.

By the time John Maynard Keynes first published his treatise on *The Economic Consequences of the Peace* in 1919, middle-class Brits—shell-shocked by the horrors of World War I—were getting an early taste of the stability and prosperity made possible by increasing investment in public infrastructure such as the Central Electricity Board, and social welfare programs like the Children's Charter and old-age pensions. Keynes openly marveled at the benefits globalization had bestowed upon the working class of his era, however problematic the colonial underpinnings. An expanding array of consumer choices and commercial conveniences—once unimaginable luxuries even for royals—was increasingly within reach, foreshadowing the "endless aisle" that many of us today take for granted. As Keynes observed, "The inhabitant of London could order by telephone, sipping his morning tea in bed, the various products of the whole earth, in such quantity as he might see fit, and reasonably expect their early delivery upon his doorstep."[10]

The businesses fueling commercial activity in these economies were among the most innovative and well funded in human history. They developed novel approaches to managing complex global supply chains, accommodated more generous labor policies, and learned to respond to the dynamic tastes and preferences of their increasingly affluent customers.

But much like modern India or China, dynamic and fast-growing emerging economies like the United Kingdom and the United States also had an Achilles' heel. In the excitement to sustain an era of unbridled growth, they had not yet implemented a set of economic stabilizers strong enough to avert the Great Depression. As a result, at the end of the Roaring Twenties, the global economy fell into a devastating tailspin.

With public assistance programs still in their infancy, families once again became the primary source of security and support. On both sides of the Atlantic, multigenerational households were forced to pool scant resources, with younger members seeking jobs wherever they could find them while their elders watched over the children—common strategies we still find today in emerging and frontier economies.

It would take President Franklin D. Roosevelt and his New Deal to launch the first truly advanced economy. His audacious package of stimulus spending, industrial policy overhauls, and robust market regulations aimed to strike at the root causes of the Great Depression while mitigating its most devastating effects. These included a new portfolio of public institutions, such as the Federal Deposit Insurance Corporation (1933), the Securities and Exchange Commission (1934), and the Social Security Administration (1935), each designed to address a different form of common market failure. With renewed political will, these new agencies immediately began to stabilize markets for labor, capital, and goods, ushering in the most extended period of peace and prosperity the world has ever known.[11]

The newly minted advanced economies, including the United States, the United Kingdom, and Canada, were humanity's best attempts yet at balancing the invisible hand of private capital and the visible hand of good government. Unintentionally, their investments rendered many of the historical benefits of family obsolete, because protections against food insecurity, labor insecurity, housing insecurity, and physical insecurity were now enshrined more directly and systematically in constitutional rights and freedoms.

Ever since, as countries have migrated further up the Hierarchy of Stability, and governments have taken on more responsibility for enabling well-functioning markets for goods, labor, capital, and information, businesses have been able to focus more on their products and customers than on their security and access to capital. Consequently, they tend to rely less on family as a source of opportunity and support. In contrast, when countries lurch suddenly from peace into war, or are caught between dueling regimes, or are plunged into economic chaos, the pursuit of growth becomes secondary to survival, and the stabilizing benefits of familial networks naturally grow.[12]

In the advanced economies, such stability can flourish for seventy-five years or more, roughly the length of a human lifetime. Stability allows entire generations of citizens to live out their full lives in relative peace and prosperity. At the same time, it leaves many business leaders without much intuition about how to deal with existential risks when they inevitably reemerge. By now, anyone not in their nineties will only ever understand the events of the Great Depression and World War II secondhand. That leaves fewer of us who can broadcast to younger generations the rare privilege that comes with being citizens in an advanced economy, as well as the dangers of losing faith in our public institutions and democratic ideals. Not surprisingly, many younger citizens have become more easily dissatisfied with a status quo that isn't working well for them, yet they don't have a visceral sense of how much worse conditions can get. They are thus increasingly likely to agitate for revolutionary change.[13]

Contrast this with emerging economies like China and India, where eras of sustained peace and prosperity may last a decade or two, but rarely longer. Such "golden ages" are often triggered by rapid industrialization, as was the case in nineteenth-century Europe, followed inevitably by some massive market failure or political crisis. Under these conditions, fewer institutional stabilizers (such as social security programs and monetary stimulus policies) are available to support a speedy return to business-as-usual, so businesses and families are often better prepared.

The most enduring enterprises learn to thrive while the sun is shining, and to leverage reserves of family capital and investments in organizational resilience whenever political or economic systems break down. In emerging economies, there's still a visceral sense of "what it was like" to live and work in a frontier economy, and consequently a deeper commitment to investing internally in stability in the present while still keeping one eye focused on the future.

Meanwhile, at the base of the pyramid, in frontier economies such as Lebanon or Nigeria, stability is the rare exception to the rule, so survival requires constant strategic vigilance. Much like Europe at the turn of the seventeenth century, these contexts are rife with commercial activity but lack many of the external stabilizers present in more affluent economies. As a result, enduring enterprises are forced to invest significantly in their own internal stability.

To do so, they deploy a portfolio of strategies to anticipate and mitigate future disruptions (which we'll introduce in Chapter 4) while also leveraging the familial resources and networks that form the foundations of humanity's most ancient social and commercial traditions. As our research confirmed, in more turbulent conditions, these often overlooked and underappreciated familial assets can make the difference between mere survival and enduring entrepreneurial success.

THE ORIGINS OF INTERNAL STABILITY

In a sobering 2015 article on the promise and perils of life in modern Mexico, *The Economist* made a provocative statement: "Without enforceable laws and contracts, public services that make taxes seem worth paying and a political establishment that serves the national interest, the only institution that most people can rely on is the family."[14] This observation resonates not only with our own experience in Mexico, but also more broadly.

Family is the first laboratory within which humans develop the capacity to adapt, collaborate, and trust. A healthy home life provides a unique source of stability, particularly in turbulent times. For enterprising families, such resilience often begins at home, then projects into their organizations, and ultimately out into the world. As we mentioned earlier in the

The Family Factor Is More Pronounced in Less Stable Environments

Familial structures have a greater impact on organizational design and resilience

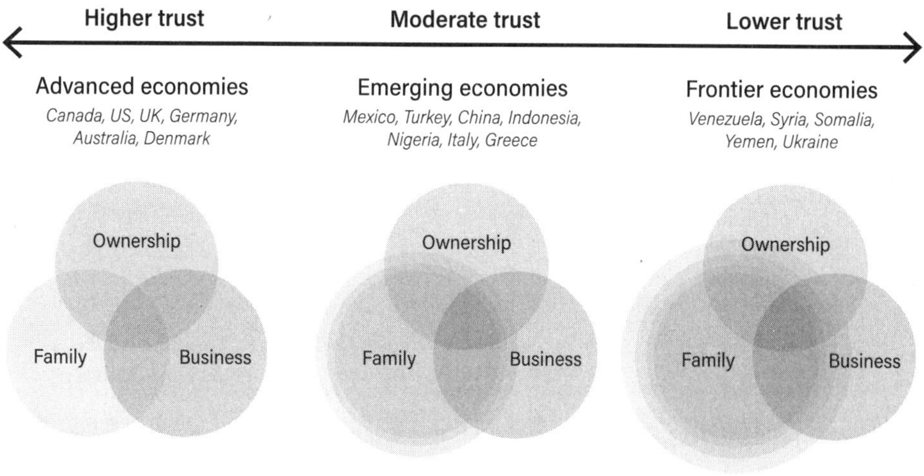

book, this influence is particularly impactful in lower trust environments, where external stabilizers are scarce and unreliable.

That enterprising families are able to grow successfully in emerging and frontier economies, while holding tens and in some cases even hundreds of cousins together under a common strategic vision, is a truly remarkable achievement. Consider the Castillo family from Guatemala, with over 1,300 descendants, a consortium of cousins who have successfully stewarded the family's entrepreneurial legacy, a regional beverage and food conglomerate, for over 137 years. By fostering the active participation of shareholders in management and governance roles, and by gradually evolving their governance structures and processes to allow for an optimal balance of professional merit and family representation, they have managed to sustain unity and commitment to their common legacy despite a highly turbulent context. They are a wonderful example of what a client of ours refers to as "nepotism with excellence."

The important role that these extended familial networks play in the resilience and economic success of families in frontier regions cannot be overstated.[15] Familial networks are a fundamental source of support, vital knowledge, and information. Given the size of frontier families, and the premium they place on loyalty and mutual support, the ongoing curation and strengthening of these extended networks can offer significant competitive advantages that help mitigate the risks of operating in these volatile environments. When a family exceeds the number of members that can be adequately cared for, it is not unusual for some of the children to be sent to extended family members to be looked after. Grandparents, aunts and uncles, and godparents take these "excess" children in and raise them as their own, sometimes in the same community where the parents live and sometimes in locations farther away, where they may have occasional contact with their families of origin.

Mapping how these familial networks function reveals important drivers of their resilience. For instance, heads of households and business founders often spend a significant portion of their time triaging favors through their familial networks—helping family members or close friends gain access to the right medical expert; lending money to a relative in need; offering guidance on a tricky family issue, such as substance abuse or run-ins with the local authorities; providing shelter for a battered or distressed spouse; providing funding for the schooling of an ambitious young cousin; facilitating access to immigration lawyers; or offering discounted prices on products and services to financially strapped relatives. These actions create substantial goodwill throughout the network.

While there is certainly reciprocity at work, these are not, however, "tit-for-tat" exchanges. As in the Bible's Book of Ecclesiastes, when the household heads and business founders cast their bread upon these networks, they are making investments in social capital—building goodwill with loosely defined expectations of collective benefit.[16] The person who is helped at any given point in time is not obliged to give back to the more influential helper—certainly not in the short term or in an explicit way. Instead, these familial networks operate with a "pay-it-forward" mindset, in which the person helping incurs the implicit obligation to repay the favor, at some undefined point, to someone else who may be in need of assistance or help.

While there is rarely hard accounting at work, the giving and receiving that goes on typically follow a pattern of "rough justice" in order to stay in balance over the long term. Those who have more are expected to give more. Those with less are expected to give back with their loyalty to the family, and to reciprocate when called upon to help with a particular assignment or task.

For those building businesses, such familial networks also serve as tools for scouting and recruiting talent. Cousins who excel at delivering results when tapped can be amply rewarded and recognized. The best are often brought into roles in the business. So the ebb and flow of influence that moves through these networks helps to sort out who can be trusted with sensitive matters, such as the family's finances and personal security. Again, the active curation of these networks greatly simplifies the demands placed on families in challenging environments, providing a durable source of internal stability.[17]

In short, the family itself is an essential source from which some remarkable enterprises derive the resilience needed not just to survive but to thrive in turbulent times. Family permeates all aspects of their functioning, including the values that define their highest priorities and the culture of the businesses they build, the vision and long-term goals that provide direction and purpose to their enterprise, and the strategies and tactics needed to succeed.

THE EVOLUTION OF ENTERPRISING FAMILIES

So far we have demonstrated how a stable and predictable context provides the institutional scaffolding that makes large-scale commercial activity possible. We've also argued that it is easy for those of us fortunate enough to have been born in societies in which these external stabilizers exist to take them for granted—until they fail us and we get caught by surprise.

Such economic entropy is always lurking in the background. As we learned in the previous chapter, the more complex and interwoven our societies become, the more energy needs to be invested to sustain external stability. But in circumstances where public institutions are unreliable or under threat, the more this investment needs to shift internally.

Those at the helm of the most enduring enterprises understand this intuitively. They are a rare and special breed, and we can learn a lot about resilience from how these families emerge, evolve, and endure in the face of chronic adversity.

Their stories typically begin with a remarkable and charismatic entrepreneur—someone who emerges from the periphery rather than the establishment.[18] They're often new arrivals in the capital from the countryside, or immigrants from a distant shore, whose hunger, sheer ambition, and wherewithal fuel extensive experimentation. Frontier capitalists are typically "pushed" into entrepreneurship out of necessity, rather than "pulled" by a preconceived vision of an enterprise they are aspiring to build. Their vision, insofar as they have one, is simply to succeed and to provide for their family.

This path is often littered with early failures that nurture their experience—and resilience. These founders are typically graduates from the university of life, not schooled intellects. Life in survival mode is a powerful teacher. What distinguishes the founders who succeed from those who do not is precisely the capacity to extract useful learning from a stream of failures and successes that simultaneously motivate them and gradually improve their odds of success. What may start out as a process of trial and error, with its addictive random reinforcement schedule, evolves with some luck into an entrepreneurial learning machine.

The most successful founders enthusiastically embrace the inherent risks of seemingly insurmountable odds and deconstruct them into a stream of smaller but achievable challenges. They continuously tweak their small ventures and adapt them to the immediate constraints they face as well as to the evolving needs of their customers. The kernels of their entrepreneurial ideas come from many places—an innovative approach to a product or service that's customized to the needs of the local culture, a previously imported product that is no longer available but for which there's pent-up demand, an innovative idea learned on an apprenticeship or trip abroad, or a serendipitous encounter with people in power that opens access to information and opportunities.[19]

While some founders are natural strategists, most are master tacticians, capable of pivoting in whatever direction success points. Like adept sailors, their strategy is to remain flexible so they can tack as the wind and currents change. That said, they all share two common denominators—the raw ambition to succeed, and the grit to achieve it. Their risk-taking builds confidence, and in some cases even a false sense of mastery. As a founder once explained it to us, the secret for succeeding in frontier environments is an "endless capacity for denial."

With little time to socialize, for many frontier founders the business itself becomes a conduit for potential life partners. Trusted employees, suppliers, or even loyal customers can become eventual soulmates. They are pulled into the gravitational field of the founder's entrepreneurial dream and find an orbit that resonates with their own ambitions and aspirations. Some serve as traditionally supportive spouses, nurturing the founder's ambitions and overseeing the development of the next generation. Others become full-fledged business partners and collaborators, tending seamlessly to both familial and business responsibilities. In some instances, the spouses themselves inherit the leadership role if the founder dies unexpectedly or becomes incapacitated. In these cases, a spouse's role may shift from home builder to business leader. The spouse's own entrepreneurial capacities come to light and are deployed to sustain and grow the family's commercial legacy.[20]

In these companies, the founder's assumptions about how the world works form the deep foundation upon which the culture and structure of the enterprise is built.[21] But these assumptions also shape the family's internal structures—particularly those related to parenting. In the early stages, there are often few boundaries between the family and the fledgling enterprise. Children are brought to work and work is brought to the home in an uninterrupted flow of activity in which everyone participates in some form. The children are often assigned tasks—arranging window displays, greeting customers, helping to stack inventory, tidying up the production or office space, or, later, overseeing the cash register or helping with the bookkeeping. This work can feel more like shared household chores than formal organizational responsibilities.

As they grow up, children born into these privileged but complex environments must find a path to differentiate psychologically under the shadow of a heroic founder—a challenging developmental task under any circumstances, but particularly so in family enterprises in frontier markets, where paths for gaining independence are often constrained. In these societies, when you come from a prominent entrepreneurial family, the expectation is that you will work for your family's business. It is often framed as a matter of loyalty.

But while all families share much in common, each is also unique. Consequently, the early values of the founders influence the opportunities and obligations of future generations. For instance, the more autocratic the founder's parenting style, the more likely it is that members of the family will compete with one another to ingratiate themselves with the founder and exploit each other for personal gain—as in a Shakespearean drama or an episode from the HBO series *Succession*. In contrast, those founders whose parenting styles are more democratic are more likely to induce relationships in which everyone works to further the interests of the whole family.

Over time, the stability and opportunity generated by sustained entrepreneurial success tend to hold these growing tribes together far longer than what is experienced by families without shared business interests. As a result, families in frontier markets tend to be large, and their sheer size can become an important source of individual and collective resilience. For instance, larger families offer abundant cheap and loyal labor. They also provide a wide array of complementary skills that can be put in service of a growing enterprise. Additionally, larger families offer long-term protection for aging seniors in environments with poor health and social services, as well as insurance for high mortality rates among children.

As entrepreneurial activities unfold, much of the acquisition of business skills in the family happens by doing, without much awareness that learning is actually taking place. The business nurtures the resilience of the family, and the family nurtures the resilience of the business, in a mutually reinforcing web of collaborative opportunities and obligations. If managed well, this symbiosis can harness the innate talents of a family and deploy them in service of wealth creation, ultimately benefiting all key stakeholders in the system.[22]

At the same time, these experiences can also leave a deep imprint in the minds of family members. Threats to the business are often experienced as threats to the family. The mismanagement of production, the mistreatment of customers, the mishandling of inventories, or the fear of disappointing the never-ending demands of often loving though stern founders are all experienced as challenges both to the business and to the family. This dynamic adds even more pressure to succeed and helps to fend off feelings of disappointment and shame.

If the business gains some lift and continues to grow, founders' extended families are often recruited to fulfill a variety of functions and organically evolving roles. Some are tapped for seed capital, while others supply raw materials at favorable rates, or become useful as general fixers, or serve as liaisons to the local authorities. Still others are tasked with sensitive roles in the business that typically involve the handling of money—bookkeeping or the oversight of inventory—all of which require high levels of trust, a rare commodity in frontier environments.

The next developmental challenge occurs at the end of the founder's tenure. By then the children have had to find their place inside (or outside) the enterprise, and the need to begin separating business and family responsibilities and formalizing roles and procedures necessary for growth becomes increasingly apparent. In some families, the impetus to hold the business and the family together exerts a powerful binding force, making the sustainability of a viable business possible. In others, the wear and tear of building a business in a hostile frontier environment strains family relationships, making it evident that sustaining the continuity of an integrated enterprise is not a viable option.

In cases when the siblings' personal and professional aspirations are not in alignment, and the costs of continuing to work interdependently under a single umbrella outweigh the benefits of staying together, the prospects of continuity rapidly fade. Just as family *unity* is a source of strength and resilience in frontier markets, family *disunity* and mistrust compromise adaptability. Frontier markets are unforgiving, and enterprises that took a lifetime to build can lose their footing and disappear in moments if the family breaks down into rival factions.

Those that are able to persevere—successfully evolving from a system of centralized authority in the hands of a founder into a partnership of siblings in which decision-making authority is effectively shared—are faced with another fundamental challenge. Building the capacity to collaborate effectively in service of realizing a shared vision is an essential ingredient for continuity. Sibling partnerships can only work when they harness collaboration in service of mutual benefit. For these systems, the adversities of frontier markets become a common threat—a shared enemy of sorts—that evokes an instinctive collaborative capacity and collective resilience. Effective sibling partnerships are those in which the siblings manage to build complementary roles through which they can add value to the enterprise, and respond effectively to shifting external contexts, while genuinely satisfying their unique professional and personal aspirations.[23]

If successful for long enough, these enterprises also invariably reach a critical juncture in the developmental road as the transition to the next generation looms large. In these moments, they can either work to put the governance structures in place that are needed to hold together a complex cousin consortium, or they can sell and divide the enterprise, returning to a consolidated ownership structure. For some sibling groups, the investment necessary to sustain their collaboration into the next generation proves too burdensome or complex. Demographics often become a significant driver of these decisions, as families with only a few siblings in the second generation can balloon rapidly into an extensive network of cousins by the third.

As ownership fragments with the passing of generations, and the ability of any single individual or subgroup to impose their will on others becomes increasingly tenuous, the adoption of more formal governance structures, policies, and practices becomes imperative. Like the third law of thermodynamics, as the complexity of a family enterprise system increases, so too does the energy needed for sustainable integration.[24]

Enterprising families that have flourished through tactical opportunism must confront the need for structures, policies, and processes that by their very nature constrain the creative improvisation needed to respond to the ever-shifting demands of frontier environments. As a client from Mexico stated succinctly, "Now that we're so many owners, we absolutely need structures and policies. And our first policy must be to remain flexible." Learning to manage this paradox effectively becomes a competitive skill.

In these larger family systems, much energy is also invested in governing the "ungovernables"—those who continuously break the rules in service of advancing their own personal objectives. The enforceability of agreements is a common challenge, particularly in environments dominated by legal informality, and can pose a serious threat to the continuity of any cousin consortium. However, this dynamic is particularly acute in regions where charismatic personal leadership—rather than institutionalized systems for decision-making and enforcement—is deeply ingrained into the collective DNA.[25]

A more nuanced view of families, as sources of both stability and instability, is therefore critical as we build a greater understanding of the preconditions for enduring success. In the next chapter, we'll introduce our first case study—the Carvajal family from Cali, Colombia—whose inspiring entrepreneurial journey illustrates how certain families provide precisely this type of stability across multiple generations in spite of intense political, economic, and social headwinds. Their story will also introduce us to a portfolio of stabilizing strategies—forged in volatile conditions—that all leaders and organizations can deploy to increase their chances of thriving in both tranquil and turbulent times.

KEY INSIGHTS

- Building an enduring enterprise requires understanding the origins of both external and internal stability.
- External stability is impacted by the breadth and quality of public institutions, which are designed to create greater stability and predictability, and ultimately to foster large-scale commercial activity.
- Early feudal economies lacked incentives for innovation and investment until the emergence of commercial law and institutions such as joint-stock companies and fractional reserve banks.
- The Commercial Revolution marked a major inflection point in the evolution of modern capitalism, establishing a foundation for business activity at an unprecedented scale.
- These changes ultimately brought about the Industrial Revolution, which fueled a period of rapid economic growth for some emerging economies, driven by advancements in technology and the creation of novel institutions to help keep this accelerating development on track.

- Emerging after World War II, modern advanced economies typically prioritize both prosperity and stability, and they have been successful at sustaining these conditions for nearly a century.
- However, recent global events, including pandemics and political conflicts, are harbingers of a New Age of Uncertainty, which is threatening external stabilizers at all levels on the Hierarchy of Stability.
- This is precisely where internal stabilizers become critical—with families providing a natural internal source of strength and resilience, particularly in turbulent times.
- Strong extended family networks can provide businesses with invaluable support, information sharing, and access to talent.
- Enduring enterprises are often started by resourceful and adaptable founders who build their ventures from the ground up, learning from failures and adapting their strategies based on scarcity and local needs.
- Family members play a crucial role in supporting and growing these businesses, where spouses become partners and children grow up involved in the business, fostering a sense of shared purpose.
- As families develop across generations, governance structures become essential, and balancing flexibility with structure is a crucial challenge.

4

INVESTING IN STABILITY

The most important aspect of the work we do at Carvajal, and as a family, is to live our purpose every day. It's how our family overcame crisis in the 1930s, World War II in the 1940s, and a host of challenges connected to Latin America in the decades that followed. Our firm sense of purpose enables us to confront whatever obstacles and disruptions lay ahead.

—Pedro Carvajal

One of the privileges of our work is the opportunity to meet remarkable enterprising families from around the world. We have featured many of these inspirational cases throughout the book, each one demonstrating a different approach to navigating turbulent times. However, one family in particular exemplified so many of these fundamental building blocks that we chose to leverage their story to introduce our model of entrepreneurial endurance.

For over a century, Carvajal has been a role model for the type of agility and resilience necessary to survive under a variety of adverse conditions—from chronic political dysfunction to paramilitary insurgency, runaway inflation, and currency chaos. During periods of relative stability, its leaders have pursued world-class strategic planning and operations management across their portfolio of businesses. However, the company's real competitive advantage shines during a crisis—whether it is a civil war, a political coup, or narco terrorism—when conventional business models break down.

Carvajal was founded in Cali, Colombia, in 1904—a challenging time for the South American nation. Like many of its neighbors, Colombia was still struggling to define its identity after centuries of colonial servitude under Spanish rule. The country had just endured a period of intense civil strife known as the Thousand Days' War—a conflict mostly between the Liberal and Conservative Parties over the future of the nation.

It was precisely this turbulent backdrop that prompted Manuel Carvajal Valencia, then fifty-three, to convince his wife to sell a property she had inherited and buy a printing press to start *El Dia*, a weekly newspaper. His early foray into publishing was hardly coincidental. A lawyer by profession, Manuel's real calling was politics, and *El Dia* was a means to disseminate his ideas and further his successful run for public office.

Manuel initially recruited two of his sons—Alberto, twenty-three, and Hernando, twenty—to help print and distribute his political pamphlets. They dutifully supported their father, but also realized that the press was mostly left idle throughout the week. So they launched a separate contract printing business—what today we might call a side hustle. This formed the foundation of the Carvajal family enterprise we know today.

At the time, the closed economy promoted by the ruling Conservatives made it possible for domestic champions like Carvajal to leverage their early entrepreneurial successes, allowing them to diversify into a wide array of industries and products unhampered by direct foreign competition. Alberto and Hernando invested considerable time and resources scouring international markets for new ideas and technologies. They traveled extensively throughout Europe, especially Germany, and brought back printing machines that were at the cutting edge of the publishing industry. The brothers also recruited German technicians with the specialized know-how needed to operate sophisticated lithography machines. These early bets established a culture of innovation that helped the young company to distinguish itself from peers, adapting global technologies, products, and services to meet the unique needs of Colombian consumers.

What makes this phase of the company's growth all the more extraordinary is that it took place against the backdrop of *La Violencia*—a period of great conflict in the 1940s and 1950s that killed over 200,000 citizens. The first wave of violence was sparked by the assassination of the popular Liberal leader Jorge Eliécer Gaitán, which once again pitted supporters of the Liberal and Conservative Parties against one another. In 1958, a power-sharing agreement established the National Front, temporarily stabilizing the political situation, though it failed to address underlying ideological tensions. This set the stage for decades of ongoing conflict involving government forces, paramilitary groups, and guerrilla organizations such as the Fuerzas Armadas Revolucionarias de Colombia (Revolutionary Armed Forces of Colombia, FARC) and Ejército de Liberación Nacional (National Liberation Army, ELN).

Throughout this period, the Carvajals' reputation for being generous corporate citizens in Cali and its surrounding communities insulated them from much of the turmoil. In fact, care for the community has been part of the family's core values since Manuel's first foray into public life. It provided an early and powerful internal stabilizer in the face of chronic external chaos.

For instance, at the height of *La Violencia*, the family launched the Fundación Carvajal (Carvajal Foundation), its philanthropic arm, initially donating 40 percent of its equity in the business. The stated purpose of the foundation was to help "vulnerable families" in Cali and beyond, demonstrating the family's deep conviction that "there cannot be a healthy business in a sick society."

Remarkably, this generous reallocation of capital didn't limit the company's growth prospects in the least. Under the leadership of the third generation, the Carvajal family continued its strategic expansion, producing personalized stationery and printing phone books. The lucrative market for Colombia's first yellow pages—in many ways the Google of the twentieth century—became a critical driver of Carvajal's growth for the next half-century.

It was only in the early 1960s, after consolidating its market leadership in Colombia, that the Carvajals began to experiment with international expansion. They established a new printing plant in Puerto Rico at a time when American policymakers were eager to promote the island's development. An incentive program was established to encourage the pharmaceutical industry to build plants near the country's abundant sugarcane plantations, a key ingredient in the production of many medicines. Importantly for the Carvajals, pharmaceutical products required highly technical packaging and safety information—most importantly in Spanish, which no existing American printers were able to produce at scale. The Carvajals' sophistication and advanced machinery, coupled with their eloquent command of Spanish, allowed them to service the industry's niche demands. Building on this early success, they migrated into other adjacent countries where local competition was sparse, political and economic conditions were familiar, and their reputation for excellence preceded them.

Their international expansion took place despite waves of turmoil in Colombia—where the company still generated the vast majority of its profits. In many ways, it happened precisely because of it, as the family members sought to diversify exposure to their volatile home market. Throughout the 1960s and 1970s, the FARC and the ELN continued their campaigns of armed resistance to Colombia's central government, targeting infrastructure, disrupting transportation, and creating an overall climate of insecurity and uncertainty. Kidnappings and extortion became commonplace, adding an additional layer of danger for the family, its customers, and its loyal employees.

As if the security situation wasn't challenging enough, the 1980s also saw the meteoric rise of narco traffickers, most notably the Medellín Cartel led by Pablo Escobar, and the Cali Cartel led by the Rodríguez Orejuela brothers. These criminal syndicates amassed tremendous wealth and power, corrupting all levels of the Colombian government and law enforcement. Violent turf wars pitted them against each other and the state, further contributing to the chronic logistical and operational disruptions affecting Carvajal's most essential operations.

Endemic security issues only exacerbated the already volatile economic situation. At the time, fluctuating commodity prices for certain major exports, such as coffee, put a strain on government finances, while inconsistent fiscal policies triggered periods of high inflation and currency depreciation.[1] It became increasingly difficult for the company's executives to secure financing and craft long-term strategies, let alone for average citizens to afford to feed their families.

When faced with persistent external instability, the Carvajals draw strength from within, working hard to live up to a core set of enduring values, including ethical integrity, respect for customers and employees, and a deep commitment to their communities, that have been part of the enterprise since its founding. The family's relentless pursuit of the public's best interests has helped them rise above the chaos that plagues so many of their operating markets. Corrupt politicians, local guerrilla thugs, and narcos know that tempting the Carvajals with graft or appealing to greed is futile.

Alfredo Carvajal, who has served in various public roles, including as mayor of Cali, told us confidently that the family's reputation provided insulation from shady business dealings. In all his time in public office, he was never once offered any underhanded deals. "While corruption is certainly a problem, it is also true that there are many officials in government who conduct themselves ethically. The key is to carefully select with whom you associate yourself"—advice the company's leaders have followed assiduously over the years.

By the end of the twentieth century, having navigated successfully through periods of growth and turmoil across the continent, the company approached its one hundredth anniversary with a new set of challenges to both internal and external stability. The family was in its fifth and sixth generations and boasted a sprawling tribe of nearly 200 members. Carvajal's leaders recognized that maintaining consistent economic returns would become increasingly important to sustaining the commitment and engagement of this expansive community of owners, especially as many of them no longer lived in Colombia or had close emotional connections to the business and the foundation. Additionally, technological changes presented increasing threats to the enterprise's dominance across many of its conventional markets.[2]

As a result, in 1998 the family created Inversantamonica SA, an investment vehicle completely separate from their operating companies. Its express purpose was to grow a secondary pool of funds from which dividends could be paid to shareholders in the rare event that the operating businesses were unable to do so. In addition to providing greater asset diversity, Inversantamonica generated an additional stabilizing benefit that Carvajal's leaders called the "Social Dividend." This private safety net, established to provide all family members with access to health insurance, support with educational expenses, and housing assistance, was a direct response to the lack of public stabilizers in Colombia that are common among advanced economies.

The new collective nest egg also funded a family office, which was created to assist family members with personal financial matters and a variety of additional support services. Importantly, these benefits were offered equally to everyone in the family as long as they maintained a minimum proportion of their ownership in Carvajal. Building on a strong family culture, Inversantamonica helped to reinforce the unity and commitment of the shareholders as the size and complexity of the family increased. Gustavo Carvajal shared with us his strong conviction that "the Social Dividend has kept the family together throughout these very complicated times."

For over a century, this iconic enterprising family has demonstrated a willingness and a capacity to overcome the political, economic, and social turmoil that bankrupted many of their competitors and chased away countless multinationals. By shedding their dying yellow pages business in the 1990s, then reinventing the company as a lead player in the packaging and real estate industries, the Carvajals have shown remarkable resilience and adaptability. Today, their various business lines generate over US$1 billion in annual revenues, with operations in 14 countries and over 19,000 employees. Even still, the Carvajals aren't immune to the generic challenges that afflict all family companies, including generational transitions and succession, too much (or too little) governance, the increasing pace of technological disruptions, and the weight of an ever extended and dispersed network of family members.

Like all frontier capitalists, Carvajal will have to manage these evolving internal pressures while also responding effectively to the ever shifting sands that typify the external environments within which they operate. As with the cases we will feature throughout the book, they provide inspiration for leaders everywhere who are likely to experience greater uncertainty in the years ahead. But most importantly for this book, they help us introduce a unique portfolio of stabilizing strategies that together form the basis for enduring success.

BUILDING BLOCKS OF STABILITY

Obviously there are many paths to surviving and thriving in turbulent times, but the *seven stabilizing strategies* we lay out below represent the most common and replicable approaches we've observed. Over the past three decades, in our study and work with leading businesses around the world, we've witnessed firsthand how each of these strategies can be deployed successfully in a variety of contexts—from the earliest onset of a crisis, through its darkest hours, and onward until a "next normal" emerges. They align with the latest research among behavioral and social psychologists, developmental economists, historians, and evolutionary biologists, and will likely resonate with anyone who has spent time leading organizations through crises and turmoil.

We intentionally use the term "stability" rather than "adaptability" because these strategies are designed to introduce greater predictability into otherwise turbulent environments. Such investments should not, however, be confused with "rigidity" or "inertia." If anything, as we learned in the previous chapter, greater stability (up to a point) is an essential driver of commercial speculation and economic development.

Like ballasts on a ship, these seven strategies are designed to provide greater control and strategic intent—the precondition for all planning and progress. They are of little use when seas are calm, but essential during a storm. As we enter the New Age of Uncertainty, we believe leaders everywhere—particularly those with little experience navigating choppy waters—should at least test out a few of these stabilizing investments.

Let's begin with *differentiation*, a strategy that involves supplying an underserved niche in conditions that are often hostile to foreign competition or devoid of capital or technology. Throughout history, enterprising families in frontier environments have focused their entrepreneurial energies on acquiring or developing local alternatives to products and services that aren't readily available. For instance, Carvajal's flexible packaging unit

Introducing the Seven Building Blocks of Stability

Enduring enterprises leverage these strategies to support resilience and performance

Differentiation	Supplying an underserved niche in conditions hostile to traditional competition
Modularity	Developing a network of partnerships that operate autonomously and share resources seamlessly
Redundancy	Coordinating actions and sharing resources across nested or interdependent systems
Symbiosis	Investing in backup resources and processes for all essential systems and activities
Migration	Moving into new markets as resources become scarce and conditions more hostile
Simplification	Reducing complexity to cope with chronic resource scarcity or societal instability
Diversity	Developing a broad array of capabilities and resources to minimize risk of systemic collapse

deployed differentiation to solve the unique problem of distributing milk in developing countries. In the tropics milk spoils quickly, limiting its broad use as an essential source of nutrients. This is particularly problematic in impoverished communities, which lack access to refrigeration and reliable power. By identifying and adapting the latest aseptic packaging technology available in advanced economies, Carvajal managed to dramatically extend the shelf life of milk—from just a few days to over three months, satisfying a niche need and opening up lucrative new markets. As we'll learn in Chapter 5, differentiation comes in three distinct flavors, and it is among the most pervasive of the stabilizing strategies we've seen in practice.

Modularity involves the sharing of risk and opportunity across a network of strategic partners—the original "buddy system" of capitalism. As we learned in Chapter 3, such partnerships extend the frontiers of stability by encouraging greater collaboration; supporting the development of increasingly larger networks of information, resources, and expertise; and ultimately expanding the scale and scope of commercial activity. The Carvajal family successfully deployed this strategy by nurturing over twenty joint ventures around the South American continent, becoming the dominant distributor of yellow pages throughout Latin America. As Alfredo Carvajal shared, "You absolutely need local know-how—people with the connections and particular knowledge of each market." As we'll learn in Chapter 6, managing and sustaining these partnerships effectively requires its own unique expertise—particularly in turbulent times—skills that the Carvajals had honed over generations.

Symbiosis has been deployed in every political economy on the planet by enduring enterprises. It involves developing close relationships with public officials, business leaders, and communities to provide islands of stability within otherwise mercurial markets. Symbiosis is pervasive in the natural world—where unrelated species interact to compete for resources or to seek mutual protection against common threats. But as we'll see in Chapter 7, this strategy can also be extremely effective in business, particularly when external stability is elusive and patrons remain in power for extended periods of time. In the case of Carvajal, Manuel's early career in politics laid the foundations for a close relationship between the family and the political establishment, and many of his descendants have since served in public office—including in key cabinet posts and prestigious ambassadorial roles under a number of administrations. The Colombian government was also one of the company's most important buyers of printing products, including the paper ballots used for elections. Just as importantly, the family's commitment to local communities has been a core value of the enterprise and critical to its success, including the many philanthropic activities of the Carvajal Foundation.

Redundancy involves building backup systems and resources in an effort to protect against disruptive events and ensure operational continuity. It typifies the conservative mantra "just in case," rather than the vaunted "just in time." As we'll explore in Chapter 8, dependence on a single resource or relationship can be fatal during a crisis, so resilient firms often secure multiple providers, maintain surplus inventories, and build backup infrastructure (such as power generators or even secondary facilities). It is especially valuable in remote locations where traditional infrastructure is either nonexistent, expensive, or unreliable. The Carvajal family's Social Dividend is an innovative example of financial redundancy. This strategic nest egg has helped the enterprise meet shareholder obligations whenever cash flows in their operating businesses have been limited. It has even allowed the family to take on additional risk in their main businesses, knowing that there is a safe reserve of uncorrelated assets available.

Migration is one of the most natural reactions to worsening operational conditions: seeking calmer waters or greener pastures. It requires quickly pivoting into new markets when conditions become so hostile that exit is the best or only option. As we'll learn in Chapter 9, there are countless stories of family firms forced to migrate away from home, often due to political persecution and regime change, but also as a strategic response to changing regulatory and market conditions. Once again, Carvajal provides a remarkable case study of investing in the building blocks of stability, this time in defense of its 80 percent market share of printed notebooks in Ecuador. Responding to new protectionist measures in 2015 that increased tariffs on nearly 3,000 Colombian and Peruvian products, in a matter of days Carvajal's leaders secured a Colombian printing machine, physically loaded it onto a truck, and migrated it to the Ecuadorian capital of Quito. Several years later, after a change in government, the import restrictions were lifted, and the company quickly migrated the equipment back to Cali, where they could operate it more efficiently and profitably.

Simplification is most effective when rapidly changing environments leave no other option but to brace for impact and ride out the storm. As we'll see in Chapter 10, under these conditions leaders are left with little choice but to prioritize the company's most essential products, services, and processes until conditions improve and resources become more available to support a return to scale and complexity. For instance, during a rapid depreciation or change in a currency regime, businesses can lose access overnight to foreign markets for capital and raw materials. Wars can have a similar effect, shrinking industrial activity and forcing leaders to scrounge for resources until external conditions stabilize. Throughout

Carvajal's history, there have been many instances that called for a dramatic organizational simplification because of political turmoil or market failure. Military coups across Central America over the years intermittently shut down the company's yellow pages business as governments tried to prevent citizens from communicating with each other. The situation required a radical simplification of their internal operational footprint until conditions eventually improved.

Diversity involves promoting greater breadth in key products, services, suppliers, customers, regions—and critically, talent—to help minimize acute risks to individual segments of a business, and to generate synergies and innovation across a portfolio. Deploying this strategy effectively goes well beyond the Nobel Prize–winning theories of Harry Markowitz, which mostly ignore the possibility of imperfect markets. As we'll see in Chapter 11, imperfect markets grow increasingly common further down the Hierarchy of Stability, forcing leaders to manage industry and country risks not through external capital markets, but through the internal expansion of business activities. Since the Carvajal brothers' very first side-hustle into commercial printing, the family's entrepreneurial investments in a wide array of businesses and markets have infused diversity directly into its core operating model. As Alfredo Carvajal put it, "We survived mainly because we diversified." Importantly, the company's commitment to diversity goes well beyond its physical and financial capital, and fully embraces the benefits of a diverse array of human capital. Non-family executives and employees are empowered to rise to the highest levels of management, strategically widening the pool of available leadership talent. Additionally, their fiduciary board includes a majority of independent directors deliberately selected for their diverse domain expertise, ensuring that rich strategic dialogue is built into all layers of the company's governance architecture.

As the Carvajal story suggests, families often function as experiential laboratories in which the stabilizing strategies are first tested and then fitted to their unique personal, familial, and organizational preferences and conditions. Eventually, as the family matures, this process provides the foundation for how the strategies are applied within the broader enterprise. In particular, it's important to recognize that few families deploy all seven strategies simultaneously. Rather, as the family evolves and circumstances change, different strategies come to the foreground as emergent pathways for adaptation. The choice of a given strategy often reflects the dynamics of the family itself. This includes its history, the quality and strength of its relationships, the level of trust among its members, how well differentiated individuals are, the gender and age composition of the family, and how authority, cooperation, and rivalry are handled. Each of these factors can influence how adaptive strategies are selected, deployed, or abandoned.

For instance, whom the family selects to migrate to a new territory, manage a joint venture partnership, or lead a simplification campaign, often depends on factors such as birth order, gender, and the level of trust that the senior family leaders place on individuals in the next generation. Consequently, the choice of strategy is not necessarily conscious, though it is often informed by preconceived notions about a family's shared vision for the enterprise and by the roles that founders and leaders envision for their children and descendants. We're simply pointing out that internal circumstances within the family can also stimulate the adoption of particular strategies at a given point in time.

CONTEXT MATTERS

Throughout their long and remarkable history, the members of the Carvajal family have deployed each of the seven building blocks of stability many times over, both instinctively and with strategic intent. Gustavo Carvajal summarized the company's approach: "The only sure thing in Latin America is continuous change. So you have to be adapting all the time." We're not claiming that these investments alone are a guarantee for enduring success, but they do provide a wonderful illustration of how the rules of engagement can be very different depending on where we sit on the Hierarchy of Stability, and how they inevitably evolve over time.

After all, Colombia was a very different place when Manuel Carvajal Valencia imported the company's first lithographic press at the turn of the twentieth century. As economies become more affluent, companies require fewer internal stabilizers, because the external context is intrinsically more predictable. For instance, fewer kidnappings, hyperinflationary episodes, and political coups require less redundancy, simplification, and symbiosis. Of course, the same is also true in reverse. When countries slide down the hierarchy—and are suddenly and unexpectedly faced with geopolitical shocks, economic turmoil, political dysfunction, or natural disasters—conventional strategic intuition is at best obsolete and at worst dangerous.

This logic is obvious to leaders and citizens who have lived and worked further down the Hierarchy of Stability and cope with elevated uncertainty all the time. Like Carvajal, their organizations are built for agility rather than speed. Without reliable public institutions and infrastructure, private companies and citizens have no choice but to invest in stability themselves. In contrast, those who lead organizations in advanced economies are almost exclusively focused on efficiency and profitability, since stability is provided by the external environment rather than originating from within. But as the Stanford economist W. Brian Arthur has argued, "When a system is optimized, all its parts need to work properly, and some are going to be working at their limit. . . . If things go wrong, even minor disruptions can set off a cascade of failures."[3]

Like drag cars racing in straight lines down manicured tracks, these marvels of Six Sigma engineering can be sent into a tailspin by even the slightest turbulence. This is precisely why Formula 1 vehicles look and function differently from drag cars, given their greater requirements for lateral movement and controlled deceleration. Similarly, nimble rally cars are designed for off-road trails, and need to prioritize handling and shock absorption over blistering acceleration. In these rough-and-tumble environments, even a lowly Subaru will trounce a multimillion-dollar Ferrari. Throw a little rain or fog into the mix, and features designed for speed become even more of a liability, forcing greater vigilance and agility behind the wheel. The same is true for businesses: the strategies used to navigate must complement the demands of the environment in which they operate. When our operating environment is filled with hairpin turns and gravel trails, more stabilizing investments are necessary.

Obviously, advanced economies are not impervious to risk, nor are frontier economies devoid of predictability. We're simply emphasizing an important point that often goes unaddressed in the management literature: that leaders need to invest both in growth and stability if they want to create an enduring enterprise.

KEY INSIGHTS

- The Carvajal family business, founded in 1904 by Manuel Carvajal Valencia in Cali, Colombia, offers a fascinating case study in family business endurance.
- From its humble beginnings with one printing press, Carvajal blossomed into a multifaceted holding company spanning multiple industries and countries.
- Carvajal's success can be attributed to seven stabilizing strategies that all leaders can deploy to increase their resilience and performance:
    - *Differentiation* involves supplying an underserved niche in conditions that are often hostile to foreign competition or devoid of capital or technology.
    - *Modularity* involves the sharing of risk and opportunity across a network of strategic partners—the original "buddy system" of capitalism.
    - *Symbiosis* involves developing close relationships with public officials, business leaders, and communities to provide islands of stability within otherwise mercurial markets.
    - *Redundancy* involves building backup systems and resources in an effort to protect against disruptive events and ensure operational continuity.
    - *Migration* involves quickly pivoting into new markets when conditions become so hostile that exit is the only option.
    - *Simplification* involves scaling back and prioritizing the company's most essential products, services, and processes until adverse conditions improve and resources become more available to support a return to scale and complexity.
    - *Diversity* involves promoting greater breadth in products, services, suppliers, customers, regions—and critically, talent—to help minimize acute risks to individual segments

of a business and to generate synergies and innovation across a portfolio.

- Context clearly matters when deploying any strategy—not all approaches are fit for all seasons.
- In turbulent times, these seven stabilizing strategies are an excellent defense against extended periods of adversity.

PART 2
STABILIZING STRATEGIES IN ACTION

A genius is the person who can do the average thing when everyone else around them is losing their mind.

—Napoleon Bonaparte

One of the core themes of this book is how exposure to uncertainty and adversity elicits a special form of resilience. In Part 1, we learned how the Kongōs and the Carvajals responded to a variety of existential threats by making careful investments in stability, both anticipating and reacting to frequent shocks within their operating environment. Leveraging these investments like a form of self-insurance, they were able to navigate decades and even centuries of turbulence, often while others were losing their minds—not to mention their businesses.

In Part 2, we'll take a deeper dive into each of these seven stabilizing strategies and illustrate how they can be deployed effectively by leaders everywhere under a variety of conditions and contexts. Within each chapter, we'll begin by introducing an iconic enterprising family whose origin story takes place within an exotic frontier economy—from Peru and Saudi Arabia to Korea and India. We'll then examine the underlying mechanics of how their investments in stability supported greater organizational resilience, and how these lessons can be applied more generally. Finally, we'll end each chapter with a few conditions and caveats to support further reflection and application.

As these stories will reveal, strategic leadership in the face of persistent uncertainty is both a multidisciplinary and cross-cultural phenomenon. In fact, it is an ancient and universal tradition. The term "strategy" itself is derived from the Greek word *strategos*, or "general." The earliest *strategoi* were not only military commanders, but also political leaders with the power to make life or death decisions for their communities. In the millennia since, strategic leadership has become both an art and a science, focused on planning and executing complex operations in pursuit of territory or treasure.

Astute business strategists—particularly those operating under chronically adverse conditions—have long sought wisdom and inspiration from some of history's leading military thinkers, from Sun Tzu to Bonaparte to Eisenhower. They recognize the need for plans that are flexible enough to adapt to rapidly changing circumstances, but coherent enough to guide and inspire the actions of large and diverse teams.[1]

Yet with a growing host of destabilizing events haunting the daily news cycle, we're surprised that more leaders in advanced economies aren't seeking inspiration from these less conventional sources—places and times where the risk of disruption and organizational failure is constantly elevated, and where enduring success requires a greater focus on what could go wrong, rather than what should go right. Instead, many of them have buried their heads in the sand, remaining focused on shorter-term profitability and eschewing investments in longer-term resilience.

In 2023, professional services juggernaut PwC captured this paradox in a survey of 1,812 business leaders worldwide about their risk management practices. In the study, 91 percent of respondents said they had experienced at least one disruption in addition to the COVID-19 pandemic. Furthermore, 76 percent claimed this disruption had a medium to high impact on operations, affecting "critical business processes and services and causing downstream financial and reputational issues." Yet, despite the fact that disruptions are becoming more frequent and severe, only 20 percent of these organizations had an integrated resilience program in place, and only one-third of these initiatives were sponsored directly by the company's CEO.[2]

A Strategic Wake-Up Call

Disruption is becoming more frequent and severe

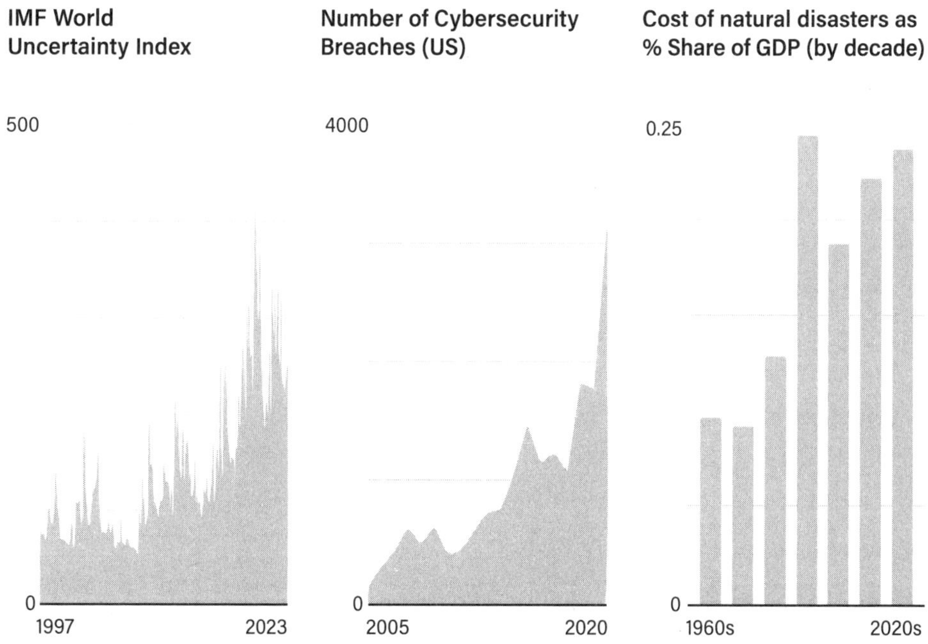

Source: Federal Reserve, Statista, Our World in Data, World Bank, CyberEdge, Swiss Re

These findings are not surprising, if you consider the limited incentive for investing in stability under conventional operating conditions. But it seems downright irresponsible as we enter a protracted period of polycrisis. It would be akin to waging war without first taking the following steps:

1. Adapting tactics and equipment for unique battlefield conditions (differentiation)
2. Organizing your troops into agile networks of platoons, companies, and brigades (modularity)
3. Building allies to expand influence and provide collective defense (symbiosis)
4. Reinforcing supply chains for protracted conflict (redundancy)
5. Relocating troops along the shifting frontiers of combat (migration)

6. Streamlining communication to support efficient and effective decision-making (simplification)
7. Developing a broad array of defensive and offensive capabilities and equipment (diversity)

Though they may be less familiar to those living and working in advanced economies, whenever the daily grind of business begins to resemble the fog of war, as it does further down the Hierarchy of Stability, these seven preemptive strategies can significantly increase the odds of organizational survival and success. Their value lies not in the fantasy that they can prevent business failures, since these are inevitable on the frontiers of capitalism, but in the fact that they can help us minimize the damage and bounce back faster.

One final note before we dive in: while each of the chapters in Part 2 will focus on a single stabilizing strategy, it's important to remember that they are not mutually exclusive. In fact, many enterprising families deploy them simultaneously in varying combinations over time, as both the Carvajal and Kongō families have already demonstrated. When taken collectively, these investments increase an organization's "absorptive capacity" to endure external shocks and traumatic events that would otherwise threaten continuity.[3]

That said, depending on the circumstances, different strategies come to the foreground as natural pathways for adaptation. For instance, when your assets have been expropriated by a new and hostile regime, and your family's safety is at risk, sometimes migration is the only viable option. However, the choice of which strategy to deploy isn't always conscious and proactive, and leaders often have preconceived notions of which would be most effective at any given point in time.

Even a decade into our research, we are still learning how enduring enterprises develop, deploy, calibrate, and shed these strategies—that is, under what conditions some are more effective than others. But one insight has already become abundantly clear: like sports coaches strategizing at key junctures in a game, or generals campaigning for victory, all business leaders growing their organizations over time should consider a portfolio approach to deploying these strategies in the face of chronically elevated uncertainty.

Whether it is before the next crisis strikes, after all hell breaks loose, or as conditions return to something approximating normal, it is important to consider using these strategies actively and dynamically. The more enduring enterprises we meet, the more confident we become that these tools will enhance your decision-making, particularly as we all slide a few notches down the Hierarchy of Stability in the years to come.

5
DIFFERENTIATION

Ignore the conventional wisdom. If everybody else is doing it one way, there's a good chance you can find your niche by going in exactly the opposite direction.

—Sam Walton

Like many of its Latin American neighbors, in the late 1970s Peru was a political and economic powder keg. Chronic inflation and internal unrest pitted the poor and the middle class against a few privileged families who ran the country's most influential institutions. By the time the country's military government held elections in 1980—for the first time since 1963—the polarizing Shining Path rebels (*Sendero Luminoso*) had already been mobilizing for over a decade.

Founded in 1969 by philosophy professor Abimael Guzmán (aka Presidente Gonzalo), the group first rose to prominence as a revolutionary communist party. But it later became notorious as one of the most brutal terrorist regimes in the Western Hemisphere. The rebels brought chaos to everything they touched, disrupting society and commerce across vast swaths of the Peruvian countryside.

One fateful day in 1988, that chaos visited Eduardo Añaños and his wife, Mirtha, in the warm, dry lowlands of San Miguel Province. The couple mourned the destruction of their hacienda and farmland at the hands of the Shining Path, which frequently targeted educated and entrepreneurial landowners for their complicity in the capitalist conspiracy. Elsewhere, in their home state of Ayacucho, one of the poorest in the country, the guerrillas were destroying property, murdering citizens, and cutting off major transportation corridors. Only minimal traffic was able to flow back and forth, disrupting supply chains for food, medicine, and other necessities of provincial life.

Many of Eduardo and Mirtha's neighbors left their belongings and fled to the relative safety of Lima, Peru's capital city, 500 kilometers away. However, the Añaños family chose a different approach, one that changed the fortunes of the family and the region for decades to come.

Carlos, the youngest of Eduardo and Mirtha's six children, pointed out that soft drinks were among the many modern conveniences that were displaced by the Shining Path. The country's largest suppliers, Coca-Cola and Pepsi, stopped sending delivery trucks into the region because the rebels took a special interest in hijacking and destroying vehicles owned by foreign companies. They accused the multinationals of marketing their products only to the privileged elite in Peru who could afford them, making no effort to service lower socioeconomic classes.

Undeterred by these hostile conditions, and fully committed to supporting their local community, the Añañoses saw an opportunity amid the chaos. Jorge, their eldest son, was the most enthusiastic. He worked as a distributor for a local brewery, and suggested to the family that they repurpose empty beer bottles and start brewing soft drinks to fill the obvious gap in their local market. Jorge reasoned that many locals were too poor to have tasted the big American brands, and the rest would likely embrace a homegrown, low-cost, refreshing alternative.

Eduardo and Mirtha were impressed by the prospect and undeterred by the rebels. As one former executive explained, "It was quite a difficult time, [but] when many people saw problems and risks, the Añaños siblings found an opportunity and took advantage."[1] They immediately sold the family's agricultural equipment for US$8,000, and mortgaged their land to a local bank for US$22,000 more. Aided by their son Carlos's knowledge of chemistry, the Añaños clan developed a cola-style drink in the back courtyard of their home in Ayacucho using basic kitchen equipment.

The Shining Path's Destabilizing Impact on Peru

The rebellion destroyed lives and livelihoods, causing lasting uncertainty

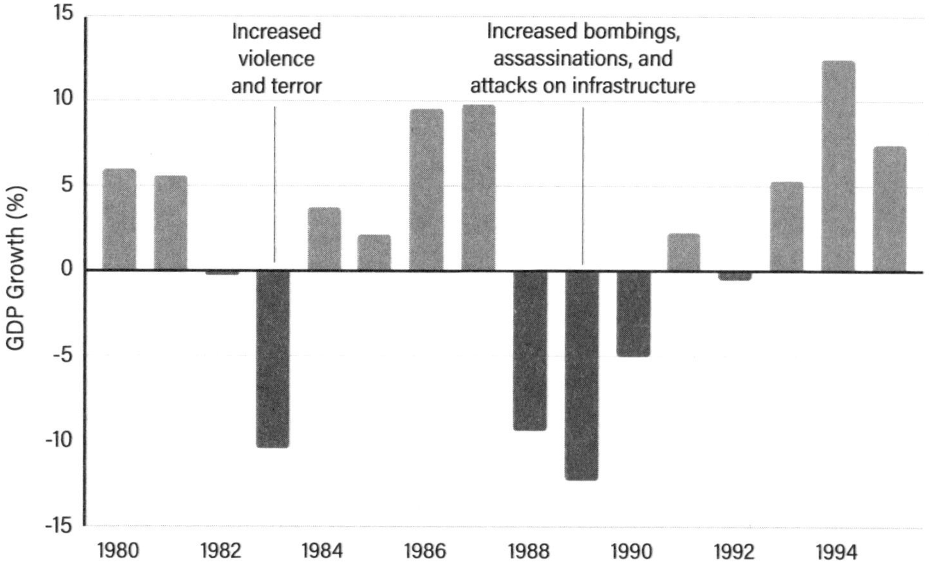

Regional Activity and Impact Spread Over Time

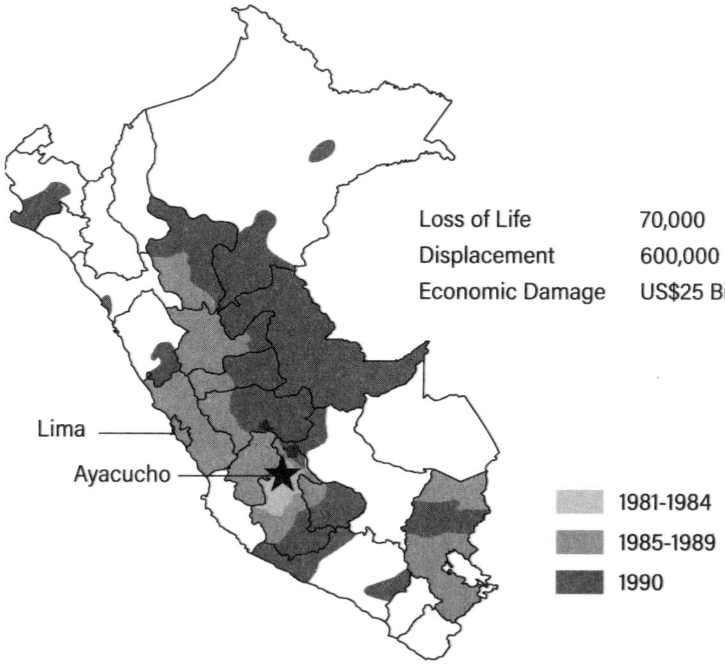

Loss of Life	70,000
Displacement	600,000
Economic Damage	US$25 Billion

Source: World Bank data, Pols 448: Terror Group Profile (Sendero Luminoso) by Meredith B. Watkins

This technique not only allowed the family to reliably supply their isolated market with locally sourced materials but also eliminated the cost of beverage concentrate, which ate up about 20 percent of Coca-Cola's revenues. Additionally, in order to survive without access to imported bottling equipment, Jorge designed a simple, homegrown substitute (nicknamed "Atahualpa," after the last Incan emperor) that would enable the fledgling business to keep up with early demand from friends and neighbors.

These innovative brewing and bottling techniques helped the family launch its first mass market product in 1988, a low-cost orange-flavored drink called Kola Real. It competed directly with popular soft drinks such as Fanta and Crush and offered customers a large two-liter bottle for less than half the price of smaller Coca-Cola or PepsiCo products. The brand promise was clear and printed right on the label: "Calidad a precio justo" (Quality at a fair price). Customers could get more for their money without sacrificing taste: it was both a commitment to creating shared value and a not-so-subtle jab at foreign soft drinks that were framed as shamefully overpriced.

Though the idea was initially quite successful, it wasn't without risk. The Añaños family knew little about the soft drink industry. They were operating on a shoestring and unsure whether violence in the region might affect them. On the other hand, in a niche market, it helps to have home field advantage. The family was well liked and well respected in Ayacucho and sustained close connections throughout the local community. As a result, family members naturally understood the needs and motivations of lower-income families—a unique and valuable asset when launching a new product targeted precisely to these households. This alignment with rural communities helped the company build an early and faithful following, providing a stable customer and employee base that fueled subsequent growth.

Consider that two-thirds of Peru's 22 million citizens at the time lived outside metropolitan Lima. These communities were largely peasant farmers who were naturally price sensitive, surviving day to day without many modern conveniences or discretionary indulgences. Like many emerging economies, Peru has long struggled with socioeconomic inequality, and consumer wants and needs are often left unsatisfied. In that special context, the AJE Group (as the business was eventually renamed) helped to increase the size and diversity of these provincial economies. As Carlos Añaños put it, "Many of our customers had never tried a soft drink before. They could not afford to buy the big brands, but they were the majority of the population. With our products they became part of the market. Our mission was to expand the market, not to fight against anyone or become number one. Everyone was a winner with this approach, even the big brands."[2]

At first, the family sold Kola Real door-to-door to residents and mom-and-pop convenience stores, recruiting local citizens eager to earn a living as sales representatives. They couldn't afford advertising, so the product's early success or failure would rely on word-of-mouth endorsements and prompt delivery. As demand grew beyond their most loyal customers, they began to subcontract distribution to microentrepreneurs with privately owned trucks, providing even more locals with hard-to-find work. This new and proprietary network of local resources was cheaper than creating their own regional logistics system, and it had the added benefit of providing much safer and more predictable passage on highways actively patrolled by the Shining Path.

By the time the Peruvian military finally made gains against the rebels and captured the Shining Path's Guzmán in 1992, AJE had already expanded its distribution capabilities to nearby small cities such as Huancayo, Bagua, Trujillo, and Sullana, and built bottling plants in several distributed locations. The family continued this slow but steady expansion throughout the Peruvian countryside until finally reaching the capital city of Lima in 1999, roughly a decade after launching door-to-door delivery of Kola Real. By that time, they had built up significant infrastructure and a devoted customer base, presenting a very legitimate threat to Coca-Cola and Pepsi in the more affluent urban markets.

Even still, the Añaños family, painfully familiar with the unpredictable actions of governments and guerrillas, decided to expand into foreign markets to ensure that their growing enterprise wasn't entirely dependent on Peru. That same year, the AJE Group expanded into Venezuela (quickly capturing 17 percent of the market), and two years later it entered the Ecuadorian market (where its early market share was an impressive

12 percent).[3] These countries were chosen deliberately because of their socioeconomic similarities to Peru at the time, increasing the odds that the family's niche business model could be adapted relatively seamlessly.

It wasn't long before the international business media began running stories about the extraordinary success of the nimble family business from a small developing nation that was taking on some of the world's most powerful companies—and winning. "We thought that if the business model in Peru was sustainable in Mexico," CEO Angel Añaños told a journalist, "it would be sustainable anywhere."[4] The next wave of expansion went to Costa Rica, Guatemala, and Nicaragua before pivoting to Asia with operations in Thailand, Vietnam, and Indonesia. AJE approached each new country with the same basic principles that had made it successful in the heartland of rural Peru—providing "quality products at a fair price" and supporting education and entrepreneurship wherever they operated.[5]

Today, the AJE Group operates in more than twenty countries while remaining focused on a distinct socioeconomic niche at the "bottom of the pyramid." Its revenues have only grown as a result, reaching US$1.5 billion in 2021, which earned the company a Top 10 spot in a global market for soft drinks estimated to be worth nearly US$1 trillion annually.[6] The company is currently the fourth-largest global producer of soft drinks by volume and directly and indirectly employs over 13,000 people.

From its humble beginnings recycling beer bottles during a brutal guerrilla war to its bold moves to open up new markets in emerging and frontier economies, the Añaños family has demonstrated how focusing on an underserved niche can generate considerable commercial success and drive broader economic development. That said, if AJE's experience was a rare entrepreneurial miracle—the result of being at the right place at the right time with the right idea—then this story would simply be an inspiring anecdote and nothing more. However, as we studied hundreds of enterprising families around the world, we quickly realized that Eduardo and Mirtha's courageous and entrepreneurial response to the destruction of their agricultural business was actually quite common—particularly in environments that are hostile to commercial activity, but where locals are nonetheless willing to take risks and innovate.

FRUGAL INNOVATION

It turns out that many enduring enterprises in emerging and frontier economies have been successful at developing homegrown alternatives to products and services readily available in other markets, or solutions to unique challenges and obstacles not found anywhere else. Due to geographic constraints, unreliable infrastructure, limited security, rampant corruption, and resource scarcity, these markets are often underserviced by large multinational firms. This creates opportunistic gaps for local entrepreneurs to explore and exploit.

As with each of the stabilizing strategies, nature provides us with an elegant metaphor to help explain this phenomenon. Evolutionary biologists have discovered that new forms of life will fill the gaps in every imaginable ecological niche, from the deepest seas to the hottest deserts to the coldest mountain tops. These unique environmental idiosyncrasies provide natural barriers to entry, making it easier for some species to become big fish in small ponds.[7]

Interestingly, the process of differentiation is also naturally built into the way families evolve and adapt. For instance, every child enters the family at a different juncture and encounters a unique set of opportunities and constraints. The wider the age span between each child, the more different the circumstances. In effect, the emotional and economic context is never the same for any two children—and that, in turn, drives their instincts for differentiation. Like Charles Darwin's famous finches, siblings engage in a kind of competition that enhances the variety of personalities and skills available within the family.[8] This differentiation, in turn, supports the family's potential to explore a variety of niche opportunities, until one eventually achieves breakthrough success. At that point, as with the Añaños family, scarcity turns to abundance, and these entrepreneurial successes are then shared with the rest of the "tribe."

Many of the oldest entrepreneurial families in our study got their start in precisely this way, as niche purveyors of innovative local products and services—from beverages to textiles to housewares. Whether they remained in these original businesses or not, their origin story was made possible by the astute recognition of a unique market opportunity where competition was sparse and conditions favorable for enduring success.

As we saw in Chapter 3, one of the miracles of advanced economies is their capacity to make critical resources more abundant—maybe not guaranteed, but certainly easier and cheaper to acquire. However, there are many places where reliable access to bare necessities, such as shelter, electricity, and potable water, is still a privilege, and procurement remains unpredictable, at best. Consider the many war-torn, impoverished, and underdeveloped communities where chronic necessity breeds a form of *survivalist entrepreneurship*. Under these grueling circumstances, families must leverage their scarce resources and boundless resourcefulness to address chronic market failures.

This activity often begins at the microenterprise level, with a type of informal, small-scale import substitution. Local entrepreneurs begin by identifying a set of goods and services that are currently imported from outside the community, and then they develop a local alternative—what Harvard management guru Clayton Christensen would call "market-creating innovations."[9] For the Añaños family, that process involved an early recognition that soft drinks could be produced more affordably, sustainably, and reliably in Ayacucho, at least as long as the Shining Path rebels were disrupting transportation corridors and scaring away international competitors. It also involved innovative bottling and recycling techniques, new chemical formulations, pioneering distribution channels, and inclusive stakeholder relations—all of which combined to sustain the family's early success and support their efforts to scale.

These challenging conditions, emblematic of life at the base of the Hierarchy of Stability, have produced some of the most innovative and impactful solutions to humanity's most persistent structural challenges. This phenomenon is perhaps best studied in South Asia, where the Indo-Aryan concept of *jugaad* has a long tradition. The term refers specifically to indigenous innovations and simple work-arounds for common problems using and combining resources in novel and unexpected ways.

As one might expect from any niche adaptation, the origin of *jugaad* is tied to the unique socioeconomic and cultural context of the region in which it evolved, in this case India. In the absence of well-funded and trustworthy institutions, families in India are often exposed to daily challenges such as poverty, corruption, and violence. It is precisely the will to overcome these destabilizing forces that can catalyze a wide variety of creative and flexible solutions. The ultimate goal is to create greater economic stability and generate opportunity with the resources locally available. Most importantly, the path to achieving that goal is only limited by our ingenuity and grit.

Consider just two examples to whet your curiosity. In 1976, Dr. Govindappa Venkataswamy, inspired by the McDonald's business model, invented the Aravind Eye Care System, a family-run network of eye hospitals that provides high-quality and low-cost eye care to millions of people in India and abroad, performing more than 300,000 cataract surgeries per year at an average cost of US$15. Similarly, in 2008, the Tata family launched the Nano, the world's cheapest car, to cater to the needs of the emerging Indian middle class. Selling for only US$2,000, it boasted a remarkable fuel efficiency of 25 kilometers per liter (or nearly 60 miles per gallon).[10]

Though there are countless instances of frugal innovation throughout India and beyond, there is no formulaic recipe for deploying *jugaad*—just like there isn't a guaranteed recipe for any other form of innovation, despite many best-selling books to the contrary. That said, Navi Radjou, Jaideep Prabhu, and Simone Ahuja, a team of scholars who have studied this phenomenon extensively, have found common themes and applications among the most complex environments and enterprises. In their book *Jugaad Innovation*, they highlight examples from Siemens, Tata, and dozens of others who all practice *jugaad* by seeking opportunity in adversity, doing more with less, and thinking and acting flexibly.[11]

Given the calculus of surviving and thriving in these niche environments, it's no wonder this strategy is so pervasive. According to a survey by the Legatum Institute, 81 percent of Indian businessmen said *jugaad* was the key reason for their success.[12] But as the AJE case has shown, this isn't exclusively an Indian invention. Leveraging dancing landscapes to inspire innovative commercial solutions is truly a global phenomenon.

In Brazil, the term *gambiarra* (or "creating through improvisation") is used to describe enterprising Brazilians who develop innovative strategies to repair or create what they need with whatever resources they have available. In Kenya, the locals use the term *jua kali* (or "fierce sun" in Swahili) to refer to the more than 700,000 Kenyans who work in the informal sector and can make, fix, and solve whatever their customers need. In China, a similar concept is known as *zizhu chuangxin*, or "indigenous innovation," and is used both by policymakers and entrepreneurs to encourage domestic innovation specifically targeting the Chinese market.

Israel also offers a powerful demonstration of the frugal resourcefulness that comes as a natural byproduct of chronic uncertainty. In the 2009 book *Start-Up Nation: The Story of Israel's Economic Miracle*, authors Dan Senor and Saul Singer ask a provocative question: How is it that a country of 7.1 million people, only sixty years old, surrounded by enemies, in a constant state of war since its founding, with no natural resources—produces more startup companies on a per capita basis than large, peaceful, and stable nations like Japan, China, India, Korea, Canada, and all of Europe?[13] The authors cite a dynamic blend of *chutzpah* (extreme self-confidence or audacity), *bitzua* (commitment to getting things done), and *rosh gadol* (literally "big head," or a "can-do attitude") as major contributors to Israel's economic dynamism, all of which have clear echoes in *jugaad* and its many regional variants.

Before we move on, let's consider one final example from an extreme frontier market where commercial life still manages to thrive. Along the border between China and North Korea, a thriving ecosystem of enterprising families has emerged to supply beleaguered citizens with products not otherwise available. Opaque politics, strict regulations, minimal infrastructure, and United Nations sanctions are all natural barriers to entering this volatile market. Yet despite the risk and uncertainty, a community of opportunistic *donju* (or "money masters") have figured out how to make an entrepreneurial living within one of the most closed and centralized economies in the world. Lured both by profit and purpose, they play a critical role as economic intermediaries, helping the struggling citizens of North Korea access key goods and services that would otherwise remain unobtainable.

We're not suggesting that such high-risk frontier capitalism is for everyone. We're simply providing evidence that innovation comes naturally under conditions of scarcity, and that enterprising families are well positioned to capitalize on these opportunities. As the saying goes, "Necessity is the mother of invention."

LEAPFROGGING

Early on in our research, we identified a second form of differentiation that involved solving for gaps in the local market. However, rather than inventing and scaling new domestic ventures, these resourceful families differentiated themselves by importing superior equipment and know-how from abroad, often a low-cost solution that is readily available and easily deployable. Initially, this approach requires more capital and connections, but in the long run it can generate significant returns. Importing reliable next-generation infrastructure and processes confers unique advantages in terms of the quality, quantity, and diversity of the goods that can be produced relative to older domestic alternatives, many of which haven't evolved as quickly in the absence of global competition and capital.

This concept, sometimes called "leapfrogging," was originally developed in the fields of industrial organization and economic development, where it describes how new entrants can bypass established firms by adopting radical innovations from abroad. It also recognizes the opportunity for developing countries to "skip" over traditional stages of development (or create alternative paths) by leveraging products and services already available in more advanced economies.

The most familiar examples are related to mobile telecommunications. Many developing countries, for instance, have deployed next-generation wireless networks without first investing in expensive and antiquated landline infrastructure. This strategy proved to be a massive driver of economic development and commercial opportunity in frontier economies, where communication was previously limited, costly, and unreliable. With the leap ahead into mobile technologies, citizens gained access to mobile payment systems, which expanded financial inclusion and enabled new forms of transactions and savings for hundreds of millions who previously lacked access to formal banking services. Similarly, China's early imports of Western manufacturing equipment helped to kickstart the country's industrial modernization in the 1980s, and Africa's imports of advanced agricultural technologies and machinery have helped to increase crop yields (though less so than in South Asia).

Recall that Carvajal successfully deployed this strategy when importing its first lithography equipment from Germany in the early twentieth century. The move set it apart from competitors and allowed the company to outcompete on print resolution, flexibility, and price. This technology was so specialized and "foreign" that the family needed to import not only the machinery itself, but also German lithographers and experienced typesetters to keep it running smoothly (since people skilled in these areas were not yet available in the domestic labor market—another common challenge). But in the absence of any natural competitors, the Carvajals quickly became the biggest fish in the small Colombian pond, which set them up for future expansion throughout Latin America and beyond.

Many enduring enterprises have replicated this model in industries ranging from beverages to building materials to banking. What they all have in common is the capacity to identify the transformative potential of new outside technologies and business models, then successfully adapt them to unique local conditions. Interestingly, while leapfrogging is most common within emerging and frontier economies, in recent years advanced economies have been increasingly seeking inspiration further down the Hierarchy of Stability, where technologies such as mobile payments and drone delivery have already become essential infrastructures.

ARTISANAL CRAFTSMANSHIP

Among the world's oldest companies, a third form of niche differentiation is by far the most pervasive. These enterprising families have focused on a single trade or craft and built a reputation for excellence that spans generations. Like our favorite temple builders, Kongō Gumi, these ancient lineages of master artisans have found ways to preserve unique traditions and skills while adapting to dramatically evolving conditions across many centuries. Such craftsmanship goes beyond a mere trade or occupation. It becomes a way of life, reflecting a deep respect for the materials, environments, and people involved in production.

Craftsmanship fosters a sense of pride, identity, and communion with customers. Such loyalty increases the probability that artisans and their clients will continue to transact reliably during wars, natural disasters, and other disruptive events that were frequent centuries ago, providing greater stability for both producers and consumers.

Surveying the world's oldest institutions, the trend is abundantly clear. Italy's Pontificia Fonderia Marinelli has been producing bronze bells for churches, cathedrals, and monuments since at least 1339. Staffelter Hof in Germany's Rhineland, founded by monks in the 860s and run continuously by the Klein family for seven generations, is among the oldest wineries. Nishiyama Onsen Keiunkan, considered to be the oldest hotel, was founded by Fujiwara Mahito under the shadow of Mount Fuji in 705. Each of these companies has survived wars, plagues, fires, and economic crises without ever compromising the quality of their craft, the continuity of their business, or the integrity of their family.

Japan has incubated more of these ancient artisanal houses than anywhere else. The country is currently host to several members of Les Hénokiens, an international association founded in 1981 composed exclusively of bicentenary families—that is, families that have operated their companies continuously for at least 200 years. In the association's own words, many of its member families have successfully deployed the artisanal flavor of differentiation across multiple generations:

> Because of their extraordinary longevity, Henokiens Association members are an exception to the economic landscape. The specific characteristics of their respective backgrounds, the common values which unite them, such as respect for product quality and human relationships, know-how transmitted with passion from generation to generation, and the continuous questioning of achievements, all these constitute a message of hope for all family businesses, especially those forming the economic and social fabric of the future.[14]

During a recent visit to Japan, we met with representatives of this illustrious tribe, members of the family that runs the Toraya Confectionery Company, fine purveyors of *wagashi*, or traditional Japanese sweets. The Kurokawas trace their entrepreneurial origins back to the early sixteenth century in Kyoto, where they became the preferred vendor to the Imperial Court during the reign of Emperor Go-Yōzei. Rather than leveraging this connection to expand into other sweet indulgences, the family honed its artisanal expertise in *wagashi*. This focus helped Toraya endure many challenges over the years, including a massive fire that destroyed the Imperial Palace (and their shop) in 1788, the political and economic upheaval that followed the Meiji Restoration in 1869, and the devastation of two world wars—to name just a few. Throughout that time, the Kurokawas have remained committed to perfecting the fine craft that first brought the family fame and fortune, using ancient Japanese techniques that have been passed down for generations. Today, its beautiful wooden headquarters are still just a stone's throw from the walls of the Imperial Palace, and its sweets are available to discerning clients internationally.

Such niche craftsmanship is an ancient tradition—from blacksmiths and potters to violin makers and tailors. That said, in today's complex global economy, craftsmanship extends well beyond the antique arts, from ethnic restaurants and bike shops to video game studios and veterinary clinics. In fact, most family companies fall into this category, at least at their inception, because transmitting niche mastery from generation to generation is part of our universal heritage and, for many of them, one generation is simply not long enough to perfect their craft.

CONDITIONS AND CAVEATS

As we've argued throughout the book, none of these stabilizing strategies is a panacea. Crises can strike unexpectedly, and even well-prepared companies can fail through no direct fault of their own. However, niche adaptations can certainly increase the odds of success, particularly in environments where resource constraints limit economic activity and entrepreneurship. Under these conditions, differentiation can help enduring enterprises punch well above their weight class.

In his 2015 book *David and Goliath: Underdogs, Misfits, and the Art of Battling Giants*, best-selling author Malcolm Gladwell celebrated precisely this dynamic, explaining how underdogs can, and often do, triumph over seemingly insurmountable odds. Gladwell drew inspiration from the biblical story of David, a young shepherd who defeated the giant warrior

Goliath with some frugal innovation, using nothing more than a sling and a stone. Gladwell used the story to make the case that our initial disadvantages can be leveraged to achieve unexpected success. This is as true for little-known beverage companies reaching international success as it was for T. E. Lawrence's successful guerrilla campaign against the Turks during World War I. He reminds us that "David's victory over Goliath, in the Biblical account, is held to be an anomaly. It was not. Davids win all the time."[15]

The moral of the story for niche markets is that if you can't win by being bigger, faster, or stronger, win by being different. Focus on your unique strengths—those attributes innate to your core values, organizational culture, and resource endowments. Make the most of your physical, financial, human, and social capital. You may not have what it takes to compete on scale and scope with global titans, but in these niche environments, you often don't have to. Create products and solutions that defy conventional logic, even if they don't look or function like anything we've ever seen before. It's one of the reasons we chose to write this book—we spotted a unique domain of inquiry where we found few competing ideas to help explain the phenomenon we were observing, then utilized our available skills and resources to frame a novel approach to understanding business continuity.

As you explore options for strategic differentiation, remember that a car in Chennai doesn't need to look or function like a car in Chicago, nor does a mall in Mali, or a hospital in Hyderabad. Don't fall into the false trap of seeking to reverse engineer a local version of Apple or Tesla. We can certainly draw insights from their massive investments in product and process engineering, but recognize that solutions built for advanced economies are designed to leverage more predictable infrastructure and more plentiful resources. Instead, seek inspiration—and stability—from your local ecosystems, building on the real structural problems and needs of your customers, suppliers, and distributors. Perhaps most importantly, at least to families like the Añaños and Carvajals, success isn't defined simply in terms of building a successful commercial enterprise, but also by solving an enduring social need that will nourish a healthy (albeit niche) ecosystem for many generations to come.

Given everything we've shared above, why don't more companies in advanced economies use this strategy more often or more effectively? The most obvious answer is that many organizations simply don't have to—they have the great fortune of operating under conditions of abundance, so they aren't forced to develop a scarcity mindset or an instinct for frugal innovation. That said, investing in differentiation is not without its challenges.

For starters, while adapting to serve a particular niche, one shouldn't confuse internal (organizational) stability with external (environmental) stability. Niche adaptations are advantageous only as long as they increase a company's fitness relative to a prevailing set of conditions. If the deep sea suddenly becomes brighter, or the high arctic suddenly becomes warmer, or the Shining Path uprising suddenly ends, survival may no longer depend on the same set of niche adaptations. In fact, attributes that were previously your greatest assets (e.g., customization and co-creation) may suddenly become your greatest liabilities (e.g., failure to compete on price or volume as global "category killers" enter the local market).

Another common risk emerges when an organization drifts away from its core expertise and market over time. When your strategic compass swings too far from tradition, perhaps seduced by growth or diversification, any unique competitive advantage can be easily lost. Remember the cautionary tale of Kongō Gumi. After more than 1,400 years and 40 generations of continuous family leadership, when the ancient temple builder diverged materially from its artisanal specialty, catastrophic failure quickly followed.

Finally, enduring success in niche markets can be difficult to reproduce or scale. Certain *jugaad* innovations may be ingenious solutions to chronic structural problems in parts of rural India, but not compatible with existing infrastructures and regulations in the country's sprawling metropolises, let alone elsewhere in the world. Other niche innovations, such as microfinance, are challenging to integrate into established banking systems, while frugal innovations such as the Tata Nano have proven to be incompatible with prevailing Western tastes and preferences. These aren't reasons to ignore the lessons and opportunities of differentiation—rather, it simply means that deploying this stabilizing strategy is not without risk, and often works better in combination with the other strategies we lay out in the chapters ahead.

KEY INSIGHTS

- Companies can achieve enduring success by investing in *differentiation*—focusing on underserved niche markets, particularly in volatile environments where resources and competition are scarce.
- The AJE Group is a prime example of how to effectively deploy this stabilizing strategy—born during a terrorist uprising, which informed its unique approach to manufacturing and distributing low-cost beverages to communities threatened by chronic instability.
- *Frugal innovation* is common at the base of the Hierarchy of Stability, where enterprising families develop local alternatives to imported products or services because of limited resources and unreliable infrastructure (e.g., AJE's leaders creating their own bottling techniques).
- *Leapfrogging*, another popular technique, involves importing more advanced technologies from abroad to accelerate development (e.g., Carvajal using German lithograph equipment).
- Differentiation is also possible by focusing on *artisanal craftsmanship*—building a reputation for excellence in goods and services across generations (e.g., Toraya, the Japanese *wagashi* maker).
- Leaders shouldn't always seek to emulate global giants (e.g., Apple, Tesla, Nvidia), but instead should consider drawing inspiration from local challenges and resources.
- As with each of the stabilizing strategies, differentiation is not a guaranteed recipe for success—even with careful planning, unforeseen events can still be disruptive, and designing an organization for a single niche environment can leave an enterprise exposed if conditions suddenly change.

6
MODULARITY

Fight for the things that you care about, but do it in a way that will lead others to join you.

—**Ruth Bader Ginsburg**

In the centuries leading up to the discovery of oil in the Arabian Peninsula, it would have been hard to believe that this desolate region would eventually play such a key role in geopolitical affairs. Commercial activity was mostly limited to oasis farming, camel herding, trade in agricultural commodities (particularly dates), and hosting pilgrims at several of Islam's holiest sites. Its most dynamic economic feature was the ancient caravan routes that moved goods back and forth between Europe and Asia—as they had since the Silk Road first connected East and West nearly 2,000 years before.

The multitude of tribes scattered across these frontier economies were each governed by distinct customs and hierarchies. Rather than working together toward common political and economic ends, they were constantly vying for influence, resources, and control over the ever-shifting sands.

Within these fragmented frontier conditions, the Al Saud dynasty emerged in the early eighteenth century as a powerful force for integration and stabilization. Muhammad bin Saud, emir of an agricultural settlement near modern-day Riyadh, forged a crucial alliance with the influential religious reformer Muhammad ibn Abd al-Wahhab, which was sealed by the marriage of their children. The strict interpretation of Islam professed by the Wahhabis, combined with the commercial and military skill demonstrated by Muhammad bin Saud, created a unique fusion of governance and faith that would lay the foundations for the modern Kingdom of Saudi Arabia.

The eventual discovery of oil, which began in earnest in the late 1930s, would alter this narrative forever—fundamentally disrupting the political, economic, and social fabric of the fledgling country, the fragile region, and the floundering global economy. In 1938, at the tail end of the Great Depression, American petro-giant Chevron began its exploration in one of the kingdom's eastern provinces. Earlier discoveries in Iran by the British had inspired exploration throughout the region, and the well known as Dammam No. 7 was the first to produce oil in commercial quantities. It was a glimpse of the high-quality, low-cost, and bountiful supply of light sweet crude that has made Saudi Arabia the world's number one producer of oil since 1971.

With the subsequent development of its vast oil reserves, the kingdom experienced economic booms (and occasional busts), with transformational consequences for every corner of Saudi society. On the path to becoming an emerging economy, the House of Saud launched ambitious efforts to shift away from its traditional agrarian roots and embrace industrialization. Ever since, big oil has dominated the domestic economy, powering foreign demand for secondary services to support these massive petrochemical investments. From supplying equipment and meals to providing transportation and housing, the oil boom represented a huge opportunity for enterprising Saudis. This was particularly true for families who spoke English fluently and could interface with Western multinationals and governments in addition to the royal Saudi court.

One of the most successful of these families is the Zamils, whose origin story begins in 1920 when the young Shaikh Abdullah Hamad Al Zamil founded a trade and services company. Under his leadership, the fledgling Zamil Group operated out of the regional hub of Bahrain, where centuries of British influence had lowered the barriers to international commerce. He quickly gained a reputation for being a trusted partner to local and foreign companies. Given this early success, it was only natural that when oil exploration arrived in Dammam, the Zamil family was among the first in the country to help foreign multinationals gain reliable access to local resources, leveraging networks of trusted relationships the family had built over decades of expanding regional trade.

Al Zamil was quick to anticipate the long-term implications of these macroeconomic tailwinds, relocating the company's headquarters to the growing eastern city of Al Khobar, just across the border with Bahrain. As Saudi Arabia continued its evolution into an emerging economy—prompted by a massive infusion of foreign capital and labor—demand for housing was growing dramatically, while public infrastructure was still limited. In a testament to the family's confidence in this expansionary boom, Al Zamil committed to erecting the tallest residential building in the city, staking a bold claim on the future of this rising economic and geopolitical powerhouse.

As his business prospects and reputation grew, so too did his family. The seamless integration and collaboration between Al Zamil's twelve sons and five daughters is one of the family's unique competitive advantages and an important source of internal stability. Though Western readers may be less familiar with this traditionally Islamic construct, these seventeen children were born to three different wives, and were all raised together and treated equally, most growing up in the same house. Abdulrahman, the second-oldest brother, describes how the siblings were "raised by a father who never felt that we were any different because we came from different mothers."[1] They worked together as an integrated, modular family system—with only minor age differences, from two years down to six months.

Mohammed was the eldest, and as was tradition in Saudi culture, he was the first to be invited by his father to join the family business. After Sheikh Abdullah's passing in 1961, Mohammed then encouraged his younger brothers to pursue higher education in the United States and the United Kingdom as each came of age.[2] Time abroad and exposure to Western education and business practices provided a variety of fresh ideas—and new relationships—to import back home, strengthening the social cohesion of the family's rising generation and providing access to new opportunities.[3]

As they graduated in waves, the brothers returned home in their own reconfigured cohorts. Rebranding themselves the "Big Four," the "Middle Four," and the "Young Four," they were seamless in their familial identity and aligned in their core values, beginning to plug-and-play within the system in diverse and complementary ways. For instance, while many of the brothers immediately joined the family business, three chose to work in government for a while before entering the business, and two chose to pursue careers exclusively in government. Though these two didn't maintain any formal roles in Zamil, they still assisted the group with strategic advice.

For instance, Abdulaziz, the fourth-oldest brother, worked at the Saudi Industrial Research Center (responsible for establishing new factories), but was still known for asking tough questions as a board member. Other brothers joined the family business directly, leveraging their knowledge of Western practices and applying them to the unique context of Saudi Arabia. Guided by a common vision for the enterprise and a core set of shared values, the large and growing family was able to remain engaged and aligned. This proprietary network of talent and influence eventually helped the brothers become domestic pioneers in a wide range of industries, including air conditioning, shipbuilding, steel, and aluminum manufacturing. Brother Khalid described it best: "We're already twelve and have very different ideas. It's a wealth of thoughts. It's a platform to test ideas."

As the price of oil continued to climb and economic development accelerated, Al Khobar's urban landscape underwent a transformation, sprouting new infrastructure projects and skyscrapers to accommodate all the people, capital, and commerce streaming into the country. To best leverage this rapid growth, Zamil became an early pioneer of modular techniques in construction—what the company today calls Total Building Solutions. This strategy involves building high-quality prefabricated components off-site, according to precise specifications, then seamlessly integrating them on-site like massive Lego blocks, making complex construction less susceptible to disruptions in weather, labor markets, or supply chains.

While the petroleum industry had been a powerful driver of growth both directly and indirectly, the Zamil family was also among the earliest of the Saudi family-run conglomerates to recognize the risk of overexposure to the oil industrial complex. As its leaders looked to diversify into less familiar waters—a natural hedge against shifting geopolitical conditions—they often did so not by striking out alone, but rather by attracting and building partnerships with global market leaders who provided both financial and strategic value.

Starting in the 1970s, the family began building a portfolio of joint ventures, initially with steel, followed quickly by air conditioning, and eventually including a diverse array of businesses from manufacturing and real estate, to plastics and chemicals, to marine services and renewable energy. Importantly, many of these partnerships are with other families based in advanced economies, and the family's commitment to Western education for its rising generation made it much easier to build these partnerships. As Abdullah, a rising leader in the next generation, shared with us, "When you can speak directly with the principals, without an interpreter, it naturally enhances trust." Importantly, these foreign partnerships also imposed more robust governance, legal structures, financial reporting, and operational covenants than were typical within the kingdom at the time, adding a level of organizational sophistication that helped them outperform their competition.

Over the years, this modular approach to growth brought greater stability and predictability to these riskier endeavors, helping the Zamils expand into new industries and regions that would have been prohibitively costly or uncertain to enter on their own. Each relationship provided new products and technologies that could be synergistically integrated into the company's expanded Total Building Solutions platform—which has supplied over 95,000 pre-engineered steel buildings to customers in over 95 countries worldwide, including Saudi Aramco, PepsiCo, Mitsui, Unilever, and BMW. Today, Zamil proudly describes itself as "the 'go-to' partner for local and international markets"—a testament to the original values and reputation of the Zamil Trading Company and the enduring value of building trusted, long-term partnerships to help inoculate against market uncertainty.

As Saudi Arabia charts a bold new course of economic, social, and cultural diversification—led by the country's young and heterodox leader, Mohammad bin Salman—the House of Saud's Vision 2030 program has emphasized that the kingdom's future prosperity will not be dependent on oil alone. So far, this has mostly meant a strong focus on construction and development megaprojects, as well as the creation of a global network of strategic and financial partners to spread out engineering and investment risk. As a result, Zamil is well-positioned to become a leading supplier for new domestic developments such as Neom—a US$1 trillion futuristic urban development seed funded by the Saudi state.

In many ways, Zamil's mission—"To work together as a strong team, harnessing the diverse knowledge and expertise in our effort to maximize value for all our stakeholders"—is a rallying cry for the enduring strategic advantage of open architecture. Over the past century, the family has demonstrated the power of deploying modular solutions in business (with its Total Building Solutions), ownership (with its joint venture partnerships), and family systems (with its growing network of cousins working within and outside the company). Together, these three forms of modularity have not only provided greater strength and stability, but also unique opportunities for growth.

In our research, we discovered that emerging and frontier economies are filled with companies deploying modular systems, flexible partnerships, and familial networks. Though these enterprises are often inherently complex, owing to their many interdependent parts, when they're all working together seamlessly in service of a common mission they can provide an enduring competitive advantage.

MODULAR SYSTEMS

One of the most successful deployments of modularity in a retail business emerged in Sweden during World War II. At the time, Sweden would have been considered a textbook frontier economy. Poverty was widespread, subsistence farming was failing, and families everywhere were struggling to cope with chronic scarcity and uncertainty about the future. In the southern province of Småland, in an effort to help his struggling family, an enterprising seventeen-year-old named Ingvar Kamprad started a mail order service for pens and watches. Though he initially had little success, his fortunes turned several years later, when Sweden's government began funding housing projects as a postwar stimulus, including loans for new home furnishings. Young Ingvar seized the opportunity and began offering his neighbors a range of low-cost, high-quality housewares, designed and built with simplicity and efficiency. It took some time before the fledgling business found its footing, but in the ensuing decades Ingvar's impact on the global economy would be profound.

Today, IKEA is a titan of home furnishings, with over 400 stores in 50 countries generating roughly US$50 billion in annual sales.[4] Its use of modular design is perhaps the company's most distinctive feature—and it is pervasive throughout the entire organization, from the design of its products to the layout of its stores to its unique approach to packaging, warehousing, and logistics. This unique operating model is what enables the mix of low prices and high quality that Ingvar first promised his customers in rural Sweden nearly a century ago.

The company's modular design principles are based on a proprietary platform of common components and fasteners, many of which are shared across entire product lines. This approach results in a diverse array of home furnishings that can be assembled, repaired, reused, and redesigned with minimal effort and expense, a benefit to both the company and its customers. Even its logistics leverages the benefits of modularity—with customers self-picking and self-transporting discrete components in "flat pack" boxes.

Given IKEA's incredible success, it's a wonder more companies haven't embraced modular innovations (though many Asian furniture manufacturers have caught on in recent years). It's even more surprising when we consider that the underlying principles of modularity have been contemplated by philosophers and enterprising families for millennia.[5]

Consider Kongō Gumi's approach to building and maintaining iconic Buddhist temples. The company's master carpenters utilized an ancient form of modular design, *miyadaiku*, that avoided the use of nails as fasteners, both to improve the overall aesthetic and to enable easier replacement of structural components over time. Similar forms of wooden joinery have been in use in Japan for thousands of years, in everything from temples to tea houses to dining tables. This ethos is captured in the Japanese concept of *tokowaka*, loosely translated as "always youthful." Unlike traditional Western castles and stone monuments, which are built by a single generation to stand the test of time, many Japanese shrines and bridges have been explicitly designed using these modular techniques, with the intention of being fully rebuilt every twenty years. It reflects a deep commitment to renewing objects in the pursuit of eternality, and serves as a way of transmitting building techniques and a caretaking approach from one generation to the next.

From Zamil's Total Building Solutions to IKEA's flat-pack designs and Kongō Gumi's interchangeable wooden components, such modular systems are inherently less susceptible to catastrophic collapse, precisely because independent components can fail without compromising the entire system. But the benefits of modularity go beyond merely enhancing operational resilience. It can also help businesses to innovate and scale. For all the fanfare and controversy prompted by Tesla's meteoric rise, the company's "gigafactories" are truly marvels of industrial engineering and epitomize the principles of modular manufacturing pioneered by Henry Ford over a century ago. The company's robotic cells can be seamlessly relocated, replicated, and swapped out as needed, and even the overall factory layout is built from standardized segments, or "pods," that can be easily copied, expanded, and combined in various configurations.

Obviously not every product or service is as complex as an automobile or a skyscraper and is therefore less amenable to modular designs. However, as the Zamil case has shown, modularity in ownership is also possible and can provide a unique and enduring source of resilience and significantly enhance opportunities for growth.

FLEXIBLE PARTNERSHIPS

While business processes such as manufacturing and engineering are perhaps the most obvious applications of a modular strategy, investments in modular ownership can also provide distinct and complementary advantages. For instance, IKEA was early to recognize the power of modular ownership, leveraging a franchise model that enabled the company to enter new markets with greater flexibility and confidence. Similarly, the Zamil family has excelled at leveraging joint venture partnerships to scale and grow while simultaneously sharing and compartmentalizing risk. As Adib (the tenth brother) shared, "The only way you can manage for the long term is to avoid sole proprietorship."[6]

In fact, the emergence of modular ownership was a major contributor to the evolution of capitalism, as we laid out in Chapter 3. Beginning with early commercial partnerships, then later through joint-stock companies, once ownership could be split between multiple individuals and families, opportunity and risk could be effectively shared for a single commercial enterprise. Such business partnerships require clear protocols for strategic planning and decision-making, which is relatively easy when all partners live and invest in the same market. However, it can be quite challenging when these relationships straddle different levels on the Hierarchy of Stability and operate in jurisdictions where the laws and customs can be substantially different.

This is one of the reasons that franchising was relatively unsuccessful until the late nineteenth century, and only really took off after World War II. Prior to the twentieth century, there were few legal and technical protocols to incentivize and regulate international agreements. It would take a new generation of multilateral stabilizers designed and funded by the first advanced economies—including the Bretton Woods monetary system and the General Agreement on Tariffs and Trade—to pave the way for Western companies to pursue growth through flexible partnerships.[7]

Among the first entrepreneurs to take advantage of this new global platform for economic cooperation and co-investment was Ray Kroc, the American businessman who originally franchised the concept for McDonald's domestically, then brought the Golden Arches to the world. These franchises represented a new form of modular ownership, one that enabled independent entrepreneurs to acquire and operate standardized units of a larger corporate brand. Kroc was a master at building out these flexible partnerships. In each new country he visited, he and his team would identify a single master franchisee, most typically an enterprising family committed to "tropicalizing" the iconic American brand (think McFalafel and Shogun Burger). The process typically required securing local licensing, building local supply chains, recruiting local workers, advertising in local media channels, and participation in all the training and development programs at Hamburger University in Chicago. Families that were already well connected in their local markets, had access to capital, and maintained strong government and public relations provided greater predictability to the McDonald's franchise team and signaled that the partnership was a good long-term fit.

This model was initially very successful, and other opportunistic American retailers were quick to follow. From gasoline stations (Exxon Mobil) to tobacco products (Philip Morris) to construction equipment (Caterpillar) to automobiles (General Motors), American companies fanned out around the globe, adding partners from emerging and frontier economies to their growing modular networks. Many of these enterprising families—including Zamil in Saudi Arabia, Al Mansour in Egypt, and Torrado in Latin America—would not stop at a single joint venture or franchise relationship. Those that were successful often found it easy to replicate the model with others, learning to effectively share information, risk, and reward across their growing portfolios.

Each of these new partnerships enabled a form of organizational "leapfrogging"—providing access to world-class business management systems, innovative products, global procurement platforms, go-to-market strategies, and human capital. Once they have some early successes behind them, enterprising families can then develop new markets and partnerships with greater confidence—and greater speed. As one family leader shared, "Understanding a market and making yourself understood is not a matter of money; it is a matter of time. Alliances speed up the process." The curation and ongoing management of these partnerships is an essential skill that highly successful enterprising families in frontier markets pass on from generation to generation—cultivating horizontal linkages among the offspring of partners and key executives.

Choose Your Partners Wisely

Four types of modular partnership

	Family	Non-Family
Strategic	Families that either run a business with strategic synergies (e.g., related industries, geographies, customers, suppliers, etc.) or invest in portfolios with complementary strategic value *Examples: Global industry leaders*	Institutions that deploy patient capital and invest in family businesses, bringing operational and strategic expertise and networks to the families in which they invest *Examples: Private equity, sovereign wealth funds*
Financial	Families looking to make minority investments in other family enterprises without taking a leadership role or providing incremental strategic value (more hands-off, interested in deploying long-term patient capital) *Examples: Family offices, investment conglomerates*	Institutions looking to place long-term capital without taking an active role in governance or strategy, focusing instead on financial metrics of performance and risk *Examples: Banks, insurance companies, pension funds*

In our research, we also identified another form of modular ownership that is particularly pervasive in emerging and frontier economies: the family holding company. From Korean *chaebol* to Latin *grupos* to Russian oligarchs, integrated portfolios of family-owned businesses are endemic in contexts where governments have either failed to enable greater access to capital, or limit market consolidation, or suppress corporate graft. By pooling resources and sharing capital across various businesses, these family conglomerates can more easily leverage their scale and financial strength to secure preferential access to capital, which is particularly advantageous in markets with underdeveloped financial systems.

To do so, they often employ a complex web of interlocking directorates and cross-shareholdings among their subsidiaries and affiliated companies, which helps them to maintain control, facilitate resource allocation, and accelerate the pace of decision-making. However, as with all modular systems, the success of these large portfolios requires clear protocols for engagement and alignment.

Consider the Japanese titan Mitsui Group: founded in 1622 in Matsusaka as a small family textile business, it has since grown into one of the world's largest conglomerates with holdings spanning a range of industries, from banks and paper to chemicals and ship building. One unique feature of Mitsui's approach to modular ownership emerged at its inception, when the patriarch, Mitsui Takatoshi, decided to combine the houses of his sons into an economic partnership. Subsequent generations added additional protocols to govern the interactions of their increasingly complex portfolio and growing family, including rules on the incurrence of debt, the use of standardized marketing techniques, and even guidelines around marriage and lifestyle. As this platform of interrelated businesses continued to grow, it was able to withstand centuries of external shocks and threats, including the eventual US occupation of Japan, a time during which family conglomerates (or *zaibatsu*) like Mitsui were systematically dismantled and culturally stigmatized.

However, in a testament to the resilience of these modular ownership systems, despite losing their formal legal connections, Mitsui's disparate operating divisions maintained a web of informal affiliations, driven by a strong familial culture and deep strategic and organizational alignment. Eventually, once regulatory conditions became more hospitable, these modular parts coalesced. Today, the Mitsui Group is a thriving *keiretsu* (or network of related companies with independent but interlocking business relationships and shareholdings), and it remains one of the largest corporate syndicates in the world.

To be clear, enhancing stability through a portfolio of flexible partnerships is distinct from diversification—a strategy which we'll explore in detail in Chapter 11. Instead, it's about leveraging a common platform of resources and a common system of governance to coordinate activities across multiple commercial entities. Most critically, it requires a shared set of structures, policies, and processes for transferring information, people, opportunities, and risks across the various discrete but interconnected nodes of these complex enterprises. That's a lot to ask of any leader or organization, but for those like Zamil, IKEA, and Mitsui who get it right, it can be an enduring source of stability and growth, particularly in more turbulent environments.

FAMILIAL NETWORKS

The final major source of modular stability we identified in our research gives a unique competitive advantage to enterprising families—that trust emerges naturally among our closest kin. Not all families are as prolific as the Zamils, but in emerging and frontier economies, many enduring enterprises actively maintain extended networks of cousins and close "family friends." These complex social networks become especially valuable during moments of adversity or uncertainty, when "circling the wagons" can provide a greater sense of collective safety and support.[8]

As we learned in Chapter 3, in environments where market dysfunctions are commonplace, families can provide reliable access to financial, physical, and human capital, often in the form of investments, gifts, remittances, resources, equipment, and labor. Their shared values, norms of reciprocity, and geographic proximity enable and even encourage disparate nodes within these large networks to consolidate and share proprietary information, which can materially influence a family's collective security and well-being.[9]

Perhaps most uniquely, families can provide a unique vector into networks of influence and power that are often beyond the reach of any individual family member. This dynamic is so pervasive globally that many cultures have given it a proper name. For instance, in China, the term *guanxi* (literally "closed system") is used to describe the process by which families develop durable relationships of mutual benefit. Grounded in Confucian values about the ideal structure of families and communities, *guanxi* networks are first built around personal bonds of trust before any subsequent business relationship can develop. Additionally, once established, these relationships are often sustained across generations, a testament to their enduring value both in good times and bad.

In the Arab world, the term *wasta* is used to describe a similar social construct, where families "pull strings" and exchange favors with powerful elites in order to derive personal and professional benefits.[10] In Farsi and Urdu, the phrase *raft amad* describes having "access"—or the privileged status of "going and coming" within another family—which is only available to trusted outsiders who are granted quasi-familial status as part of an extended tribe. Throughout Latin America, similar terms, including *compadrazgo*, *pituto*, and *jeitinho*, are used to describe how key resources are procured in contexts where public markets have failed, and where the best path to capital and information is to leverage familial connections to local elites.

Though these relationships are clearly capitalist in nature, we were surprised to discover that they were also prevalent in many former Communist states, from *blat* in Russia to *natsnoboba* in Georgia to *agashka* in Kazakhstan. In fact, the unique commercial conditions that emerge in predominantly socialist republics have attracted scholars—such as the sociologist Alena Ledeneva at University College London—who specifically focus on how these "economies of favor" help to facilitate the informal movement of goods and information between private individuals, state-owned enterprises, and government bureaucracies.

Though there is often scant evidence of these interactions and relationships in the conventional management literature, like nature's hearty extremophiles, they appear to be pervasive everywhere. That said, familial networks are especially common in places where markets lack stability, governments lack transparency, and institutions lack credibility.[11] As we enter the New Age of Uncertainty, we expect these private networks to become even more powerful drivers of entrepreneurial resilience and enduring success.

CONDITIONS AND CAVEATS

Even our ancestors recognized that when objects, institutions, and entire societies are organized in discrete, modular, interoperable pieces, stability increases dramatically. This deliberate systems-level planning consumes time and resources upfront—whether it means designing new modular systems to efficiently distribute consumer products, building flexible partnerships to form a synchronized and scalable commercial platform, or nurturing multigenerational familial networks of reciprocity and shared interest. However, once these initial investments have been made, our research suggests that the probability of enduring success increases dramatically.

As you reflect on the three forms of modularity we've outlined in this chapter, we suspect that you're already deploying at least one of them somewhere within your business, your ownership, or your family system. If you're struggling to find an example, look no further than your smartphone to highlight the many modular relationships that support our modern lives—from your mobile network to your email provider to your social media apps. Even the physical phone itself is a marvel of modular manufacturing with materials and components gathered through integrated global supply chains: gold from Peru, copper from Chile, tin from Myanmar, tantalum from Rwanda, tungsten from Vietnam, rare earth metals from China, and so forth. These materials were then combined and assembled in modular factories everywhere from Taiwan and India to the Czech Republic and the United States, many of which are controlled by companies such as Foxconn and Apple, whose modular ownership structures allow millions of investors to plug into shared commercial enterprises. In many ways, as we learned in Chapter 3, modularity is the foundational premise of modern capitalism, so it should come as no surprise that this strategy is used pervasively around the world.

From smartphones to boardrooms, we truly believe that modular systems offer several important advantages to a variety of stakeholders. First and foremost, they are explicitly designed to be flexible, scalable, and easy to repair and maintain—critical stabilizing benefits in turbulent environments. Plug-and-play platforms make it easier to add, remove, and replace individual components (products, markets, business units, and even owners) without affecting the rest of the system. This flexibility helps companies adapt more rapidly to fluctuating internal and external conditions, enabling them to identify new risks, integrate new opportunities, leverage new partnerships, and access new resources at the frontiers of their existing activities.

Yet, as with the other stabilizing strategies, there are limits to its efficacy. First, modular systems are naturally more complex to manage. As we learned in Part 1, systems that involve the independent actions and interactions of many individual agents can produce an array of outcomes that are very difficult to predict and require more coordination and oversight. The relative resilience of these networks is therefore dependent on choosing people and partners who share your values and your vision, then negotiating terms of engagement, ensuring that everyone feels they are being fairly treated and compensated.

Perhaps most importantly, without careful attention to the design of the interface (or "interlinks") between the company and its key stakeholders—partners, customers, suppliers, and distributors, not to mention the government—the increased complexity of modular systems can become a structural vulnerability that stymies productivity and consumes precious resources. This is particularly crucial during periods of acute crisis, when resources are scarce and cooperation can break down. It is precisely in these moments when familial networks of emotional support, financial capital, and social influence can become life-saving shock absorbers, redistributing organizational energy and resources where they are needed most.

As we'll explore in the next chapter, there is a particular form of modular interdependence that emerges from a single mission-critical relationship, one that overshadows all others in a successful entrepreneurial ecosystem: the relationship between business and government. In the language of networks, this interdependency is a form of *symbiosis*, since the functionality of one module depends on the resources of another. As we'll explore in the next chapter, these relationships can be positive (mutualistic) or negative (parasitic), and managing them effectively is an important strategic competency among many enduring enterprises that operate toward the bottom of the Hierarchy of Stability.

KEY INSIGHTS

- Modularity, applied strategically in business, ownership, and family systems, can be a core driver of growth and stability, particularly in uncertain environments.
- Though these enduring enterprises are inherently more complex, when their many independent and interdependent parts are working together seamlessly in service of a common

mission, such modularity can provide a powerful and lasting competitive advantage.

- The Zamil family exemplifies how these principles can be used across all three domains of business, ownership, and family to navigate a rapidly changing economic landscape and build a successful enterprise.
- In business, companies can leverage modularity throughout their operations—as IKEA does, for example, in product design, store layouts, and flat-pack logistics to offer affordable, self-assembled furniture on a global scale.
- In ownership, franchises and joint ventures enable companies such as McDonald's and Caterpillar to partner with enterprising families in emerging and frontier economies as they expand into new markets with greater confidence.
- In families, enduring networks of trusted relationships can act as a critical support system, providing access to capital, information, labor, opportunity, and even personal security in uncertain environments.
- Clear protocols are essential for sustaining and scaling modular systems over time—especially when dealing with elevated levels of uncertainty—or the increased complexity can shift from being a strategic asset to being a structural liability.

7
SYMBIOSIS

To put the world in order, we must first put the nation in order; to put the nation in order, we must first put the family in order; to put the family in order, we must first cultivate our personal life; we must first set our hearts right.

—**Confucius**

In many ways, the story of Samsung is the story of modern Korea, one shaped by civil war, industrial policy, and family enterprise. It began after World War II, when, much like Germany, the Korean Peninsula was split—in Korea's case along the 38th parallel between Western and Communist spheres of influence. At the time, the North and South were virtually indistinguishable economically. In fact, as recently as 1965, North Korean per capita income was three times greater than that of its southern neighbor, and both Bolivia and Mozambique were more prosperous.

But in the half-century since, South Korea has experienced a twenty-one-fold increase in per capita output, while the North has languished under the leadership of the Kim family's dynastic dictatorship. Today, South Korea is richer than Saudi Arabia and generates nearly four times more output per person than China, while North Korea continues to struggle to feed its growing population and remains politically and economically isolated.

This divergent path, the so-called "Miracle on the Han," began in the 1960s under the autocratic leadership of President Park Chung Hee, a peasant-turned-officer who rose quickly through the army's ranks, eventually waging a successful coup in 1961. Park's plan for Korean prosperity rested on two main pillars: protection of key domestic industries and export-oriented industrialization. To achieve this ambitious economic agenda, he formed an alliance with a fledgling community of entrepreneurial families, providing these young *chaebol* (literally "money clans") with cheap financing, protection from foreign competition, lucrative government contracts, and favorable treatment from regulators and the judiciary.

During this prodigious economic ascent, support for the country's family-run *chaebol* was rarely questioned, either by the government or the people, and with good reason. Their largest family conglomerates have since become some of the world's most successful and admired

Miracle on the Han River

Fastest growth in GDP Per Capita in modern history

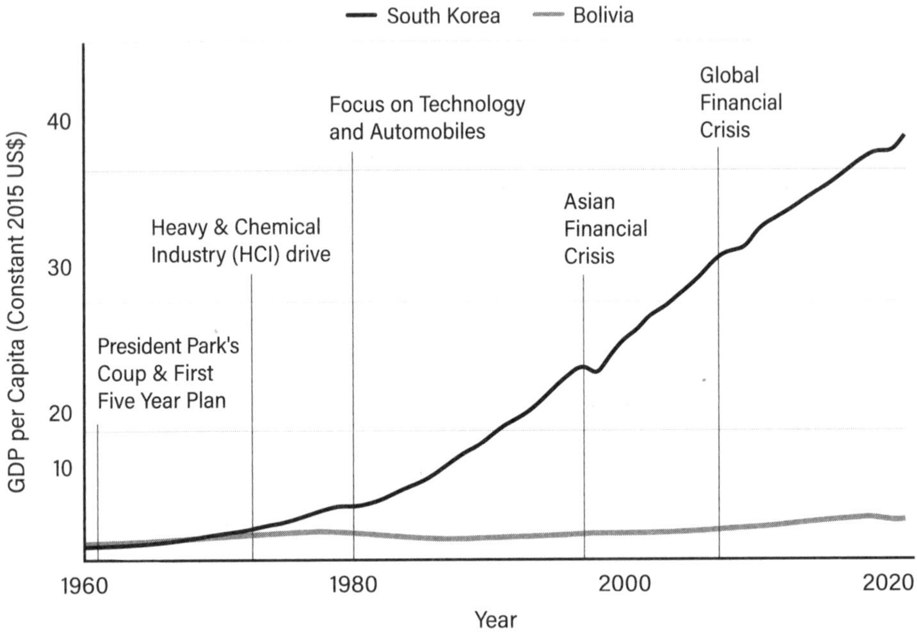

Source: Our World in Data, World Bank

brands—household names including Samsung, Hyundai, and LG. By some estimates, the top ten alone account for roughly 80 percent of the country's GDP. Without them, South Korea would look more like emerging Vietnam than developed Japan.

The global manufacturing juggernaut Samsung—established in 1938, long before the civil war—was among the first hand-picked *chaebol* to lead President Park's industrial transformation. Its founder, Lee Byung-chul, initially had little interest in entrepreneurship and few related skills. The only son in a well-off family, he was happily studying in Japan when his father died unexpectedly. Summoned home by his elders, he returned to southeastern Korea, where he used his inheritance as seed capital to start a rice milling business, but the enterprise quickly went bankrupt.

However, the young Lee, then in his mid-twenties, was undeterred. Recognizing that this wild frontier economy had many unmet needs and opportunities, he launched a new venture called the Samsung Trading Company, initially exporting fruit, vegetables, noodles, and dried fish throughout Korea and China. Lee chose the name "Samsung" based on the Korean word *sam* (the number three, which implies greatness) and *sung* (or "stars," which are vast and eternal). Clearly he had high expectations for the fledgling company, though few at the time could have anticipated the exceptional success that lay ahead.

The origins of *chaebol* like Samsung can be traced back to the period of Japanese colonial rule, when a handful of Korean entrepreneurs remodeled themselves after Japanese *zaibatsu*, such as Mitsui, whose modular networks provided a durable form of strategic stability in their own right. This was clearly the case for Lee, who was quick to expand Samsung beyond basic commodities, first into related businesses such as textiles and scrap iron, and later into other unrelated industries, including banking, insurance, and securities.

Many *chaebol* maintained close ties with the first president of the Republic of Korea, Syngman Rhee, who gained power and influence as a polished spokesman for Korean independence. His administration was known mostly for its economic mismanagement, authoritarianism, and proclivity for graft. During his leadership, a policy of kickbacks in exchange for favorable treatment from the government became entrenched in Korean commercial life.

In some ways, President Park's 1961 coup was a direct response to these failed policies. His military government, steeped in honor and tradition, initially targeted corporate leaders for corruption. But Park quickly recognized that these families were also ideal partners for rapidly modernizing the economy. His ministers would provide the blueprints and the raw materials for growth, and the *chaebol* would build out the model. As we've learned, the key to becoming an emerging economy is more inclusive institutions, and Park's new economic model was designed explicitly to benefit both private enterprise and the general Korean public.

Park and Lee both saw the opportunity for a virtuous cycle of wealth creation and economic development. To reinforce their symbiotic partnership, Lee even arranged for his sons to marry the daughters of governors and ministers. Protected by government policy, and with great access to opportunity, Samsung continued its inexorable ascent. Lee's special relationship with the government became the family's most treasured asset. In the absence of competition, and with access to cheap financing, lucrative contracts, and unrivaled state support, Samsung inevitably entered heavier industries such as shipbuilding and petrochemicals, which require abundant capital, long-term planning, and political influence. Given this remarkably synergistic relationship, it's no wonder Lee was quick to recognize "government and industry as husband and wife."

Eventually, in 1969, Lee launched Samsung Electronics, once again in response to generous government incentives. In the decades since, it has become an unrivaled symbol of the modernization of South Korea, supplying domestic and export markets first with TVs, then with refrigerators, washing machines, ovens, air conditioners, and other white goods. Then in the 1970s, Lee went further upstream and began manufacturing semiconductors, and in the 1980s, moved laterally into telecommunications. Soon Samsung was known as much for its personal computers and "hand phones" as it was for low-cost appliances.

After his death in 1987, Lee was succeeded by his second son, Lee Kun-hee. Just as his father understood in the 1970s that high-tech electronics should be the company's main focus, Lee Kun-hee successfully predicted that industrial design would become "the ultimate battleground for global competition in the 21st century."[1] He streamlined what had become a sprawling business empire, making electronics the centerpiece. By 2015, Samsung was the world's second-largest computer chip maker and held more US patents than any other company. It also became the largest mobile phone manufacturer, with its line of Galaxy smartphones outselling Apple's iPhone (while also supplying most of Apple's mobile displays). In recent years, the Samsung Group's total revenues have represented more than 22 percent of South Korea's GDP, and some pundits describe the country as "the Republic of Samsung."[2]

When Lee Kun-hee suffered a near fatal heart attack in 2014, his son, Lee Jae-yong, assumed control of the sprawling Samsung empire. His tenure began at a time when public support for the *chaebol* was waning, a sentiment shaped by accounts implicating the scions of the country's elite families in a string of scandals. With reports of their reckless disregard for

Ten Largest Companies in South Korea Are All *Chaebol*

Their combined market value represents over 40% of GDP

Rank	Name	Industry	Market Capitalization
1	Samsung	Technology	$375B
2	SK Hynix	Technology	$72B
3	LG Energy Solution	Energy	$68B
4	Hyundai	Automotive	$45B
5	Samsung Biologics	Health care	$44B
6	Kia	Automotive	$34B
7	Celltrion	Health care	$28B
8	LG Chem	Chemicals	$26B
9	POSCO	Other	$26B
10	Coupang	Technology	$26B

Source: CompaniesMarketCap.com, as of February 7, 2024.

rules and norms—in incidents involving violent outbursts against flight attendants and bribing officials to receive lenient sentences—they were no longer seen as providing mutualistic benefit to the country, especially now that it enjoyed full advanced economy status.[3]

After decades of economic development and Western influence, South Korea's public institutions were finally capable of challenging the entrenched political influence of the *chaebol* elite. New legislation to rein in *gabjil* (or "high-handedness") among the rich accompanied this shift in public perception. President Park Geun-hye, the daughter of the general who had pioneered this policy in the 1960s, and a close confidant of young Lee Jae-yong, was impeached in 2017. Convicted on corruption charges, she received a twenty-year jail sentence, sending a powerful signal to both politicians and the *chaebol* that the government would no longer tolerate behavior that wasn't expressly in the public interest.

The Samsung case clearly demonstrates that hitching the family wagon to a powerful and fast-moving regime can be a tremendous source of opportunity, wealth creation, innovation, and even economic development. To be successful, this form of symbiosis requires developing close, mutually beneficial relationships between businesses, public officials, and entire communities of workers and customers, who together help to bring stability to otherwise complex operating environments. It also leaves family firms vulnerable during moments of regime change—when patrons are replaced and community allegiances shift. A second-generation family leader in Kenya captured the dilemma: "Every time there were political pressures from politicians for support, we always remained neutral and law-abiding. Our argument was that if we support one today, what happens tomorrow when they are not in power?"[4]

This strategy is particularly precarious when societies begin to shift their views on wealth and inequality, as is the case currently in South Korea, where the privileged status of the *chaebol* is now being openly questioned. Their license to operate may be granted by the government, but losing the support of the community can be even more dangerous than regime change. As we learned in Chapter 3, when we transition up the

Hierarchy of Stability, public policies and attitudes begin to favor more open markets and globalization. Protectionism decreases as competition increases, and the stabilizing power of political patronage begins to fade—or, worse—becomes a liability. During these moments, and ideally before them, it is critical for leaders to recognize the trade-offs and choose their partners wisely.

FAUSTIAN BARGAINS

Seeking the support and protection of well-established and well-resourced patrons is a time-honored tradition. From ancient empires to modern nations, from religious leaders to cultural influencers, from military commanders to business tycoons, humans are instinctively attracted to power and influence. Whether we live in the gilded towers overlooking Central Park at the peak of the Hierarchy of Stability, or toil away at the base in the favelas of Rio, our lives are nested within ecosystems of power. As a result, our proximity to those at the top—be they mayors or kingpins—can greatly affect our access to key resources and general well-being.

Throughout history, heads of state have cultivated an entourage of courtiers, advisers, diplomats, and dignitaries who have willingly pledged their fealty in exchange for a small taste of power and stability. Being an active member of the king's court can help to insulate against the vicissitudes of life. But it comes at a steep price—including exposure to corruption, exploitation, oppression, and even violence. When the gap between the haves and have-nots grows too wide—or persists for too long—those who lack access to *guanxi*, *wasta*, and *blat* are often the earliest instigators of rebellion and revolution.

To be clear, concentrations of power and influence aren't inherently bad for society. South Korea's "Miracle on the Han" would have been impossible without its *chaebol* champions. Singapore's model of "benevolent dictatorship," albeit challenging to replicate, has been widely praised by citizens and economists. Carvajal's deep commitment both to community and country is the model of stakeholder capitalism. However, building a close relationship to power is not without risk. Like the mythical sword hanging precipitously over the head of Damocles, it simultaneously offers great power and requires great caution.

This is precisely why the Greek myth about Icarus flying close to the sun is so tragic—hubris and indiscretion drew him too close to power, and it cost him both his freedom and his life. In 1592, the playwright Christopher Marlowe captured this cautionary tale beautifully in his famous retelling of the legend of Dr. Faustus:

Swollen with cunning, of a self-conceit
His waxen wings did mount above his reach
And, melting, Heavens conspired his overthrow![5]

In many ways, Marlowe's play is a Renaissance reboot of the legend of Icarus. The protagonist, Dr. Faustus, is a brilliant scholar who has grown dissatisfied with his mediocre life. Performing a dark ritual in his study, he conjures up Mephistopheles, a servant of the devil, who offers to grant him anything he wishes. What Faustus truly craves is unlimited knowledge and power, and he signs a contract in blood, pledging his eternal soul as collateral. At first, this appears to be a phenomenally successful trade, and he relishes in "a world of profit and delight, / Of power, of honour, of omnipotence."[6] However, over time Faustus comes to regret the pact, which leaves a trail of destruction for those around him.

This narrative has been interpreted in many ways over the centuries,[7] but at its core it represents the idea that one can achieve great success—and avoid great harm—by binding one's fate to the power of others. However, this existential insurance comes at a steep price, and leaders need to analyze these trade-offs carefully before engaging in Faustian bargains. A more nuanced and granular understanding of the mechanics of symbiosis is therefore necessary in order to fully leverage the stabilizing effects of these investments.

In particular, we need to recognize that symbiosis comes in several flavors in both natural and human systems. The management literature is highly focused on *competition*, and for good reason, since it plays a significant role in shaping organizational strategy and structure, particularly in advanced economies. However, we want to focus on two lesser-studied forms—*mutualism*[8] and *parasitism*[9]—which play a larger role further down the Hierarchy of Stability. Interestingly, our research suggests that in these less competitive markets, what separates those who are focused on mutualistic relationships, which generate more prosperity for themselves and others, and those more focused on accumulating wealth and power at the expense of others, ultimately comes down to family values.

Since families are naturally hierarchical social systems—in which some individuals wield more influence over critical decisions than others—it should come as no surprise that our behavioral intuition about symbiotic relationships begins at a very early age.[10] For instance, from an evolutionary perspective, parental investment and attention is a highly coveted resource, and children naturally compete for it. Securing one's place as a favorite child by catering to the needs of parents and grandparents establishes the foundations of symbiosis not only within families—but ultimately between families and the broader society.[11]

Six Variations of Symbiosis in Nature

Not all relationships are created equal

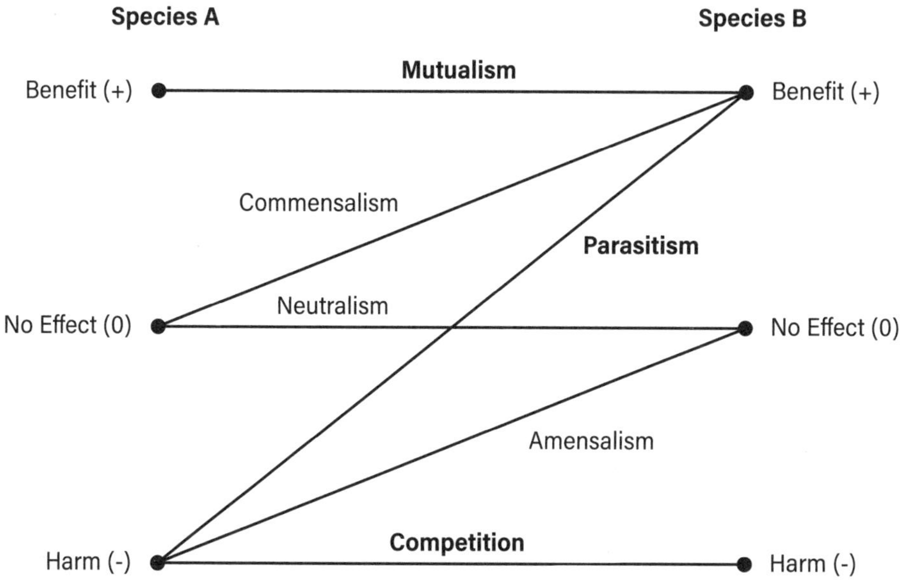

Source: "Symbiosis." Wikipedia. April 26, 2024. https://en.wikipedia.org/wiki/Symbiosis.

Consequently, when enterprising families found a new business, its organizational culture and strategy are driven by these underlying behavioral patterns and preferences. In some families, symbiotic bonds are steeped in traditions of collaboration and reciprocity, and *mutualistic* relationships abound. In others, independence and competition are nurtured, and *parasitic* relationships are more likely to unfold. Both variations can generate greater stability and help to secure access to critical resources, but they do so in very different ways.

CREATING SHARED VALUE

Mutually beneficial collaboration has a long tradition in both human and natural systems. After all, "reciprocal altruism" (as it's known in evolutionary biology) is one of the key sources of internal stability among many social species. The term was originally coined by the biologist Robert Trivers in 1971 to describe a form of cooperation that involves individuals helping each other at an initial cost to themselves, with the expectation of being paid back at some point in the future. The concept is based on the idea of "inclusive fitness," which takes into account not only the direct effects of an individual animal's actions on its own survival and reproduction, but also the indirect effects on the survival and reproduction of its relatives.[12]

To understand how this works in nature, consider the behavior of communities of male red-winged blackbirds, who defend their collective territory from predators by making alarm calls and attacking intruders—a remarkably sophisticated form of "neighborhood watch." Importantly, males reduce support for those who don't participate in this collective defense, a direct punishment for "free riding," or benefiting parasitically from a common pool of resources without contributing one's fair share.

Indeed, leveraging our instincts for reciprocal altruism has been one of humanity's superpowers, driving our social and economic development for much of recorded history—from the earliest communities of hunters and gatherers, to medieval networks of barter and trade, to the complex markets and alliances that power our modern global economy. As the father of economics, Adam Smith, first observed in the late eighteenth century, "It is not from the benevolence of the butcher, the brewer, or the baker that we expect our dinner, but from their regard to their own self-interest."[13]

Among his many talents, Smith was a keen observer of social systems, and he recognized that the economic potential of any society is determined by its capacity to incentivize these mutualistic tendencies. As we saw in Chapter 3, such "benevolence" within families is highly instinctive. However, beyond our closest kin, we often require additional stabilizing conditions, without which the incentives for mutualistic exchange can quickly break down. Enterprising families that seek stability through symbiotic relationships understand this intrinsically and focus their efforts on five key elements when selecting their partners.

First and foremost, they recognize that the strengths and needs of both parties must be complementary, generating synergies that couldn't be captured if either partner acted alone. Second, these relationships need to consistently generate shared benefits over time, providing both partners with a greater chance of survival even if in any given moment one party is benefiting more than the other. Third, mutualistic partnerships require clear communication and trust, because the synergies of collective action are only available with effective coordination. Fourth, they need to be flexible and adaptive, because environmental conditions are destined to change—particularly further down the Hierarchy of Stability. Finally, both partners must be willing to invest the time and resources necessary to sustain the relationship over time, given that these long-term arrangements may not provide immediate benefits. This last part bears repeating, since without sustained mutual benefit, all relationships will eventually break down, especially when they are under pressure from chronic environmental stress.

As the members of Samsung's Lee family and their fellow *chaebol* have proven over the past half-century, such mutualistic relationships are quite durable, particularly lower down on the Hierarchy of Stability. Under these more challenging operating conditions, where access to key resources is often limited, many enduring enterprises recognize the importance of maintaining close "upward" ties with well-established patrons. At the same time, political and economic elites are often less subject to public scrutiny, allowing these privileged relationships to survive and thrive unchecked for decades or sometimes much longer (as we saw with Kongō Gumi and Toraya).

That said, the Miracle on the Han has also demonstrated that mutualism isn't exclusively an elitist strategy. In fact, the benefits of a more inclusive, multi-stakeholder approach to continuity planning have recently begun to gain traction in C-suites and boardrooms around the world—even in advanced economies where external stabilizers are plentiful and resources bountiful.

Some look to the work of Harvard's Michael Porter as the catalyst that set these wheels in motion. Over five decades, Porter has contributed significantly to the field of strategic management, pioneering groundbreaking theories that have helped managers and policymakers understand how to create and sustain competitive advantage in a wide array of industries and contexts. However, it was a seminal 2006 article in the *Harvard Business Review*, which he wrote in collaboration with Mark Kramer at the Harvard Kennedy School, that introduced the concept of Creating Shared Value (CSV), defining a new framework to help "corporations turn social problems into business opportunities."[14]

Porter and Kramer threw down the mutualistic gauntlet, challenging the more parasitic strain of "shareholder capitalism" to embrace a higher purpose. To prove the point, they identified a host of corporate titans who were generating substantial economic value in ways that also addressed some of society's most pressing needs and challenges—from climate change to social justice. To be clear, these activities go well beyond earlier conceptions of Corporate Social Responsibility (CSR), corporate philanthropy, or token gestures about "sustainability." They require what their fellow Harvard professor Ranjay Gulati calls "deep purpose": a fundamental realignment between a company's success and the long-term health and well-being of the communities within which the company operates.

Since these ideas were first conceptualized by Porter and Kramer in 2006, CSV (sometimes referred to as "stakeholder capitalism") has been widely adopted and praised by business leaders, academics, and practitioners as a new way to reinvent capitalism and unleash a wave of innovation and growth. However, our research has shown that this concept was alive and well long before the *HBR* article was first published. *Community symbiosis* has been a frequent source of strategic advantage for centuries at some of the oldest and largest family companies. This more inclusive approach to stakeholder relations has helped to bring greater stability to places and times when both businesses and societies have faced structural threats or sustained uncertainty.

A shining example is the renowned soy sauce manufacturer Kikkoman, a family-run company since its founding in 1603 in the Chiba prefecture just east of Tokyo. We met with members of the Takanashi family—one of the company's eight founding clans—in Noda at their traditional ancestral home. Like Toraya, the Takanashis are a privileged supplier to the royal court. This standing is a treasured asset—a relationship that has both benefited the royal family and enhanced the company's fortunes. However, the Takanashi family's embrace of mutualism goes beyond the "upward" relationship with its Imperial patron and extends deeply into the local community.

When we asked the family's leaders about the largest crises they had faced throughout their long and storied history, without hesitation the response was a series of famines—in the 1730s, 1780s, and 1830s—which devastated crops and threatened the region with starvation and collapse. During these sustained shocks, the Takanashi family "Master" took direct responsibility for managing relationships both with the royal court and local officials. On all three occasions, the family's leaders opened up their emergency grain reserves to help feed the starving locals.

To this day, a stone monument sits next to the family's tea house as an enduring token of gratitude from the community. Kikkoman's role in providing assistance during the famines has endeared the company to its loyal customers for centuries. Their core value of community leadership has been a common thread throughout the twelve generations that have stewarded this ancient family business. It continues to guide the company's strategy today, even though Kikkoman's operations are now global and the world much more complex.

Another fascinating example comes from Venezuela—a frontier economy rife with political and economic dysfunction but also strong community values. Since its founding in 1896, the family-led distillery Ron Santa Teresa has overcome countless crises, from wars to recessions to natural disasters. But none were as destabilizing as the presidency of Hugo Chavez, who rose to power in 1999 on a campaign, backed by Cuba, to implement a socialist and "anti-imperialist" agenda in one of the world's largest oil-exporting nations.[15] These measures alienated many domestic and foreign investors, who faced expropriations, currency and price controls, and labor disputes. The regime's economic mismanagement also resulted in chronic shortages of basic goods and services, hyperinflation, and growing social unrest.

In this challenging operational context, Alberto C. Vollmer, the thirty-year-old great-great-grandson of Santa Teresa's founder, Gustavo Vollmer Ribas, was tapped to steward the family business successfully into the turbulent twenty-first century. At the time, the company was struggling financially, having loaded up on debt and facing declining sales. However, the worsening security situation presented an even more immediate threat to continuity—in many ways similar to AJE's experience with the Shining Path.

Local gangs in Aragua in north-central Venezuela began disrupting the company's supply chains, raiding their warehouses, and even squatting on their agricultural lands. In an inspirational act of community mutualism, rather than arming up and confronting the rebellious locals, Vollmer launched "Project Alcatraz," a rehabilitation program for young people trapped in the parasitic ecosystems of these criminal syndicates.

The initiative was conceived in 2003, after local robbers attacked a security guard at gunpoint and held him hostage. Rather than turning them into the authorities and perpetuating the cycle of misfortune endemic to the country at the time, Vollmer instead offered them jobs. Then he introduced them to rugby, a sport he was passionate about, and which encourages mutualistic values such as teamwork and respect. Since then, *Proyecto Alcatraz* has helped more than 200 former gang members reintegrate into society as workers, coaches, and mentors to at-risk youth. It also propelled Ron Santa Teresa's reputation, nurturing loyalty and expanding markets for many of its products worldwide.

Vollmer proudly shares his confidence in the stabilizing power of symbiosis, which helped bring about the unlikely success of his family business in the face of seemingly insurmountable odds. “The guys from the gangs are used to risking everything,” he told a reporter. “So, when you give them a chance to do something positive in life and they take it, they become an extraordinary force.”[16]

It takes a lot of courage to trust others in these tumultuous conditions, particularly those who might harm or cheat or steal from you without hesitation. That level of trust certainly isn’t for the faint of heart. But it is possible, and can even be mutually beneficial. Whether you’re a massive multinational looking for triple bottom-line returns, or a resilient enterprise looking for solutions to thrive in turbulent times, co-investing in the communities you serve can pay huge dividends—under the right cultural conditions. The rest of the time, as we’re about to explore, *mutualism* remains an exception to the rule.

CRONY CAPITALISM

Whatever our perceptions about frontier economies—from exotic treasures to treacherous swamps—corruption is clearly endemic. As a Venezuelan business owner once told us, “The only thing that has been successfully privatized in this country is the justice system—it functions as a perfect market!” Among advanced economies, *political symbiosis* is merely rebranded as “influence peddling” or “lobbying.” As legendary Federal Reserve chairman Alan Greenspan once observed, “Corruption, embezzlement, fraud, these are all characteristics which exist everywhere. It is regrettably the way human nature functions, whether we like it or not. What successful economies do is keep it to a minimum. No one has ever eliminated any of that stuff.”[17]

The further we shift down the Hierarchy of Stability, the more pervasive these dynamics become. Some families, including the Lees, the Takanashis, and the Vollmers, spend decades and even centuries taming these complex and ever-changing environments. They recognize that long-term success is more likely when powerful friends abound, and that these friends aren’t grown overnight. As the Japanese say, “When you’re thirsty, it’s too late to start digging a well.”

Others have neither the patience nor the privilege to incubate these kinds of relationships. Instead they seek the Faustian bargain—more immediate access to resources and prosperity, though, like deals made with the infamous Godfather in Mario Puzo's book, at the expense of eternal fealty. Interestingly, our ancient brains are wired to make this trade by default, particularly when resources are scarce. It's tough to turn down a tree full of figs on an empty stomach, even if it comes with ominous strings attached.

Such temptations help to explain why *parasitic symbionts* are so prolific. They can be found anywhere power leaks from ivory towers into public squares, providing a treasured competitive advantage to those fortunate enough to secure these privileged relationships. But they are especially prevalent in frontier economies, where public institutions are scarce, and, consequently, accountability and transparency are elusive.

Consider the case of Russia, which lurched from communism to capitalism virtually overnight, with few external stabilizers to support the transition. Mass privatization presented a once-in-a-lifetime windfall for a new class of oligarchs (literally "rule by few") who nurtured close ties with the Kremlin in the years leading up to the fall of the Berlin Wall. As a result, they were able to purchase state-owned assets for kopeks on the ruble, using their newfound wealth and influence to control key sectors of the economy—as long as they supported overall Kremlin policy.

A popular Russian expression emerged to capture this phenomenon: "Never ask about the first million." Such systemic cronyism is sometimes referred to as the "original sin" of modern capitalism—a necessary byproduct of economic development. These transitions create vast wealth for a few privileged insiders. But as with all Faustian bargains, they come with a catch. The quasi-legal origins of the wealth are used as leverage to keep these new industrial titans in check as their power and wealth grow.

In modern China there is a saying that "a man fears getting famous like a pig fears getting fat." Despite millions of followers and billions in wealth, the power that parasitic symbionts wield is clearly derivative. It can be withdrawn at a moment's notice at the whim of the ruling regime.[18] But that still leaves many undeterred. One of the surest paths to wealth in twenty-first-century China is political office. By some estimates, there are at least a hundred billionaires in China's ruling party, and their combined wealth is an order of magnitude larger than that of the entire US Congress.

A fascinating case from India highlights the challenges of navigating environments with the kinds of incentive systems and risk profiles that are so pervasive in emerging and frontier economies. In early 2023, the Adani Group, a business empire closely associated with India's president, came under serious attack in the stock market. This was prompted by the release of a damning report by Hindenburg, a market research firm that specializes in short-selling overhyped stocks.

In a startling turn of events, this industrial conglomerate—spanning power generation and transmission, mining, airport operations, natural gas, food processing, and more—lost a jaw-dropping US$100 billion in market value in the days following the initial press release from Hindenburg.[19] This came after a meteoric rise over the previous five years, during which the value of the company even outpaced Elon Musk's Tesla and other high-flying American tech companies. For a brief moment, its founder, Gautam Adani, was the second-richest person on the planet.

The fall of Adani's empire put the spotlight on India's opaque political economy, which is plagued by crony capitalism and a concentration of wealth and power. While critics argue that this model is stifling competition and creating monopolies, others can't imagine India achieving its ambitious modernization goals without at least some consolidation of power and influence. Consider the impossible task of running a functional democracy in a country of over 1.3 billion people and 23 languages.

Adani began his entrepreneurial journey in 1988, importing and exporting raw commodities. The family, in other words, started out much like the Lees, Zamils, and countless others who sought their fortunes in commerce and trade in nascent frontier economies. Then in 1990, to help expand this business, the Adanis were selected by the regional government to build a port in the coastal city of Mundra, in the state of Gujarat. At the time, the chief minister of India's most industrialized state was a relatively unknown but ambitious young politician named Narendra Modi. The careers and the power of these two provincial upstarts have been inextricably intertwined, with Adani rising to the heights of economic power while Modi consolidated political authority as president. Together, their focus on India's modernization has built more infrastructure—and generated more wealth faster—than virtually any other company in history. These symbiotic dividends allowed Adani to underwrite Modi's growing political ambitions. Ever since, the two families have remained members of the same intimate familial network, helping to modernize Gujarat, lifting millions out of poverty—and minting billions in the process.

This cozy and mutualistic relationship—both between Adani and Modi and between their families and the country—isn't what caught the attention of Hindenburg. After all, symbiosis is pervasive at the base of the Hierarchy of Stability. However, the Adani Group's skyrocketing shares attracted a lot of domestic and international attention. As analysts began to scrutinize the company's convoluted legal and financial structure, they noticed some irregularities that sent troublesome signals about the integrity of the entire Adani empire—and about the mutualistic benefits of India's reliance on symbiosis more generally. As the *Financial Times* noted in 2020, several years before the release of the Hindenburg report, "Some argue the concentration of economic power in family-run conglomerates is a way to fast-track India's economic development, like the *chaebol* did for postwar South Korea. But critics say the rapid consolidation of state assets is creating monopolies and stifling competition."[20]

Some enterprising families like the Lees and the Adanis can begin as mutualistic contributors to their communities. But over generations, if they don't maintain and nurture this deep purpose, the shared value they once created can easily foster narcissism and become captive to private interests. This usually doesn't end well for dynastic elites—as the imprisoned scions of several Korean *chaebol* have clearly demonstrated in recent years. In other cases, such as that of Russia's oligarchs, parasitism was present right from the start, embodied in willful acts of state-sanctioned larceny by friends of the KGB. Yet when Putin's era of authoritarian rule comes to an end, whatever replaces it will inevitably favor new constituencies that have been patiently waiting their turn to feast at the trough.

Whether these changes happen by choice or by force, the stability generated by parasitism is always transitory. The only flavor of symbiosis that generates enduring prosperity is mutualism, particularly as countries migrate up the Hierarchy of Stability. Though it involves sharing value creation with others, in the long run healthy stakeholders make wealthy shareholders—and ultimately advanced economies.

CONDITIONS AND CAVEATS

The stabilizing benefits that come with proximity to power are not a modern phenomenon, nor are they isolated to any region or society. As we explored earlier in the book, nested hierarchies of power are integral to families and to the human experience more generally, connecting back to our earliest settlements and spanning all cultures and times. The security, stability, and influence that comes with access to authority has been a treasured asset for those brave enough to seek it, those fortunate enough to secure it, and those skilled enough to sustain it.

To be clear, some form of symbiosis is table stakes, even in advanced economies, because the blessing of public authorities is required when founding a business, and the support of a wide array of stakeholders is required for it to thrive. In the Global North, such *political mutualism* is essentially "government relations," while *community mutualism* is akin to "corporate social responsibility." Extracting parasitic rents from the government is still possible (and quite lucrative) through lobbying and influence peddling. But these ties are less structural and permanent than they were a century ago, when dynastic elites still directly appointed members of the US Senate, and much of the work of government policy and procurement took place away from prying eyes. As information markets have grown more pervasive and advocacy groups more active, it has become much harder for businesses in advanced economies to sustain parasitic relationships for long without reprisal.

If anything, as a 2023 article in *The Economist* succinctly captures, today's governments are growing increasingly critical of private enterprise. "They want to correct the problems of globalization by winning back manufacturing jobs. They want to enhance national security by protecting vital technologies. And they want to fight climate change by speeding up decarbonization."[21] These growing interventionist tendencies challenge a half-century of accumulated wisdom and experience about what it takes to sustain healthy business-government relations and make long-term planning significantly more challenging.

As we enter the New Age of Uncertainty, business leaders around the world, and enterprising families in particular, are faced with a stark choice—seeking strength from above (i.e., through relationships with the governments they serve), or building stability from below (i.e., through support for the communities they serve). Increasingly, these two strategies seem to be incompatible. On the one hand, the pursuit of government favoritism can provoke the ire of consumers, workers, and competitors, as many of them lack these same privileges and opportunities. On the other, having to earn the loyalty of citizens can be seen as a threat to the power and influence of public officials, who will need the support of these same voters to sustain their political status. In the face of this intractable dilemma, how can a greater understanding of symbiosis help to inform strategic planning and insulate against the rising tide of uncertainty? Our research and experience suggest that there are three common approaches that all leaders should consider.

Symbiosis in Business Also Comes in Several Flavors

All four can be lucrative, though mutualistic interactions are more enduring

	Mutualistic	Parasitic
Political	Private benefits support state development *Examples: Samsung in Korea, Carvajal in Colombia*	Private benefits undermine state development *Examples: oligarchs in Russia, Gupta in South Africa*
Community	Private benefits support public well-being *Examples: Santa Teresa in Venezuela, Kikkoman in Japan*	Private benefits undermine public well-being *Examples: Wagner Group in Africa, narcos in Mexico*

First, they should invest actively in the resilience of their communities. Whether out of genuine care for others or enlightened self-interest, the health of all key stakeholders is a critical driver of long-term success in any enduring family enterprise. Business continuity requires healthy relationships with customers and workers, reliable suppliers and distributors, effective public and private institutions, well-functioning markets, and stable environmental conditions. This might seem like a lot more responsibility than what typical corporate leaders currently have on their desks—and it is! But from the perspective of continuity and strategic planning, does it really make sense to retreat into a gilded fortress and ignore what's happening outside the castle walls? In the turbulent years ahead, if emerging and frontier economies are any indication of what's to come for companies operating everywhere, this broader stakeholder approach will become basic table stakes for organizational resilience. As the renowned Spanish philosopher José Ortega y Gasset eloquently commented, "I am myself and my circumstance, and if I do not save it, I do not save myself."[22]

Second, business leaders (and even more importantly, family business owners) need to choose their dance partners wisely. If modularity is like friendship, symbiosis is like marriage—requiring deeper and more structural integration. Symbiosis thus naturally requires an alignment in core values and organizational purpose as well as a commitment to investing in healthy intergenerational relations. Like succession planning for a single leader, symbiosis requires mutual assurances that these strategic contacts will be well managed and stewarded over time. People come and go, and power ebbs and flows, but Samsung's commitment to South Korean development, Kikkoman's commitment to the health of its communities, and Carvajal's commitment to Colombian democracy were so impactful precisely because they were able to persist across generations. The returns on social capital compound over time much like they do with financial capital. Similarly, if a relationship isn't a good fit or brings more risk than opportunity, then it's better to bring closure sooner than later. Enduring enterprises foster political and community allegiances that support their performance and resilience—and are quick to sever the ties that don't.

Third, it's essential that leaders and owners clarify their ethical frontiers—and align them with their organizational structure and strategy. Drawing clear red lines will ensure that everyone in the company can operate without ambiguity when they are confronted with decisions such as whether to pay bribes to expedite construction permits, prioritize profits over employee safety, or build protectionist tariffs into product development plans. Businesses like Carvajal that choose to operate with full moral integrity on the frontiers of ethics openly signal this commitment to all stakeholders, and thus they are able to sidestep much of the ethical ambiguity that is endemic to commercial life in emerging and frontier economies.[23] In the years ahead, enterprising families in advanced economies will need to remain more vigilant as well, given how easy it is to slide down the slippery slope of ethical transgressions during a polycrisis. Just ask the leading German families who were active in the 1930s, when Hitler and the Nazis seized control of the economy.[24]

One of the most disorienting aspects of operating during these volatile turning points in history is that moral goalposts are constantly in motion. Companies are more likely to remain better hedged against these risks if they operate in places where their core values are rewarded, and avoid places where they aren't. Compliance means something very different in Dhaka than in Dallas, and enduring family enterprises that manage symbiotic relationships on either side of an ethical frontier are particularly vulnerable, since their divided allegiances are bound to disappoint both sides at some point. As they grow, enterprising families must double down in transferring their values and ethical principles to the next generation, and in heightening collective awareness that the family's reputation and goodwill—the essential source of its social capital—constitute a shared asset for which everyone in the family must take personal responsibility.

To be clear, we fully recognize that not all organizations may need—or want—to rely on external parties to provide additional stability in the absence of more pervasive and inclusive institutional support. As we'll explore in the next chapter, another alternative is to avoid codependency altogether. Instead, strategic reinforcements can come from within.

KEY INSIGHTS

- Symbiosis is a powerful stabilizing force in nature and business, allowing two related parties to share resources, opportunities, and protection within otherwise turbulent environments.
- Samsung benefited greatly from a symbiotic relationship with the South Korean government—which provided cheap financing, protection from competition, and lucrative contracts in exchange for driving the country's rapid economic development (e.g., the "Miracle on the Han River").
- The relationship between Samsung and the Korean state helped generate stability and growth for decades, though in recent years public support for *chaebol* has waned, and the government and the general public are becoming increasingly critical of their privileged status in South Korean society.
- There are different flavors of symbiosis—some relationships are *mutualistic* (beneficial to both parties), and others are *parasitic* (accretive to one party while damaging to the other).
- The most enduring relationships are mutualistic—built on trust and reciprocity.
- The most profitable relationships, at least in the short run, are often parasitic—built on extractive self-interest.
- Family businesses are well positioned to develop symbiotic relationships both "upwardly" with governments (political symbiosis) and "downwardly" with their key stakeholders (community symbiosis).
- Codependency can be both a source of strength and a vulnerability—if these relationships suddenly sour, or are threatened by others, as with the Adani Group in India, a company's most lucrative asset can quickly become its greatest liability.

8
REDUNDANCY

Neither should a ship rely on one small anchor,
nor should life rest on a single hope.
—Epictetus

On January 12, 2010, shortly before 5 p.m. local time, a 15-second, magnitude 7.0 earthquake struck the small country of Haiti on the Caribbean island of Hispaniola. It was followed by aftershocks that lasted for days, leaving an estimated 300,000 people dead and as many as 1.6 million homeless. A subsequent cholera outbreak, triggered by broken sewage and water treatment infrastructure, made millions ill and killed another 10,000. Sadly, this catastrophe was merely the latest in a long series of unfortunate events that have tested the resilience of the Haitian people over the centuries, from economic exploitation to environmental degradation to political instability.

Initially of minor importance to the French Empire, the colony of Saint-Domingue was transformed into a booming economic powerhouse in the late seventeenth and early eighteenth centuries with the introduction of sugarcane plantations. Leveraging a steady supply of African slaves and an insatiable demand from emerging economies on both sides of the Atlantic, Saint-Domingue became one of the richest colonies in the world. By 1789, it was producing roughly half of all the sugar and coffee consumed in Europe and the Americas and was the crown jewel in France's colonial portfolio.

Despite this bountiful economic success, the "Pearl of the Antilles," as it was known at the time, was a poster child for parasitic symbiosis. The booming commodities trade significantly enhanced the wealth and power of France, but it did little to protect or support the colony and its people. Eventually the locals revolted, culminating in Haiti's independence in 1804. However, sovereignty came at a steep cost. In exchange for diplomatic recognition, France imposed a crippling indemnity on Haiti for the loss of its slave-based wealth, plunging the fledgling nation into a cycle of debt and economic hardship from which it has never fully recovered.

The early years of independence were not marked by a political or economic renaissance, but instead stoked a rivalry between the many former slaves and the few free people of color who held a disproportionate share

A Tale of Two Islands: Dominican Republic vs. Haiti

Centuries of mismanagement have had lasting consequences in Hispaniola

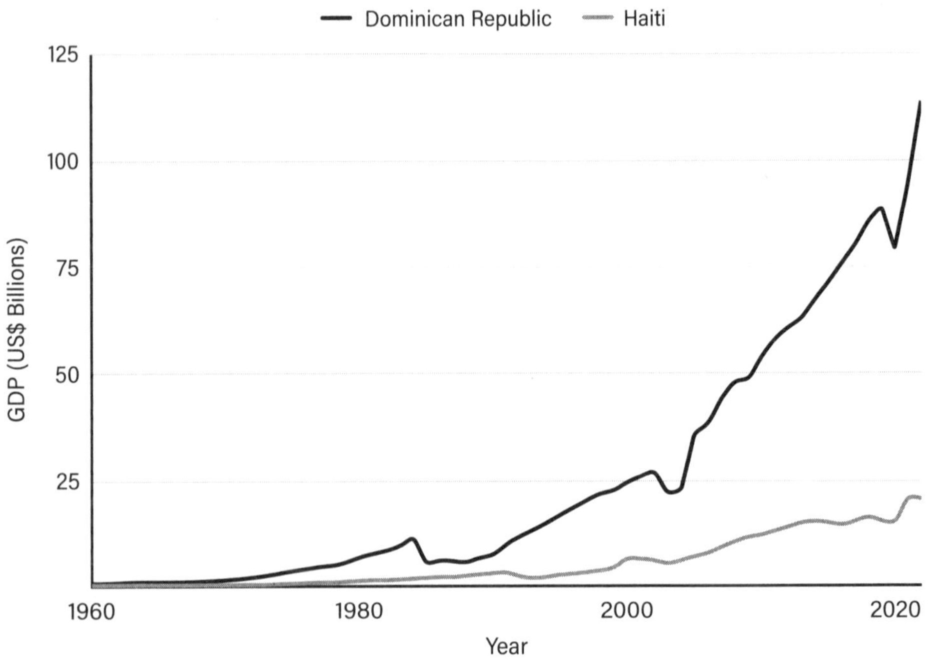

Source: World Bank national accounts data

of wealth and power. This structural tension has persisted for centuries, producing a succession of dictatorships, coups, and military regimes. Given this backstory, it's no wonder Haiti is one of the poorest and most politically unstable countries in the Western Hemisphere.[1]

Under these challenging conditions, Haiti has remained a struggling frontier economy. Anywhere else, an earthquake of the magnitude that struck in January 2010 would have registered as among the worst natural disasters in a nation's history. In Haiti, it was but one of a long list of natural and man-made calamities over the centuries plaguing its people and hindering its progress.

With that context in mind, let's reconsider the events that unfolded in the weeks after the 2010 quake. As aid organizations and the media converged on Haiti's capital city, Port-au-Prince, many foreigners needed to establish a stable base from which to begin the important work of humanitarian aid and reconstruction. That work would require reliable access to basics—water, food, and shelter, as well as secure connections to electricity and a telecommunications infrastructure, enabling greater coordination within and outside of the country. Personal security, a consideration in Port-au-Prince in the best of times, was also an issue, as desperation in the wake of the disaster was driving even greater levels of civil unrest than usual.

In that context, the destination of choice—at least for the lucky few able to secure a room—was the historic Le Plaza Hotel, which stood virtually undamaged despite the devastation all around it. As Agnès Pierre-Louis, a third-generation member of the family that founded the hotel, remarked several years after the quake, "Many believe it was a mystical blessing. Others pointed to the number of old trees on the property, whose deep roots held firmly onto the earth. Or we simply got lucky."[2] Fortune may have been a factor, but it only explains part of the reason this family-run institution has survived and thrived for decades in an inhospitable frontier economy.

The history of this storied hotel begins in the mid-1950s, when Therese Pierre-Louis founded a modest, six-room guesthouse in the Haitian capital. For years, the business subsisted on a slow trickle of local and foreign guests, while dynastic despots and undercover death squads chased away all but the most intrepid tourists.

In 1961, one of Therese's two children, Fred, began working with her to help grow the struggling business. Under their collective stewardship, it evolved from a small bed and breakfast into a sprawling ninety-five-room hotel. Between 1981 and 1998, it operated under the Holiday Inn banner—an early test of modularity and an effort to attract more American tourists to the exotic French side of Hispaniola. However, chronic political and economic dysfunction made it increasingly hard for the hotel to survive, and few travelers were willing to trade the pristine beaches and safe compounds of Punta Cana for a more frontier experience in Port-au-Prince.

The situation was so bad that in 2004 Fred was forced to close the hotel and rent it out to the United Nations as a base camp. It was a real turning point for the family and the business—one that tested their commitment to continuity. At one point a few years later, when the political climate appeared to be stabilizing, Fred asked his daughter, Agnès, who had a degree in hotel management in Switzerland and a master's in business administration from the Kellogg School of Business, to come back to Haiti and run the business with him. In time, Fred's son Marc joined as well, and together the Pierre-Louis family committed to turning their family business around and leading this Haitian landmark boldly into the twenty-first century.

Leveraging lessons from the United Nations' brief occupation of the premises, the Pierre-Louis family deployed one of the oldest, simplest, and most reliable strategies for stabilizing otherwise turbulent environments. Redundancy has a long history of success in situations where threats abound. Using backup systems and resources to protect against disruptive events may seem obvious after a crisis has occurred, though before a crisis, they're often seen as costly or wasteful.

Consider how many families in your neighborhood keep backup parts on-site for their furnace or fridge, anticipating that supplies may not be available the next time it breaks down. Or how many households subscribe to multiple telephone, power, and internet utilities, just in case one fails during an important video conference. Or how many of your neighbors have redesigned their homes so there are no exterior windows, because thicker building materials will deflect any stray bullets that might be flying by. Our guess is, not many—unless, of course, you happen to live in Haiti or another fragile state.

At the Le Plaza Hotel, the Pierre-Louis family invested in each of these structural redundancies, creating an oasis of stability for their guests within a broader ocean of discord. As Marc Pierre-Louis explained, "We tend to be extremely resilient and have a variety of contingency plans to ensure our staff and guests are well taken care of."[3] For instance, tucked behind its double-gated courtyard walls and surrounded by fruit trees and tall palms, Le Plaza has installed US$500,000 in backup generators alone, along with backup water supply systems and backup telecom providers. Even the water in the pool is used as a backup for any fire emergencies.

Additionally, after the 2010 earthquake, the banking system completely shut down, so all transactions needed to be settled in cash. For weeks the family was forced to keep surplus amounts on hand—despite the added security risk. This required explicit police protection, which the family procured through close relationships with authorities that it had fostered over decades. Retail supermarkets also remained closed, their owners fearing that shops would be raided by hungry locals and opportunistic gangs. So the hotel procured and warehoused a large inventory of essentials, supplied by multiple vendors, to ensure that guests and staff would have access to most of the basics during their extended stays.

As a result of these many redundant infrastructures, and the vital stability they have provided during Haiti's frequent crises, the Le Plaza Hotel is seen by many locals as "an island within an island." We fully recognize that not every business will need to take all of these same precautions, and that excess redundancy can be wasteful, particularly in resource-rich settings at the peak of the Hierarchy of Stability. However, we have also seen how strategic redundancy—in just the right dosage—can make the difference between survival and failure in resource-scarce environments. Such investments can generate greater stability in virtually any situation where enduring success is dependent on mission-critical systems prone to disruption or failure, whether you operate in Port-au-Prince or Paris.

JUST-IN-CASE VS. JUST-IN-TIME

Consider for a moment what you would do in the unlikely event that the telecommunications grid goes down for more than a few hours. Whether it's triggered by a terrorist hack, a solar flare, or a ferocious storm may have long-term implications worth considering. But in the meantime, you've lost contact with everyone in your life who isn't within earshot. Without immediate, real-time access to our loved ones, colleagues, and business partners, your emotional and professional life would grind to an immediate halt. Extend that situation for days, and it would likely be perceived by most as a catastrophic event, sowing chaos and uncertainty until communications were restored.

Now consider how much you might be willing to invest today to prevent that undesirable outcome. That's before even considering the broader systemic impact of failed communications grids on payment processing, traffic signals, 911 emergency services, and so forth. As the experience of the Pierre-Louis family demonstrates, building backup systems and resources can provide a vital line of defense in the effort to protect against disruptive events and ensure continuity of operations. So why don't more companies embrace the simple and ancient wisdom of "just-in-case," rather than the more contemporary logic of "just-in-time"?

The inventory and manufacturing system known today as "just-in-time" (JIT) first emerged as a unique form of differentiation during the resource-scarce conditions that prevailed in post–World War II Japan. At the time, the country lay in ruins—its government dismantled, its infrastructure shattered, its resources depleted, and its industries crippled. Every material—and every minute—counted as the country sought to rebuild. Japanese industries were compelled to make the most of their limited resources, and within this crucible, they pioneered JIT—first as a survival tactic, and only later as a strategic management philosophy.

Inspired by the ideas of the economist and engineer W. Edwards Deming, the Toyota engineer Taiichi Ohno observed the American supermarket model during a visit to the United States. He was struck by the practice of stocking just enough products to meet consumer demand at any given time. Ohno envisioned applying a similar system to manufacturing—holding just enough inventory at each stage of production to meet the minimum requirements of the subsequent stage. This would allow the company to manufacture cars based on customer demand rather than static forecasts, saving handsomely on warehouse costs.

Sure enough, when Toyota put the idea into practice, its JIT system drastically minimized stock levels, as expected. But it also reduced manufacturing inefficiencies, and it even improved production quality. By the late 1970s, the success of the Toyota Production System had caught the attention of manufacturers worldwide. In the wake of the oil crisis of 1973, the timing was ripe for a global paradigm shift. JIT emerged as more than just a Japanese novelty—it became the standard operating system for many of the largest companies in the world.

Despite their clear benefits, and the incredible commercial success of Toyota and other loyal adherents, JIT systems were never widely adopted in uncertain environments. The reason is simple—these approaches are

JIT Accelerated Japan's Economic Growth for Decades

...until the oil shock of 1973, when advanced economies finally took notice

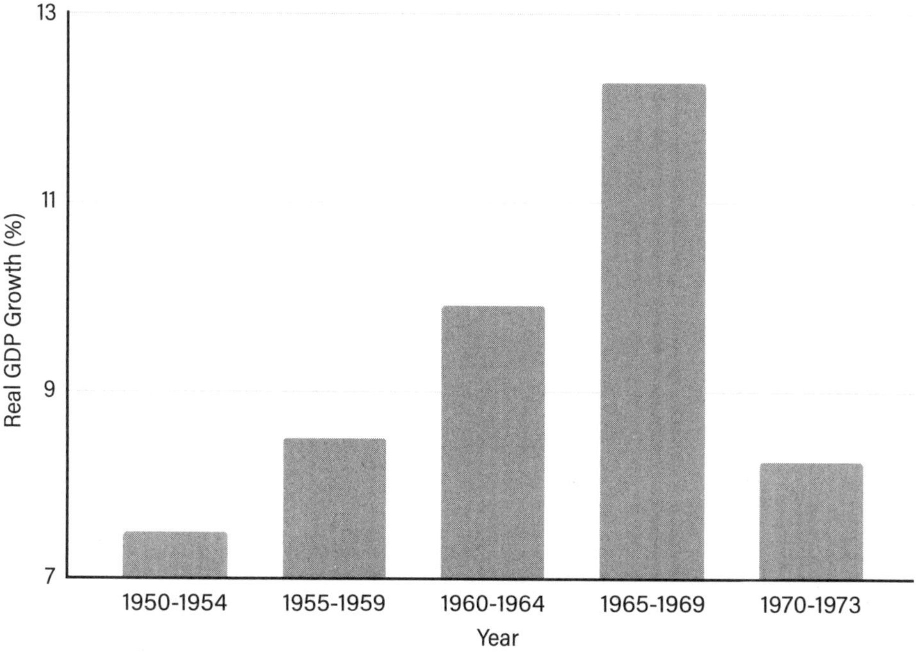

Source: World Bank national accounts data

the industrial equivalent of a Swiss watch, operating smoothly and reliably under the normal conditions pervasive in advanced economies. But it is the Timex watch—designed to "take a licking and keep on ticking"—that provides a better metaphor for the redundancy in process design that is suited to more turbulent conditions.

This is precisely the paradox of JIT—the same lean systems that provide agility in times of calm also provoke fragility in times of crisis. During these moments, JIT systems are prone to significant vulnerabilities, particularly around their lean supply chains, where any minor disturbance—whether by natural disaster, strike, geopolitical tensions, or currency devaluation—can grind operations to a halt.

Additionally, their limited flexibility can make it difficult for businesses to adapt to rapid changes in demand or supply, particularly when an important component becomes unavailable. In such highly engineered systems, having 99 percent of the parts needed to assemble a car is insufficient to deliver the final product. Even minor disturbances in procurement can leave a company vulnerable and dependent on external stakeholders whose actions are beyond its control.

These risks were clearly exposed during the COVID-19 pandemic, perhaps nowhere as obviously as within the automotive industry itself. For nearly half a century, all the major manufacturers followed Toyota's lead, relying heavily on lean production systems. But when faced with severe supply chain disruptions, from chip shortages and plant shutdowns to logistical bottlenecks, manufacturers were forced to halt production. This resulted in billions of lost revenue and delayed deliveries for customers around the world.

Given that we expect greater uncertainty in all economies over the coming years, companies need to adopt a more balanced approach. Getting the dosage right—between just-in-time and just-in-case investments—doesn't come naturally to companies weaned for decades on a diet of stability. It involves more than just adding another warehouse to store spare parts. It requires a systems-level review of operations—identifying all the processes, infrastructure, and people that are critical for success. Then it entails designing and implementing backup plans, contingency measures, secondary resources, and even regular fire drills to ensure that these systems will continue to function in a variety of both probable and unlikely scenarios.

Carrying all of this extra organizational "weight" can be expensive, as the Pierre-Louis family knows all too well. But it's also essential for survival—particularly for those who make a living in environments where it's wise to plan for catastrophe. Like firefighters heading into a burning high-rise, with heavy tanks of breathable air strapped to their backs, business owners often find that these investments are worth their weight in gold.

BELTS AND SUSPENDERS

As one of the most ancient and pervasive of the stabilizing strategies, redundancy naturally has a long tradition in both economic and military affairs. Countless battles throughout history have been lost or won based on access to essential resources at pivotal junctures, and some of the greatest innovations in military strategies and systems often happen far from the front lines. While historically we are more likely to write songs about heroic soldiers, brilliant generals, and decisive battles, much of Sun Tzu's advice thousands of years ago had little to do with battle itself. Most conflicts, he argued, are won before they are fought, and have more to do with managing resources and people than firing arrows and swinging swords.

In *The Art of War*, Master Sun was especially concerned with extended conflicts because they inevitably exhaust our most precious resources, including weapons, money, energy, and food. Under these conditions, without deliberately planning for redundancy, troops will fail, battles will be lost, and kingdoms will fall. This fate is particularly likely during wars of attrition, a grueling form of long-term combat that involves wearing down the enemy until defeat or surrender—what Carl von Clausewitz called "exhaustion of the adversary."[4]

While military and civilian approaches to strategic planning, scenario analysis, and leadership development have converged since World War II, approaches to logistics have been fundamentally divergent. Supply chains within the armed forces are deliberately designed around "just-in-case" scenarios, while much of the developed world has become intently focused on the leaner "just-in-time" approach. Just-in-case preparation obviously comes at a higher cost, but given that success for armies is measured in lives, whereas for companies it's measured in livelihoods, the incremental resources required are often well worth the investment.

In the military, this form of *strategic redundancy* is often described as taking a "belt-and-suspenders" approach. Either one of these fashionable accessories can hold up your trousers, but having both ensures that you won't be caught with your pants down if one ever fails. It's similar to the common military idiom that "two is one, and one is none." Having only a single backup for communication systems, or weapon systems, or fuel reserves, can leave a campaign vulnerable to failure. If those backups ever fail, the lives of soldiers and the fate of entire wars can be compromised.

Strategic redundancy can take one of two principal forms: layers of offense and layers of defense. One striking example of *offensive redundancy* comes from World War II, when the US Army set up the "Red Ball Express." This innovative truck convoy system was designed to supply Allied forces moving quickly through Europe after D-Day. Aware of the importance of uninterrupted supply lines, redundancy was built into the strategy as a feature rather than a bug, maximizing the probability that supplies would be available where and when they were needed most. At its peak, the Red Ball Express operated nearly 6,000 vehicles—from trucks to ships to trains—and moved over 12,000 tons of supplies every day, sustaining 28 divisions within the advancing Allied campaign.[5]

Defensive redundancy can also help to protect against persistent external threats. For instance, modern missile defense systems typically include an overlapping portfolio of ground-based interceptors, naval assets, and airborne deterrence systems. If one layer fails, the next takes over, adding a strategic buffer to help absorb shocks and make the system more resilient. This concept—sometimes called "defense in depth"—is intended both to discourage and to delay the advance of an attacking force, helping to exhaust enemies, deplete their resources, and ultimately make them more susceptible to counterattacks. A layered approach to defense is also common in biological systems, despite nature's ruthless efficiency—a testament to its enduring value. We're all familiar with humanity's many paired organs, such as eyes, ears, lungs, and kidneys. Though they obviously require additional resources to "build" and maintain—and don't always serve an identical function—backup organs increase the chances of survival in case of injury, disease, or congenital defects.

Both forms of redundancy—offensive and defensive—have a long history of use among armies, where life-and-death contests clearly require a conservative approach to risk management. But they are also viable strategies for businesses, where failure to compete may result in bankruptcy, the commercial equivalent to catastrophic defeat.

In particular, the further down the Hierarchy of Stability we move, the more valuable redundancy becomes, and consequently, the more often we find it in use. Le Plaza is a poster child for the level of extreme redundancy that can be essential in frontier economies—offensively with their procurement systems and defensively with their surplus infrastructure. In emerging economies, the value of redundancy is often self-evident, though emergent institutional stabilizers, such as electoral systems, courts, financial markets, and public utilities, are more reliable, so fewer investments are needed in order to sustain an organization in the event of a crisis.

Consider the Mexican multinational building materials behemoth Cemex, which has implemented a robust logistics and distribution system to ensure reliable delivery of its products to customers even in remote or hard-to-reach areas. In 2004, the third-generation family CEO Lorenzo Zambrano explained, in his annual letter to shareholders, "We do not see volatility as an occasional, random element added to the cost of doing business in an interconnected global marketplace. We plan for volatility. We prepare for it. We have learned how to profit from it."[6]

Contrast this with advanced economies, where companies are naturally built for speed and global conquest, and shock absorbers are nice accessories but mostly dead weight. Like training wheels on a bike, investments in redundancy are considered by many executives to be unnecessary or even distracting. In these environments, as with JIT systems, having too much redundancy is often a bigger threat than having too little.[7]

But even stable and prosperous economies can be thrust into chaos, at which point preemptive investments in redundancy can be the difference between life and death. The Bata family provides an archetypical case. They founded a successful shoe company in Czechoslovakia in 1894, which was then still a frontier economy. Its early successes were punctuated by frequent crises, including World War I and the Great Depression, but they managed to continue their regional growth in spite of geopolitical and economic turmoil.

By 1939, Czechoslovakia had become one of the top ten economies in terms of industrial production,[8] and the Bata family's growing shoe business was in good health, though dark clouds were forming on the horizon. In a remarkable act of strategic foresight, the family members at the helm of the business, Jan Antonín Bata and his nephew Thomas Bata, sensed the threat of Nazi invasion and decided to move to Canada to head up a new division of the company.

Thomas built this satellite operation in a new town he called "Batawa," staffing it with 100 Czech families who had migrated with him. A few years later, when the company's European operations were first bombed and then nationalized by the Soviet Union, the fledgling Canadian subsidiary became the new headquarters for the company's global operations overnight. Thanks to this preemptive investment in redundancy, Bata was able to avoid catastrophic failure. It went on to become one of the world's biggest shoe manufacturers, at its height selling over 300 million pairs a year.

In short, wherever a company operates on the Hierarchy of Stability, it's worth at least considering the idea of building some strategic redundancy into its organizational planning. All senior leadership teams need to acknowledge that destabilizing events are happening with increased frequency—from cyberattacks to supply chain disruptions. As a result, identifying opportunities for investments in redundancy should become part of every continuity planning exercise. Whether leaders ultimately choose to invest or not is then a matter of financial planning and risk appetite, but at least the decision will be made with strategic intent.

NEST EGGS

Such intention is the hallmark of the enduring enterprises that thrive in emerging and frontier economies, where investments in redundancy often extend beyond the business. Recall the Carvajal family's commitment to building a secondary pool of assets completely decoupled with its principal business, generating a "Social Dividend" that was available to support the family in good times and bad. Such reallocations of capital are certainly easier said than done, particularly as families grow larger, their financial needs become greater, and their businesses grow more complex. Over time, resisting the temptation of raiding the family's "piggy bank" becomes harder. However, as with just-in-case process design, and belt-and-suspenders backups, we believe all enterprising families should at least consider building an uncorrelated reserve fund into their overall risk management plans as a hedge against unforeseen shocks.

Think of these investments as a form of existential insurance—a long-term "nest egg" that can be activated in the event of catastrophic failure. This particular term, and the concept it represents, has fascinating agricultural roots that date back to a simple but ingenious practice in poultry farming that has been in use since the seventeenth century. Farmers discovered that placing a real or fake egg in a hen's nest would encourage her to lay more eggs. In essence, the decoy acted as a psychological cue for the hen, convincing her that the nest was secure, thereby increasing her production. Rather than consuming or selling the egg as usual, the farmer instead placed it aside, deriving value indirectly from its impact on the changing behavior of the hens.

In the centuries since, the concept has evolved beyond agriculture, and now symbolizes any financial cushion or redundancy fund that protects against unanticipated future challenges. Having access to backup resources—ideally placed safely in lower-risk countries and assets—frees leaders from short-term financial pressures and encourages greater risk-taking and innovation when thinking about the future. This isn't about hoarding resources or avoiding redeploying capital in the business. Such strategic redundancy is a deliberate and judicious allocation of capital that enables—and even encourages—the pursuit of growth by providing a backstop in case the future doesn't unfold as planned.

The entrepreneurial journey of the Hayel Saeed Anam (HSA) Group provides an inspiring illustration. This family business based in Yemen epitomizes resilience, and among the cases we studied, has utilized strategic redundancy in some of the most innovative and unexpected ways.

Founded in 1938, HSA began as a small trading business, but the family soon translated its early successes into an increasingly diversified portfolio of over 70 companies, ranging from dairy and flour to cement and hotels, and employing over 35,000 people. This enduring success is even more remarkable when you consider that it's been achieved against the backdrop of a protracted civil war. Today, Yemen has the dubious distinction of being one of the few countries in the world doing worse than Haiti on the Fragile States Index.[9]

Over the years, HSA has invested in redundancy on countless occasions, intuitively understanding the benefits of anticipating changing conditions. For instance, the family built a backup headquarters in Dubai, which came in handy when the civil war broke out in 2014. It also bought up all of the unused hotels and empty buildings near its manufacturing facilities in Taiz, then offered them to workers to help them avoid crossing sniper fire on the way to work. Even the company's policy for admitting family members into the business had layers of defense against nepotism, requiring interested candidates to earn two degrees plus spend ten years working in another business before considering them for employment.

But in our opinion, the Saeed family's most innovative and inspiring display of redundancy began long before rising sectarian tensions in Yemen erupted into outright civil war. During the Arab Spring in 2011, as security conditions worsened, the family activated an innovative continuity plan—which involved airlifting 167 family members to Egypt, the only friendly neighbor that didn't require entry visas. There, the family would be transported to a safe neighborhood, where a series of homes had been procured as a backup in case conditions in Yemen reached unsafe levels—even by this resilient family's standards. Investing in personal security for family members is quite common in countries with chronic instability—from armored cars to teams of private security guards—providing safety, albeit at considerable expense. However, securing an entire neighborhood as a backup base of operations, particularly for a family of this size, is an impressive act of strategic foresight. This Egyptian nest egg allowed the Saeeds to continue investing in HSA and the Yemeni community while having peace of mind, knowing its nonoperating family members were out of harm's way.

CONDITIONS AND CAVEATS

To be clear, while we're advocating for leaders everywhere to consider building more strategic redundancy into their organizations, as with the other stabilizing strategies there are limits to its utility, and also diminishing returns. Backup parts, generators, telcos, and servers alone cannot guarantee 100 percent uptime. After all, parts expire, and even backup equipment can fail. Moreover, tripling down on all key infrastructure can lead to needless inefficiency, and managing duplicate infrastructures, headquarters, and supply chains can dramatically increase organizational complexity.

Still, many companies operating in advanced economies are likely to have less redundancy built into their businesses than prudence would suggest. Those in emerging economies are more likely to have layers of defense and offense built directly into their business models, though the more ambitious may be seduced into chasing greater efficiency in the quest for global leadership, leaving them more vulnerable to inevitable disruption. Those in frontier economies are likely investing in redundancy instinctively—both operationally and financially—but must remain vigilant, since the weight of these investments can accumulate over time, starving the company of growth capital if not managed dynamically and proactively.

Striking the right balance between the pursuit of resilience and the pursuit of growth is an eternal challenge. As a general rule, the more disruption one expects in the near future, the more valuable investments in redundancy will be. For instance, companies operating in advanced economies might keep three to six months of expected cash outflows in a liquidity reserve, recognizing that local banks are backed by the full faith and credit of the most credible governments and central banks in the world. In emerging economies, where fewer institutional stabilizers are in place, six to twelve months of cash flow would likely help to sidestep any transitory economic or political hiccup while funding a nest egg in a safe haven financial center such as New York, London, Zurich, or Singapore. In frontier economies, anything less than a year's worth of on-demand liquidity could be a recipe for insolvency, and having a safe on-site filled with high-value commodities can become part of any rapid getaway plan.

Enduring Enterprises Deploy More Redundancy Than Peers

They take on less debt and maintain higher cash reserves than industry averages

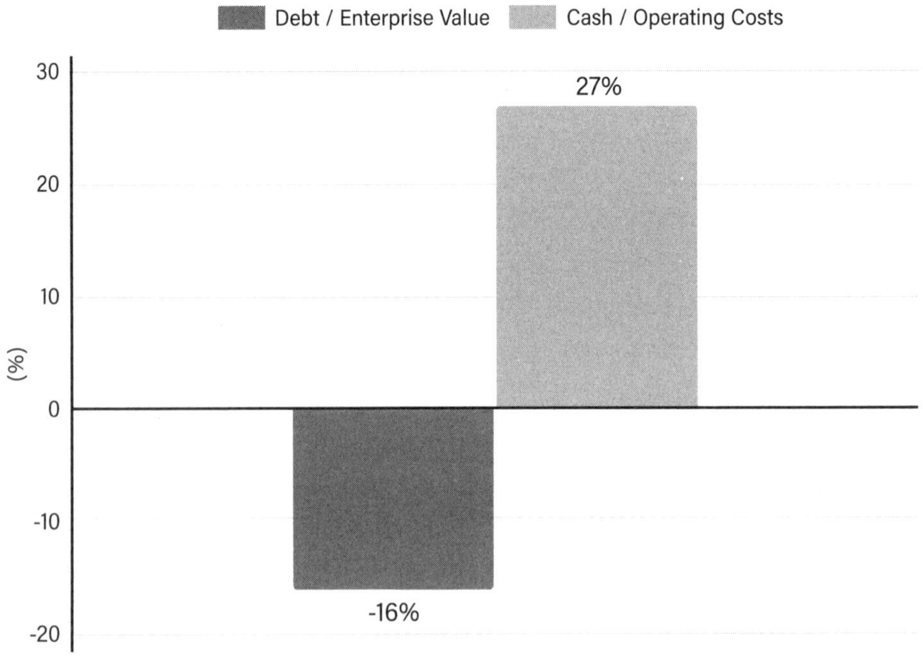

Source: BCG Henderson Institute

Additionally, it's useful to remember that redundancy is also integral to the ways that families develop and the choices they make to ensure the genetic and cultural continuity of their members. While household size has declined globally with the availability of contraceptives and the increase in fertility education, family size varies considerably depending on economic and cultural conditions. Just as in contemporary monarchies, in enterprising families worldwide the notion of "an heir and a spare" is still quite prevalent, and in frontier environments the tendency to ensure multiple heirs is deeply ingrained. Large families are often desirable in order to have many hands available to help with basic familial tasks—such as child-rearing and caring for the infirm and the elderly. Enterprising families also want to provide an education for the members of the next generation. These are tasks that all families must perform effectively if they are to launch a new generation of adults capable of "love and work," as Freud succinctly described an "effective" human being.[10]

In terms of timing, redundancy is most effective when it is deployed before a crisis strikes. As the COVID-19 pandemic illustrated for households, companies, and entire countries, once markets become dysfunctional and shortages are exposed, it's already too late for action. Anticipation and initiative are essential preconditions for outperformance. That means mapping out risks, assigning probabilities, then reinforcing key systems to address the highest vulnerabilities.

So if disruption is the new normal, and redundancy is the new necessity, how can leaders identify their lowest-hanging fruit? One easy mental experiment is to consider what changed the most within your life at the onset of the pandemic. Where did you feel most vulnerable? Where did you feel most secure? Which of your key relationships were most helpful? Which were the most problematic? What did you wish you had more of?

This same mental checklist works in individual, family, and business contexts. Those items that rise to the top of that list are where to focus investments. Not only do they provide peace of mind, but they can also inspire greater risk-taking elsewhere in the enterprise. Consider your entire supply chain, and your suppliers' supply chains. Then think about your distributors, customers, executives, and potential successors. Review all of your banking relationships, joint venture partnerships, and government relations. At the end of the day, the logic of "belts and suspenders" is a helpful guide. For every major supplier, seek out at least two additional sources. For every irreplaceable leader, identify at least two potential successors, and so forth. Obviously this approach can become more granular with time and experience. But for starters, consider that all key systems, people, and resources need at least one backup, and ideally two.

Contrast this strategic hypervigilance with the wasteful hyperventilation of doomsday prep making the rounds among the super-rich—what we might describe as "unproductive paranoia." From LinkedIn cofounder Reid Hoffman to PayPal cofounder Peter Thiel, ultra-high-net-worth individuals have lately been buying up islands, stockpiling weapons, and securing food and medical supplies to ride out what they believe to be an imminent apocalypse. As Hoffman has argued, "Saying you're 'buying a house in New Zealand' is kind of a wink, wink, say no more. Once you've done the Masonic handshake, they'll be, like, 'Oh, you know, I have a broker who sells old ICBM silos, and they're nuclear-hardened, and they kind of look like they would be interesting to live in.'"[11]

Generally speaking, we don't anticipate the type of apocalyptic event to unfold that might make New Zealand the only safe place left on the planet. However, history is littered with examples of contexts becoming so hostile that nothing, not even strategic reserves, can guarantee survival. Under those conditions, the only option left for an enduring enterprise is to pick up and move. As we'll learn in the next chapter, these migrations are often incredibly destabilizing at first, both for the business and for the family. However, when done well, they can also create unique opportunities and help enduring enterprises sustain their success across generations.

KEY INSIGHTS

- Investments in redundancy help to insulate an enduring enterprise against disruptive events—the more unstable the environment, the more valuable these investments are.
- The historic Le Plaza Hotel and the Pierre-Louis family inspired our earliest thinking about redundancy—with their proactive investments in backup generators, water supply systems, telecom providers, and other critical supplies, all helping them to overcome the persistent shocks and volatility endemic to business in Haiti.
- Just-in-time (JIT) systems are efficient but fragile, and useful in more stable environments, while just-in-case (JIC) systems are more robust but expensive, and more effective in turbulent times.
- Leaders can leverage the military's "belt-and-suspenders" approach to redundancy—implementing multiple layers of backup and fail-safe mechanisms to ensure that all mission-critical systems remain functional even if one part fails or is damaged.
- Many enduring enterprises also invest in "nest eggs"—financial reserves or assets placed in safe locations to act as a buffer in case of emergencies, which can encourage greater risk-taking in the primary business.

- As with investments in the other stabilizing strategies, striking the right balance with redundancy is also crucial—too much can be expensive and hinder growth, while too little leaves an organization vulnerable to unnecessary losses or even failure.
- The optimal level of redundancy depends on where on the Hierarchy of Stability you operate, and consequently the expected frequency and amplitude of disruptions to normal business operations.

9
MIGRATION

The first step towards getting somewhere is to decide that you are not going to stay where you are.
—John Pierpont Morgan

The Fertile Crescent, a vast swath of land stretching from the eastern shores of the Mediterranean to the northern coast of the Persian Gulf, has hosted human settlements continuously for at least 12,000 years. Many great civilizations—from the ancient Sumerians and Persians, to the classical Phoenicians and Romans, to the modern Ottomans and French—have recognized and capitalized on its geostrategic importance.

Throughout the millennia, Syria's capital—one of the world's oldest—has remained a critical trading hub connecting Europe, Africa, and Asia. In the bustling souks of Damascus, merchants peddled silk from China, spices from India, and olive oil from the Mediterranean, laying the earliest foundations of Syrian entrepreneurship. For nearly six centuries under relatively stable Ottoman rule, its largest cities became prosperous nodes within the empire's sprawling modular trade networks. Many enterprising families sought their fortunes within these thriving medieval markets, where competition was fierce and opportunities abounded.

It was within this primordial nineteenth-century frontier economy that the Baalbaki Group first emerged. Founded by Izzo Baalbaki as a textiles manufacturer in the 1870s, the fledgling business grew slowly and steadily in the twilight years of the Ottoman Empire. At the time, the industry was a confluence of tradition and innovation, featuring age-old weaving techniques inherited from generations past while absorbing new influences from global trade that integrated European designs and Asian silks.

Rapid industrialization in Western Europe inevitably introduced lower-cost goods to Middle Eastern markets, and Baalbaki and his sons—Sobhi, Rushdi, Kamal, and Omar—were forced to consider their strategic alternatives. Like many frontier capitalists at the time, they pursued opportunities across the textiles value chain, eventually opening a department store in Damascus. This allowed the family to sell quality products made by others in addition to their own proprietary brands. Their first strategic pivot paved the way for the enterprising Baalbaki family to continue to explore and exploit opportunities outside the garment industry—albeit at a time of massive political and economic change.

When the Ottoman Empire finally collapsed at the end of World War I, it left a fragmented quilt of diverse societies spanning a region from Algeria to Ukraine to Iraq. These dominions were initially carved up by the Allied powers, paving the way for the French Mandate in Syria beginning in 1920. Early administrations introduced new political structures and supported infrastructure projects like ports and transportation systems. As with Haiti and elsewhere, these were largely designed for France's parasitic colonial benefit. However, as the economy integrated these new institutions and stability increased, enterprising families such as the Baalbakis were well positioned to ride the wave of growth.

Despite this disruptive shift in governance, the Baalbaki family's commercial portfolio continued to grow, eventually expanding across the southern border into Jordan. By the mid-1940s, as the third generation was getting ready to join the family business, the Baalbaki brothers oversaw a diverse range of companies, including ones specializing in office equipment and oil and gas consulting. Yet they were all connected in some way to their core Syrian operations.

This diverse set of activities helped them successfully navigate Syria's disruptive push for independence after World War II, particularly through regional expansion. By the late 1950s, Omar and his son Ihsan were ready to test out a more modular ownership structure, launching joint ventures with German multinationals Linde AG and Mauser GmbH. Together they built one of the first factories in the Middle East producing "white goods"—refrigerators, gas ovens, steel furniture, and other durable appliances. Meanwhile, another son, Hassan, took the family's textile business public in one of the region's first initial public offerings.

The future was looking bright both for the business and the family. Then, on March 8, 1963, the country suffered a military coup, later known as the "March Revolution," that completely reset the rules of engagement for all Syrian businesses and citizens.[1]

Starting in 1964, Ba'athist authorities began a nationalization campaign, starting with the oil and gas industry, and followed by commercial

Economic Volatility During the Early Ba'athist Years

Planning and operating are more challenging when economic conditions are so erratic

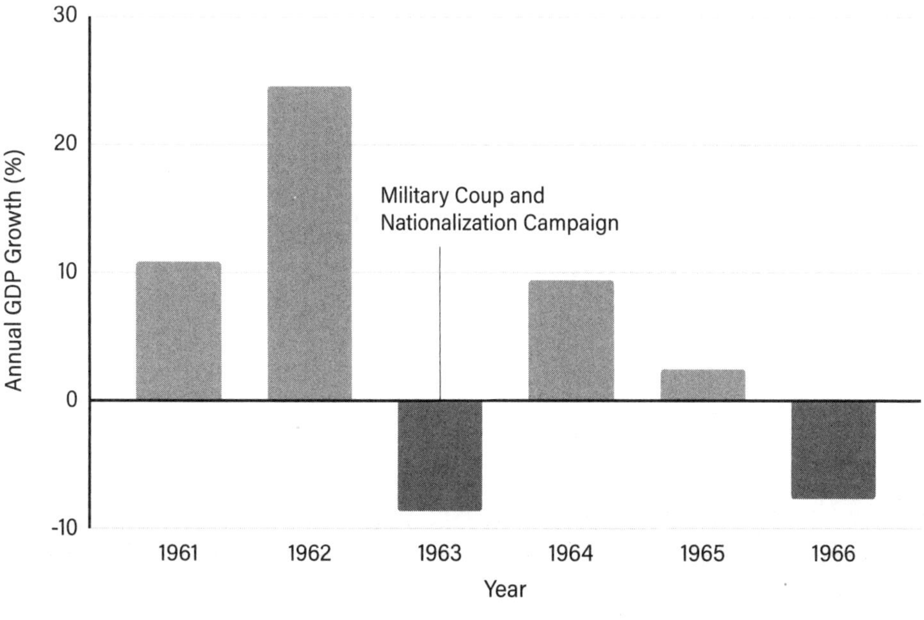

Source: World Bank national accounts data

banking and insurance. As the economy transitioned virtually overnight into state control and central planning, many heavy industries and manufacturing facilities were expropriated without any compensation, including those of the Baalbaki Group. One day families owned and operated their enterprises in a relatively free and fair market, and the next they were left with nothing.

The Baalbakis had managed disruption and turbulence for nearly a century—in many ways it had become a core competency—but this was their first experience with expropriation, and it was truly existential. Yet when faced with the challenge of starting over again from scratch, the family responded with courage and resolve—understanding from their own legacy that "turmoil creates opportunity." Family leaders had already survived the dissolution of the Ottoman Empire and both world wars without losing their entrepreneurial spirit. While much of the Baalbaki Group's physical and financial capital was nationalized, its human and social capital was still very much intact—and the family leveraged both brilliantly in the years that followed to make the most of this desperate situation.

First, like many business owners who felt stifled by Syria's socialist policies, family members relocated to Beirut, which was still open for business. Once they were settled in neighboring Lebanon, they prepared to relaunch the next chapter in the family's dramatic entrepreneurial adventure. Fortunately, as with Bata in Batawa, Ihsan Baalbaki had recently established a satellite office in Beirut. It was after migrating to this auxiliary headquarters that Baalbaki would reinvent itself in the years that followed.

Starting virtually from scratch, the family jumpstarted its efforts by launching a marketing consultancy, leveraging its human capital (knowledge of the appliance industry) and social capital (trusted relationships with global partners) to help other companies enter and grow their manufacturing footprint in the Middle East. Within a year, the company had been retained by thirty leading partners in the refrigeration industry, which supplied it with the cash flow necessary to begin rebuilding its industrial footprint. Reviving its joint venture with Linde AG, the firm launched Linde Middle East, reentering the lucrative white goods market at a time when these appliances were finally achieving mass adoption throughout the region. This was followed by the development of a real estate portfolio and reentry into financial services.

Once the company's financial and physical capital base was solidified in Lebanon, the family made its first foray into the polyurethane industry, providing spray foam insulation for the refrigerators it was manufacturing. Under Hassan's leadership, this new chemicals division was extremely profitable and quickly became the core business of the Baalbaki Group's diversified holdings, helping the family to further expand its footprint throughout the region.

Today the Baalbaki Group is a diversified giant in the Middle East with operations reaching into Europe and the United Kingdom and a fourth generation of family members helping to sustain and grow the enterprise. Reflecting on his family's long and winding road to success, Ihsan Baalbaki captured the challenges well: "During the past 50 years we have survived and prospered despite experiencing nationalization in Syria; a civil war and devaluation in Lebanon; regime changes in markets where we were active; and the equally dangerous transition from generation to generation in our management and ownership."[2]

When we first encountered the family early on in our research into frontier economies, we were immediately struck by their equanimity. Not many leaders would describe nationalization and succession planning as equivalent risks to their enterprise—especially not when operating in such a rough neighborhood. But Ihsan was absolutely right: continuity in these environments certainly takes the kind of strategic planning, operational excellence, and effective leadership taught in every business school around the world. But it also requires the capacity to identify ever-shifting pockets of stability amid the chaos, and the relentless tactical agility to transition between them—skills like those of a surfer riding the crest of a massive wave. Under these conditions, leaders need the vigilance to monitor and anticipate when markets are no longer viable, and to recognize when the path to continuity requires a pivot away from danger and into new products, markets, geographies—or even new business models altogether.

Leaving the familiar can be emotionally challenging even when we're traveling somewhere amazing. But it's especially taxing when there is little chance of a safe return. The same can be said for leaving a legacy business, product, or market behind—one for which there is deep emotional connection and a reassuring familiarity.

Yet such migrations are a common feature in human affairs. Consider the estimated 10 million Ukrainians who fled their homes in the wake of Russia's invasion, out of a population of roughly 40 million, and the impossible decisions they had to make about where to go, what to bring, how to get there, and what to do to support themselves once they arrived. Or, if you prefer, consider the more than 160 million migrant workers around the world who are living far from home in an effort to build a better life for their families.

Whether the decision is strategic or existential, migratory pressures emerge from two basic sources: either the current environment flips from hospitable to hostile for an extended period of time, or an even more attractive opportunity emerges in a nearby market. Those who choose to stay put and adapt to the changing circumstances can deploy any of the other stabilizing strategies we've outlined throughout the book. However, those who choose to migrate can seek comfort and insight from the experience of the Baalbaki family, and countless others who have left their homes behind in search of safety and fortune.

PUSH AND PULL

Mass migrations, both in human societies and in the natural world, are seminal events that shape the course of history and the evolution of entire ecosystems. They are driven by a combination of external forces and internal motivations to either stay or go. Those that resist greener pastures still need to invest in greater stability internally, for instance via redundancy or symbiosis. Those that choose to address new threats not by changing themselves, but by changing their scenery, are often responding to the fundamental force in all biological systems—reliable access to resources.

Many species of animals, particularly migratory birds, relocate between regions as seasonal changes affect the relative scarcity and abundance of their primary sources of nutrition. Their innate mobility and endurance make it easy for them to explore and exploit more distant ecosystems featuring different resource endowments.[3] Humans have a long history of responding in similar ways to shifting environmental cues and conditions. From modern "snowbirds" who spend their winters in the south to refugees fleeing disasters in search of peace and prosperity, migration has been a core feature of our evolutionary story.

Fossils of *Homo erectus*—an early ancestor to modern *Homo sapiens*—have been found in various parts of Europe and Asia dating back nearly 2 million years. Our mass migrations often coincided with shifting environmental conditions, including droughts and ice ages, which affected basic resources, such as water and the animal populations upon which our ancestors relied. During these extreme climate transitions, fertile new "corridors" would occasionally emerge—for instance, lush savannas across the Arabian Peninsula and frozen "land bridges" connecting previously inaccessible territories. These changes opened up vast new and uncharted ecosystems for our curious ancestors to explore and plunder.

Success in these new and unfamiliar environments required new strategies for procuring food, water, and shelter, as well as the development of more advanced stone tools, not to mention the mastery of fire. Migration also leveraged an evolving set of human attributes, including curiosity, the capacity for collaboration, and the relentless pursuit of resource abundance, that are now hallmarks of all human societies. Together, these adaptations made a migratory lifestyle more viable, helping early hominins to thrive in many new and diverse frontiers.

Anthropologists often describe a mix of "push" and "pull" factors that influence such mass migrations. For instance, seasonal fluctuations in climatic conditions affected the populations and migratory patterns of large mammals—a key food source for early humans. This factor likely "pushed" our ancestors to explore new territories during certain times of the year in search of a more stable diet. Then, every few millennia, green "corridors" would periodically appear, providing extended windows of opportunity for humans to migrate. These opportunities effectively "pulled" our ancestors from Africa into Eurasia, following coastlines, rivers, and landscapes rich in resources. Importantly, these migrations weren't simply a journey from place to place but also stretched across time, as successive generations adapted to each new ecosystem, integrating their accumulated experience with migration, risk-taking, and survival into the very fabric of our DNA.

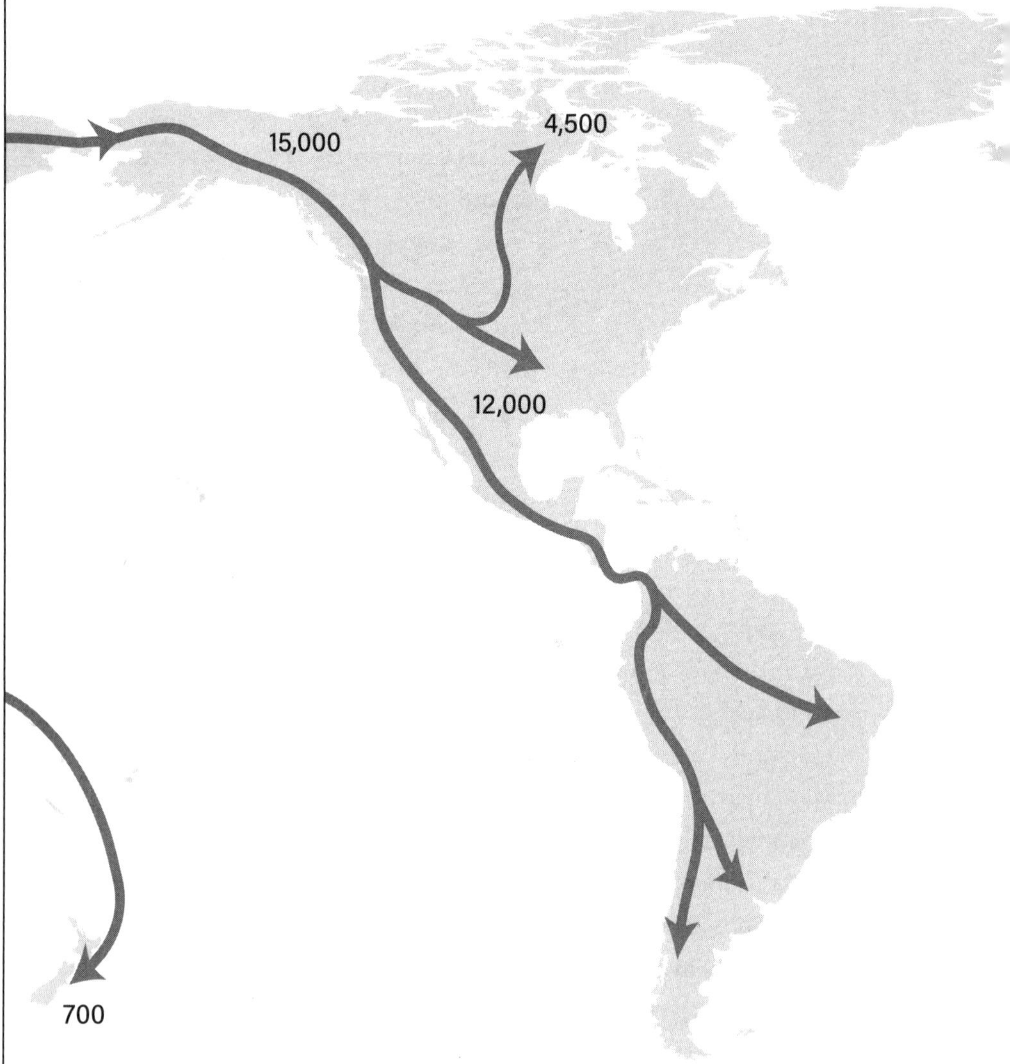

A Long History of Migration

Human survival and prosperity has long depended on adaptation to shifting environmental contexts

Source: Adapted from Wikipedia article on "Migration"

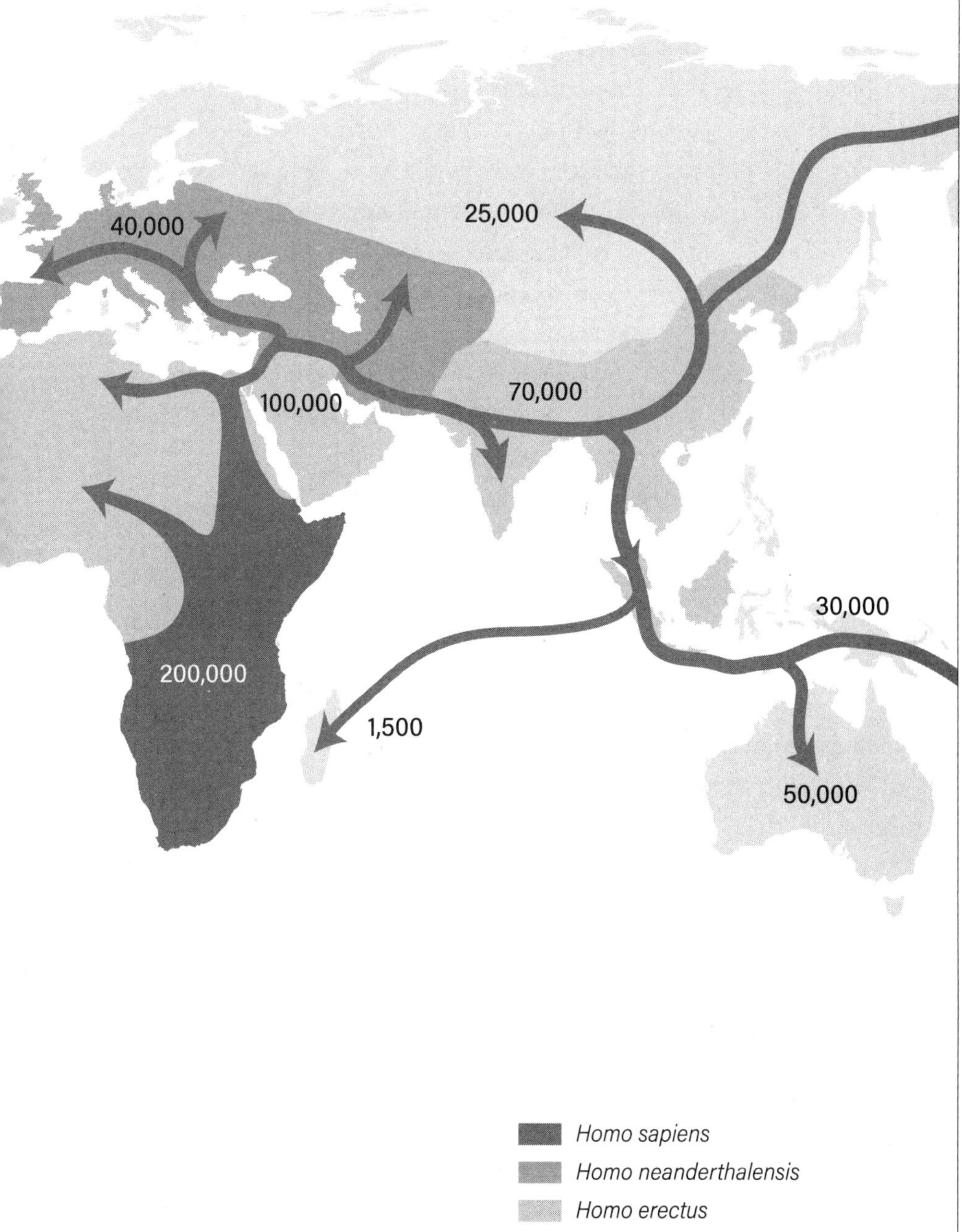
40,000
25,000
100,000
70,000
30,000
200,000
1,500
50,000
Homo sapiens
Homo neanderthalensis
Homo erectus

In a more modern context, *push factors* go beyond acute or episodic disturbances such as hurricanes and blackouts, which can be inconvenient or temporarily unpleasant. Even among frontier economies, environments need to become chronically or existentially dangerous in order to prompt us to leave everything behind—as it has been for the 110 million forcibly displaced refugees the United Nations is currently tracking.[4] Economic hardships, social tensions, political instabilities, environmental threats, and demographic pressures can often serve as the immediate catalysts to consider relocation. Examples include the many enterprising families active in India before the separation of Pakistan and Bangladesh in 1947, or in Syria after the coup in 1970, or, more recently, in Sudan, Ukraine, and Gaza.

Further up the Hierarchy of Stability, push factors can still provide strategic motivation to consider market exit. The sudden entry of new competitors or products can quickly render existing business models obsolete. Even America's greatest manufacturers of leather whips felt the heat when cars replaced horse-drawn carriages. Changing consumer behaviors and disruptive technologies have been constant forces for entrepreneurial dynamism since the emergence of the earliest frontier economies, and business leaders need to remain vigilant to the threats of obsolescence. More opportunistically, industrial migration can also be deployed to take advantage of shifting regulatory or market conditions. For instance, many companies rapidly redeployed their manufacturing capabilities during the COVID-19 pandemic, both to support public health efforts and to generate substantial windfall profits.

Burning platforms and greener pastures are obviously incentives for migratory action. But wanting to leave home is very different from knowing where to go. This is where *pull factors* come into play—conditions that attract migrants to a new region or market, much as the Arabian Peninsula beckoned to our hominin ancestors long ago. These can include the hope of a better economic future and greater political stability, or greater social connection, or even the simple pleasure of more hospitable weather.[5]

Consider Europe in the mid-nineteenth century, where religious persecution, droughts, and economic displacement led over 30 million brave souls to seek out the "New World" in search of peace and prosperity. Or the greater opportunities for education and work that have drawn millions of itinerant Chinese and Indians from remote provinces into the massive cities of Shanghai and Mumbai. Such pull factors often represent the hopes and aspirations of migrants, providing powerful motivation to make the adventure seem worth the risk.

In the case of the Baalbakis, both push and pull factors were in play. Push factors included the rise of the Ba'athist regime and nationalization of their assets. Pull factors included their auxiliary headquarters in Beirut and their strong commercial relationships in neighboring Lebanon and Jordan. A similar mix of push and pull factors motivated Toyota's strategic pivot from weaving machines to automobiles, Carvajal's pivot from printing to packaging, and Bata's pivot from Czechoslovakia to Canada.

On most days, the benefits of staying put will far outweigh the costs of leaving. But in those rare circumstances when that calculus no longer holds, we need to reach a form of migratory "escape velocity." In those moments, success will depend on two critical traits: the foresight to anticipate the forces driving us out of our comfort zone, and the capacity to choose wisely among the options that remain. Studying those who have survived the journey, particularly on multiple occasions, provides a blueprint for others to follow when the status quo is no longer viable and greater opportunities elsewhere are calling.

WINDS OF CHANGE

American country music legend Kenny Rogers captured this timeless dilemma in his classic anthem "The Gambler." Through the metaphor of a poker game, the narrator recounts advice given to him by an old gambler in exchange for a glass of whiskey, emphasizing the importance of timing an exit carefully: "You've got to know when to hold 'em, / know when to fold 'em. / Know when to walk away, / know when to run." Similarly, the first critical stage in any migration involves an explicit acknowledgment that the future will be less hospitable than the present. Being decisive in that moment can mean the difference between walking away with your business and losing your life.

The shorter-term catalysts are typically easier to spot—regime changes that are hostile to certain populations and businesses, market failures that make finding jobs or supporting families improbable, infrastructure projects or natural disasters that displace entire communities, and conflicts that threaten lives and livelihoods. Yet longer-term threats that don't manifest right away can be even more disruptive—for instance, a slow but steady stream of new competitors, the erosion of trust in public institutions, rising social tensions, chronic underinvestment in infrastructure, unregulated technological innovation, and, of course, a changing climate.

For some, tracking these longer-term risks comes naturally, more instinct than strategy, and consequently their reaction times are much faster. Consider the Syrian entrepreneurs like Baalbaki who moved to Lebanon in the early 1960s immediately after the Ba'athist coup, rather than muddling through decades of errant central planning that eventually left the economy in shambles and gave rise to the Islamic State. These pioneering families were early to recognize the writing on the wall, providing a natural first-mover advantage—both in terms of surviving the journey intact and establishing a secure platform from which to rebuild once they arrived. The Baalbakis set up their Beirut office prior to nationalization, which significantly increased the amount of capital they were able to rescue from expropriation and consequently increased their chances of survival. They were also among the first of the Syrian economic migrants to capitalize on new opportunities that Lebanon offered, accelerating the pace of their early growth.

For others, sensing the winds of change requires deliberate and strategic intention. After all, the most common source of resistance to migration is organizational inertia, an understandable combination of our natural human tendency to avoid change and the operational rigidity that comes from investing in physical assets that are logistically difficult to move.

A second source of resistance is "path dependency," or the reality that past decisions can have long-lasting effects on organizations, impacting the range of future choices and opportunities. Over time, as organizations make plans and decisions, the costs of reversing or shifting them inevitably increases, encouraging leaders to double down on the established trajectory even as danger is escalating. The social psychologists Daniel Kahneman and Amos Tversky captured precisely this cognitive vulnerability in their early conceptualization of "prospect theory," which

Kahneman and Tversky's Prospect Theory

Humans fear losses more than we seek gains

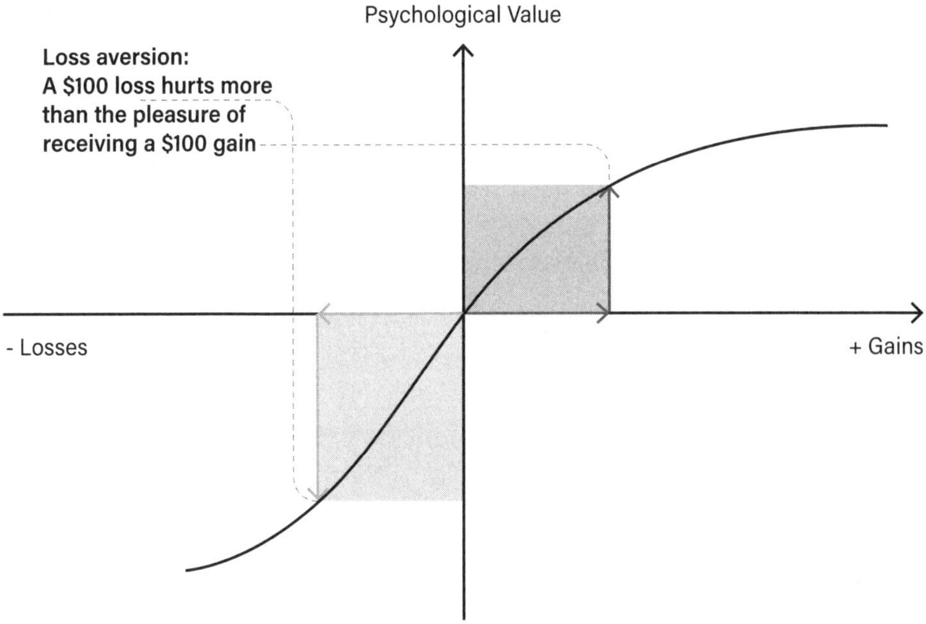

Source: Adapted from Kahneman and Tversky, "Prospect Theory: An Analysis of Decision under Risk." *Econometrica* 47, no. 2 (1979)

highlights our tendency to be more motivated to avoid losses than excited to pursue gains.[6]

Families are particularly vulnerable to these psychological barriers to exit, because their businesses are often so closely linked to their communities. As a result, their leaders need to pay special attention to rising threats, intermittently reevaluating whether external market conditions are still aligned with internal goals and objectives. In frontier economies, every six months is a reasonable frequency, given how dramatically conditions can change on a dime. In emerging economies, such a review every two or three years is typically sufficient, since these environments are less prone to systemic collapse or sudden regime change. Meanwhile, in advanced economies, organizations can often go a decade or more without reassessing the health of their key markets—though not forever.

Whether you're fleeing persecution and civil war, or a global tech giant has decided to eat your lunch, the psychological and practical barriers to exit are very similar. In fact, despite the obvious differences between operating in Damascus versus San Francisco, we also found interesting parallels that can help leaders better decide when to hold 'em and when to fold 'em.

PIVOT OR PERSEVERE

In many ways, the entrepreneurial ecosystem that emerged in Silicon Valley in the 1970s—then accelerated in the 1990s and early 2000s—popularized the art of launching and relaunching businesses under conditions of scarce capital and resources. Operating at the brink of insolvency has been the catalyst for many transformational turnarounds, including some of the most iconic companies of the twenty-first century, from Apple to Tesla to Airbnb.

Enterprising families operating in emerging and frontier economies face similar pressures and constraints to these bootstrapping startups, whose leaders often live month to month as they struggle to keep their commercial dreams alive. It is not uncommon for these organizations to be just one misstep away from disaster. This makes sustained growth, swift decision-making, and adaptability not just strategic virtues but necessities for organizational survival.

As we reflected on these similarities, we recognized that all organizations experiencing existential threats face similar challenges when they're pinned against the ropes. In these tenuous moments, leaders must decide whether to continue down their existing path and risk failure, or radically reinvent their business in an effort to stave off total collapse.

For instance, when Baalbaki had its manufacturing assets seized, it could have continued operating in Syria with some of its other service businesses in the hope that they might not also be nationalized. Instead, the family chose to leave the country with whatever assets weren't seized by the government or bolted to the ground.

This critical decision—to pivot or persevere—is often the difference between continuity and bankruptcy. Persevering only makes sense when there is a reasonable probability of success, if conditions aren't expected to get substantially worse, or if you're willing to suffer the potentially existential consequences. Having the foresight and the fortitude to pivot at the right moment is critical for any successful startup—and for any successful migration. Abandon ship too soon, and you risk leaving a good thing behind. Depart too late, and you risk getting left behind.

In this sense, strategic planning for a white goods manufacturer in Damascus has more in common with a couch-surfing startup in Palo Alto than an appliance manufacturer in Berlin. All organizations that operate in frontier environments are kindred spirits. They're used to conditions where access to capital is intermittent, competition is fierce, markets are fickle, and continuity is a luxury few can obtain. Consequently, they can leverage lessons from the high-stakes world of venture capital, where resources are scarce and failure rates are as high as 95 percent.

In a world bewitched by high-tech unicorns and eccentric billionaires, we often forget about the many challenges that startups face on the path to continuity. Serial entrepreneur and author Eric Ries was among the first to provide practical guidance to these embryonic businesses, whose fragile ecosystems of commercial activity are constantly under threat of extinction. Leveraging the metaphor of a basketball player who keeps one foot in place while shifting the other around rapidly to shake off the competition, he encourages businesses to consider a strategic pivot, which he defines as "a special kind of change designed to test a new fundamental hypothesis about the product, business model, and engine of growth."[7]

This concept of an organizational "pivot" is particularly resonant in contexts undergoing significant structural change—whenever a current business model is no longer feasible, and the strategy for achieving an entrepreneurial vision needs to be reimagined. Whether, as Ries put it, the focus is on "creating a new product or business under conditions of extreme uncertainty," or—as in the case of the Baalbakis and other frontier entrepreneurs—merely on sustaining and growing an existing business in turbulent times, the strategic dilemma is virtually the same: Should we pivot or persevere?[8]

Neither approach can guarantee success. But in any resource-scarce environment, leaders should at least engage in frequent "pivot or persevere" discussions with executives and owners. When times are tough and uncertainty spikes, key stakeholders need to gather regularly to realistically assess the current trajectory of the enterprise and discuss the major risks and opportunities of staying the course or charting a new path forward.

FINDING SAFE HARBOR

Once the strategic decision to exit has been made, a new chapter in the entrepreneurial adventure begins—one that has much in common both with mass migrations and with the painful decision to pivot a nascent business in a new direction to stave off collapse. These moments are often deeply emotional, a blend of the excitement that comes with starting anew and sadness for what gets left behind.

Success during these transitions requires a rational and pragmatic assessment of any potential destinations. After all, not all new markets are equally bountiful or well suited to a company's unique value proposition—let alone its culture, values, and language.

Enterprising families searching for a new market—whether by force or by choice—have to figure out which destinations are most feasible, given both the practicalities of financing and the chances of survival. They also must decide who from the family will migrate and how they will manage the challenges of straddling multiple locations—raising children in divergent cultures who might ultimately shed their mother tongue and even risk losing their psychological connection to their native land, their family, and their shared enterprise. Of course, leaders must also consider the receptivity of new customers and communities, the availability of resources, the reactions of incumbent competitors, the infrastructure to support operations, and the hospitality of all layers of government.

High-tech startups face a similar dilemma. Once the decision to pivot has been made, the business may need to concentrate on identifying new markets or operational methods: for example, it can target new customer needs, new organizational designs, new growth engines, new distribution channels, or a new technology stack. Airbnb's early shift from renting air mattresses to offering furnished suites and entire homes was a logical adjacency worth exploring. Had it leapt straight into curated experiences, or the formal hotel industry, it may not have become the $80 billion juggernaut it is today.

In many ways, the choice to pivot or persevere comes down to two basic options: Should we take the safer path and *exploit* the familiar, or strike out bravely and *explore* a new frontier? Leveraging the Hierarchy of Stability as a menu, there are three potential destinations for any migration, each with its own unique characteristics and requirements for success. The first is certainly the easiest and most seamless to reach: leaders can seek new markets in locations that share a similar level of stability. These environments will often have many of the same characteristics as the point of origin, especially in terms of the ease of doing business, the sophistication of consumers, the presence of competitors, the availability of infrastructure, the role of regulators and compliance, levels of taxation, and so on. As a result, they are by far the most common choices among the hundreds of families we researched. An example would be Baalbaki's initial decision to expand into Jordan, then its later decision to migrate more fully to Lebanon, instead of other nearby emerging markets with less in common like Turkey, Egypt, or Israel.

Success in these *lateral migrations* certainly requires strategic adaptation to local norms, customs, and resources, though the adaptation needed

Three Strategies for Migration

Lateral moves are most familiar and common

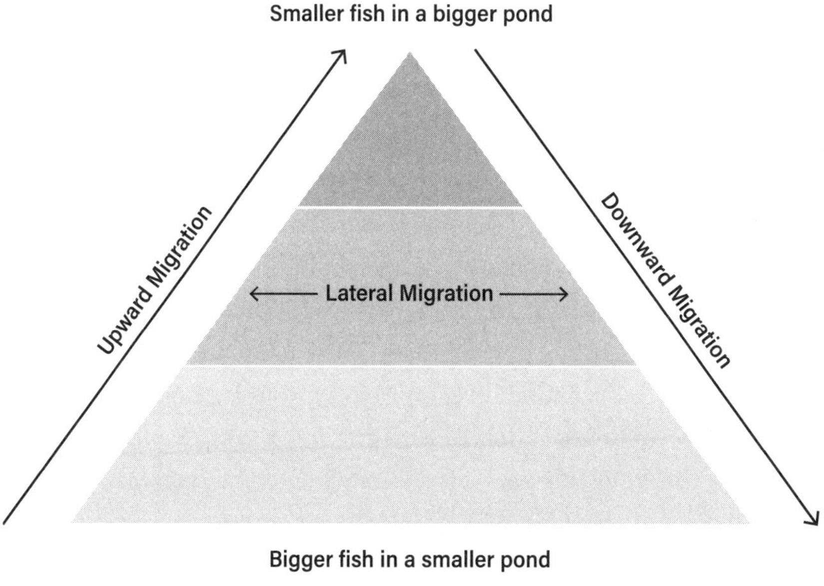

is typically quite minimal. Many peer countries are already members of regional trading blocs, making it easier for leaders to accelerate the pace and effectiveness of their efforts to localize their business model for these new environments.

A second approach is to seek the greater stability that is endemic to more developed contexts. This holds both for companies migrating from frontier to emerging economies and for those migrating from either of those to an advanced economy. Such *upstream migration* offers the promise of more reliable infrastructure, more transparency in institutions, and more legal protections, but also stiffer competition, greater consumer discretion, and more sophisticated accountability and compliance requirements.

Mexico's Carlos Slim, head of the family enterprise Grupo Carso, faced precisely this challenge. For several decades, his success throughout Latin America knew no bounds, yet when he attempted to migrate capital and grow his business in the United States, he exposed his conglomerate to billions of dollars in losses and was ultimately forced to retreat. A similar challenge awaits frontier families looking to move upstream into emerging economies. While competition may be less fierce than in advanced economies, not to mention governments less strict and consumers less spoiled by choice, the largest companies are still incredibly sophisticated. As we saw in Chapter 6, many have engaged in joint ventures with Western partners, learning and leveraging cutting-edge business practices, which places them at a significant competitive advantage relative to those migrating up the Hierarchy of Stability.

The third potential approach is to move in precisely the opposite direction—further toward the more exotic frontiers of capitalism, where volatility and instability are often the biggest barriers to entry, and where opportunities abound to better service the bulk of the world's population subsisting at the base of the economic pyramid. The logic of *downstream migration* is quite intuitive and familiar, particularly for established businesses in advanced economies seeking expansion. It provides a natural way of tapping into large pools of new customers who may not yet have domestic access to goods and services, and also offers opportunities to take advantage of lower-cost labor, or to secure access to important key resources not available in one's home market.

There are plenty of companies that have mastered this approach—McDonald's, Caterpillar, Danone, and Procter and Gamble, to name just a few. These companies have strategically migrated further down the Hierarchy of Stability through joint venture agreements, franchise partnerships, and even direct investments in subsidiaries with highly skilled local teams and infrastructures. Critical for the success of these efforts is the capacity to adapt all aspects of their business to these downstream markets, rather than trying to colonize them with products and processes honed for more advanced economies.[9]

Contrast the success of Ray Kroc with Home Depot's expansion in China. The retail giant largely failed because it tried to replicate its American business model in a downstream market without accounting for Chinese consumer preferences (for example, for smaller neighborhood stores), or the tendency in China to opt for do-it-for-me (DIFM) solutions rather than the do-it-yourself (DIY) ethos popular among Western consumers.

The unforced errors a company can make in downward migration abound, whether it's failing to adapt to local market tastes, trying to exert too much control from faraway corporate headquarters, overlooking local community values, or neglecting to develop regional training centers to create deep pools of reliable talent. But one thing is clear: bringing a colonial mindset to twenty-first-century emerging and frontier economies is a guaranteed recipe for failure.

CONDITIONS AND CAVEATS

Beyond the operational complexities of adapting business models, products, and services to any new environment, there is an additional challenge inherent to expansionary upstream and downstream migration. Companies that attempt to operate simultaneously at two different rungs on the developmental ladder are essentially signing up to perpetually manage the following dilemma: Which of our operating environments will anchor our culture, values, and strategy?

Some families operating across both advanced and emerging or frontier economies will choose to project Western standards of business ethics and excellence throughout their organizations. This has the benefit of protecting the enterprise's reputation across its entire operating portfolio, though it will inevitably mean that certain business opportunities will be lost to domestic competitors whose moral compasses point in a different direction.

Carvajal exemplified this situation when its leaders made the decision not to take on a lucrative magazine printing contract with a known narco-trafficking syndicate. Others may take a more fluid approach to managing ethical frontiers but risk backlash in more advanced countries where consumers, governments, and the court of public opinion can significantly punish any ethical transgressions.

Walmart's operations in Mexico provide a cautionary tale, where playing by local rules led to significant financial and reputational consequences. The case came to public attention in 2012, when it was reported in US media outlets that Walmart's Mexican subsidiary had paid more than US$24 million in bribes to officials to facilitate permits and accelerate approvals for new stores—an illegal but common practice in many emerging and frontier economies.[10] Following these allegations, investigations were initiated by the US and Mexican governments, resulting in Walmart paying a sizable fine—US$282 million.[11] Walmart has since undertaken efforts to strengthen its anticorruption compliance program worldwide, but only after suffering considerable reputational and financial damage.

Companies that migrate upstream or downstream—or that are successful enough to end up with operations that straddle multiple levels on the Hierarchy of Stability—need to weigh the promise of accessing new markets with the perils of regulatory compliance, and the risk of losing face in the court of public opinion when deciding on an ideal destination. Understanding these trade-offs comes more naturally when operating on your home turf, particularly after generations of success.

This is precisely why lateral migrations are, in our experience, by far the most common. Entering a new market is hard enough on its own—but doing so while the goalposts are constantly shifting is an exceptionally difficult task for any organization, especially those that have just endured a traumatic series of events.

Regardless of the destination, leaders contemplating migration can either do so proactively or reactively. As with most planning, being proactive, like the Baalbakis and the Saeeds, is the gold standard, but it isn't the only path to success.

Proactive planning involves a strategic assessment of new markets to analyze their fit with the existing business model and product portfolio. Having these in place before a crisis occurs is one of the best ways to survive a catastrophic event in your home market. This exercise also adds value even when conditions are relatively stable, as it encourages business leaders to examine fertile new markets that are ripe for expansion. Some businesses even use this kind of analysis to discover opportunities for proactively migrating to countries with more promising macroeconomic characteristics, more favorable regulatory environments, or more stable political situations—a strategy sometimes referred to as "regime-hopping."

Proactive planning for market exit and entry can also add value in situations where potentially catastrophic long-term risks are looming, but there is less of a sense of urgency in the short term. Consider companies that operate in coastal communities threatened by rising sea levels. The Maldives—which could be entirely submerged in the Indian Ocean by the turn of the next century—has been anticipating this disruptive event for decades. The Maldivian government has developed a variety of plans in the event that the country's 300,000 citizens need to be permanently resettled, from planting mangroves to building futuristic floating cities to relocate those citizens most at risk.

Obviously, not all countries—or companies—are so directly exposed to rising sea levels. That said, any leader or community with coastal assets ought to at least consider the potential benefits and risks of migrating to higher ground. Recent estimates suggest that by 2100, more than 680 million people and over US$14 trillion in assets will be at risk from rising sea levels alone, with vulnerability across the entire Hierarchy of Stability.[12] Think about all the major American cities that lie along the coast—from New York and Boston to Miami and Los Angeles—artifacts of our earlier maritime economies, when access to the sea was an asset rather than a liability. Port cities in Europe, from Amsterdam and Copenhagen to Hamburg and Marseille, are similarly exposed.

Any organization committed to multigenerational continuity needs to acknowledge the very real possibility that coastal maps will look very different for our grandchildren and their grandchildren than they do for us, and that the only way they might enjoy the Maldives—not to mention parts of Lower Manhattan or the City of London—may be through scuba goggles.

For those unwilling or unable to engage proactively, *reactive migration* remains a viable escape path in the event of sudden or gradual degradation in their operating environment—whether from natural events or human actions. This approach simply increases the risk of a failed response and diminishes the range of feasible alternatives.

For those who resist any form of migration at all, despite worsening conditions at home, all hope is not lost. In these moments, the other stabilizing strategies can still help to increase the odds of survival and success. However, in the face of acute and existential threat, one strategy in particular—simplification—is absolutely essential. It is the organizational equivalent of "battening down the hatches" in the face of a severe storm—tying off all essential items, tossing everything else overboard, and hoping to simply survive long enough for conditions to return to some kind of normalcy. Though the risks of this strategy are extremely high, as we'll explore in the next chapter, when the seas finally settle, the few who resist migration and manage to survive the harrowing storm may be left with a bountiful new niche to exploit.

KEY INSIGHTS

- When resource conditions shift dramatically and our active environment is no longer hospitable, sometimes the only alternative to extinction is relocation.
- The human story is filled with tales of migration, both voluntary and forced—moving in search of a better life, fleeing hardship, or being drawn to new opportunities.
- Businesses can face similar pressures to adapt or relocate in order to survive and thrive.
- The family members at the helm of the Baalbaki Group successfully managed the nationalization of their business by

strategically migrating to neighboring Lebanon and rebuilding their business from scratch.

- There are two types of forces that drive such migrations, both for people and for businesses.
- *Push factors* are driven by a difficult current situation (e.g., economic hardship, political instability), while *pull factors* occur when a new location seems attractive (e.g., better economic opportunities, greater stability).
- When faced with existential threats, enduring enterprises, much like fledgling startups, must decide whether to adapt their business model (pivot) or continue with the existing strategy (persevere).
- Once the decision to leave a market is made, careful consideration needs to be given to choosing a new location—assessing factors such as the similarity of the customer base, competition, available resources, and government regulations.
- It is also critical for leaders to determine whether to migrate laterally, upwardly, or downwardly on the Hierarchy of Stability, as this decision powerfully influences the likelihood of surviving the transition and achieving enduring success.

10
SIMPLIFICATION

As [one] simplifies [one's] life, the laws of the universe will appear less complex, and solitude will not be solitude, nor poverty poverty, nor weakness weakness.

—Henry David Thoreau

Argentina is a country of many paradoxes. Over the past century, its politics have lurched from democratic populism to military dictatorship, and its economy has alternated rhythmically between central planning and neoliberalism. Its culture is a unique mix of indigenous and European heritage—producing the tangos of Carlos Gardel, the literature of Jorge Luis Borges, and the spectacle of Diego Maradona. Though its modern economy is anything but stable, it was once one of the wealthiest nations of the world.

Yet up until the late eighteenth century, Argentina was mostly a political wilderness on the frontiers of the global economy. Its meteoric rise began at the height of the Industrial Revolution, when Buenos Aires—situated strategically near the Rio de la Plata (or "River of Silver")—became a reliable exporter of livestock and agricultural products to feed the rapidly growing populations of Western Europe. For the next century, as speculative Western capital poured into the country, new infrastructure, including railroads, ports, parks, and modern schools, helped Argentina become one of the most prosperous and productive emerging economies. To put that in perspective, in 1900, its GDP per capita was roughly equivalent to that of the United States, just shy of the United Kingdom, and greater than both Germany and France.

In many ways, the early twentieth century was Argentina's golden age, and many countries aspired to replicate its export-oriented model. Unfortunately, the Great Depression brought a swift end to a century of increasing stability and prosperity. Collapsing asset prices and soaring unemployment in Europe and the United States triggered a massive drop in demand for Argentine exports. World War II only accelerated the economic decline, prompting the rise of a new populist movement under the presidency of Juan Perón. The so-called Peronists promised to address the country's protracted economic hardships by supporting the working classes, establishing state control over the economy, and demonstrating minimal fiscal constraint.

Large deficits, heavy borrowing, and money printing became the policy tools used to achieve this lofty populist agenda. As a result, bouts of hyperinflation, frequent currency devaluations, and persistent foreign exchange controls plagued the economy for decades. Consequently, Argentina now holds the dubious distinction of defaulting on its sovereign debt more than any other country in history—nine times between 1827 and 2020.

Considering its long demoralizing slide back down the Hierarchy of Stability—one of the few countries in modern history to do so—it is perhaps surprising to learn that domestic entrepreneurship is still alive and well, as it has been throughout the country's long journey from frontier economy to emerging economy and back again.

One family business that exemplifies Argentinean resilience is Grupo Arcor. This global confectionery giant is a shining example of how simplification can generate greater stability during prolonged periods of economic turmoil. Fulvio Pagani founded the business on July 5, 1951, in a rural town in the province of Córdoba. It was inspired by the small bakery his father had run in Italy a quarter of a century before. While working together for their father in their youth, Pagani and his brothers would dream of running a factory that could produce 10,000 pounds of candy a day.

At the age of twenty-five, Fulvio and his siblings recruited two external partners and built a small candy plant, naming it Arcor—a combination of the first two letters of their hometown, Arroyito, and the first three letters of the province of Córdoba. Less than a decade later, Arcor was already producing 130,000 pounds of confectionery daily—an order of magnitude more than the brothers had ever imagined as kids.

Their focus on sweets provided a natural hedge against the chronic turbulence affecting Argentina's economy. As Luis Pagani, Fulvio's son, would later recount, "The idea was based on British American Tobacco's distribution model, which complemented cigarettes with the distribution of Eveready batteries and Gillette razor blades. Then, it was Arcor that provided the complement of the sweets. They were these four items that all commerce in the interior should have: cigarettes, batteries, razor blades and Arcor sweets. They were all high-turnover products that had a good profit margin."

During those early years, Fulvio and his leadership team focused on distributing their "essential" products in the interior regions of the country—away from the coasts and the capital. Like the AJE Group in Peru, only once the company's core manufacturing and distribution model in the interior was refined did the Pagani family begin to target larger cities, including the lucrative but highly competitive market of Buenos Aires.

To enable rapid expansion and greater quality control, Arcor vertically integrated some of its key upstream inputs, such as sugar and milk. This first wave of simplification would later prevent substantial losses during bouts of hyperinflation, when procuring these commodities externally would have been prohibitively expensive. During the 1950s and 1960s, despite the country lurching between democratic populism and military despotism, the company also remained well insulated from political interference, since neither of these movements stood to gain from standing between the people and their "just desserts."

By the mid-1970s, fueled by its focused and highly efficient model, Arcor was already supplying 20 percent of the Argentine candy market and 8 percent of the chocolate market. To help diversify its exposure away from the dysfunctional Argentine economy, the company began to

Argentina's Long Fight with Price Stability

Persistent inflation punctuated by hyperinflation challenges strategy and operations

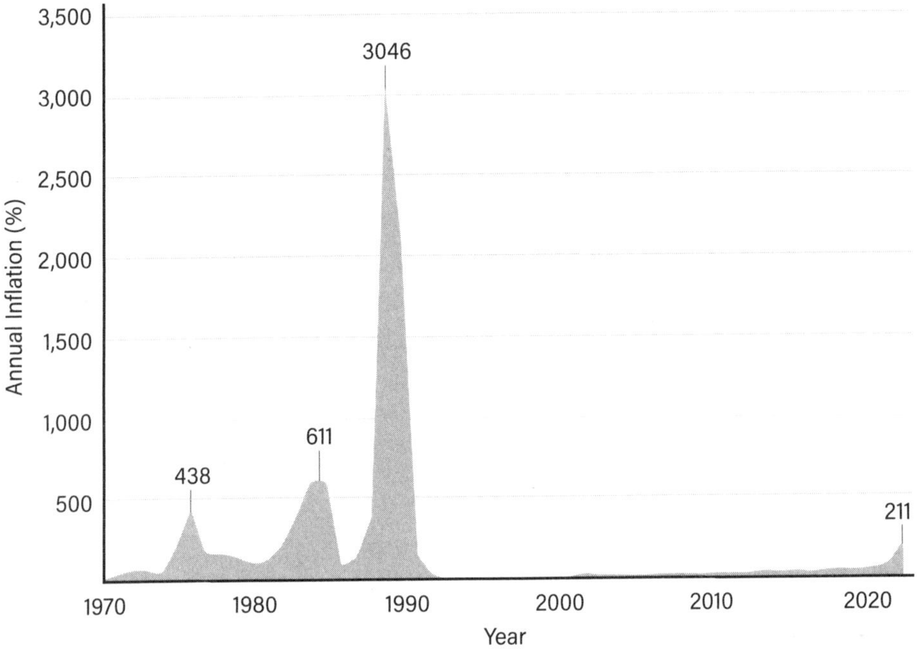

Source: Instituto Nacional de Estadística y Censos (INDEC), Trading Economics

expand laterally on the Hierarchy of Stability, first into Paraguay, then Uruguay, Brazil, and Chile. Even still, Arcor's fortunes remained tethered to its home market, where annual inflation was as high as 100 percent in 1981, over 400 percent in 1983, and a staggering 3,000 percent by the end of the decade.

Then unexpectedly, in 1990, sixty-five-year-old Fulvio died in a tragic car accident. As though the economic situation in the country were not bad enough, now the family and the business were forced to grapple with how to navigate the promises and perils of regional expansion without the visionary leadership and passion of their beloved founder.

Fulvio's oldest son, Luis, then only thirty-five years old, assumed responsibility for leading Grupo Arcor after a successful tour of duty as a regional sales director. This change in leadership prompted the family to pursue another wave of simplification, which then fueled a new string of focused investments and acquisitions. As a result, Arcor's sales rose by nearly 300 percent between 1991 and 1999, compared to only a 39 percent increase in Argentina's GDP.[1] By the start of the new millennium, Arcor controlled more than half of the Argentine candy market and a third of the chocolate market. However, two critical headwinds were blowing that would force the company to shift its focus from growth to survival once again.

First, by the mid-1990s the company's success was beginning to attract international competition from global heavyweights such as Kraft, Danone, and Cadbury Schweppes. These multinationals used their deep pockets to enter the Argentine market, acquiring major local companies that were pushed out of business by the economic turmoil. Second, Argentina chose to default on US$132 billion in sovereign debt in December 2001, and its subsequent move away from fixed exchange rates produced a "controlled devaluation" of nearly 50 percent in 2002, transforming the entire economy overnight. These two forces made it extremely challenging for Arcor to meet its financial obligations to workers, suppliers, and lenders. The crisis also threatened the company's loyal customers, who were struggling under the crippling weight of another Argentine Great Depression.

Thankfully, this was not Grupo Arcor's first rodeo. As Luis confided years later, "In Argentina, we have developed expertise in inflation.... Our people had experienced these kinds of circumstances before, so we didn't panic."[2] Since the company's inception, Arcor had embraced strategic cost reduction as one of three core pillars of its DNA (the other two being productivity and industrial know-how). Throughout that time, the company had weathered multiple inflationary episodes. So its leaders understood what was needed to keep costs and operations under control while price stability was eroding.

For instance, they were keenly aware that their customers were suddenly less affluent than they had been before the collapse, and that buying patterns were likely to change. Executives explored ways to appeal to these new price sensitivities, including reducing the size of their most popular products, idling operations, and running machinery less than twenty-four hours a day, seven days a week. As customers began to demand cheaper prices, Arcor also needed to find more cost-efficient processes in order to pass on these savings.

One innovative solution was to streamline the quantity and mix of key inputs, which were among the largest drivers of overall costs and margins. Arcor's leaders decided to reduce the amount of chocolate in its candies, adding more wafer, cream, and other fillings that were cheaper and easier to procure. For instance, they shrank the layer of chocolate in their best-selling "Bon O Bons" from 11 percent to 8 percent, and reduced the number of pieces in packaged gums and candies to keep the overall price point down for cash-strapped consumers.[3]

Finally, Arcor tightened its payment terms for retailers, which had traditionally been quite generous—as long as 120 days in some cases. In the context of a depreciating currency, a generous receivables policy significantly decreases the amount of working capital available. So Arcor shortened its collection window to 35 days and stopped delivering to outlets that did not comply with its new terms—a radical simplification in policy, but one that critically helped the company stay cash-flow positive when it mattered most.

Throughout these years of painful macroeconomic reckoning, Luis ensured that the company made every interest payment, delivered every shipment, paid every salary, and—thanks to its ultra-lean and agile operations—still managed to turn a profit. He even raised employee wages by 20 percent and increased donations of food to the community to alleviate effects of the peso devaluation on the most vulnerable.

Once its product portfolio was retooled, and its financial performance stabilized, Arcor's leadership team didn't waste any time to survey the landscape for opportunity. In the years that followed, the family went on an acquisition spree. Financed by its efficient operating model, it was able to buy up the assets of its failed competitors, and even expand into new markets, without taking on any outside capital. Today, the company is active in over 120 countries on 5 continents, with more than 20,000 employees and global sales of over US$3.5 billion—celebrating its best year ever in 2022.[4]

At the time of writing, Argentina is once again facing a fight with hyperinflation. Prices for key household items, including milk, tea, and apples, are increasing more than 10 percent every month.[5] Its voters elected a libertarian president promising radical reforms, but enduring economic stability will take more than populist rhetoric. Business leaders are rightfully anxious. As Luis Pagani put it, they worry "that Argentina has split in two—a country that consumes and another that doesn't make ends meet."[6] Only time will tell if these reforms will bring lasting stability. In the meantime, Arcor's leadership team knows the drill—first simplify and reinforce the core strengths of the business, then buy up the assets of competitors who failed to prepare adequately or adapt effectively.

STABILIZE THE CORE

Whenever our context shifts from abundance to scarcity—and our experience from feast to famine—conventional wisdom no longer holds. Those stranded in the desert must learn not to waste water. Those trapped in the cold must learn not to waste heat. Such extreme shifts in climate provide an obvious metaphor to frame the imperative for simplification under extreme environmental stress, since they quickly highlight the most essential drivers of survival.

Among the various exotic species we studied to better understand this phenomena, *tardigrades* are by far our favorite—they are the quintessential example of biological minimalism. First described by the German zoologist Johann Goeze in 1773 as *Kleiner Wasserbären*, or "little water bears," these fascinating creatures were given their current scientific name by the Italian biologist Lazzaro Spallanzani, who coined the term *Tardigrada*, or "slow steppers," based on their unique form of locomotion. Usually measuring less than one millimeter, tardigrades are microorganisms with segmented exoskeletons and eight stubby legs. Yet despite their diminutive size and adorable appearance, their real claim to fame is that they are one of the most resilient animals in the known universe. They can survive without food or water for decades, withstand temperatures approaching absolute zero and above boiling, resist pressures six times greater than the ocean's deepest trenches, and even endure in the vacuum of outer space.

These incredible acts of biological resilience are enabled by an innate capacity for radical simplification. When faced with conditions that are hostile to normal metabolic functioning, tardigrades enter a so-called *tun* state, an extreme version of hibernation. This transformation is structural—much more than simply napping when food is hard to find. Instead, such cryptobiosis involves complex molecular and metabolic changes that allow animals to preserve organ function and prevent tissue damage long enough for conditions to improve. During torpor, for instance, the metabolic rate of small animals like house mice can decrease by up to 95 percent, significantly enhancing their resistance to starvation.[7] Over evolutionary time scales, these seasonal variations have allowed some species to survive in conditions that would otherwise force them toward extinction.

Scientists have made remarkable discoveries and advances by studying how these hearty little creatures manage to punch so far above their weight class in nature's relentless existential tournament. They have inspired research into new technologies for preserving organs and tissues before transplantation, and offer potentially revolutionary breakthroughs in the field of cancer research. They are even providing astrobiologists with insights into how life might persist in other inhospitable environments throughout the universe. Most importantly for our purposes, nature's lesson for business leaders is clear: identifying and prioritizing your most essential systems is a prerequisite for survival whenever critical resources become scarce.

As with Arcor during Argentina's many bouts with hyperinflation, when cash flow and capital become precious commodities, any organization committed to continuity can take a page out of the tardigrade playbook and immediately find ways to reduce its complexity. Such strategic simplification involves prioritizing basic or essential products, services, and processes until conditions improve and new resources become available to support a return to scale and complexity. Though this inevitably requires making difficult choices about which assets and activities to keep and which to shed—the strategic equivalent of chopping off the hand to save the arm—it is often the only viable path forward.

Consider a fascinating example from the United States during an earlier stage of its long march up the Hierarchy of Stability, while it was still an emerging economy. The country's thirteen-year experiment with Prohibition in the 1920s and early 1930s forced all but one domestic distillery out of business. Family-owned Brown-Forman was able to survive these turbulent times by focusing on the production of medical alcohols—one of the few legal uses for spirits at the time. The company obtained a federal license—one of only a handful that were issued—permitting them to manufacture medicinal whiskey. Once Prohibition was repealed in 1933, the company was able to reanimate its core business of producing consumer spirits (like Jack Daniel's Tennessee Whiskey) with relative ease. Brown-Forman now proudly stands as "the only U.S. spirits company existing today that bottled, aged, and distilled whiskey before, during, and after Prohibition."[8]

There are many other brand name examples of enterprising families deploying this strategy throughout history and around the world, like the retailer Groupe Casino in France during World War I, the energy giant Hess in the United States during the Great Depression, and the Japanese beverage giant Suntory during World War II. COVID-19 can now be added to this list of disruptive events as well. If nothing else, the pandemic exposed our very natural tendency to prioritize "essential services" during times of crisis at every level of society—from governments to private enterprise to individual households.

Since we only learn from the dangers we survive, it becomes crucial for every enduring enterprise to identify its most vital processes, resources, and services, then protect them at all costs. Common sources of internal stability, such as cash reserves, supply chain diversity, insurance products, and risk management systems, are not frequently cited as organizational superpowers. But in times of scarcity, not having them in place can easily become our kryptonite.

Consider Arcor's decades-long campaign for operational efficiency. If this relentless focus on simplification had not already been built into the company's DNA, it may have faced the same fate as its competitors, many of which failed during the first few critical months following Argentina's 2001 default. Waiting until a hurricane hits to pack your bags makes it much less likely that you'll escape with your most precious belongings, let alone your life.

One framework we've found particularly useful to help distinguish between organizational needs and wants was first introduced in the late 1990s in the book *The Alchemy of Growth*.[9] It was written by a trio of McKinsey consultants for an entirely different purpose: to help companies balance investments in current performance while maximizing opportunities for future growth. However, the basic premise also provides a useful perspective for company leaders on how to identify their organizational "grab bag"—that is, those core activities that provide a financial lifeline in turbulent times, and which in good times fund more aspirational activities related to innovation and growth.

The original model is quite intuitive, advocating that leaders focus simultaneously on all three "horizons" of growth, rather than pursuing each sequentially over time. "Horizon One" involves optimizing current operations that are the existing profit centers, focusing on improving efficiency and effectiveness in the short term. "Horizon Two" emphasizes the medium term, where the spotlight shifts to emerging opportunities, and how to leverage current capabilities to explore adjacent markets. "Horizon Three" is aligned with the long-term vision of the enterprise, encouraging experimentation and innovations that have the potential to revolutionize the business.

Strategic Simplification in Action

Enduring enterprises dynamically adjust investments across these three horizons

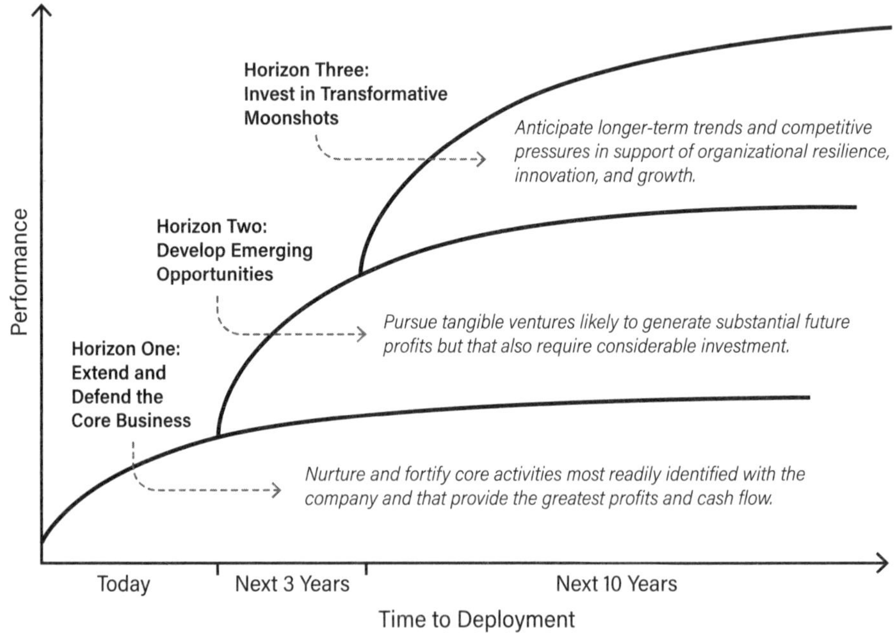

Source: LGA, Model adapted from *The Alchemy of Growth* by White, Baghai, and Coley

While many companies—particularly those with established research and development teams—have used this framework effectively to drive growth during eras of relative stability, we have found that the model naturally breaks down during periods of crisis, when resources are scarce and success more elusive. As a result, Horizon Two and Three projects are often paused or canceled altogether. However, going through the exercise of identifying Horizon One activities is among the fastest shortcuts to identifying an organization's most essential needs.

This is precisely how Grupo Arcor navigated through the 2002 crisis. Having been through inflationary periods before, its leaders already knew which markets were most impacted by price sensitivity, which inputs would react more dynamically to inflationary pressures, and which of its best-selling products could be simplified to drive operational efficiencies and sustain consumer demand. They also understood that expansionary plans needed to be put on hold until these changes had been implemented successfully, so that the core business wouldn't be starved of cash at a time when both domestic and foreign capital markets were essentially closed, and all operations and investments would need to be financed internally.

Like the intrepid tardigrade, Arcor initially shrank down to its most essential Horizon One functions until conditions stabilized. Then its leaders took advantage of the failures of their competitors—who hadn't been proactive in planning for the crisis and protecting their core—first by acquiring their assets at fire-sale prices, then by reanimating various Horizon Two (i.e., Latin American expansion) and Horizon Three (i.e., African expansion) initiatives.

AN OUNCE OF PREVENTION

Many enduring enterprises have pursued a similar approach—downsizing during crises—though the degree to which this is done out of desperation or proactivity significantly affects the outcome. For instance, during the 2008–2009 Global Financial Crisis, in the face of a catastrophic drop in consumer demand and the loss of cheap and plentiful financing, family-controlled Ford was the only major American automobile manufacturer to avoid bankruptcy and restructuring. The automaker's ability to weather the crisis can be attributed to a series of strategic moves initiated before the crisis even began, demonstrating the importance of a proactive and strategic form of simplification.

Under the leadership of CEO Alan Mulally, and with the full support of the Ford family, in early 2006 the company launched a restructuring strategy called the "Way Forward" that focused on reducing costs and streamlining the company's financial and operational portfolio.[10] This included a focus on producing quality vehicles that met growing consumer demands for higher fuel efficiency; pursuing a global platform strategy that would reduce costs and manufacturing complexity through standardized production; and selling off non-core assets to concentrate on its Ford and Lincoln brands. The company also borrowed over US$23 billion to finance this strategic simplification, which provided a significant financial cushion and helped the company endure the crisis without seeking even a penny of government aid.[11]

Mulally's proactive thinking allowed Ford not only to survive but to emerge even more focused and competitive just as the disruptive electric vehicle revolution was about to take hold. Avoiding government support also enhanced its reputation among consumers, banks, and investors, providing it with a competitive edge both during and after the crisis.

Contrast Ford's experience with IBM's more *tactical simplification* in the early 1990s. At the time, Big Blue's troubles stemmed from the rapid changes taking place in the technology industry, culminating in a massive US$8 billion loss in 1993—the largest in the company's then eighty-two-year history. Under the leadership of Lou Gerstner, IBM underwent a deep and costly restructuring that involved shrinking its workforce by over 60,000 (or roughly 15 percent) and reducing layers of management and bureaucracy in the hopes of promoting quicker decision-making and a more entrepreneurial culture.[12]

Its product portfolio was downsized and consolidated as well, with a shift away from consumer hardware and toward business services and software. Gerstner also pursued a range of direct cost-cutting measures, including the consolidation of manufacturing facilities and the reduction of operational expenses. Former executives shared with us that these austerity measures were so severe that employees starved of budgets for office furniture were paying out of pocket to procure their own ergonomic chairs to supplement the otherwise spartan workplace designs.

This ruthless campaign for efficiency certainly helped IBM stave off collapse, and some management scholars still praise these efforts as producing one of the greatest turnarounds in tech history. However, we would argue that Gerstner's reactive approach still left the company a step behind its major competitors. After all, it would take nearly two decades for Big Blue's financial performance and market share to recover—with a brief glimmer of success in 2010 and 2011, followed by another twenty-two successive quarters of declining revenue and relevance.

As Ford and IBM clearly demonstrate, these same basic principles can be applied to all enduring enterprises—whether they are family owned and operated or not. Inspired by the scholarship of Jim Collins and his colleagues, let's briefly consider the contrasting experience of American Airlines and Southwest Airlines in the wake of 9/11.[13] These terrorist attacks obviously had a profound impact on the entire airline industry, but they affected different companies in radically different ways, depending on whether they used simplification reactively or proactively.

American Airlines, which was directly involved in the tragedy with two of its planes hijacked, faced immense operational and financial challenges in the days and months that followed. Demand for air travel was significantly reduced, forcing American to cut flights and lay off thousands of employees. These savings in variable costs were more than offset by rising operational expenses, particularly the sharp spike in insurance premiums, fuel prices, and the cost of security. As a result, the company reported a net loss of US$1.8 billion in 2001 and another US$3.5 billion in 2002. The damage to the company's business model was so severe that it would take until 2005 before the airline was able to generate even a modest profit.

In stark contrast, simplification was already an explicit strategy of Southwest Airlines long before the terrorist attacks, allowing the company to weather the storm with far less disruption to operations and financial performance. For instance, Southwest's model focused on the use of a single aircraft type, the Boeing 737, which significantly simplified maintenance, scheduling, operations, and crew training.[14] The airline's more

A Tale of Two Airlines

How strategic simplification drives performance during a crisis

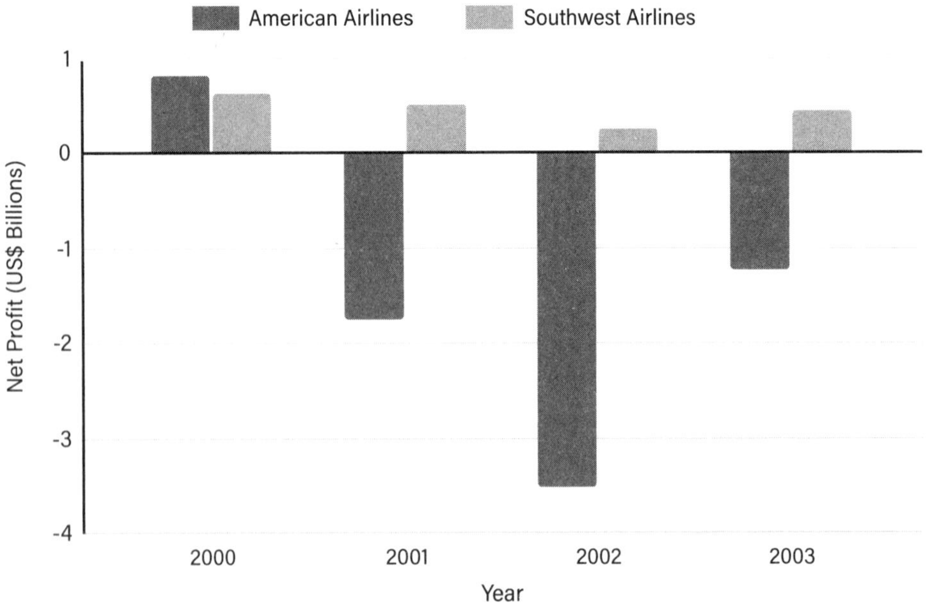

Source: Company financial statements.

streamlined point-to-point service model was also far less complex than the traditional hub-and-spoke system used by American Airlines and others, because it allowed for easier scheduling and quicker turnaround times. Additionally, a prudent hedging strategy shielded the airline from the steep hike in fuel prices seen in the years following 9/11, enabling it to control costs more effectively than many of its competitors. While Southwest also experienced a downturn in passenger traffic, it was the only major US airline to record a profit in 2001 and 2002.

These examples illustrate the main differences between tactical and strategic simplification. The former, more reactive approach is clearly better than no downsizing at all. But the latter creates more stability during a crisis, and, as Arcor, Ford, and Southwest Airlines all discovered, also positions an organization for greater success once conditions eventually stabilize.

A POUND OF CURE

Not all companies, in all crises, across all contexts, are willing and able to be proactive in their efforts to simplify—reinforcing the critical systems vital to the survival and success of their enterprises. That said, any company in any situation is capable of being tactical. How leaders respond to these choices can often mean the difference between survival and failure—or at the very least between modest profits and massive losses.

While strategic approaches to simplification necessarily begin long before a crisis, a tactical approach is more about reacting with speed and conviction to the most urgent organizational threats. These difficult choices often include short-term cost reductions, temporary layoffs, and quick pivots into alternative revenue streams that are viable in the short run but may not be sustainable. Such tactical actions tend to focus on the "here and now," leveraging existing resources and quick wins to steady the ship. They are also most often used as a last resort—once all other stabilizing strategies have been tried, or when the existential threat is so overwhelming that it becomes the only way to stave off total organizational collapse.

To help us make this distinction, let's revisit the case of the Venezuelan distiller Ron Santa Teresa, which has deployed both tactical and strategic simplification over the past several decades. A few years before Alberto Vollmer launched his now famous Project Alcatraz, the company was in dire straits. Fluctuations in the Venezuelan bolivar made its products more expensive in export markets while making imports from global competitors relatively cheap. Sales were falling steadily, and operating losses were piling up, making it difficult to meet financial obligations to banks, suppliers, and even the tax authorities. Several board members believed the company was no longer viable and recommended defaulting on these obligations and winding down the business. Others suggested that Alberto's father consider selling out to a larger multinational. But Alberto was unwilling to give up on his family's proud entrepreneurial legacy.

On February 7, 1999, Alberto and his brother, then thirty and twenty-eight years old, boarded a flight to Rome to meet with their father and reassess the future of the business. They recommended a swift management takeover followed by a process of radical simplification. Alberto pleaded with his father, saying he didn't want to be the last generation to run their iconic family business—he couldn't stand the thought of telling that story to his grandchildren. While they may have missed the opportunity to administer an ounce of prevention, the two young brothers were ready to endure a painful but life-saving pound of cure.

The restructuring plan they presented to their father the next morning—nicknamed "Operation Conuco"—included the removal of most of the company's board members and senior leadership team. It also required a laser focus on its own Santa Teresa brands, shedding less important or less successful products, targeting core domestic markets, and negotiating repayment plans with creditors on favorable terms. The initial phase of this "slash-and-burn" simplification was quite traumatic, particularly for the company's workers. By the end of 2001, only 205 remained out of nearly 650 employed just a year earlier. The brothers were also forced to radically streamline their outsourced distribution channels down to just two.

It was only after the company's dire financial and operational situation was stabilized that the brothers were finally able to launch a more strategic second phase in their ambitious plan. The company's current values, mission, and vision emerged at a time when Venezuela was just beginning its decades-long descent into Communist mismanagement and economic hardship. However, this time around, the company was fully prepared for crisis. After their previous near-death experience, simplification is now built intentionally and strategically into their organizational design.

Deploying tactical simplification has reliably saved companies like Ron Santa Teresa from total collapse many times throughout history. Whether triggered by terrorist incidents, financial pressures, competitive obsolescence, or natural disasters, when an organization's very survival is questioned, this becomes the surest (and often the only) path to continuity.

The underlying logic is both simple and obvious. Under stable conditions, "visions" and "strategies" can be useful for organizing large teams in service of lofty goals. But in moments of acute crisis, one goal becomes crystal clear and connects deeply and intuitively with our most primal instincts for survival. As with the fictional spy James Bond, the basic game plan is to avoid destruction long enough to "die another day."

To stave off total collapse when our backs are against the wall, individuals, families, and entire organizations are able to do things that nobody thought possible. Consider how unlikely it might have seemed just a few short years ago, before the COVID-19 pandemic, to have so many employees working remotely, or entire sectors of the economy deemed nonessential and effectively shut down. Remember how surreal it was to have field hospitals active in New York's Central Park, empty football stadiums hosting live professional matches, and much of the world's manufacturing capacity throttled or shuttered, while researchers rushed to develop a portfolio of safe and effective vaccines.

In many ways, the types of frugal innovation and entrepreneurship we studied in Chapter 5 are born of moments like these. However, many organizations enter these traumatic periods with legacy assets, processes, structures, policies, cultures, and leaders trapped in the past. Before they can innovate and thrive, they first need to simplify and survive.

CONDITIONS AND CAVEATS

In many ways, the pandemic was a natural reminder for every institution on the planet that the future can't be taken for granted. Some organizations have the foresight to plan ahead for disruptive events—particularly the further down they operate on the Hierarchy of Stability. Whether they're facing existential threats, transitory business discontinuity, or simply increased competition, we've seen how their investments in simplification can yield both financial and operational dividends.

Consider Carvajal's use of the pandemic to conduct a thorough review of its organizational design, shrinking the number of operating companies from 163 to 50. This decision significantly reduced organizational complexity—particularly for the company's Shared Services Center—with fewer boards and leadership meetings to arrange, fewer financial statements to prepare and consolidate, and less regulatory compliance to observe. It also helped Pedro Carvajal and his team focus their attention on the activities that mattered most during those precarious first few months of the crisis, when there was very little sense of how long the disruption would last and how deeply it would affect macroeconomic conditions.

Applied judiciously, strategic and tactical simplification can each enhance organizational stability, though in slightly different ways. Strategic simplification ensures that the organization keeps sight of its long-term objectives and retains its core value propositions, while tactical simplification allows it to effectively maneuver through its most pressing challenges. In both cases, the desired outcome is the same: to emerge from a crisis more streamlined and focused, with the resources and momentum to thrive.

That said, the payoff on proactivity is significantly higher. As the American polymath Benjamin Franklin captured artfully, "An ounce of prevention is worth a pound of cure." Franklin originally coined the phrase in the eighteenth century in reference to public safety, at a time when urban fires were among the most dangerous and preventable hazards in the bustling metropolises of New England.[15] Despite their cost and inconvenience, Franklin repeatedly made the case for citizens to keep buckets of water and ladders readily available to help limit the spread of indoor fires, which at the time were both indispensable and treacherous. His sage advice applies both to fighting fires and simplifying businesses—that is, there are significant benefits to investing in stability before a crisis strikes. Savvy business leaders should always prefer to pay up front for an ounce of prevention, rather than having to clean up a mess with a pound of cure.

With such obvious advantages in both the short and longer term, why aren't all companies engaging in proactive simplification campaigns? What might prevent or delay companies from integrating this simple tool into their broader strategic planning activities?

For starters, all change-management efforts can be risky affairs. Employees, customers, and strategic partners may all resist or even reject the wisdom of these investments, giving executives pause, and reinforcing the status quo bias of "If it ain't broke, don't fix it." There's an additional risk of losing our most distinguishing capabilities—for instance, pockets of innovative research and development—that may be critical for future growth in Horizon Two or Three, even if they aren't "essential" for survival in Horizon One.

Investments in Simplification Can Take Three Forms

Each has a different impact on performance

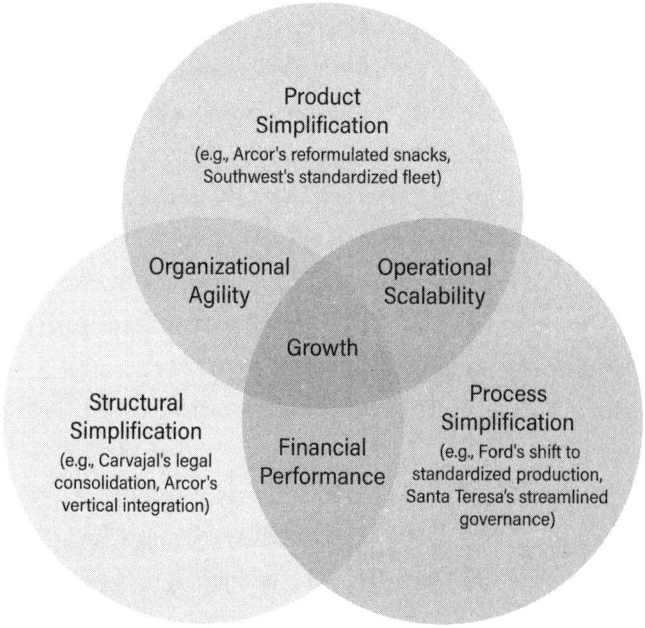

Source: Model adapted from Know How Innovations, "Business Simplification"

Enterprising families also face a unique form of cultural resistance to simplification, particularly when the cuts that have to be made involve units that are under the leadership of family members, or are related to legacy assets that carry significant emotional value. Consider the case of a European media company at the dawn of the digital age. The CEO's plan to shed the company's high-end printing division—a central part of the family's legacy since the 1700s—was almost abandoned because three of his cousins in senior leadership roles strongly resisted the thought of working for a multinational if the deal went through. After considerable family conflict, the deal proceeded. Then, shortly after the sale, the market for high-end publishing collapsed. While the three cousins did lose their jobs, all members of the family (including the resistant cousins) were grateful that their wealth was protected and could be redeployed into more lucrative businesses with stronger long-term prospects. It was like cutting off a finger to save the hand.

Extreme simplification campaigns can also increase fragility—particularly around supply chains, as we saw in our exploration of redundancy in Chapter 8. There are certain areas within any business where greater efficiencies are possible, and even desirable. But strategic simplification needs to be wielded more like a scalpel than a hammer. We shouldn't start knocking down walls until we know what they're holding up.

For instance, cybersecurity and workplace safety aren't areas where you want to trim back investment—unless, of course, these aren't high-priority threats or vulnerabilities. Similarly, supply chains need a little "slack" or they risk triggering cascading dysfunction. But juicy R&D budgets filled with nonviable pet projects, layers of administrative bureaucracy that have accumulated like plaque over generations, and cushy benefits for senior leaders untethered to long-term performance are often natural places to start.

Grupo Arcor, Ron Santa Teresa, Carvajal, and others have proven that simplification can be well worth the effort. They drive greater financial performance, increase organizational resilience, and can even catalyze innovation in business design. Squeezing a camel through the eye of the needle may seem a dangerous or even impossible task, particularly in the midst of a crisis, but it's often far better than the alternative.

We encourage all leaders who want to build an enduring enterprise to push through the natural resistance that comes with any organizational change and invest the time and resources necessary to identify and fortify their most "essential services" long before they become truly "essential." In the years ahead, we believe this exercise will become a regular feature of any resilient organization's portfolio of stabilizing strategies—though, like all the others, not sufficient on its own. The next and final chapter in Part 2 will explain how a systematic approach to diversity can provide another reliable path to prosperity in turbulent times.

KEY INSIGHTS

- Simplification, an intuitive approach to surviving external shocks and instability, involves focusing on essential products, services, and processes until conditions improve.

- Simplification doesn't always come naturally to companies accustomed to operating in prosperous times, because abundant resources often mask any underlying organizational vulnerabilities.
- Companies that implement simplification strategically and proactively by streamlining operations and optimizing resource allocation are inevitably better positioned to weather storms and can emerge even stronger following a crisis.
- Grupo Arcor, a confectionery giant, deployed this strategy superbly across decades of economic mismanagement in Argentina, managing to stay afloat during periods of hyperinflation and currency chaos—and even to expand—while their competitors floundered and failed.
- All enduring enterprises must focus on three horizons of growth—Horizon One (optimizing current operations), Horizon Two (emerging opportunities), and Horizon Three (long-term innovation)—though during a crisis leaders need to sharpen their focus on Horizon One to ensure survival.
- *Strategic* simplification is proactive and emphasizes long-term resilience and performance—involving a pre-crisis evaluation of core functionalities and a focus on strengthening those critical aspects of the business.
- *Tactical* simplification is reactive and focuses on survival through austerity—involving short-term cost-cutting measures such as layoffs or temporary pivots in product lines—though it doesn't necessarily position the company for future success.
- For any simplification campaign to be successful, leaders will have to make tough decisions about what to keep and what to shed, and communicate effectively with all key stakeholders to ensure the structural integrity of the enterprise during moments of significant change.

11
DIVERSITY

It is the part of a wise man to keep himself today for tomorrow, and not venture all his eggs in one basket.

—Don Quixote

The Indus River Valley has been a cradle of civilization since the early Bronze Age. Four thousand years ago, ancient cities such as Harappa and Mohenjo-Daro already hosted as many as 40,000 residents and featured sophisticated grid plans, markets, public baths, and even water and sewage systems that would have been the envy of medieval Europe. The fertility of these great plains spawned a vibrant tradition of complex metropolitan life and commercial activity that has characterized India ever since.

Sharing resources in such dense communities—without resorting to violence—doesn't come naturally to humans. But the Indus Valley Civilization managed to sustain conditions of relative peace and prosperity for millennia, inspiring some of the earliest thinkers in political philosophy. This included renowned Indian treatises like the *Arthashastra* (literally "Statecraft"), documented in South Asia during the fourth century BCE when Rome was still a fledgling village. It laid out remarkably clear guidelines for governance, economics, and trade that helped to build and sustain a level of trust among strangers that endured for centuries.

Artisanal guilds dominated commercial life in these early cities—organized groups of makers and traders who later became known as *shrenis* in Sanskrit. Each guild followed well-defined operating principles drawn straight from the *Arthashastra*, including rules for collective bargaining, price controls, and even quality assurance. Importantly, families often supplied both the intellectual and human capital that powered them, handing down craftsmanship and acumen from generation to generation. In many ways, these *shrenis* and their predecessors laid the foundations for modern India's vibrant culture of family entrepreneurship.

It would take the eventual rise of the British East India Company to disrupt this ancient tradition. In contrast to the mutualistic Mughals they displaced, British colonists were unapologetically parasitic. The British Raj heavily favored the import of English goods, often at the expense of local Indian industry. It also introduced an extractive new land tax of up to 50 percent, which threw the agrarian economy into disarray, leading to widespread poverty and famine.

One of the few silver linings of this imperial exploitation was India's first taste of modern manufacturing, particularly in key export commodities such as cotton, tea, indigo, and jute. Many Indians experienced hardship under colonial rule, but as the British invested hundreds of millions of pounds in infrastructure, irrigation, and industry, new opportunities also emerged for the country's many enterprising families.

Few capitalized on this unique moment in Indian history quite like the Tata Group, one of India's largest and most respected conglomerates. The family's entrepreneurial legacy begins with Nusserwanji Ratanji Tata. Born in 1822 into a family of Zoroastrian priests, his ancestors had been exiled from Persia centuries earlier during the Muslim conquests, and they subsequently migrated to India. Despite the expectation that Nusserwanji would become a priest, continuing the family's long religious heritage into the sixteenth generation, he instead found his calling in the ancient Indian tradition of commerce and trade.

Nusserwanji initially sought work within the Parsi community in Gujarat before moving to Bombay (now Mumbai), where he established himself in the bustling commodities business just as the Industrial Revolution was taking hold in Western Europe. He specialized in high-volume goods for import and export, which included jute and even opium—an unsavory detail often omitted from official Tata Group histories, although trade in opium was quite common.

As his reputation grew and his business flourished, Nusserwanji eventually invited his son Jamsetji into the fold. Thanks to his father's commercial success, and early propensity for math, Jamsetji received a British education and spent a considerable amount of time abroad—both rare privileges among his contemporaries. His travels took him from Japan and China to Europe and the United States, where he studied the market dynamics of each of the key commodities his father was trading. These experiences also afforded him a taste of the diverse landscape of cultures and technologies powering the Industrial Revolution.

Inspired by his travels, upon returning to India Jamsetji founded his first new enterprise, buying up an aging oil mill and converting it to process cotton. He made it his goal to learn how to compete effectively in the burgeoning textiles business, and two years later he sold the mill at a profit. He then used the proceeds and the knowledge he had gained to launch his ambitious plan to revolutionize India's entire textiles industry.

Leveraging his observations of Manchester's sophisticated manufacturers, and over six years of research into India's shifting industrial landscape, Jamsetji set up the "Central India Spinning, Weaving and Manufacturing Company" in Nagpur—a remote village over 800 kilometers (500 miles) northeast of Bombay.

At the time, Nagpur was considered to be a provincial backwater with limited industrial potential, and he was ridiculed by the business community for not locating the mill near the rest of his competitors in Bombay. But Jamsetji recognized the strategic significance of the location, which featured a diverse range of critical resources including cheap land, bountiful coal and water, and a large community of artisanal hand loomers who could supply skilled labor.

Most importantly, Nagpur was situated along a new rail corridor that promised quick and reliable access to Bombay. Trains were still a relatively unknown technology in India, but Jamsetji recognized that railways would eventually transform the region and the world, and he was confident in the long-term advantages Nagpur would provide. He also invested heavily to get the best machinery, then manufactured in Germany, to power his new mill. This heavy equipment could only be moved by ship or rail, so once again the new location proved to be ideal.

Leveraging this strategic foresight, both the quality and quantity of his company's textiles quickly established a new global standard for Indian exports. Within a decade, having already launched his fourth mill, he was well on the way to becoming the country's market leader. As a formerly skeptical banker would later remark, reflecting on those first bold bets in Nagpur, it was like "taking out earth and putting gold in the ground."[1]

Beyond a keen business mind, Jamsetji was also known for his revolutionary mission to provide for the holistic well-being of his employees, irrespective of their race or religion. His understanding of the benefits of diversity and mutualism, particularly with respect to the community, was remarkably progressive. He ensured that each of his employees had access to clean water, sanitary working conditions, credit at local stores, medical aid, accident compensation, maternity benefits, a free library, and even pension funds.

These compassionate innovations, and countless others, were virtually unknown to industrialists of that era on any continent. Jamsetji's values set global benchmarks for employee welfare over a century ago, instilling a corporate philosophy that seamlessly blended profit and purpose. As he observed just a year before his death, "In a free enterprise, the community is not just another stakeholder in business, but is in fact the very purpose of its existence."[2] Generations of Tata family members have followed these foundational principles ever since, demonstrating the unique capacity for enterprising families to drive long-term, systems-level change.

Toward the end of his life, Jamsetji articulated four diverse goals he believed would help India become an independent nation. First, he wanted to create a national iron and steel business, laying the foundation of heavy industry. Second, he advocated for launching a world-class Indian university, providing the scientific and technical training necessary to power economic progress. Third, he wanted to encourage greater tourism by building world-class luxury hotels. Finally, he desired to bring clean, low-cost hydroelectric power to Bombay, to protect the city's notoriously poor air quality, regardless of the cost.

By the time of his death in 1904, Jamsetji had succeeded at only one of these diverse and ambitious goals, having launched the Taj Mahal Palace, a luxury hotel, in Bombay.[3] Even still, it was an impressive achievement. When it first opened, it was the only hotel in India featuring electric lighting and elevators. It was also one of the few hotels in the city where Indians were treated as first-class citizens—a rare experience under British colonial rule, and an inspiration for the push toward Indian independence that followed.

Picking up the mantle of his father's ambitious nation-building agenda, Jamsetji's son Dorabji took over the business in 1904. In less than a decade, the former athlete and journalist completed the other three pillars of his father's unfulfilled mission. While managing the rest of the Tata Group's businesses and philanthropic activities, Dorabji and his brother Ratanji launched the Tata Iron and Steel Company in 1907. The company has since become one of the top ten steel manufacturers in the world, supplying the raw materials to fuel India's industrialization for over a century.

A few years later, Dorabji deployed 7,000 loyal Tata workers to help build the Tata Hydroelectric Company, leveraging his father's diverse relationships to procure pipelines from Germany, waterwheels from Switzerland, generators from the United States, and cables from England. Once the first generator began operations in 1910, it had an immediate impact on air quality in Bombay and increased the reliability of electricity supply to the city's existing coal-powered textile mills. It also generated a handsome profit for the growing Tata conglomerate, one which was uncorrelated with the performance of its manufacturing business by design.

The very next year, Dorabji launched the Indian Institute of Science (IISc), fueled by his father's domestic and international connections, and funded by his philanthropic endowments. Today, the IISc is regarded as the "MIT of India," supplying both the company and the country with some of the most skilled engineers and scientists in the world.

But Dorabji's entrepreneurial aspirations and exploits went far beyond his father's vision. Inspired by Jamsetji's commitment to stimulating the Indian economy through a diverse mix of industrial and philanthropic entities, he eventually launched a cement manufacturing division, a construction company, a life insurance firm, and a variety of consumer goods businesses.

Over the years, this diversity helped to insulate the group's portfolio of activities against a variety of macroeconomic and political headwinds, particularly those that emerged during and after World War I. No company is completely immune from these shocks and crises, but having a diverse portfolio of activity certainly diminishes the risk of total organizational collapse. For instance, Tata Steel nearly went bankrupt in 1924, after a string of operational and supply chain challenges, natural disasters, and geopolitical tensions forced the company to suspend dividends for twelve out of thirteen years. But Dorabji was able to rescue the struggling division, in part by reallocating surplus resources from elsewhere in Tata's diversified commercial empire.

When Dorabji died in 1931, he was succeeded by his cousin Nowroji Saklatwala, who served as Tata's chairman from 1932 until his sudden death in 1938. Saklatwala navigated the company through the difficult years of the Great Depression, maintaining stability and ensuring growth despite a prolonged era of global turmoil. He consolidated the group's many disparate businesses under a single Tata umbrella with a renewed focus on synergy and efficiency. Like Grupo Arcor, this strategic simplification further strengthened the company's core competitive advantages—particularly vertical integration—and positioned the streamlined portfolio for continued success.

After Saklatwala's untimely death in 1938, thirty-four-year-old Jehangir Ratanji Dadabhoy Tata, known universally as JRD, was appointed chairman, setting in motion another explosive era of diversity and growth. JRD's father was Jamsetji's first cousin, but his mother was French, and he had been born in Paris. As a result, his educational background and worldview were perhaps even more international than any of his predecessors'—by the time he took the helm of the company he had already spent time in London, Tokyo, and Bombay. Throughout his career, he had proven himself to be hardworking, shrewd, and willing to delegate responsibility to those he felt knew more than he did—precisely the type of leadership necessary in a sprawling conglomerate. When he assumed leadership of the Tata Group in 1938, there were fourteen businesses and assets of US$101 million. When he retired in 1991, there were ninety-five businesses with assets of more than US$5 billion.[4]

At the start of his career, much like Saklatwala, JRD was focused on steering the firm through a period of great instability. The fight for India's independence and the end of the British Raj in 1947 forced the Indian business community to learn to navigate a new strategic landscape. The independent Indian government placed a strong focus on economic nationalism and managed industrial policy. As a result, forging a healthy alliance with the government and aligning with national priorities (or political symbiosis) became table stakes for all private business activity.

Generations of Tata family members had excelled at the art and science of government relations. Even still, Tata's airline and insurance businesses were both nationalized during this era, sending a powerful signal to the business community that no corner of the economy would be safe from government influence. New legislation in 1970 made matters worse, requiring all subsidiaries of large corporations to be independent entities controlled by their own boards. For an enterprise like Tata, with fifty manufacturing companies and a hundred associate companies, that meant the group board would lose explicit control.

Fortunately, JRD had already delegated a great deal of authority to talented and loyal executives across the group's portfolio. Much like Mitsui and the other disintegrated *zaibatsu* in Japan after World War II, these disintegrated businesses were able to leverage their long traditions of horizontal collaboration and coordination, even without any formal legal or governance ties.

When JRD finally retired in 1991, after more than fifty years heading the company, he was succeeded by Ratan Tata, whose father had been adopted into the Tata family, and whose mother was one of Jamsetji's nieces. Following in the footsteps of Tata's many iconic leaders, Ratan also spent his formative years studying abroad, accumulating a diverse range of experiences before returning to lead the family business, including an architecture degree from Cornell University. JRD had proven the importance

Growth and Diversity at the Tata Group

From humble roots to a diversified conglomerate

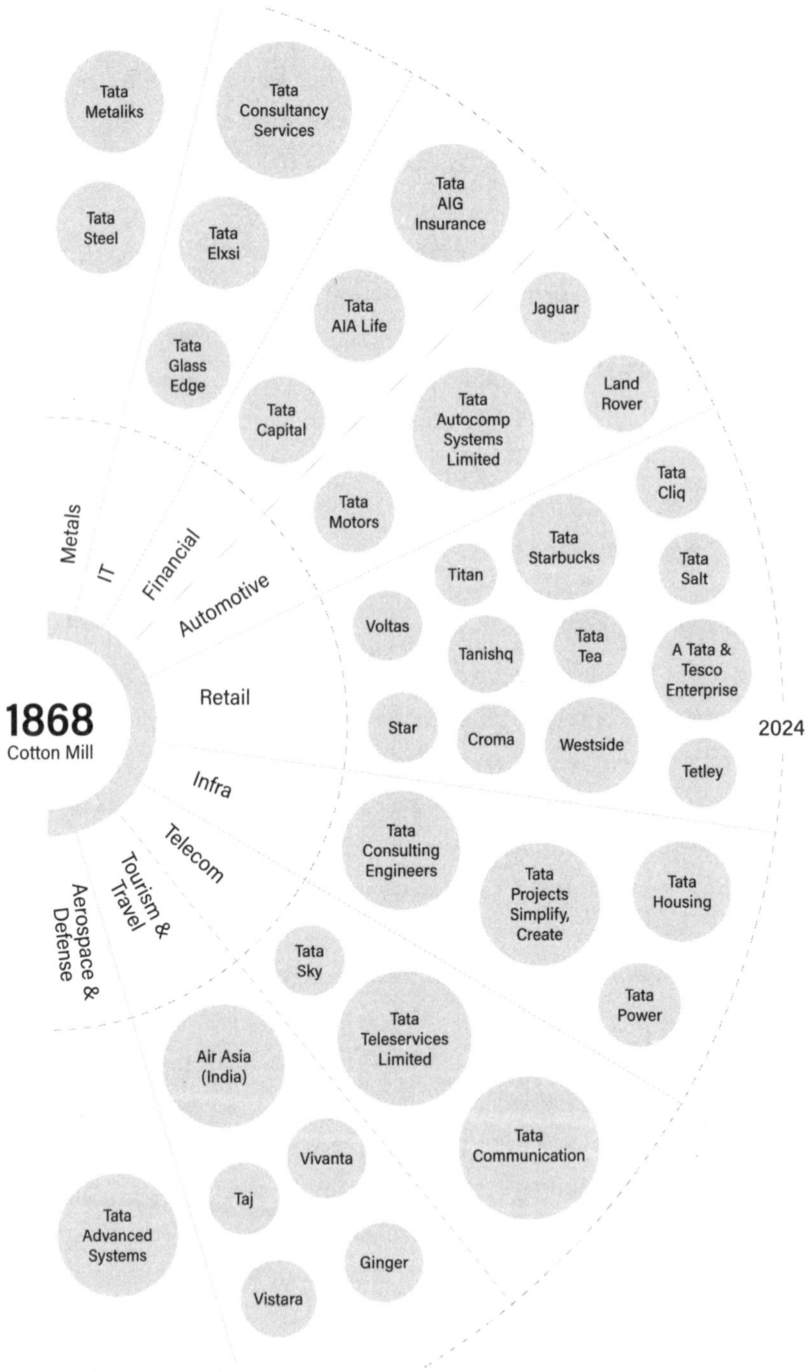

Source: Tata Group.

of agility by establishing a decentralized system of governance under intrusive government oversight. But by the 1990s the operational environment in India was fundamentally different, and Ratan recognized the need to pivot.

After the fall of the Soviet Union, economic liberalization returned to India for the first time in nearly half a century. As the world opened back up to India, and India opened up to the world, the globe-trotting Ratan embraced the next wave of growth and diversity for the Tata Group through a portfolio of new modular partnerships. Tata's insurance arm began collaborating with the US giant American International Group (AIG), while Tata Motors began a partnership with the German automaker Daimler, and Tata Consumer Products began a joint venture with Starbucks. Ratan also initiated a string of acquisitions, increasing Tata's stake in a number of firms, including the Tetley Group, the steelmakers Cronus and NatSteel, General Chemical Corporation, and the British premium automaker Jaguar Land Rover Limited.

Today, the Mumbai-based conglomerate is led by lifelong employee and non-family executive Natarajan Chandrasekaran. The Tata Group is one of the largest single contributors to India's GDP, generating annual revenues of over US$150 billion and collectively employing more than one million people.[5] In many ways, Tata's commitment to diversity has been a core strength throughout its long history. From Jamsetji's earliest exposure to a diverse array of global ideas, technologies, and perspectives to the various nation-building efforts of his son Dorabji, the assorted businesses launched by Saklatwala and JRD, and the many global partnerships and portfolios led by Ratan in the modern era, the Tata family enterprise has survived and thrived by tapping an incredible breadth of resources and inspiration. They have also deployed their entrepreneurial energies in service of a broad cross-section of stakeholders, understanding that the strength and innovation needed to overcome turmoil derive not from following conventional wisdom but rather from divergent thinking.

To be clear, we're not suggesting that diversity is destiny, or that more is always better. Diversity is neither a guarantee of long-term gain nor a perfect hedge against short-term pain.[6] However, when leaders are more intentional about integrating a diversity lens into their strategic filters for opportunities and risk—within their business portfolios and leadership teams, and among suppliers, customers, products, and markets—it can help to elevate the quality of decision-making and diminish the threat of systemic collapse.

EGGS AND BASKETS

The incredible longevity and success of the Tata Group is a useful reminder of two related but independent concepts that we'll now explore in greater detail. The first is the idea of *diversification*, which has been an integral strategy for survival and growth since prehistoric times. The second is *diversity*, which has long been prized in nature, but is less prevalent in business than we might expect.

As we learned in our brief tour of the history of capitalism, agricultural societies have dominated our economic landscape for more than ten thousand years. Initially, these farming settlements were highly vulnerable to a range of environmental shocks, including droughts, floods, and pest infestations, any one of which could result in devastating famines and economic ruin. The absence of advanced technologies for storage, transportation, and communication further exacerbated these risks, as communities had limited means to warehouse their surpluses or seek help from neighboring regions. The failure of a single crop could spell disaster, leading to malnutrition, social unrest, and even the collapse of entire communities. The ancient wisdom of agricultural diversification wasn't just a matter of increasing crop yields, but a crucial strategy for survival in a hostile environment.

The earliest recorded evidence of strategic crop rotation comes from the Middle East, in civilizations such as the Sumerians and Babylonians around 6000 BCE. After generations of alternating between periods of feast and famine, their leaders discovered that planting certain crops in rotation helped to prevent soil depletion and control devastating pests. Though they didn't fully grasp the underlying chemistry, the outcomes were undeniable. As a result, these practices were quickly adopted across many prehistoric societies, supporting humanity's earliest growth and territorial expansion.[7]

Such ancient wisdom eventually transcended agriculture and entered the world of commerce, initially via trade. As we learned in Chapter 3, early merchants who invested all of their capital in a single voyage could be wiped out completely by storms, pirates, robbers, or simple misfortune. This was an inescapable risk for those striking out on their first entrepreneurial adventure. Seasoned merchants understood the wisdom of spreading out their risk across a diverse mix of caravans, captains, and cargoes.

Later, Dutch and British innovations, such as joint-stock companies, corporate bonds, and securities markets, allowed merchants and financiers to pool resources and spread risks across a variety of business ventures. These early frontier capitalists understood how uncertain the future could be, and how speculative it was to put all of their eggs in one basket, without any certainty about which ventures would ultimately succeed or fail. Through diversification, investors could reduce their exposure to any one asset or industry, and increase their chances of growing their capital over time.

Interestingly, the concept of "eggs" and "baskets" made its way into popular culture around that same time. The idiom first appeared in the writings of the Spanish novelist Miguel de Cervantes in his masterpiece of romantic fiction, *Don Quixote*. In the novel, first published in 1605, the errant knight's pragmatic sidekick, Sancho Panza, wisely cautions his master "not [to] venture all his eggs in one basket." Quixote's obsession with chivalric quests often required putting all of their efforts, time, and resources into pursuing singular and unrealistic outcomes, such as slaying imaginary giants. Panza's wisdom, an attempted foil to Quixote's boundless idealism and recklessness, provides a timeless and cautionary tale not to stake everything on a single enterprise.

Despite its popularity at the time of publication—and its intuitive wisdom—this pragmatic idiom did little to discourage illogical speculation in any number of investment bubbles that emerged during that period, from Dutch tulips to colonial trading companies.[8] However, these euphoric episodes galvanized generations of investors in their understanding that diversification reliably increases risk-adjusted returns, and it quickly became the bedrock principle of early portfolio theory.

Over the centuries that followed, as frontier economies evolved into emerging and advanced economies, the applications of diversification became ever more sophisticated. Institutional developments and technological advancements made it easier to invest in an increasing array of entrepreneurial ventures and asset classes, each with its own unique profile of risk and reward. Ever since, choosing among these options has become the defining challenge of business leaders and asset managers.

The Nobel Prize–winning economist Harry Markowitz was among the first to conceptualize a strategy for how to deal with this growing paradox of choice, and is often credited with saying that diversification is "the only free lunch in finance." With the Great Depression—and the decade-long stock rout it produced—still resonant in the minds of investors, Markowitz outlined his early vision of Modern Portfolio Theory (MPT) in 1952.[9] In the paper outlining the theory, he proved mathematically that investing in a range of assets can achieve a desired level of expected return with less exposure to volatility and risk. This strategy involves diversification, but goes well beyond drawing random cards from a deck. MPT specifically requires the selection of assets based on how their valuations moved *in relation to one another*. In other words, it's not enough to randomly combine a bunch of risky and less risky securities in a portfolio—the correlation *between* them must also be carefully considered.

Half a century later, this logic seems obvious. But at the time it was like financial alchemy—the modern equivalent of crop rotation miraculously increasing both the quantity and predictability of agricultural yields. In the decades that followed, legendary management scholars such as Peter Drucker and Michael Porter would begin to extend this same logic beyond investment portfolios and into operating businesses themselves. They identified diversification as a key strategy both for innovation and growth, specifically encouraging companies to pursue *correlated* investments—that is, entering into businesses that built on existing core competencies, leveraging existing knowledge and resources, and moving up and down their existing value chains. These actions are often driven by the opportunity to generate material "synergies"—that is, the enhanced efficiency, profitability, and competitive advantage achieved when different components of a diversified portfolio or business complement each other, thereby increasing overall value and performance.

Diversification can also be deliberately focused on *uncorrelated* assets, which don't create any material operational synergies, though they can still increase risk-adjusted returns. These investments most often take the form of alternative assets like real estate and private equity; early-stage startups (sometimes pioneered by next-generation members of the family); existing businesses in need of outside capital; or those that stand to benefit from longer-term geopolitical and macroeconomic trends.

Warren Buffett and Charlie Munger mastered the art and science of this approach within their investment conglomerate Berkshire Hathaway, spawning a generation of institutional copycats. Though there is little correlation or strategic synergy between railways, jewelry, ice cream, and batteries, the whole diversified portfolio is well insulated against catastrophic threats. Like secondary crops immune to invading pests, Berkshire's uncorrelated assets serve as a natural hedge.

Whether deployed on a farmer's field, at an operating company, or in an investment portfolio, the stabilizing effects of diversification are both intuitive and inescapable. Particularly in moments of greater volatility and acute crisis, it provides a time-tested path to greater stability and long-term performance and should be considered part of any leader's strategic toolkit.

It is hardly coincidental that many of the most successful and enduring enterprises in frontier markets are diversified family businesses and family offices. Their structure enables familial engagement across a diverse array of governance and operational roles, allowing the family to provide direction, accountability, and control of portfolios that can grow in complexity over generations. Naturally, the thoughtful curation of their engagement is critical—to ensure that those from the family who hold positions of leadership have the appropriate skills and experience to perform their responsibilities effectively and in accordance with the values and objectives of the family and their strategic aspirations for the enterprise.

THE WISDOM OF (DIVERSE) CROWDS

If the narrow concept of *diversification* is about maximizing risk-adjusted returns along an investment frontier, the broader concept of *diversity* is about maximizing perspectives along a decision-making frontier. When deployed effectively, both strategies can produce superior outcomes. Like individual stocks in a portfolio, every individual in an organization brings certain benefits and carries certain biases. But when diverse communities are brought together in service of a common mission, leaders have access to a broader array of perspectives, increasing the resources available to support strategic deliberation.

This simple observation—that *social diversity* breeds better collective fitness—has deep evolutionary origins, and helped our ancestors to cope with chronic resource scarcity and existential threat.

For starters, social diversity has been linked to greater cognitive capacity, because the need to interact with a broader array of individuals requires more advanced cognitive and emotional skills. The British anthropologist Robin Dunbar has observed a strong positive correlation between the size of the neocortex among primates and the ability to process complex social information—which naturally allows for larger and more stable social groups. As a result, over generations of selective reinforcement, the brains of our *Homo sapiens* ancestors continued to grow—outpacing Neanderthals and other early hominin species. This likely supported the later development of language and symbolic thinking, more advanced tools and hunting techniques, and eventually the domestication of crops and animals within our earliest civilizations—precisely the conditions that unfolded in the Indus River Valley several thousand years ago.

Greater social diversity has also been associated with increased collective fitness. Behavioral diversity enables the specialization of labor in complex tribes, with some individuals prone to grooming and raising children, others to hunting or foraging, and still others in sentinel behavior—keeping watch for predators and threats. Larger group sizes also minimize the risks of inbreeding, as diverse groups provide more raw material for natural selection to work its evolutionary magic. Over time, genetic diversity produces a greater range of physiological and behavioral traits within a population, increasing its resistance to diseases as well as its capacity to process a wider variety of food sources. For our ancestors, a diverse diet proved essential for collective survival under conditions of perpetual scarcity.

This compelling evidence presents us with a natural paradox. Social diversity was clearly a major force in the evolution of early human societies. In many ways, life as we know it today would not have been possible without it. Moreover, research increasingly suggests that, when applied to business practices, both greater *inherent* diversity (e.g., race and gender) and broader *acquired* diversity (e.g., skills, experience, and cultural fluency) are associated with greater growth in market share, net operating margins, and profitability.[10]

Yet despite all the research—and plenty of lip service from public- and private-sector leaders—diversity in the C-suite and in the boardroom is still the exception to the rule. For instance, despite representing roughly half the population, women make up only about 5 percent of CEOs

Diversity Comes in Many Forms

Most organizations focus on only one or two, and miss out on the "wisdom of crowds"

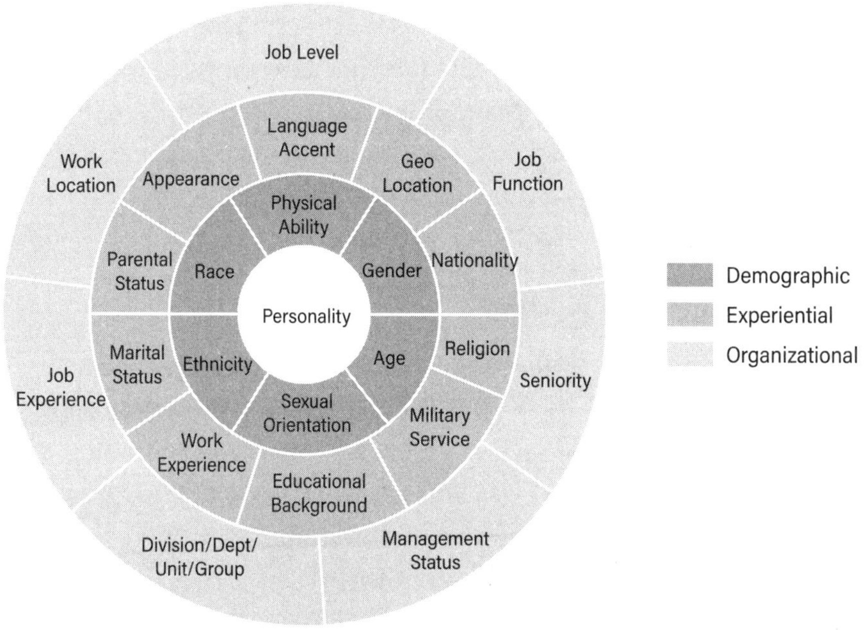

Source: Adapted from *Diverse Teams at Work: Capitalizing on the Power of Diversity* by Gardenswartz and Rowe (1994)

worldwide.[11] At the board level, the data is just as discouraging, with women currently holding a little less than a quarter of all corporate board seats.[12] Though the data is more scarce for racial and ethnic diversity, it's safe to assume the proportions are even lower.

Here again, enterprising families have a natural advantage over businesses that are not family-controlled. For instance, wives, daughters, and sisters can have a greater influence, both formally and informally, on the vision, values, and strategic intent of family-owned organizations.[13] Younger family members can also have greater influence, both formally and informally, on the diversity of perspectives informing decision-making throughout the enterprise—a unique asset that will only grow as the pace of change in the economy continues to accelerate.

However, just because families have access to these diverse resources doesn't mean they always take advantage of them. A 2023 study by PwC reported that only 10 percent of family businesses globally have a clear commitment to advancing diversity within their organizations.[14] As with non-family-owned companies, they can have entrenched cultural norms that powerfully influence the openness to diverse points of view—particularly within the traditional and patriarchal societies more common among emerging and frontier economies. But enterprising families also have the unique authority and flexibility to embrace greater diversity, often in defiance of these cultural norms. Many of the leaders we've met understand this intuitively, and we believe their diversity will become an increasingly valuable asset in the turbulent years to come.

DIVERSITY AND RESILIENCE

With any systems-level transformation, there are always competing forces at play—some in favor of change, and others resisting it. As we've learned from movements such as affirmative action, which gained momentum in advanced economies over the past half-century, we can only force greater diversity on human systems up to a point. Efforts to rebalance the scales, however just and well-intended, also galvanize resistance from those subgroups that are threatened by change. The challenge is even greater in emerging and frontier economies, where institutions are more fragile, and where laws and norms around distributive justice are not well established or enforceable.

Wherever they operate, those leaders and organizations willing to brush against the grain of history will help to prove the business case, blazing a path for others to follow. Supported by a growing body of research, their superior performance in good times, and greater resilience in tough times, can encourage other reluctant leaders around the world to at least reconsider the benefits of nurturing greater "cognitive diversity," even if the process of strategic and cultural change is hard or temporarily destabilizing. If nothing else, the business case alone is quite compelling.

Consider that diverse product development teams are more likely than homogeneous ones to design solutions that appeal to a broad array of customers. Diverse marketing teams are more likely to develop communications campaigns that reach a wider audience. Diverse sales teams are more likely to build stronger and more durable relationships with a large customer base. Perhaps most importantly, diverse leadership teams are more likely to make better decisions, integrating the interests and perspectives of a broader array of stakeholders, than less diverse ones.[15]

Aristotle once argued that "education is an ornament in prosperity and a refuge in adversity."[16] The same is true for diversity. Progressive organizations in stable environments can certainly benefit from greater creativity, innovation, and employee well-being. But the New Age of Uncertainty will increasingly reveal the fragility of more conventional organizational monocultures—and reinforce the benefits of integrating heterogeneous perspectives into risk management and crisis response.

Leaders who are able to build diversity into the very fabric of their organizations—from their front lines to their boardrooms—will be more capable of withstanding the broad array of threats that are likely to emerge in the years and decades ahead. Like healthy reefs and forests, diverse portfolios are better insulated against inflationary shocks, supply chain distress, currency fluctuations, changing tastes and preferences, and shifting industrial policies—not to mention wars and natural disasters. Enterprising families that embrace diversity are consequently better prepared for both feast and famine.[17]

Recall Carvajal's early experience operating throughout Latin America across decades of political and economic instability. When some of their biggest markets were derailed by regime change—for instance, with the rise of Hugo Chavez in Venezuela—it cost the company hundreds of millions in revenues. However, other markets, such as Mexico, were growing quickly at the time, insulating the company from catastrophic losses. Similarly, when their yellow pages business—which represented roughly a third of overall revenues by the end of the twentieth century—was replaced virtually overnight by Google, it represented a major blow to the company's operating portfolio. However, the rise of digital search also coincided with the dawn of digital commerce, which opened up huge opportunities for the company's packaging business. Products of all shapes and sizes were now being shipped by Amazon and other retailers directly to consumers, in boxes designed and manufactured by Carvajal. The business's extensive growth in this area more than offset losses from the struggling publishing division.

As we've argued throughout the book, tomorrow's leaders will need to navigate increasingly turbulent environments characterized by rapid technological changes, increased competition, inflationary pressures, and greater regulatory oversight. They will also be more exposed to an array of global uncertainties, including the kinds of protracted wars and pandemics that until recently we assumed were mostly confined to the history books. Under these new and more challenging conditions, we believe diversity will be a crucial consideration for long-term survival and resilience. It not only acts like a natural hedge against both systemic and idiosyncratic risks, but can also support growth and prosperity.

The Tata Group once again presents us with an inspirational example. Having witnessed the dangers of economic monoculture fostered by the British Raj, and the many benefits of the innovative ideas springing up across the emerging economies of the commonwealth, Jamsetji Tata built diversity explicitly into his business plans. This was perhaps best exemplified by his recommended design for the new industrial city of Jamshedpur, which would host the company's first steel plant. In a letter to his son, Jamsetji stated that the urban plan must include "wide streets planted with shady trees, every other of a quick-growing variety. Be sure that there is plenty of space for lawns and gardens. Reserve large areas for football, hockey and parks. Earmark areas for Hindu Temples, Mohammedan Mosques and Christian Churches."[18]

As a testament to the resilience fostered by this explicit commitment to diversity, when the government attempted to nationalize Tata Steel in the 1970s—not once, but twice—it was rebuffed by massive protests from the company's loyal workers and the community's grateful citizens.

Like so many of Tata's innovative ideas, Jamsetji's recognition of the benefits of both diversification and diversity were ahead of his time. They helped the company overcome regime changes, economic depressions, expropriations, restrictive industrial policies, and even challenges with governance and succession planning. That said, what worked for Jamsetji and his descendants in particular countries, within particular industries, and at particular points in history is not a guaranteed recipe for survival and success. As with the other stabilizing strategies, those looking to deploy diversity strategically need to carefully consider their context before diving in.

CONDITIONS AND CAVEATS

There are several structural reasons why conglomerates are more common and enduring in emerging and frontier economies than in advanced economies. As we learned in Part 1, developing countries tend to have weaker antitrust frameworks, which allows for greater business expansion across sectors without as much regulatory scrutiny. These economies are also prone to higher systemic volatility, which incentivizes companies to enter a variety of industries as a hedge against sector-specific risks. Larger balance sheets and diversified income streams are naturally more attractive to lenders and investors, allowing them to seek funding more easily and on better terms. This size also provides greater economies of scale, helpful for securing resources more efficiently and reliably. Finally, it's worth noting that enterprising families have a particular advantage further down the Hierarchy of Stability, since their familial resources, networks, and higher levels of interpersonal trust help them to source opportunities and coordinate larger portfolios.

The story is quite different in advanced economies, where prevailing wisdom about the benefits and challenges of building diversified enterprises has ebbed and flowed. For instance, in the immediate aftermath of World War II, American conglomerates such as General Electric and

Westinghouse, and European peers including Siemens and Philips, remained some of the primary drivers of economic growth. New markets were more likely to be developed by these large incumbents, given their deep pockets, experienced leadership teams, and strong connections to consumers, suppliers, distributors, and governments.

However, after decades of unbridled growth and limited competition, many of these diversified holding companies resembled Frankenstein's monster, with parts cobbled together haphazardly and few natural synergies between them. By the 1980s, the conglomerate fell out of favor, spurred by shifting industrial policies that encouraged greater competition, coupled with rising shareholder activism on Wall Street and beyond. This renewed interest in efficiency accompanied a growing belief that organizations should focus only on what they do best (differentiation), and either divest (simplification) or partner (modularity) in areas where they lacked distinct expertise or competitive advantage.

The Conglomerate Discount Persists over Time

Though diversity still generates enduring value beyond financial performance

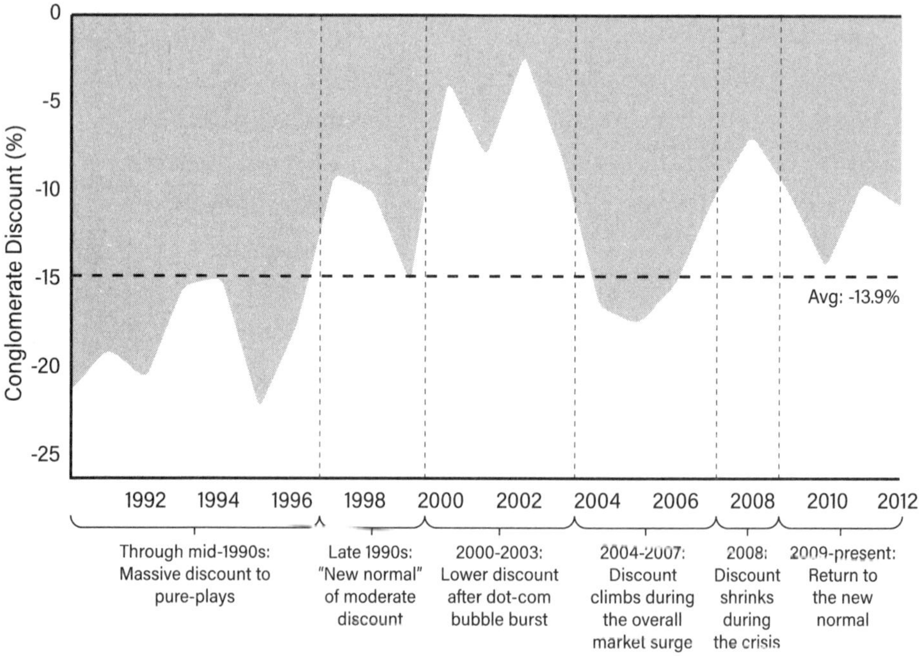

Source: BCG and HHL Graduate School of Management analysis, "Invest Wisely, Divest Strategically" by Kengelbach et al. (2014).

Research has since revealed that portfolio builders during those years were less effective at allocating capital—chronically overinvesting in stable or stagnant divisions, and underinvesting in growing business units—and often traded at discounts of between 5 percent and 15 percent relative to their more focused competitors.[19] Economies of *scope* gave way to economies of *scale*, resulting in a wave of corporate disintegrations and spin-offs as well as the rise of "pure-play" companies, from Microsoft and Home Depot to Starbucks and PetSmart, each one focused on market leadership in a single product or industry.

Over the past quarter century, these new single-industry titans amassed fortress balance sheets, allowing them to experiment with a new form of diversification—targeting related markets and projects. Consider companies like Cisco Systems, which focused narrowly on networking hardware such as switches and routers before expanding into related software, telecommunications equipment, and cybersecurity solutions. Or Amazon, which began in 1994 as an online bookstore before diversifying into other related retail categories, including electronics, music, and clothing during the late 1990s—en route to becoming one of the dominant retailers of everything worldwide. What *related diversification* lacked, however, was the same level of insulation from industry-specific threats. Disruptions in the tech sector could easily affect sales at many of Cisco's divisions simultaneously, exposing the entire enterprise to higher levels of catastrophic risk or loss.

As a result, a more nuanced view of the benefits and dangers of diversification has emerged. On one hand, rapid technological change and increased competition have encouraged companies to focus on their core competencies and prioritize operational excellence.[20] On the other hand, rising uncertainty and increasing external shocks have made the resilience of diverse portfolios more appealing once again. So as with most things in life, we advise leaders to constantly scan their environment, then consider deploying diversification in moderation. Too little leaves an organization susceptible both to targeted disruptions and systems-level shocks. Too much creates distracting complexity and threatens efficiency. Discovering the Goldilocks scenario consequently becomes a strategic imperative.

Additionally, families need to monitor and optimize the levels of cognitive diversity within their enterprises—particularly among senior leadership teams. While it may seem obvious, operating a company laser focused on a narrow range of products and markets is fundamentally different from operating a large portfolio of related businesses. The former requires focused specialists, and the latter requires nimble generalists. In both situations, leaders should be intentional about utilizing diversity throughout their organizations in order to support the type of creativity and complex problem solving that will drive survival and success in the turbulent years that lie ahead.

Finally, as we bring Part 2 of the book to a close, it's worth noting that diversity is rarely a strategy that is deployed on its own. Companies don't often begin their entrepreneurial journeys by seeding multiple business ideas simultaneously. As an old investing adage goes, "You get rich through concentration. You stay rich through diversification." Generally speaking, we would agree—with one obvious caveat: diversification alone is not enough.

It will take more than a portfolio of diverse assets and talent to achieve enduring success. As Carvajal, Tata, and others have shown, it will require a diverse portfolio of stabilizing strategies like the ones we've featured throughout Part 2. Importantly, it will also require a systematic framework for deploying them effectively and dynamically over time—such as the one we'll introduce next in Part 3.

KEY INSIGHTS

- The enduring benefits of diversity have long historical roots in ancient farming practices such as crop rotation, which eventually transcended agriculture and became a cornerstone of commercial activity.
- The wisdom of not putting all your eggs in one basket goes back centuries and applies both to business (e.g., having a variety of products and services) and to investments (e.g., spreading your money across different asset classes).
- The strategic value of diversity also extends beyond products and markets and into the realm of ideas and decision-making.
- The Tata Group has been a prime example of how diversity can fuel a business's enduring success—the company embraced

diversity systematically, both with respect to its portfolio of businesses and in its approach to stakeholder relations.

- Businesses that embrace a diversity of thought are better equipped to tackle complex problems and make sound decisions, because they can take advantage of a wider range of perspectives that can lead to a more nuanced understanding of challenges and opportunities.
- Despite these obvious advantages, women and minorities are still underrepresented in C-suite roles and on boards around the world.
- Some enterprising families are more willing to challenge the status quo than others, and to leverage their inherent diversity—encouraging wives, daughters, and younger generations to bring fresh perspectives to the table—although entrenched cultural norms and a resistance to change can also be obstacles.
- By building a wider range of perspectives and experiences, these companies are better equipped for problem solving under both stable and uncertain conditions, and are consequently better equipped to navigate turbulent times.

PART 3
NURTURING A FRONTIER MINDSET

The constant lesson of history is the dominant role played by surprise. Just when we are most comfortable with an environment and come to believe we finally understand it, the ground shifts under our feet.

—Peter Bernstein

Early on the morning of February 24, 2022, after weeks of speculation and geopolitical brinkmanship, news began to break that Russian troops had breached Ukraine's eastern border. Many were awakened by the sounds of explosions and sirens as airstrikes targeted military installations, airfields, and critical infrastructure. Panic buying ensued as frightened citizens rushed to stock up on food, water, medicines, and other essential supplies. Long lines formed at gas stations, and many families prepared to leave their homes before the fighting arrived on their doorstep.

As we've argued throughout this book, operating a large and complex business is challenging even in the best of times. But layer in an unexpected military invasion—or a natural disaster, a coup, or an economic crisis—and even the most sophisticated policies, processes, structures, and systems will provide limited stability or direction. Nor are they particularly useful for spotting a crisis before it begins.

Those who have lived through war know this intuitively. Geopolitical tensions are rarely conjured out of nothing—remember Clausewitz's observation that war is an extension of politics by other means. But few heed these inconvenient truths until the bombs begin to fall.

For those unable or unwilling to migrate to safety, life must go on—though it obviously looks and functions much differently in a war zone. As the situation escalates, sleep is increasingly disrupted by bomb blasts and sirens. Daily commutes are hampered by emergency vehicles and security checkpoints. Grocery shelves remain bare for even the most common of staples. Banks restrict access to cash in an effort to stave off broader economic collapse. Pervasive fear and uncertainty strain family dynamics, often leading to widespread anxiety and depression. By some estimates, up to 90 percent of Ukrainians today exhibit symptoms of post-traumatic stress disorder (PTSD). One can only imagine a similar impact on Gaza and Israel, not to mention other countries, including Sudan, Yemen, Honduras, and Ecuador, where civil wars and gang violence are also having a destabilizing effect.

Commercial life under these conditions is anything but textbook. Many businesses, if they aren't destroyed or repurposed for the war effort, are shut down indefinitely as a result of rampant insecurity. Those that remain open often struggle to secure the key resources, able-bodied workers, and external capital needed to continue to service the needs of the nation, as they did with great pride and profit just a few days before.

One Ukrainian entrepreneur, the head of a software engineering firm in Lviv, captured the dilemma beautifully: "Nowadays, we call it 'war-life balance'—when missiles are flying overhead; people are working from bomb shelters, basements, and bathrooms; we have no power, no internet; schools are closed, so kids are with us at home.... [T]he stress and anxiety are intense. But still, we have to find moments of joy. We have to find some way to balance work, volunteering, helping the military, and caring for family."[1]

That term—"war-life balance"—says it all. The work of securing the country's political and economic integrity is a shared responsibility, one that forces difficult trade-offs between our personal priorities, our families' needs, our businesses' success, and our countries' future. Risk and uncertainty reach new and elevated heights, often remaining at these levels indefinitely. Existing plans are rendered obsolete, forcing leaders to reconsider even the most foundational elements of their organizational strategy and design.

In these moments, it is critical to focus on the essentials, because you can only learn from the crises you survive. But it's also important to recognize that commercial life is still possible—and in fact is quite essential—even in the face of open war.

Enterprising families around the world have proven countless times throughout history that moments like these are not death sentences, and can even serve as catalysts for innovation and growth. Those willing and able to adapt to the circumstances can contribute to community resilience and national defense while still earning a generous profit (think symbiosis).

Much like American and British businesses during World Wars I and II, in the weeks following the first wave of the Russian invasion many Ukrainian businesses quickly pivoted. Textile manufacturers began producing military uniforms and protective equipment, while food and beverage companies started canning goods and other nonperishable items, both for soldiers on the front lines and for citizens under siege (think differentiation). Still others—particularly in the technology sector—expanded their operations into new markets beyond the conflict zones (think migration), leveraging the country's pro-Western culture and well-educated labor force.

Recall the case of family-owned Rozetka, Ukraine's largest online retailer. The company actually expanded its operations and logistics capabilities at the onset of the war with Russia—redistributing its supply chains among coalition partners while expanding support for war-torn communities (think redundancy and diversity). As one local venture capitalist remarked, "It's a chance to push our country forward, to invest in our country, to make sure that when this war ends, we're poised to join the ranks of truly developed nations."[2]

In the face of any crisis, a healthy war-life mix of endurance and hope is critical. Thriving under these conditions requires us to channel our fear and frustration productively. As the French novelist Marcel Proust once observed, "Happiness is beneficial for the body, but it is grief that develops the powers of the mind."[3] Throughout Part 2, we saw how some of the most innovative organizational adaptations emerge when families are faced with sustained adversity—from rebellions and hyperinflation to earthquakes and expropriation. That said, investing in stability doesn't come naturally to everyone, particularly when we're facing a new and unfamiliar crisis for the first time.

So our goal in Part 3 of the book is to introduce a simple framework that any organization can use to apply these stabilizing strategies in the wild—or to nurture a frontier mindset, if you will. We'll begin in Chapter 12 by laying out a model for understanding the general patterns of crises—how they emerge, how they evolve, how to deploy the stabilizing strategies, and how to avoid common pitfalls along the journey. Then, in Chapter 13, we'll examine how navigating crises is related to the broader practice of risk management—which is essentially about crisis prevention and recovery. Finally, in Chapter 14, we'll frame our most important lessons for leaders and forward-thinkers, providing a brief glimpse into how we're helping our clients, our global team, and our own families to prepare for and thrive in the turbulent times ahead.

12
NAVIGATING CRISES WITH CONFIDENCE

In the midst of chaos, I found there was, within me, an invincible calm.... Within me, there's something stronger—something better, pushing right back.

—**Albert Camus**

As humans we all have an instinctive sense of "crisis," helping us recognize danger and leading us to safety. For millions of years, existential threats loomed around every corner, altering the way our brains and bodies processed the many threats scattered throughout the prehistoric world. Once we began to gather in settlements and pool resources in greater numbers, our environment stopped pushing against us with quite the same force. Or perhaps, more accurately, as a species we learned to "push right back."

Though most humans are no longer at risk of predation or starvation, abrupt shocks are still an inescapable part of the human experience—from the sudden loss of a loved one to a freak accident or a financial catastrophe. As a result, we all harbor our own unique sense about how they rise and fall. The more crises we survive during our lifetimes, the more familiar they become. Much like a vaccine, some exposure inoculates us to their most destabilizing effects and helps us to respond and recover more quickly when they inevitably arise.[1]

As we studied crises from around the world and across time to better understand these phenomena, we quickly recognized that they all follow the same basic pattern. Like every good story, they have a distinct beginning, middle, and end—and as with the best stories, you often can't tell which part you're in until it's almost over. Yet whether it's Venezuela's decades-long experience with kleptocracy, Zimbabwe's twenty-six-month battle with hyperinflation, or Europe's weeks-long air travel disruption from an Icelandic ash cloud—the basic pattern is remarkably consistent, and therefore reasonably predictable.

What follows is an illustrative example. Initially, conditions are quite stable and profitable, with commercial, political, and social systems settled into a form of punctuated equilibrium. Then an event—such as a pandemic, a financial downturn, a leadership scandal, or a cybersecurity breach—triggers a spike in risk, stirring up these interconnected systems, at which point all hell breaks loose (Phase 1). Once the full extent of the crisis is revealed, an extended period of elevated volatility and uncertainty ensues,

Understanding the Typical Pattern of Crises

History may not repeat, but it certainly rhymes

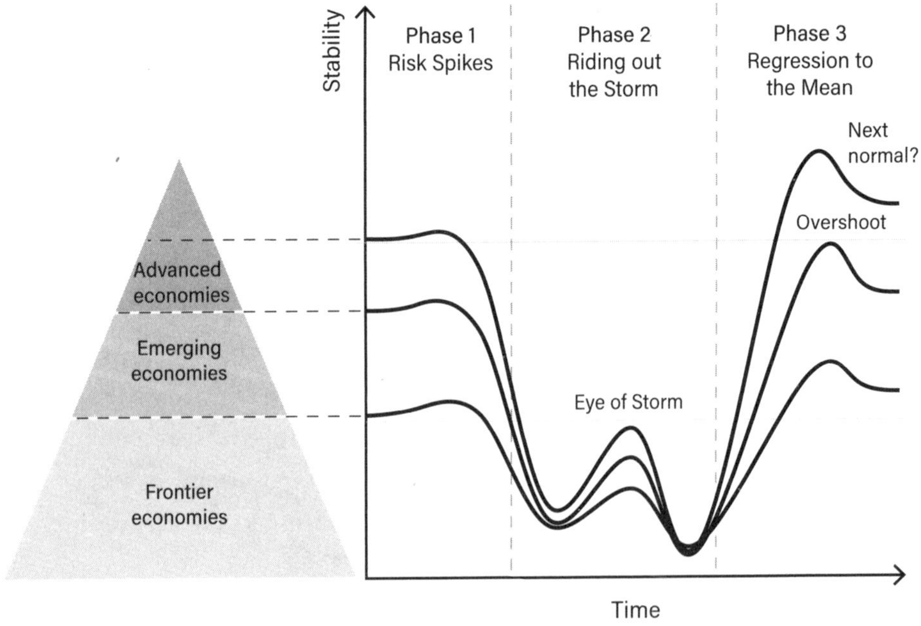

during which time the intensity and duration of the crisis remains unclear (Phase 2). At some point, owing to a combination of internal and external investments, a mini golden age of stability emerges (Phase 3). At this point the cycle resets and starts over again. This is an obvious oversimplification for the sake of orientation, but the general pattern is consistent up and down the Hierarchy of Stability, and even across time. As Mark Twain is reputed to have said, history may not repeat, but it certainly does rhyme.

The odds of success in each phase are powerfully affected by earlier actions and reactions, so it's important for leaders to track where they are on the journey. Those organizations that are able to successfully navigate all three phases of a crisis can emerge even stronger, more agile, and better positioned to grow and thrive than before. However, if they fail to recognize and adapt to worsening conditions, or resist the structural changes necessary to ride out the storm, failure on the path to the next normal is all but guaranteed.

Before we dive into each phase in greater detail, let's first take a moment to orient ourselves to the overall model, visualized in the graph "Understanding the Typical Pattern of Crises." On the horizontal axis, we track the linear progression of time, and on the vertical axis we capture the overall level of stability in the operating environment. This combination provides us with a dynamic "barometer of uncertainty," whether the crisis is triggered by external factors beyond our influence or internal factors within our control. It also reinforces the lesson that our actions over time need to reflect both our current and future context—strategy is by definition anticipatory and proactive. Of course, this is easier said than done. Change management is challenging in the best of times, but crises make people and organizations even more resistant to moving away from the status quo.

Finally, before we explore the three phases in detail, it's important to recognize that at all times, in all contexts, there is always some level of structural and seasonal volatility—the byproduct of life in a complex adaptive system. Demographics are always changing; new businesses are born while others die; politics lurch from left to right, and then back to left; and climate ebbs and flows. Together, these forces ensure that some base level of dynamism will always be present in our operating environment.

However, once some acute event triggers a collapse in the stability of our operating environment—at the border in Donetsk, on the balance sheet of a large bank, or deep under the ocean along a tectonic plate—the status quo is no longer an option and we are forced to react. In these moments, as in the metaphor of the boiling frog, we need to recognize quickly that conditions are getting worse, and leverage our courage rather than our fear to jump out of the pot.

PHASE 1: RISK SPIKES

The underlying forces that trigger crises can sometimes be months or even years in the making, and their precise timing is nearly impossible to predict. In the next chapter, we'll lay out a framework for how to anticipate them more proactively and systematically. However, once the wheels are set in motion, all crises follow a similar sequence of events.

Like the grief cycle, the earliest stages of the crisis cycle often evoke a sense of denial about the imperative for change, anger about the inconvenience, and bargaining to avoid its most destabilizing effects. Some leaders are more reluctant to accept this new reality than others, but once they do, existing plans need to be put on hold or changed altogether.

Consider your own actions and responses during the earliest stages of the COVID-19 pandemic. At the time, it was difficult to imagine a scenario in which a structural commitment to globalization would ever be challenged. Then a tiny piece of RNA, coated with some mysterious proteins, emerged in Wuhan, eventually plunging the whole world into years of uncertainty, isolationism, and loss.

It was one of those rare crises that affected all three domains—business, ownership, and family—simultaneously. In addition to learning about broken supply chains, shifting regulatory regimes, and new protocols for keeping employees and customers safe, many families also discovered that their portfolios were highly concentrated and their governance systems dangerously ineffective. Additionally, social distancing protocols forced families to reimagine what it meant to be connected and united—without exposing vulnerable family members to the physical and psychological effects of quarantine.

In advanced economies, it was a real wake-up call—shattering our illusion of control and reminding us that all stability is transitory. Boxing legend Mike Tyson is often credited with saying that "everyone has a plan until they get punched in the face,"[2] which provides a vivid metaphor for how it feels when risk begins to spike. The level of disorientation in the early stages of the pandemic was most acute at the peak of the Hierarchy of Stability, where such shocks are both rare and quickly contained by public authorities. However, unlike a simple business cycle recession, this was the macroeconomic equivalent of a haymaker—a knockout punch that has reconfigured advanced economies in ways that we're just beginning to fully understand, from growing distrust in government, to the promise of hybrid work, to the perils of molecular biology.

Contrast this experience with conditions in emerging and frontier economies, where COVID-19 was still a massively destabilizing event, but generated very different outcomes. Leaders operating in these contexts know their way around the proverbial boxing ring, and their past experience managing states of emergency and navigating threats to personal safety helped them mobilize more quickly at the grassroots level. Lower trust in public institutions also left many governments less inclined to lock down their entire economies, for fear of rebellion or revolt. Consequently, within these less structured environments, enterprising families had more degrees of freedom to react and respond.

That said, at the onset of the crisis, agile companies everywhere were able to quickly pivot, protecting their core operations and even repurposing some industrial capacity to support public health efforts—and generate windfall profits. Many enterprising families led the way with strategic differentiation—from distilleries producing hand sanitizer to textile manufacturers producing gowns and masks, industrial companies building makeshift ventilators, and of course the pharmaceutical industry doubling down on developing COVID tests and vaccines. This was all in addition to the legions of family companies that couldn't directly contribute to the frontline response, but resisted layoffs and committed additional capital to support their employees, customers, and communities, in generous acts of mutualistic symbiosis, while world leaders struggled to develop a coherent solution.

Leadership at this stage in a crisis requires the equivalent of being able to take a punch in the face without being knocked off balance. Such agility may come more naturally to those operating in the volatile markets of the Global South, but it is still possible in advanced economies as well. When leaders are able to summon grace under fire, they can significantly improve the course of events and the morale of their teams. They need to be both careful and hopeful when communicating about the rising dangers that lie ahead. Panic is an enemy, but so, too, is inaction, and the most successful leaders are able to thread this needle delicately.

Whatever the cause of the crisis—from a pandemic to nationalization to technological disruption—once "the game is afoot," as Sherlock Holmes would say, leaders need to help stakeholders throughout their entire enterprise to acknowledge that hunkering down and waiting for a storm to pass is not a feasible strategy. Inaction or even a slow reaction can lead to devastating consequences, and the accelerating pace of change during a crisis offers little time for organizations to improvise "on the fly." In these moments, rapid planning and agile execution aren't just desirable, they become indispensable. Once again, the seven stabilizing strategies provide a natural menu of options to guide your first critical steps.

Seven "Stabilizing Strategies" When Risk Begins to Spike

Differentiation	Identify opportunities to fill emergent market gaps
Modularity	Leverage partnerships for insights and capital
Redundancy	Build up reserves in anticipation of scarcity
Symbiosis	Review political allies and vulnerabilities and nurture strong connections to communities
Migration	Early "pivot or persevere" analysis
Simplification	Identify and fortify mission-critical activities and resources
Diversity	Leverage existing diversity to offset losses and threats

As Ben Franklin reminded us, deploying these strategies before a crisis strikes is far better than figuring out how to react after the fact. For instance, investments in redundancy are most effective before all hell breaks loose and access to key resources becomes a tactical nightmare. Similarly, symbiotic relationships are best nurtured during periods of prosperity, when resources are bountiful and trust is in high supply.

Even still, when it comes to investing in stability, it's better late than never. If you find yourself at the start of a crisis without a playbook, Appendix 1 provides a range of ideas on how to deploy the seven strategies with speed and confidence. In essence, your prime directive in Phase 1 is to survive long enough to experience Phase 2.

PHASE 2: RIDING OUT THE STORM

Those left standing will quickly recognize that enduring a crisis is more of a marathon than a sprint. Consequently, we begin to see a shift in strategic planning and public messaging. Temporary measures like lockdowns, furloughs, and rationing can initially sustain the integrity of an enterprise, but important changes to the allocation of resources—human, financial, and operational—will be essential in the months of disorder that follow.

As we enter Phase 2, our focus needs to shift from immediate survival to pacing and endurance. Leaders who treat crisis management as a protracted boxing match risk exhausting themselves and their teams and draining financial assets, emotional reserves, and even cognitive capabilities and decision-making effectiveness. This shift in mindset requires accepting that the organization's strategy and structure need to fundamentally change, then bracing for a long and grueling journey ahead. Along the way, some pain is inevitable, and leaders need to decide if it will be the pain of discipline or regret. As author Jim Rohn argues, "The difference is discipline weighs ounces while regret weighs tonnes."[3]

Consequently, the start of Phase 2 is often a mixed bag. On the one hand, any enterprise that has survived the first harrowing stage of the crisis naturally has something to celebrate. Not all companies will be so lucky. On the other hand, a marathon still awaits. At the very least, leaders now have a better lay of the land. The earliest financial, operational, and

Seven "Stabilizing Strategies" for Riding Out the Storm

Differentiation	Reinforce market leadership and explore adjacent gaps
Modularity	Prune failing relationships that struggle under pressure
Redundancy	Sustain reserves and strategic provisioning to provide operational buffers
Symbiosis	Engage in scenario planning around regime change and respond to evolving community needs
Migration	Consider lateral migrations within existing portfolio
Simplification	Reassess budgetary constraints and consider targeted elective activities
Diversity	Screen growth and acquisition targets for post-crisis feasibility and complementarity

cultural implications of the crisis will have already manifested, and forecasts about its ultimate duration—albeit speculative—are worth discussing among board members and senior leadership teams. The goal during this phase is to learn how to surf the turbulence like a wave—to harness its power for growth and renewal without wiping out.

If Phase 1 was defined by the capacity to absorb change, Phase 2 is defined by the capacity to endure. The frontier between them is what Winston Churchill once called "the end of the beginning."[4] Such moments are a crucible—a time when the family's shared vision, its core values, and its capacity to collaborate are put to their greatest test. Once we reach "peak uncertainty" and steady our footing, we can begin to invest in stability more proactively—less as shock absorbers and more as reinforcements. Again, in Appendix 1, we have provided some thoughts on how to deploy each of the seven strategies to help you ride out the storm with greater confidence.

Additionally, while much has been written about crisis management, especially during the depths of the recent pandemic,[5] crisis *governance* has been altogether neglected. While it is understandable that leaders must first focus on the operational and strategic issues that are most immediate and critical for them and their management teams, they must also ensure that their board and their family shareholders are kept abreast of how they are planning to respond to the crisis, as well as on the impact and efficacy of their actions.[6]

Before moving on to Phase 3, we have one final precaution. Remember that our ancient brains are hardwired to believe that the first green shoots in winter are signs of an early spring. Such intrinsic optimism allowed our ancestors to persevere through even the harshest conditions. However, this cognitive bias can also create a false sense of hope, causing us to shift out of crisis management before conditions have substantively improved. Consider the performance of the Dow Jones Industrial Average in the immediate aftermath of Black Thursday in October 1929. After several false dawns, the market only bottomed out in July 1932, nearly three years later—far later than anyone expected. It would then take another quarter

Beware the Eye of the Storm

It took the Dow Jones nearly a quarter century to fully recover from the Great Depression

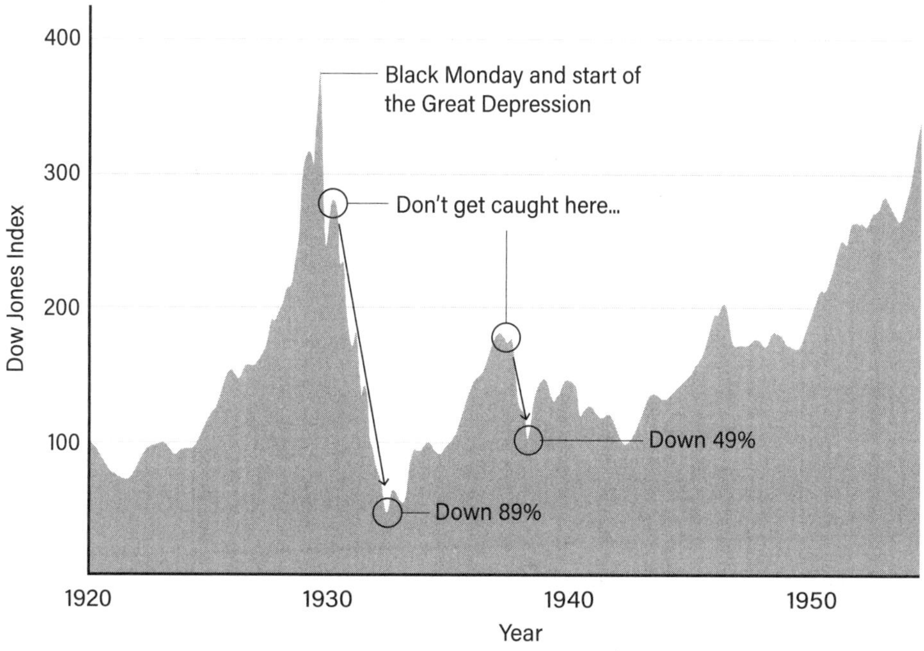

Source: Statista, Bank of America

century for valuations to fully recover their pre-Depression heights. The lesson is clear: shifting out of crisis management too early can be just as dangerous as shifting into crisis mode too late. Enduring enterprises learn to strike the right balance between optimism in pragmatism as they navigate through the eye of the storm, ensuring that essential operations are secured before investing too aggressively in the prospects of a brighter future.

PHASE 3: REGRESSION TO THE MEAN

While it's always darkest just before dawn, at some point the general contours of a "next normal" will eventually begin to emerge. In the case of a pandemic, that may mean a decline in case counts and a shift in public health protocols. In times of war, it may involve a lasting ceasefire and reengagement with genuine diplomacy. In economic recessions, it includes a jump in demand, driven both by government stimulus and emerging optimism about the future. In the wake of natural disasters, it begins with reconstruction once all the damage has finally been cleared.

In each of these scenarios, leaders are once again straddling two frontiers—one that is inherently stable and one that is not. Consequently, recalibrating the transition out of crisis planning and into strategic planning must be done with great care and intention. During these moments of transition, we find the Mandarin definition of "crisis" to be an inspiring guide, since it integrates two distinct but complementary characters: 危机—*way* for "danger," and *gee* for "opportunity." This worldview underscores the critical need to balance caution with entrepreneurial spirit, an especially relevant framing whenever we're approaching a "new normal." Recall how Grupo Arcor was able to rapidly expand its market share after each brush with hyperinflation, capitalizing on the failure of its competitors through expansion and acquisition. Similarly for the AJE Group in Peru: once the Shining Path rebellion was suppressed, the company was able to significantly expand its domestic operations, fueling the next wave of international expansion.[7]

Such entrepreneurial muscle comes naturally to enduring enterprises but can easily atrophy when you're riding out a lingering storm. In this sense, savvy business leaders are like high performance athletes, and need to start training well before the new season begins.

While every successful enterprise will have its own approach to "off season" development, we've found strategic retreats to be an easy and effective tool. If resources allow, the ideal location for such a meeting would be a nearby hub of entrepreneurial activity a little further up the Hierarchy of Stability, where conditions are more predictable and economic optimism inescapable. Like a form of strategic shore leave for worn-out leadership teams, these retreats provide a valuable and visceral reminder of the incredible possibilities that stability affords.

The most successful families we know use these moments as the educational opportunity of a lifetime, providing a deep dive into organizational resilience and the conditions and actions necessary for continuity and growth. It is particularly useful at moments like these to engage the family's institutional memory, and discuss what strategies the family has used in past crises, and in particular whether they were useful (or even harmful) during the recent crisis. Documenting such experiences not only supports thoughtful strategic planning, but can become a seminal part of a family's shared beliefs about legacy, entrepreneurship, and community leadership.[8]

Also remember that as crises begin to fade—first from reality, then from memory—a shift up the Hierarchy of Stability is inevitable. So competition will almost certainly heat up, local firms will begin to redeploy capital more aggressively, international firms will enter (or reenter) the market, and the competition for talent and resources will become more fierce. Intuition for how to handle these conventional operating conditions is often suppressed during a crisis, so acknowledging the shift back is critical for any strategic planning and organizational redesign that follows.

Finally, at the tail end of every crisis, keep an eye out for a brief "honeymoon" period, during which levels of stability often "overshoot" to near utopian highs. Whenever treaties are signed or stimulative policies are launched, "peace dividends" abound. While these moments are fleeting, they can also be quite lucrative. The American investor Warren Buffett has been through many such episodes over his long and storied career and has sage advice. "Every decade or so, dark clouds will fill the economic skies, and they will briefly

Seven "Stabilizing Strategies" When Conditions Normalize

Differentiation	Brace for competition as barriers to entry fall
Modularity	Expand healthy relationships that weathered the storm
Redundancy	Wind down reserves and revisit organizational design based on lessons learned
Symbiosis	Anticipate policy shifts and increased competition while sustaining loyalty of communities
Migration	Reconsider returning to home markets
Simplification	Document "Crisis Playbook" and fortify essential activities and resources
Diversity	Consider strategic divestment as "pure plays" back in vogue and move swiftly in war for talent

rain gold. When downpours of that sort occur, it's imperative that we rush outdoors carrying wash tubs, not teaspoons."[9] This same logic holds after any crisis, whether you're deploying capital in Canada, China, or Chad.

In short, each unique phase of a crisis requires a reassessment of your strategic playbook. Outside advisers can help orient and provide guidance, but leaders and owners ultimately need to recognize that sailing with a headwind is very different from sailing with a tailwind. Learning to navigate effectively under both conditions, particularly when the winds are changing, can make the difference between mere survival and enduring success.

CONTEXT MATTERS

All strategies—especially crisis strategies—need to be adapted to the unique contexts in which they're being deployed. Throughout the book we've provided a multitude of cases demonstrating how to create stability in a variety of operational conditions. But now that we have a more granular map of the contours of crises, we can provide a detailed description of how each stabilizing strategy can be deployed most effectively within each of the three distinct phases.

These different "flavors" for each strategy evoke a related concept from the natural sciences—the isotope—which explains how unique forms of the same elemental atom can have distinct properties. Consider hydrogen, the most abundant element in the universe. It has three different isotopes: protium, deuterium, and tritium. All three feature a single proton, which gives them similar chemical properties. They also each have the capacity for a single electron, leading to similar bonding behaviors. However, because of subtle differences in their atomic mass, each of these three isotopes exhibits a distinct set of physical properties that make it useful—or harmful—in certain conditions.

Humans are most familiar with the protium isotope (H1), which is an essential component of water and all organic compounds. It represents roughly 99.98 percent of all the natural hydrogen in the universe. A rare form of "heavy water" made from deuterium (H2), however, has higher melting and boiling points than common water, making it useful in nuclear fusion research and spectroscopy. Tritium (H3), which is exclusively lab-made, has medical and industrial applications, including self-luminous "glow-in-the-dark" devices. It's also naturally radioactive. So while "tritiated water" might look and feel like nature's finest, exposure to large amounts of it can increase the risk of cancer and have other detrimental health effects.

Like their chemical analogues, *strategic isotopes* can be both life-saving or fatal depending on the context, so it is critical to understand both what to deploy and when to deploy it. In Appendix 1, we have laid out three variations for each stabilizing strategy, making it easy to figure out which could be most effective in any given situation. Choosing a strategy simply requires answering three questions:

1. Which phase of the crisis am I in now?
2. Which stabilizing strategies have worked in the past?
3. Which stabilizing strategies could be most effective in the future?

Whether you are increasing your use of these strategies during the earliest stages of a crisis, tweaking and sustaining them as you ride out a storm, or unwinding and recalibrating as conditions stabilize, remember that each isotope requires special handling and care. The in-depth study of all twenty-one permutations in Appendix 1 is intended both for those who are curious and want to be more proactive, and for those actively navigating crises and seeking immediate guidance on how to respond.

Leaders in advanced economies have an additional challenge. Beyond the natural vacillations of the typical business cycle, or the havoc of one-hundred-year storms, they often have limited intuition about investing in resilience, and sometimes little interest. Their organizations are so purpose-built for speed and efficiency that shifting course at the onset of a crisis can be extremely disorienting. Consequently, when a crisis does eventually strike, they face a longer and steeper drop in performance, require greater investment in stability to ride out the storm, and must endure a longer climb back to good health once conditions improve.

Contrast this with the resilient citizens of Gaza, for whom many of these strategies are second nature. Even in the best of times, access to basic necessities such as water, fuel, and food requires proactive planning, agile problem solving, and familial support. So when bombs began to rain down in late 2023 in response to the conflict between Israel and Hamas, ordinary citizens intuitively understood how to navigate these existential disruptions. In a telling interview with *The Economist*, a young Palestinian shared, "My male relatives and I go out each morning to see if any supermarkets are open so we can buy tinned food. We each try to go to a different supermarket, so that if one is hit by an air strike we will minimize the loss to the family."[10]

When a fresh crisis emerges in Gaza, Caracas, or Kabul, familial networks are immediately activated, and procurement routines are rapidly adjusted—coping strategies honed over generations of navigating uncertainty as a tribe. These enterprising families brace for impact long before most businesses in London or Shanghai have even acknowledged that dark clouds are gathering on the horizon, and have much to teach all leaders about thriving across the crisis cycle.[11]

CRISIS PREPAREDNESS

Regardless of where you operate, investing in stability still requires proactive planning. Those in advanced economies often need to start from scratch, while those in emerging and frontier economies can simply tweak and adjust. Think of the seven strategies more like dials than switches, allowing leaders to scale their investments up and down as uncertainty waxes and wanes.

Leveraging this idea, one practical tool to assess our preparation for the future is to conduct an "Endurance Health Check"—the strategic equivalent of walking into a doctor's office and asking for an annual physical. But rather than a full body scan, you're testing for two critical organizational variables: (1) the degree to which you're currently deploying any of the stabilizing strategies, and (2) how you expect to deploy them in the near future.

So, for instance, if you're operating in a typical advanced economy during a typical year, your use of redundancy is likely limited on both counts. However, if you're operating in Nigeria, you likely have multiple layers of defense, from liquidity reserves to offshore assets to private security, which need to be dialed up and down as conditions dynamically fluctuate.

The resulting analysis generates a simple spider graph that captures a family's crisis preparedness at any given point in time. Below we've included a sample of what that might look like for Carvajal, based on the information we've shared so far throughout the book. Preparing this analysis is relatively simple. Just ask yourself the following two questions for each of the strategies:

1. How are we deploying this strategy today?
2. How should we be deploying this strategy over the next year?

Then answer using the following four-point scale:

1. Never used it
2. Used in the past but no longer
3. Using occasionally—but only intermittently
4. Using extensively—built explicitly into our structure

Endurance Health Check: Carvajal, SA

Understanding current and future investments can guide crisis preparation and response

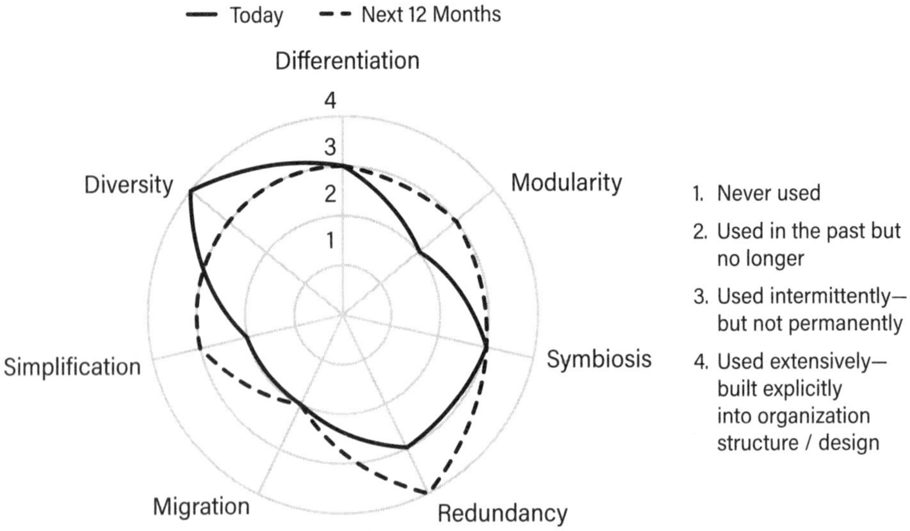

The end result is a simple visual representation of their uses and gaps. For instance, at Carvajal, where all seven strategies have been deployed over time in varying degrees, the rings of the graph are already spread out from the core. Importantly, given major elections in several of the company's key markets this year, stockpiling key manufacturing inputs around these potentially contentious events seems prudent. Similarly, a continued focus on strategic simplification might affect diversity in the company's portfolio of fully owned subsidiaries, which the family can offset by growth in its network of joint venture partnerships. These examples are purely illustrative, but they provide a sense of how this simple exercise can challenge us to consider both the context for crisis in the year ahead and how we might respond. Building this rigor into your annual strategic planning process can help your company to better anticipate, react to, and recover from crises, regardless of their underlying source.

This raises an important final lesson—that the best time to plan for a crisis is always before it begins. Throughout the book, we've made the case that proactive planning is essential to both survival and success. From Ben Franklin's advice about "an ounce of prevention" to the Scout motto of "Be Prepared," our capacity to endure is predicated on an acknowledgment that crisis is an inescapable part of life, despite our best efforts to contain it.

That said, most people don't like talking about risk when it isn't staring them right in the face. And who can blame them? In many cultures, contingency planning is like "tempting the devil" and often avoided altogether. This is one of the reasons why people don't like writing wills or engaging in succession planning.[12] But crisis preparedness is a critical component of a family's overall continuity planning—one that often gets far too little focus both in the C-suite and at the board level. These patterns of history are ignored at our peril, and understood to our advantage.

So if you're starting conversations about risk in the middle of a crisis, you're already behind the curve and should head straight to Appendix 1. For everyone else, combining proactive prevention, agile response, and adaptive recovery can significantly increase your chances of both survival and success.

In the next chapter, we'll integrate these three crisis management tools into a broader framework—one we've developed to guide leaders and organizations at all levels on the Hierarchy of Stability seeking to build an enduring enterprise. Deploying a more systematic approach to managing risk may be an unfamiliar or uncomfortable experience. But we're also confident that it will be among the best investments you ever make.

KEY INSIGHTS

- Crises are an inevitable part of life, and the ability to adapt and change is essential for survival in any context.
- Leaders need to be proactive in planning for crises—particularly as their frequency and intensity seem destined to increase in the years ahead.
- Every crisis has three distinct phases:
    - In *Phase 1*, when risk begins to spike, leaders need to brace for and absorb the initial shock, and the speed and clarity with which they respond are key drivers of survival.
    - In *Phase 2*, leaders need to shift their focus to endurance and pacing, accepting that the organization's strategy, structure, and resource allocation will need to fundamentally change.

    - In *Phase 3*, as the crisis begins to subside and a "next normal" emerges, leaders need to calibrate their transition out of crisis mode and rebuild their strategic planning muscle in order to capitalize on the exciting opportunities that lie ahead.
- The seven stabilizing strategies can be deployed across all three phases of the crisis cycle, though in slightly different forms we call *strategic isotopes* (see Appendix 1).
- The Endurance Health Check, a tool for family businesses to assess their crisis preparedness, highlights the strengths and weaknesses of a business's current approach to crisis preparedness and helps to identify which strategies can be deployed to provide greater stability and resilience.

13

MANAGING RISK IN AN AGE OF UNCERTAINTY

The dogmas of the quiet past
are inadequate to the stormy present.
—Abraham Lincoln

On the afternoon of March 11, 2011, at 2:46 p.m. local time, a 9.0 magnitude earthquake struck off the east coast of the Tohoku region on the island of Honshu, Japan. It was the most powerful quake ever recorded in the country, generating waves of up to 10 meters high and causing widespread destruction. It also triggered one of the worst nuclear disasters in history at the Fukushima Daiichi power plant, where radioactive fallout continues to affect local communities and complicate international relations over a decade later.

In hindsight, there were plenty of warning signs that could have helped authorities prevent this disaster. For starters, the monitoring of tectonic movements is common in Japan, given its vulnerable location along the "Pacific Ring of Fire." Since the founding of Kongō Gumi over 1,400 years ago, nearly 150 destructive tsunamis have been recorded in the country's coastal areas, with some waves cresting as high as 90 meters (300 feet).[1] As a result, the Japanese now deploy some of the most sophisticated seismic sensors and predictive algorithms in the world. Yet predicting the timing, location, and magnitude of a major earthquake remains a significant challenge.[2]

During our study of this catastrophic event, we were fascinated to discover that the Japanese had another more ancient technology available to help guide their decision-making—a network of "tsunami stones" that have dotted the coast for centuries. Though clearly less dynamic than their high-tech replacements, these ancient stones, some over 600 years old, were placed at the highest elevations affected by previous tsunamis, indicating safe elevations for future settlements. They were inscribed with warnings to future generations in simple yet powerful prose: "Do not build your homes below this point" and "If an earthquake comes, beware of tsunamis."[3]

Despite the unambiguous language, this ancestral wisdom was ultimately ignored by urban planners in Fukushima Prefecture—lost to the economic conveniences and aesthetic appeal of coastal living. Fumihiko Imamura, a professor in disaster planning at Tohoku University, captured it well, observing, "It takes about three generations for people to forget. Those that experience the disaster themselves pass it to their children and their grandchildren, but then the memory fades."[4] Japan will never be rid of tsunamis—its geology virtually guarantees it. But knowing this, Japanese businesses and communities need to better plan and prepare.

The Fukushima disaster is just one example of a category of high-impact risks that most of us should see coming from miles away, but somehow manage to ignore. The author Michele Wucker coined the term "gray rhino" in 2013 to describe precisely these scenarios—obvious dangers lumbering right toward us, with potentially devastating consequences, but which we willfully choose to ignore.[5] Cybersecurity breaches, crumbling infrastructure, ticking time bombs of debt, and a changing climate—it's not that we can't see or understand these threats. We just find them inconvenient to acknowledge and address, because that would force us to make difficult choices and face our fears with open eyes.

So instead, we roll the dice. We bury our heads in the sand and hope the rhino changes direction, or somehow fails to notice us. Such willful inertia is more common further up the Hierarchy of Stability, where fewer crises and disruptions make us naturally less vigilant. We build homes and nuclear power plants at elevations below the tsunami stones—then cross our fingers and hope the rhino doesn't charge.

But such a strategy in frontier economies would be both dangerous and irresponsible. In turbulent times, preparing for disruption is essential. All of the enterprising families we've featured in the book, from the Añaños to the Zamils, demonstrate proactivity in spades. Recall Arcor's many brushes with macroeconomic stability, which provided a playbook for rapid simplification and galvanized the company against the corrosive effects of hyperinflation. Likewise, Le Plaza's many layered investments in redundancy were a direct response to the unrelenting economic, social, and environmental shocks that have plagued Haiti for decades.[6]

Managing risk comes naturally to those who routinely navigate crises. Their intuition develops like a sixth sense, honed by experience. Having survived countless crises, they learn to perceive the subtle tremors that precede an economic avalanche, as well as the telltale shift in wind before a political storm breaks. As a result, they have much to teach us about how to thrive in turbulent times.

FROM NAVIGATING CRISIS TO MANAGING RISK

Enterprising families in frontier economies recognize that greater vigilance isn't a strategic indulgence, but a core competency. Carvajal's proactive fire drills accelerated the company's response to the COVID-19 pandemic. Samsung's proactive management of government relations sustained its privileged status despite multiple regime changes. The leaders of resilient organizations make sure that even when risks aren't present, there are policies, processes, and structures in place for when they inevitably reappear. Like those who erected the ancient tsunami stones, these leaders take an institutional approach to managing risk that will help future generations anticipate shocks and threats, then respond to them more effectively.

Seeing the world through this lens helps organizations brace for gray rhinos and prepare for black swans. It manifests in behaviors and decisions that take place before, during, and after a crisis in a recurring "endurance cycle" that unfolds at all levels on the Hierarchy of Stability.

The Endurance Cycle

Strategic risk management happens before and after a crisis

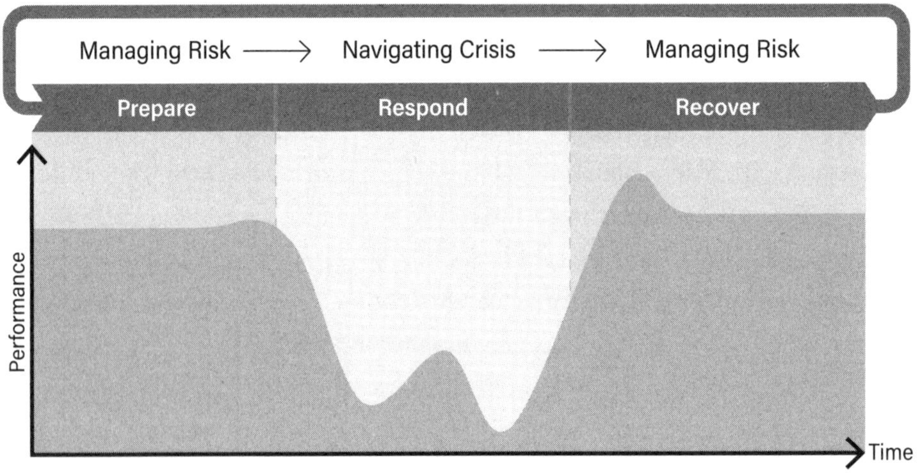

For those who want to be intentional and systematic about preparing, we developed a Family Enterprise Risk Management (FERM) framework for building an enduring enterprise. It was inspired by the many cases we researched for this book as well as the many families we know and have worked with who thrive under the toughest conditions. It was also a reaction to many off-the-shelf enterprise risk management (ERM) frameworks—knee-jerk reactions to the Global Financial Crisis focusing more on containing specific financial risks than on promoting systems-level resilience.[7]

We'll begin by guiding you through an exercise to identify and prioritize the key risks facing your organization given your specific circumstances. We'll then equip you with tools to understand how stakeholders already perceive these risks, both individually and collectively. Next we'll lay out a variety of structures, policies, and processes that will produce greater risk intelligence throughout the enterprise. Finally, we'll reinforce the importance of stress-testing our assumptions about the future—a critical hedge against poor decision-making in the New Age of Uncertainty. Once assembled, this five-step process forms the basis for a robust FERM framework that can help any business better manage risk and navigate turbulent times.

FERM Framework for Enduring Enterprises

A systemic approach to managing risk and navigating crises in all seasons

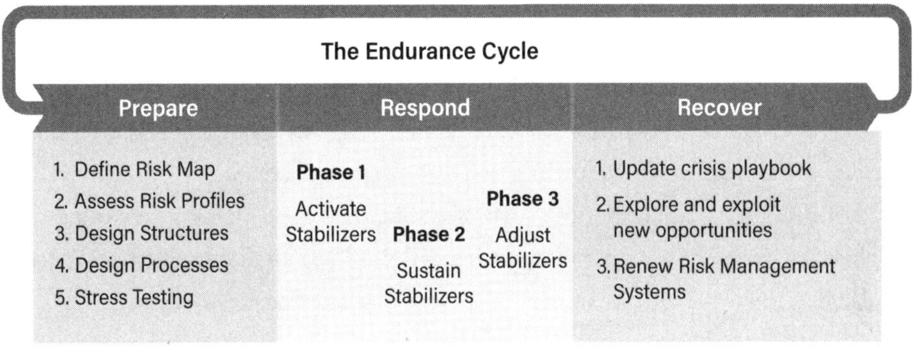

MAPPING RISK

Let's start by taking a moment to consider the single biggest risk facing your enterprise right now. It could be any number of internal or external factors, from a new and disruptive technology to a transformational acquisition, or perhaps an imminent economic crisis. It could even be a dispute among family shareholders that's been simmering for years, or the failure to plan for an orderly succession. At any given moment, there are likely to be at least a few issues that keep you up at night.[8]

Each of us has our own innate sense of what those risks are, how probable they may be, and who should address them. But in our experience, too few organizations have a structured process for mapping and prioritizing these risks and perceptions across their entire enterprise. Without such a map, the capacity to prepare for and prevent crises from emerging is significantly compromised, derailing the resilience cycle before it even gets started.

In order to create this map, we need to consider two critical dimensions for categorizing risks. Let's first consider our perceived *degree of control*. This concept was first proposed by the physicist Chauncey Starr a few years after he joined the faculty at the University of California at Los Angeles. In his seminal 1969 paper "Social Benefit Versus Technological Risk," Starr argued that people are generally willing to accept greater risks if they feel they have more control over them. For instance, the risk of dying while driving a car is significantly higher than any number of other potentially dangerous activities (including flying in an airplane), yet people generally accept it because they feel a greater sense of control when they are sitting behind the wheel.[9]

Beyond the novelty of these early behavioral insights, this idea of ranking risks based on degrees of control is crucial. It helps us focus our attention on risks where we have agency, while still tracking those beyond our influence.[10] Peter Bernstein, the honorary dean of the field, argued that this awareness forms the basis for all risk management efforts. We should maximize efforts where we have some control, and minimize damages where we don't.

Applying that logic visually, we developed a map of all the risks we are able to identify, clustering them by degree of control as a method of triage (see "A Systemic Map of Enterprise-Level Risks" diagram). The map features three concentric circles—each one representing a different degree of control. Allocating known risks across these three bands helps us to prioritize those that require attention and identify those that can be safely ignored.

For instance, among the world's few advanced economies, tech disruption and succession planning are common threats, while kidnappings are relatively rare. In frontier economies, personal security requires constant vigilance, while the biggest disruption to technology comes from frequent power outages. Clearly each of these risks is present everywhere—they simply manifest in different proportions across the Hierarchy of Stability.

Let's begin with the external layer and work from the outside in. In this band we capture systems-level forces such as the health of the economy, the stability of the political system, and the nature of geopolitics. These "external risks" are often structural, long-term trends that drive major inflections in global affairs, though importantly, they are also forces over which even the most powerful have little or no control. Nevertheless, they are important to acknowledge and integrate into our planning, because they define the limits and opportunities of our enterprise.

The vast majority of the risks highlighted in annual reports from the World Economic Forum and other such organizations fall into this category.[11] They provide the vital backstory for each of the enduring enterprises we've featured in the book—families who survived and thrived

A Systemic Map of Enterprise-Level Risks

Clustering risk makes it easier to assess exposures without being overwhelmed

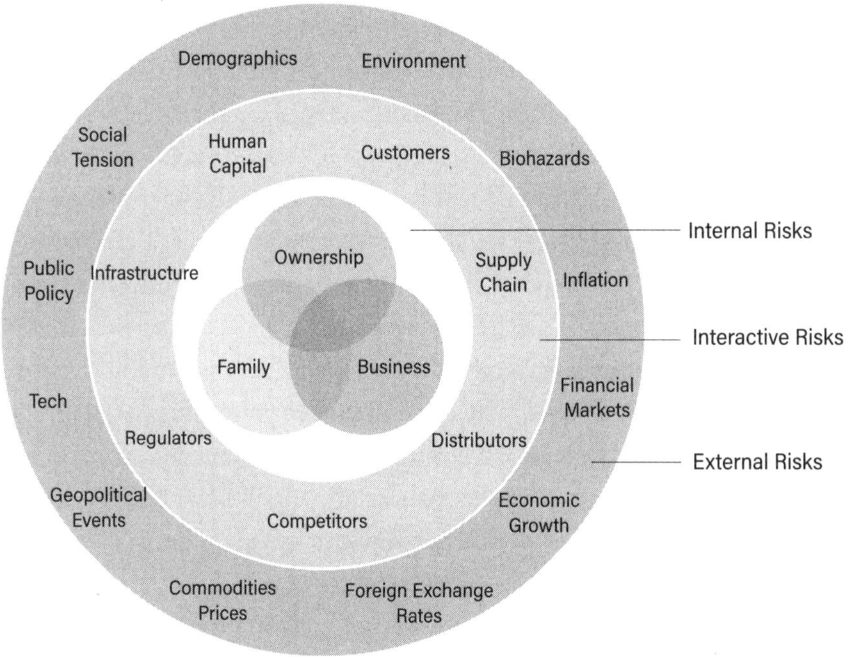

despite an array of destabilizing social, commercial, and environmental factors that were beyond their control.

The popular acronym **PESTLE** can help us to cluster the vast array of these impactful external forces, helping to simplify the outer ring into six major categories:

- Political risks (e.g., corruption, populism, polarization)
- Economic risks (e.g., inequality, market failure, price instability)
- Social risks (e.g., demographics, nationalism, secession)
- Technological risks (e.g., cybersecurity, digital disruption, reliability)
- Legal risks (e.g., taxation, intellectual property, international trade)
- Environmental risks (e.g., extreme weather events, climate change, biodiversity)

In contrast, within the middle ring of the map, we capture those interactions with the outside world where we have at least some degree of influence, even if we lack full control. These "interactive risks" are shared with our strategic partners—key suppliers, distributors, and customers—in the regular course of business. They also reflect our reliance on trustworthy infrastructure, justice systems, and labor markets in order to sustain normal business activities.

As we explored in Chapter 3, shared risks are more benign in advanced economies thanks to stronger institutions and the rule of law. Conversely, they are chronically elevated in frontier economies, where infrastructure, courts, and labor markets are less developed and dependable. Recall how the Zamils' investments in partnerships helped the family gain access to global talent, supply chains, and customers that weren't yet available in Saudi Arabia at the time. Also consider Tata's pioneering investments in hydroelectric power and higher education, which provided more reliable electricity and skilled workers to support India's growing industrial activities.

Finally, at the center of the map, we capture all of the remaining risks over which we have a much higher degree of control, since they are essentially decisions we make about our own businesses and families. To help map out these internal risks, we prefer to use the "Three Circle Model"—a systems-level framework that has dominated family business theory for decades.[12] It helps us to consider an otherwise long list of more familiar business risks while also challenging us to consider others more related to owners and family.

On the map, you'll immediately notice a range of these common *business risks*, such as cybersecurity and workplace safety—ones you would learn about in any business school or leading any organization. They include the typical threats to operations, reputation, and culture that are present in every enterprise. However, we also encourage families to track important *ownership risks*, including asset concentration, liquidity needs, and ineffective governance. In addition, the FERM map captures a variety of *family risks*, such as conflicts among owners, shareholder disengagement, disputes over inheritance, the sudden death of a significant family member, divorces, and family scandals. These two additional

Key Internal Risks for Family Enterprise

Most risks outside the business circle aren't factored into conventional ERM programs

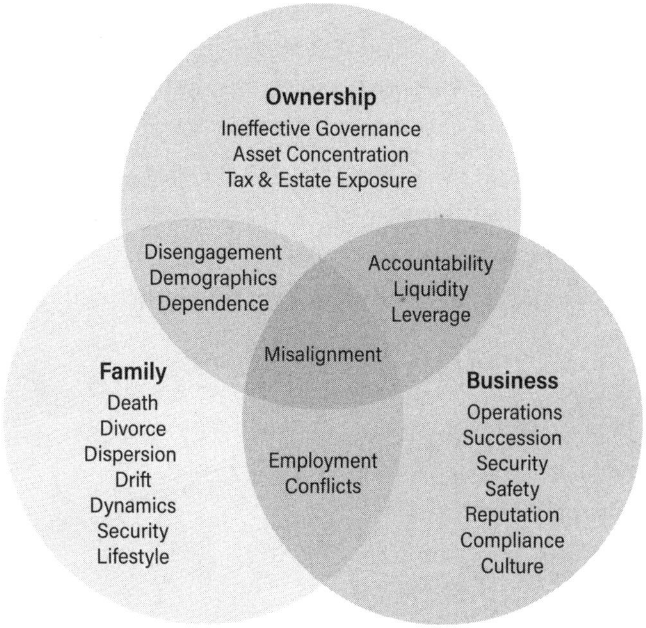

categories—ownership and family—are often overlooked during conventional strategic and continuity planning. Yet in our experience, failing to create effective governance architecture or anticipate the loss of an essential leader can be just as destructive as a failed product launch or a cybersecurity breach. Consequently, a more systematic approach to mapping out these risks becomes an essential first step in any risk management exercise.

Wherever we sit on the Hierarchy of Stability, the overarching goal is clear: to identify potentially disruptive or destabilizing forces that could threaten our continuity. Every family and every business will have its own unique sensitivities or vulnerabilities, but the approach to managing them is essentially the same. We first need to map out all the risks, both the proverbial "wolves at the door" and the "termites in the walls."[13] This may sound like a daunting task—particularly for large, complex family enterprises. But realistically, identifying and categorizing risks is the hardest part, and lays the groundwork for a more systematic and strategic response.

FIVE OPTIONS

Once our risk map is ready, the next step is to understand how our key stakeholders perceive these risks in terms of potential impact. This perception is inevitably biased in a variety of predictable ways, but still provides leaders with a useful barometer of exposures and concerns.

The most effective way to gather data is via a survey of the system—from owners to managers to frontline workers, and even major suppliers, distributors, and loyal customers if possible. We often ask the following questions when we're working with families to help prime the pump for these discussions:

- What are the top five risks facing your family enterprise right now?
- Of these, which one is the single most pressing risk?
- Why is this most pressing?
- Who is currently responsible for managing it?

This simple exercise helps leadership teams build a common understanding of their highest priorities and concerns, and an awareness that we don't all experience risk in quite the same way. In general, those items in the top five will require constant vigilance and care, while those further down can be safely delegated or even ignored. After this initial exploratory conversation, a more detailed survey can help to flesh out a more comprehensive assessment—with a focus on all three categories of external, interactive, and internal risks. Assessing them together also makes it easier to compare and contrast risks that otherwise don't have much in common, such as supply chain disruption and leadership succession.

When we graph all of the responses, we generate a visual "heat map" of risk exposures, highlighting general areas of concern. Additionally, gathering data from multiple stakeholders also reveals the diffuse perceptions, biases, and challenges that exist within each of the different subsystems that make up the enterprise. Armed with this information, leaders can then review each risk, beginning with the most pressing, and ask themselves the following question: Should we avoid it altogether? Or accept it as necessary in the pursuit of our mission?

Choosing to avoid risk can certainly help to avert significant losses—not investing in active war zones is one obvious example. But a complete avoidance of risk is both impossible and impractical. All decision-making involves risk-taking—or staring out into an unknowable future, gathering data, assigning probabilities to a range of outcomes, then taking the plunge. However, when we follow the FERM framework, leaders can be more systematic about which risks we take and which we avoid.

Two follow-up questions can help leaders make this critical choice. First, can the risk be effectively managed with our current resources and capabilities? To draw from Chauncey Starr's work, as humans we are more amenable to taking on risks when we have some agency in mitigating their impact—for instance, by deploying some combination of the seven stabilizing strategies. Second, what is the opportunity cost of avoiding the risk? Choosing not to operate in a particular country, industry, or market can help us steer clear of known complexities and dangers. But it also limits our access to opportunities.

Illustrative Risk Map

Clustering risks based on control and impact helps leaders prioritize effectively

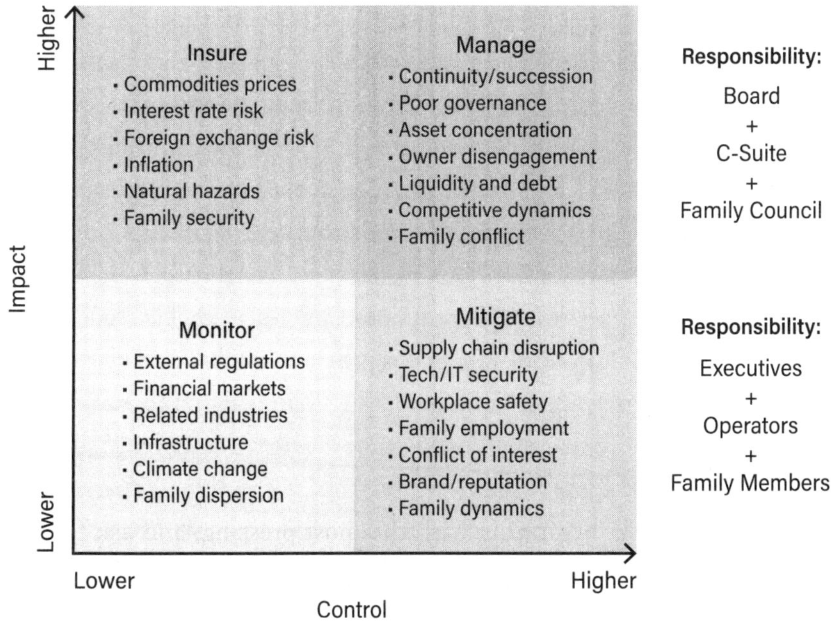

Once we've made the calculated decision to accept a given risk, with the expectation of receiving some commensurate benefit, we are left with only four strategic options. Leveraging our two dimensions of control and impact, we can easily build a two-by-two matrix to categorize and allocate the risks, which provides a simple way of distributing them across the four remaining options. In the diagram "Illustrative Risk Map," we provide an example.

As with many two-by-two frameworks, the top right box commands the most attention. In this case, it represents all the risks with a high potential impact on the enterprise over which we have a high degree of control. As a result, these risks can and should be actively *managed* by senior leaders, since their outcomes often mean the difference between continuity and failure. From succession planning to asset concentration or family conflict, these risks ultimately involve decisions that we get to make. We can manage them by investing in continuity planning, improving our governance, and rebalancing our portfolios—or we can ignore them at our peril.[14]

For those high-impact risks over which we have less control, leaders can explore opportunities to *insure* against any potentially negative outcomes. Every advanced economy hosts a thriving community of financial institutions and investors who specialize in managing these risks, allowing companies to contractually outsource their exposure. These specialist counterparties—insurance and reinsurance companies, hedge funds, commercial or investment banks, and some family offices—have developed an expertise in risk assessment honed through years of data collection, statistical modeling, and actuarial science. Additionally, enterprising families can "self-insure" by investing in stabilizing strategies such as redundancy, which often includes stockpiling key inputs to provide an internal hedge against supply chain volatility.

For lower-impact risks over which we have greater control—including workplace safety, cybersecurity, and conflicts of interest—leaders can design stabilizing processes and policies to *mitigate* their frequency and disruptive potential. These "known unknowns" often don't require ongoing executive attention, as long as management teams are empowered to monitor and address them within their day-to-day workflows. Carvajal's "fire drills" are an excellent illustration of designing and testing these internal systems, as are Grupo Arcor's proactive campaigns of strategic simplification, which streamline essential processes and structures throughout the entire enterprise.

Finally, the risk mapping exercise may have identified other less impactful risks that don't require our active attention, but which we would still be wise to *monitor.* These might include anything ranging from the health of the banking system to the longer-term impacts of climate change, or the evolving demographics of the family. Building in an opportunity to review these risks intermittently is at least reasonable. Like a cancer that has gone into remission, they can easily grow out of control if neglected.

Several important insights emerge from this "Five Options" exercise. First, it raises our awareness of a broad catalog of risks that could affect the performance and continuity of the enterprise over time. Second, it provides a new language to help teams discuss, prioritize, and problem-solve around those risks. Third, it helps leaders assign responsibility for each risk across the system. Finally, it raises an interesting paradox: building awareness of all these risks can heighten both our sense of vulnerability and our psychological readiness to address them proactively.

RISK APPETITE

As we learned with the stakeholder survey, each one of us has a unique risk profile that shapes our preferences about which risks to take and which to avoid. Consequently, once the enterprise's key risks have been identified, mapped, and categorized, leaders need to gather two additional pieces of information from their owners and management teams in order to better understand the social psychology of risk within the system.

This step involves diagnosing two related concepts—*risk appetite* and *risk capacity*—that have long been deployed by the wealth management industry to help individual investors structure their portfolios and plan for the future. The premise is simple: our appetite to take on risk, and our capacity to absorb risk, should be actively calibrated. For instance, if we are willing to assume greater risk with our investments—such as by operating further down the Hierarchy of Stability—we should ensure that we have sufficient capacity to absorb any losses that might realistically occur by actively investing in the stabilizing strategies.

This logic works fine if there is a single decision-maker—as is often the case during the founding of a business. But add multiple owners and leaders into the mix, whose perspectives each need to be considered, and the equation breaks down. Our personal attitudes and approaches to managing risk become just one factor in a more complex equation, and we must consider the interactive social dynamics of decision-making in teams.

In any large group, there will be a distribution of perspectives about *everything*—from musical tastes to political preferences to strategic aspirations. This is just as true for managers, owners, employees, and customers as it is for virtually any other social group. Yet all human beings are also fundamentally wired to avoid risk—an instinct honed over millions of years of survival in the toughest conditions. Those of our ancestors who were more risk-averse had a greater chance of surviving than extreme risk-takers, and therefore of passing down their genes to future generations.

As a result, specific brain structures, such as the amygdala, have evolved to play a crucial role in how we assess threats and make decisions, particularly under conditions of uncertainty. These structures form part of our limbic system, the brain's emotional center, which activates our sense of fear and caution. It's one of the reasons humans are naturally afraid of the dark, loud noises, spiders, and other ancient sources of existential risk, no matter where we live on the Hierarchy of Stability.[15]

But despite this shared physiology, humans also differ in how they process dopamine—the body's "feel good" chemical—and in the strength of our fight-or-flight instincts. These opposing biological forces keep our risk-seeking and risk-averting behavior in a state of dynamic equilibrium, though at a different level for every individual.

As we studied these differences in risk appetite, and how they cluster reliably across gender, age, culture, and wealth at the individual level, we were surprised at how little attention is paid to how groups experience risk together.[16] Companies spend fortunes trying to understand their customers, but shockingly little time understanding the unique psychology of risk among their primary decision-making teams, and how it affects an organization's most important choices about strategy and governance.

We all know some leaders who are predisposed to living life on the edge, and others who take a more pragmatic approach. When combined, this cognitive diversity can broaden our perspectives and improve decision-making. But it can also make it more difficult to reach consensus,

Risk Appetite Varies Across Individuals

It's not binary—but rather exists along a continuum

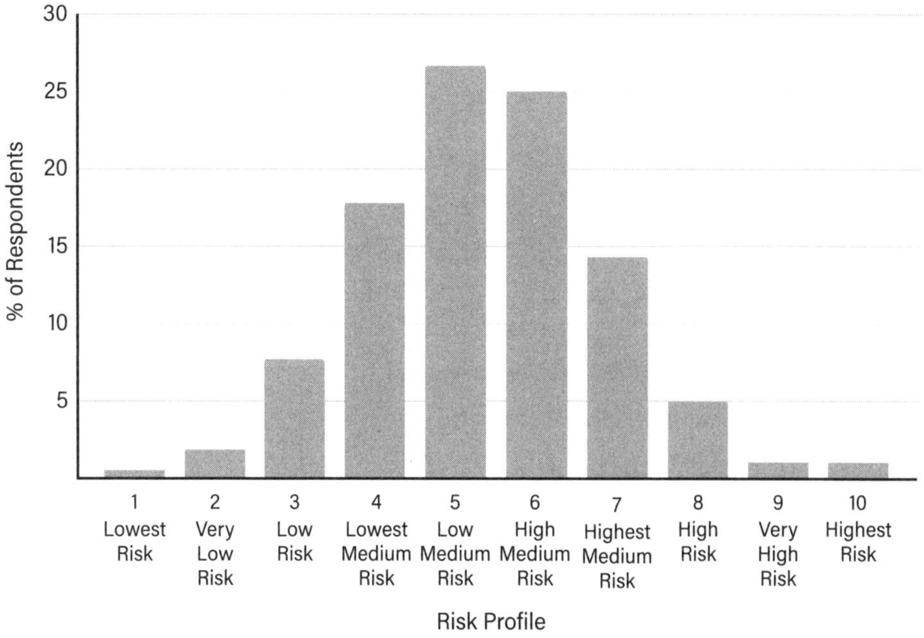

Source: Oxford Risk

complicating and delaying our planning.[17] In this way, many strategic disagreements are ultimately reflections of our different appetites for risk.

Leveraging the pioneering work of Oxford Risk, a research group founded at Oxford University in 2002, we discovered that risk appetite across any community of diverse stakeholders produces a remarkably consistent bell-shaped curve.[18] We have replicated this phenomenon countless times in boardrooms and classrooms around the world. With remarkable consistency, among any group of humans, most will be risk-neutral—neither drawn to it nor repulsed by it—with far fewer daredevils and scaredy-cats on either side. This is true both for risk appetite in general and for any given risk.

In Appendix 2 we have included a simple tool for assessing the risk appetite of your key stakeholders. You can use this tool to help your leaders gain a better understanding of your organization's willingness to accept risk in the pursuit of its strategic aspirations. But also remember that risk appetite is only half the equation. Our subjective tolerance for any given risk must be calibrated with our objective capacity to bear this risk without total failure. We need to understand both dimensions to know whether our enterprise is taking on too much risk, or perhaps too little.

RISK CAPACITY

Like many innovations around risk, the concept of Value at Risk (VaR) was pioneered in the late 1980s in response to a crisis—in this case the massive stock market crash in October 1987. As global portfolios collapsed by an estimated US$1.71 trillion on Black Monday alone, the first generation of data-driven "quantitative investors" began to ask themselves whether there might be some threshold of losses beyond which their organizations might not survive.

VaR quickly became a proxy for our innate "risk capacity"—a financial safety net that helps an enduring enterprise absorb unexpected shocks and losses. It's a way to quantify and manage a worst-case scenario, helping leaders assess how much risk they can comfortably take on while still safeguarding the company's long-term continuity and success.

Calculating VaR is easier for investment portfolios than for businesses, since there is a substantial body of market data to help generate these calculations. Like risk appetite, investment returns conform to a familiar bell curve, with a high probability of modest gains, but a remote chance of either a massive gain or a large loss. The key question is how well-equipped the portfolio is to weather a black swan event.

This same concept can also be applied to operating portfolios. It simply involves less fancy mathematics, instead relying on descriptive scenario planning. Take a relatively generic risk like *succession planning*—an issue endemic to every enterprise committed to continuity, regardless of its status on the Hierarchy of Stability. If the worst possible outcome is an emergency succession that would threaten the strategic integrity of the business, induce massive liabilities and uncertainties from the forced transfer of ownership, and prompt a tournament of infighting among the family, then one could argue that the system has little capacity to bear that risk. As a result, both succession and contingency planning should become strategic priorities.

In contrast, when clear succession and contingency plans are already in place, redundancy has been built into all leadership functions, estate

Understanding "Risk Capacity"

All investments require an understanding of our capacity to absorb shocks

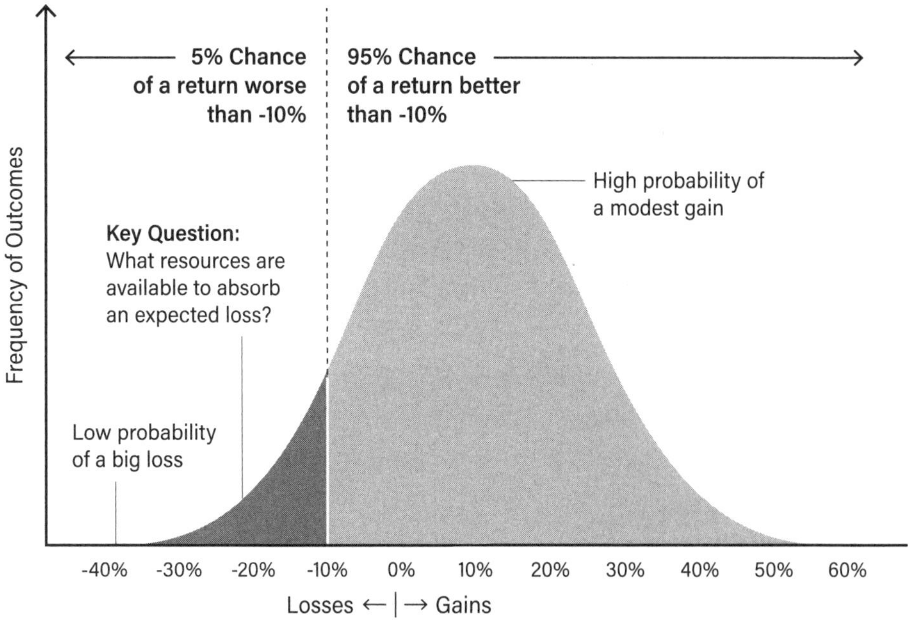

plans and legal structures are clear to all parties, and the family is investing actively in its unity and well-being, then the system's capacity to bear the risk of suddenly losing its current leader is considerably higher. Such enhanced risk capacity then allows resources and attention to be deployed in other areas, where they can be used to invest in greater stability and pursue new opportunities for growth.

This same exercise can be replicated for each of the risks in your map. The goal is ensuring that you have sufficient absorptive capacity available, at the very least for those with the highest potential impact. Here again, the seven strategies can be a powerful tool, generating greater internal stability to help absorb shocks and other adverse outcomes—from common threats, such as succession and cybersecurity, to more destructive black swans and gray rhinos.

For instance, within the business, the higher the quality and quantity of assets available (that is, redundancy), the higher the capacity to absorb losses without critically endangering the company's structural integrity.

Similarly, lower debt levels and more predictable cash flows (that is, simplification) can increase risk capacity because they improve the probability of honoring contractual commitments, even during periods of financial distress. In terms of ownership, longer investment horizons (differentiation), offshore nest eggs (redundancy), coordinated estate planning (symbiosis), and various forms of insurance (modularity) can also provide greater insulation against these destabilizing risks. Within the family, "softer" attributes, including ever-changing demographics, lifestyle needs, and retirement planning, can affect the system's risk capacity as well.[19]

Fewer internal resources are typically needed in advanced economies to hedge against systemic volatility, because these societies invest collectively in managing risks such as market failure, contract enforcement, and personal security, leaving more resources available to pursue growth and profit. In frontier economies, where access to redundant resources both on-hand and offshore are essential for survival, it's precisely the opposite. Enhancements to risk capacity in these societies obviously come at a price, lowering returns and limiting growth. But like carrying a spare tire or a good insurance policy, they help owners hedge against the variety of risks that can erupt unexpectedly in turbulent times.

CALIBRATING RISK

Armed with a better understanding of the system's collective appetite for risk, and its capacity to bear risk, the next important step is to understand whether these factors are broadly in a state of balance. Each stakeholder in the system has a unique equilibrium, or "risk profile"—both with respect to individual risks, such as succession, asset concentration, and family harmony, and more generally.

In our work with enterprising families, we've come across four recurring profiles that map naturally against these two dimensions, and you'll find representatives of these same archetypes distributed throughout your enterprise. One will likely resonate with you personally, and you can likely think of others who manifest the rest. More important than the categories themselves, however, is an awareness of how your fellow stakeholders are distributed across these profiles.

- **Trailblazers (High Risk Appetite / High Risk Capacity):** These natural risk-seekers are characterized by a pioneering spirit and an appetite for exploring uncharted territories. They are often innovators, disruptors, and fearless entrepreneurs who are not just comfortable with uncertainty and volatility—they seek it out as the crucible in which transformative ideas are tested and forged. But like Roald Amundsen in his quest for the South Pole, trailblazers also invest considerable time and resources preparing for the adverse conditions that inevitably emerge in the pursuit of their bold ambitions. This higher risk-seeking behavior is both brave and well calibrated.
- **Guardians (Low Risk Appetite / Low Risk Capacity):** These stakeholders are naturally risk-averse, valuing stability and predictability wherever possible, both in their professional and personal lives. Change is approached with caution, and decisions are made with a heavy emphasis on minimizing potential losses rather than maximizing gains. Guardians are often the older members of the family and seek to transfer wealth and power to younger generations. They tend to favor harvesting and preserving what they have accumulated over time, rather than reinvesting in novelty and growth. Their lower risk-seeking behavior is both cautious and well calibrated.
- **Speculators (High Risk Appetite, Low Risk Capacity):** Some are easily seduced by the high stakes of speculative ventures, though, unlike trailblazers, they do so without an adequate safety net to protect against adverse outcomes. Speculators often overestimate short-term opportunities and underestimate longer-term vulnerabilities or consequences. They are easily drawn to the latest investment fads and business ventures without sufficient capital or safety nets in place. Their moves are bold and often impulsive, reflecting a high-risk appetite that exceeds their actual capacity to absorb potential financial setbacks. These individuals present the most pressing risk to the continuity of an enterprise, particularly when they hold seats of authority for extended periods of time.

- **Skeptics (Low Risk Appetite, High Risk Capacity):** This archetype represents those who have ample capacity to take on risk, such as substantial savings and assets, but whose personal disposition leans toward caution. They often hesitate when faced with significant investment decisions, even though they could likely withstand considerable volatility and large potential losses. Skeptics are typically willing to forgo higher returns, which often leads to the underutilization of resources. Their challenge is not in taking on too much risk, but rather, in taking on too little.

Needless to say, people do not always fall strictly into these categories, and you may find that some stakeholders are more of a hybrid. But in general, the first two archetypes are intrinsically balanced, while the second two are not. This highlights the dissonance that can occur when there is misalignment between a system's financial capacity to handle risks and the willingness of its leaders to take them.

Four Risk Archetypes

Understand how your key stakeholders are distributed across these archetypes

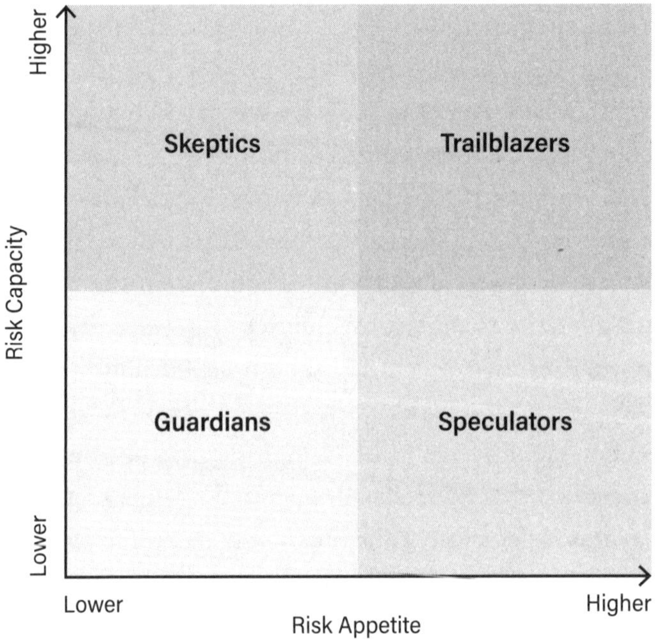

To be clear, we introduce this framework without judgment about the particular risk profile of any given enterprise. We've seen incredibly successful organizations with an extremely high appetite for risk, innovating relentlessly at the vanguard of their industries and economies. We've also seen organizations with a careful and conservative approach to continuity.

When we facilitate these conversations with families and their leadership teams, often the most important insight to emerge is that no organization is monolithic: each one has its own unique distribution across all four of these risk profiles. Recognizing this cognitive diversity helps us understand why certain strategies resonate with some but not others. It also helps boards and executives work together more effectively, deciding when to invest in stability and when to invest in growth.[20]

One might expect families operating in frontier markets to be inherently more conservative than those in advanced economies, because the context calls for greater prudence. However, in our experience, the inverse is often true, with those operating at the base of the Hierarchy of Stability demonstrating both thicker skin and a trailblazing spirit. Another counterintuitive insight emerges when we look at demographics. For instance, older generations in frontier economies are often more risk-seeking than their children, having survived and thrived in turbulent times for decades. Meanwhile, their kids are often sent away to train at elite Western schools, then return home with unrealistic expectations about what it's like to operate outside of these islands of stability and trust. Contrast this with older generations in stable economies, who tend to be more conservative than their children, and are often resistant to innovation and change.

What complicates matters is when clusters of stakeholders are distributed across all four archetypes, rather than concentrated in one or two quadrants. This is especially the case when key stakeholders, such as founders, CEOs, and board chairs, are outliers—out of sync with the risk profile of the rest of the system. In these situations, their disproportionate influence can lead the organization to take on either too little risk or too much—both of which can threaten the unity and alignment of the whole system.

This is one of the reasons why we find risk calibration exercises so valuable. They provide a simple framework and visualization that helps leaders understand why achieving strategic alignment can be so elusive, and how management teams and their boards can balance shorter-term aspirations of growth with longer-term imperatives of resilience.

ENTERPRISE RISK MANAGEMENT

On their own, any one of the tools outlined above can help you prepare for, survive, and bounce back better from unexpected shocks. But combined, their benefits are significantly amplified. So why don't more organizations deploy them? The most challenging part, as with any process of change, is integrating new behavioral patterns into your organizational DNA. Thankfully, as we'll outline below, the task isn't insurmountable, and the benefits are well worth the effort.

The process begins with the risk matrix, and asks leadership teams two critical questions: (1) How much of each risk should we take? And (2) what is our capacity to bear that risk? Armed with this data, leaders then need to design structures and assign responsibilities for managing each of them.

The general rule is that business-related risks—along with most interactive risks—should be managed by the C-suite. Ownership risks and external risks should be overseen by corporate governance structures: the board, its related committees, and any legal fiduciaries. And family risks should be managed by the family's formal or informal leaders—councils, foundations, assemblies, wise elders, and so forth. Together, an integrated ERM system can help any family sustain their commitment to a common mission, both during good times and bad.[21]

After these structures have been set up, they need processes and policies to bring them to life. How will the data about risks be tracked? How will leadership teams use this information to inform their strategic planning and decision-making? One actionable tool we often recommend is building a risk management dashboard, like the one shown in the table here (see "The FERM Dashboard"). You'll immediately notice that this isn't simply a "Top 10" list of the first few risks that come to mind. It's designed to be comprehensive—capturing all of the rich data from the risk survey, including appetite and capacity for each risk. It also includes a traffic-light rating of current risk levels, along with an indication of the

The FERM Dashboard

Enduring enterprises monitor and manage risks actively and systematically

Approaching Boundaries of Risk Appetite   Outside Boundaries of Risk Appetite

Risk	Category	Risk Appetite	Risk Capacity	Risk Level	Trend	Owner	Mitigation Strategy
C-Suite succession	Business	Low-Med	Med		↔	Board/Ctte.	Succession planning
Reputation & brand	Business	Low	High		↘	CMO	External monitoring
Workplace safety	Business	Low	Low		↘	COO	Ongoing training
Cybersecurity	Business	Med	Low		↗	CTO	Firewall investment
Supply chain risk	Business	Med	Med		↘	COO	Procurement study
Earnings volatility	Ownership	Med-High	High		↘	CFO	New dividend policy
Leverage	Ownership	Low-Med	High		↔	CFO	Fiscal prudence
Portf. concentration	Ownership	Low-Med	Low		↗	Audit Ctte.	Exploring acquisitions
Board functioning	Ownership	Low-Med	Low		↘	Gov. Ctte.	Kellogg Exec Ed.
Owner development	Company	Low-Med	Low		↔	Family Cncil	FB advisor
Family conflict	Family	Med	Low-Med		↗	Family Cncil	Strategy retreat
Disengagement	Family	Low-Med	Low		↗	Family Cncil	Family Assembly
Family employment	Family	Low	Low		↔	HR Ctte.	Career dev. Ctte.
Inflation	External	Low-Med	High		↔	CFO	Contract flexibility
Supply chain	Interactive	Low	Med		↗	COO	Project Onshore

general trend, a designated owner for each risk, and the strategies that have been put in place to mitigate them.

Last but not least, the final piece of any robust ERM system is comprehensive stress-testing. Even with all the other pieces in place, if we don't challenge our assumptions about risk, and integrate new information and alternative perspectives, the enterprise will remain vulnerable both to occasional disruptions and to catastrophic threats.

This exercise can be as simple as asking your executive teams or board to consider the worst possible thing that can happen to the enterprise in the next six to twelve months, then creating a contingency plan. Or it could involve reassessing risks that you believe your organization is better prepared to manage than your competitors. Or it could start with a basic question: How would you respond if one of the world's largest platform companies—Amazon, Tencent, or Alphabet—decided to enter your market? We believe every board should have at least one strategic debate each year about potential disruptors to their core business model, including the impact of autonomous vehicles, AI and machine learning technologies, 3D printing, climate change, geopolitical turmoil, and so forth.

To conduct this thought experiment effectively, and avoid the cognitive complacency that comes from the same people sitting in the same room discussing the same set of risks over and over again, leadership teams with an *inside-out* view often find it helpful to be provoked by experts outside the system. These organizations tend to believe that their own resources, capabilities, and internal environment are the drivers of their success. Without mechanisms to ensure legitimate testing of assumptions, they are prone to insular thinking and a strong availability bias—both dangerous forms of groupthink ill-suited to rapidly changing environments.

In contrast, leaders who take an *outside-in* perspective eagerly seek input about risk from a variety of external sources—including customers, suppliers, distributors, and the marketplace. As a result, they are more responsive to change, continuously realigning their enterprises with evolving external conditions. Those in emerging and frontier economies do this intuitively. For them, one of the few constants is change, so building the rigor to consistently scan the external environment for threats is table stakes for survival.

The problem, as with most other crucial decisions, isn't the absence of available information. It's the tyranny of our ingrained perspectives. We cling to what we "know" even when the data whispers otherwise. But especially in turbulent times, gathering this external information is mission critical. Outside-in perspectives open the aperture between our enterprise and the world. The best ones help us sense the bigger tectonic movements that are quietly—and sometimes not so quietly—shaping our future.

In the next and final chapter, we'll revisit five of these gray rhinos—lumbering, unavoidable forces, such as demographics and climate change, that will fundamentally reshape the global economy in the coming decades. We'll also provide a variety of recommendations on how best to prepare for those moments when the rhinos inevitably charge.

KEY INSIGHTS

- Risk-taking is a natural by-product of all decision-making.
- One of the principal responsibilities of family leaders is to make effective decisions about the future of their enterprise—staring out into an unknowable future, contemplating a range of potential outcomes, and ultimately deciding to proceed or pass.
- In enduring enterprises, managing risk isn't an occasional exercise—it is built into the deep operating systems of the organization.
- They map out and prioritize their *external risks* (e.g., macroeconomic, geopolitical, environmental); *interactive risks* (e.g., suppliers, distributors, regulators, competitors), and *internal risks* (business circle, ownership circle, family circle).
- They pay particular attention to risks within the business circle (e.g., supply chain, reputation, safety, cybersecurity) where executives focus instinctively.
- They also track various ownership risks (e.g., asset concentration, poor governance, lack of estate planning) and family risks (e.g., disunity, dispersion, death, divorce, disengagement) that often go unattended, but can easily destabilize even the most high-performing businesses or family offices.
- The unique psychology of risk among the system's key stakeholders is also a major influence in decision-making, both at the individual and collective level.
- Measuring individual risk appetite and risk capacity can expose major gaps across an enterprise (e.g., among board directors, within the C-suite, between spouses, among siblings, across generations, and with external partners).
- However, measuring collective risk appetite and capacity requires more than just calculating the "average" of these individuals—leaders need to understand how they are distributed across the four most common risk profiles (e.g., trailblazer, guardian,

speculator, and skeptic), with the goal of maximizing alignment between owners, boards, and executives.

- Those who aspire to build an enduring enterprise can integrate these various tools and interventions into a formal Family Enterprise Risk Management (FERM) system.
- Such a program requires durable *structures* (e.g., risk committees, risk dashboards) and *processes* (e.g., regular board and C-suite reviews, communication chains, stress tests, family surveys, hedging programs) that create the conditions necessary for effective risk management in both good times and bad.
- Together, these efforts can nurture risk awareness and resilience throughout an enterprise, helping it both to prepare for and recover from the inevitable shocks and events that can threaten business continuity at all levels of the Hierarchy of Stability.

14

BUILDING AN ENDURING ENTERPRISE

If we have learned one thing from the history of invention and discovery, it is that, in the long run—and often in the short one—the most daring prophecies seem laughably conservative.

—Arthur C. Clarke

We wrote this book to introduce a counterintuitive notion—that leading companies in the most advanced economies, which many consider the gold standard for organizational excellence, have much to learn about survival and success from family-owned companies operating further down the Hierarchy of Stability. Four central ideas inform this thesis. First, as we argued in Part 1, exposure to chronic volatility and uncertainty can boost organizational ingenuity, adaptability, and resilience. Second, as we explored in Part 2, enterprising families that have endured these strains and stresses for generations have developed stabilizing strategies for navigating crises with greater skill and confidence. Third, as we proposed in Part 3, organizations everywhere can enhance their performance under these conditions if they engage proactively in managing risk, a systematic approach that will increasingly become a vital function for leaders no matter where they are located. Fourth, as we reinforced throughout the book, whenever polycrisis has threatened the prevailing world order, a New Age of Uncertainty begins, and sustained periods of turbulence inevitably follow.

This last point is particularly salient, since external risks are often the triggers that set protracted crises in motion, from political assassinations to speculative bubbles to revolutions against dynastic elites. In each case, the catalyst is different, but the outcome is the same—a renegotiation of the social contract between private citizens, private enterprises, and public authorities that can dramatically alter the conditions for commercial survival and success.

Throughout the book, we have introduced five such disruptive forces—revolutionary technologies, demographic changes, social tensions, market failures, and climate change. Each is its own gray rhino, slow-moving in pace but far-reaching in impact. Ominously, all five seem to be gathering simultaneously on the horizon for the first time in nearly a century.

In this final chapter, we'll revisit these critical megatrends, recognizing that they are likely to affect all of us to varying degrees in the years and decades ahead. Then we'll provide our best recommendations on how to prepare your business, your ownership, your family, and yourself for whatever unfamiliar conditions lie ahead.

THE GREAT ACCELERATION

Let's begin with disruptive technologies, a buzzword both in Silicon Valley and on Wall Street. Throughout history, some of the most transformative revolutions have been triggered by the invention of new tools, from the aqueduct to the printing press, to the steam engine, to artificial intelligence. Such technologies have been key drivers of social and economic development for centuries. But like all gray rhinos, their short- and long-term impacts were poorly understood by their earliest proponents.

This phenomenon was first identified in the sleepy suburbs of Palo Alto, California, at the Institute for the Future (IFTF). Founded in the late 1960s, long before Silicon Valley became a global hub of innovation and speculation, the IFTF was committed to helping leaders brace for change and make better decisions about the future. One of its founding members, and among its most influential thinkers, was the futurist Roy

Amara, who served as IFTF's president for a quarter of a century between 1971 and 1996. Among his many inventions and achievements, Amara is perhaps best known for his observation that humans are predictably poor at forecasting the impact of technological changes over any time scale.

In particular, he observed that we often expect too much change to come from new technologies in the immediate future, and too little in the distant future—a quirk of human cognition since memorialized as "Amara's Law." It was built upon the earlier musings of inventor and author Arthur C. Clarke, and it inspired subsequent tech enthusiasts such as Ray Kurzweil and Bill Gates, who have made similar observations about humanity's propensity to consistently misinterpret the long arc of scientific progress.

One striking example is the telegraph, invented in the nineteenth century and now seen as a precursor to telephones and the internet. Its early proponents predicted the complete demise of traditional mail. Others had visions of instantaneous financial transactions across continents, which whipped up a speculative frenzy. However, setting up and maintaining telegraph lines across vast distances proved to be costly, hindering their widespread deployment. Operating the telegraph also required specialized knowledge, restricting its use to trained professionals. Meanwhile, traditional communication methods—such as mail and carrier services—remained cost-effective and efficient for bulk and personal communication, slowing the adoption curve predicted by the telegraph's earliest enthusiasts.

However, the really transformative impact of the telegraph unfolded over a much longer time scale and extended far beyond even the most ambitious early predictions. For instance, the ability to transmit news rapidly through telegraph lines laid the foundation for real-time reporting, allowing events to unfold before the eyes of the public on a national and even international scale. This change dramatically altered the rugged landscape of news media, influencing public opinion and shaping the course of history. Commercial life was also revolutionized, as faster communication between businesses across vast distances allowed for improved coordination between disparate operating divisions and provided a better awareness of market trends.[1]

A more modern case is the slow-motion revolution unleashed by artificial intelligence that first began over half a century ago. The concept for AI emerged in the early 1950s, when a group of researchers at Dartmouth College in New Hampshire coined the term and held a summer workshop to discuss the potential for machines to learn and reason like humans. A decade later, the first chatbot, ELIZA, was developed at the Massachusetts Institute of Technology (MIT). ELIZA was trained to mimic a human psychotherapist with only 200 lines of code.[2] Yet despite many brilliant minds contributing ideas and experiments over the decades that followed, the technology remained mostly abstract and theoretical.

It was only in the late 1990s that a few small breakthroughs began to emerge outside of these initial academic settings. Interestingly, many of them took place in the domain of gaming—stable environments that provided clear rules and objectives within which brute computational power could be tested against the dynamism of human creativity.[3] IBM's

The AI Gold Rush Is Just Getting Started

Over the past decade, nearly US $1 trillion has flowed into AI companies

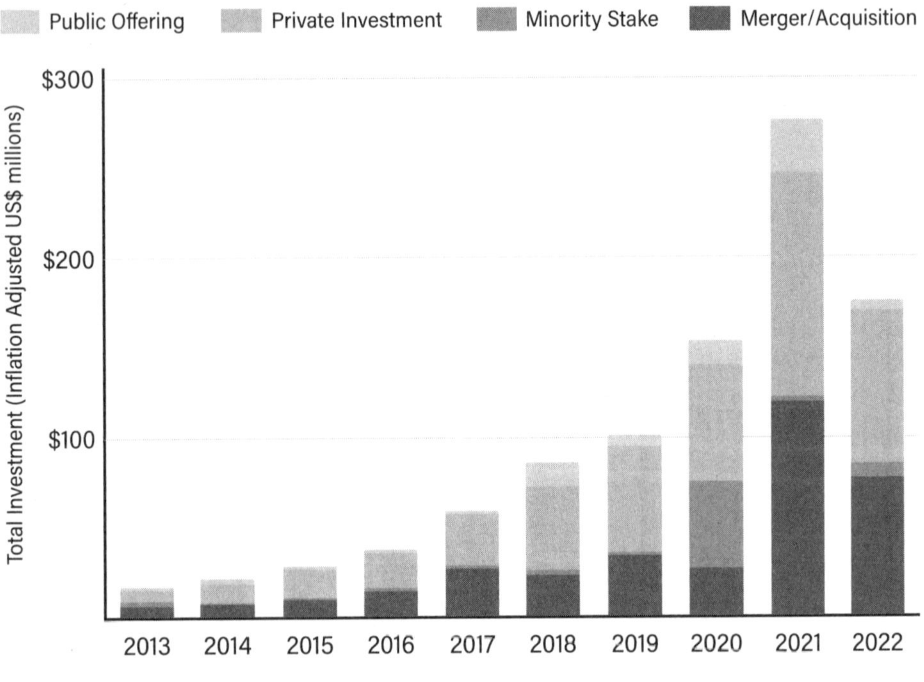

Source: Our World in Data, Annual global corporate investment in artificial intelligence, by type.

impressive triumphs at chess and *Jeopardy* aside, these early AI models would languish for another few years without a natural commercial application, mostly relegated to making predictive "recommendations" of products to buy, songs to hear, and shows to watch in the rapidly growing domain of e-commerce.

That all changed in late 2022, with the public release of next-generation large language models, including OpenAI's ChatGPT and Google's LaMDA, among countless others, in rapid succession. ChatGPT, in particular, took a commanding lead in the field, quickly becoming the fastest-growing platform in the history of the internet. It generated over 100 million active users within its first two months, and then over 100 million per day only two months later.

In the years ahead, few industries will remain untouched by these new tools and technologies—as in the case of the telegraph two centuries ago—though not without their fair share of controversy. While some take a rosy view, predicting that AI will lead to a three-day workweek and allow all humans to flourish as members of a new twenty-first-century leisure class, others fear how AI-wielding tech firms might transform modern culture and even warfare.[4]

This dichotomy between hope and harm exists in other high-tech industries as well. For every new mRNA vaccine developed to help us fight diseases, from coronavirus to cancer, elsewhere rogue scientists are using controversial gene editing technologies such as CRISPR that could accelerate the evolution of our species in ways we're only beginning to imagine.[5] Yet disruptive new technology is only one of the megatrends we think all leaders should be tracking in the years ahead, particularly as the pace of change continues to accelerate.

Let's consider demographics, the second of these five grinding forces in the long arc of human affairs. It is distinctively slow in pace, but inescapable in impact. The trope that "demography is destiny" reflects our deep understanding that populations are constantly evolving, ever so slowly, in mostly predictable ways. After all, every day we each get a day older (if we're lucky). Over billions of people and hundreds of years, that makes forecasting long-term trends relatively easy—certainly compared to predicting the weather or commodities prices even a few days in advance.

As a result, over the past few centuries actuaries have learned how to predict population-level outcomes such as life expectancy and fertility rates with astonishing accuracy. Trends in these two data points alone will have major implications for organizations and institutions everywhere in the years ahead. Yet too few of us pause and consider how and when these slow-moving tectonic plates will unleash the next civilizational earthquake.

For instance, the World Bank recently branded 2018 as a demographic turning point. For the first time, there were more humans aged sixty-five years and over than children under the age of five.[6] As waves of experienced workers suddenly shift from being net contributors to net beneficiaries, younger generations and public institutions will be forced to support a growing population of seniors on a shrinking tax base. Painful adjustments will be needed in health, pension, and tax systems to address this persistent redistributive gap.[7]

Interestingly, though these inconvenient truths are relatively easy to predict even decades in advance, policymakers and voters around the world have been reluctant to acknowledge or address them. Growing demographic pressures haven't been attended to structurally, and, as with AI, their consequences will become increasingly difficult to ignore in the years ahead.

This issue will be most acute among advanced economies, where fertility rates have been declining at an accelerated pace while lifespans have been increasing. At the time of this writing, wealthy countries, including Japan, Italy, and Germany, are already feeling the demographic pinch, with nearly a third of their populations over the age of sixty-five.[8] In the United States, it's only one in six, but this cohort of seniors has grown by roughly 1,000 percent over the past decade—five times faster than the total population and the fastest pace since 1890.[9] Even labor-friendly France has forced through deeply unpopular legislative changes to raise the retirement age, reducing pressure on a strained pension system and helping combat a shrinking workforce—particularly in conventional blue-collar careers such as carpentry and plumbing that have fallen out of favor with younger workers.[10]

As with AI, these changes are likely to alter the structure and performance of enterprising families. Consider, for instance, how functional longevity is likely to affect succession planning. Senior generations are remaining actively involved in leadership roles much longer than in the past—Warren Buffett is in his nineties, for instance, and when Charlie Munger died in 2023, at the age of ninety-nine, he was still going strong.[11] With leaders living longer, there is sure to be a significant delay in how generational transitions unfold in family businesses.

Indeed, the prospect of having members from three (or even four) generations simultaneously involved in ownership and management roles poses new questions and dilemmas that our field has not even begun to contemplate. For instance, might the prolonged delay of these transitions complicate the process by which rising generations establish their own credibility and authority? Might it also increase the risk of seniors retaining control well beyond the limits of their own cognitive abilities? Sumner Redstone's destructive departure from National Amusements and ViacomCBS in 2016 at the age of ninety-two, amid claims that he was suffering from dementia, painfully illustrates the problem.[12] Alternatively, how might the continued leadership of wise and experienced elders like Warren Buffett and Charlie Munger enhance the performance of their organizations in the turbulent years ahead? Given the rising tensions between the United States and Russia, not to mention China and Iran, how many CEOs active today can say that they have experience operating successfully during a Cold War, let alone a hot one?

This same demographic phenomenon is also shaping trends in broader society and policymaking. Look no further than the recent presidential election in the United States to see that we are becoming a species dominated by individuals in the last decades of their lives, with all the social and economic consequences that entails. One fascinating explanation for the relatively swift and substantial response to the COVID-19 pandemic, relative to slower-burning crises like climate change, is that this particular virus disproportionately threatened the oldest members of our species, who still dominate the corridors of political and economic power. In contrast, climate change is more likely to directly affect younger generations and those yet to be born, so the political will to address these risks hasn't successfully materialized.

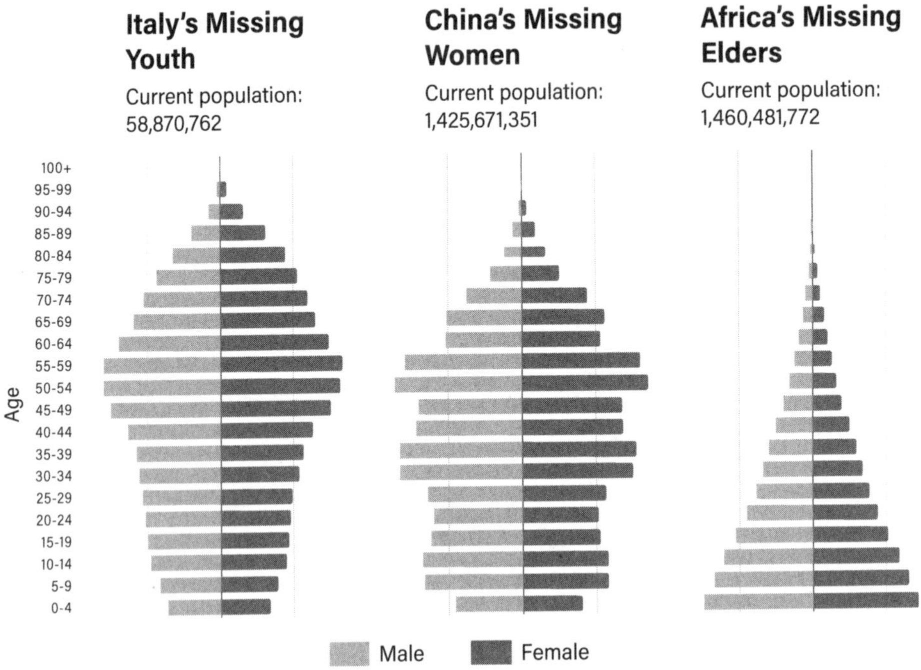

Source: PopulationPyramid.net, UN Department of Economic and Social Affairs, Population Division.

Meanwhile, the inverse demographic trend is true for many developing nations, especially in Africa, where over 40 percent of the population is still under the age of eighteen, and fewer than one in twenty people are older than sixty-five. Such youthful societies lack some of the generational wisdom that accumulates over time in the elders of the tribe. But they can also harness the unique "demographic dividend" of a young, mobile, and energetic workforce—provided that quality education and job opportunities are abundant. However, without this critical infrastructure, persistently high youth unemployment can trigger social unrest—along with billions in economic damages.[13]

As we learned in Chapter 9, migration is one potential response to the mismatch in labor conditions, though it is far from a panacea. Labor mobility was one of the great promises of globalization, and over the past half-century, young workers left their jobless home countries in record numbers, looking to supply the talent and tax base that aging societies increasingly required.[14] But opportunities have become more scarce and the future less certain, and support for immigration has recently turned from enthusiasm to intolerance.[15]

As a result, in recent years the frontiers between countries have become more hostile to human transit, even though migrants continue to stream up the Hierarchy of Stability in record numbers. It isn't yet clear which of these two opposing forces will prevail. In either scenario, the gray rhino of demographics seems destined to destabilize both economic and international affairs in the years ahead.

These growing pressures interact with a third systemic development we've been tracking closely—an alarming rise in *social tensions*. As we've argued throughout the book, trust is a vital lubricant in human affairs. Georg Simmel once described it as "one of the most important synthetic forces within society."[16] But in recent years, research by the renowned Edelman Trust Institute has revealed that trust in business, government, the media, and even nonprofits has plummeted.[17] This trend is exacerbated by technological innovations such as smartphones and digital media platforms, which are undermining our psychological well-being and social cohesion.[18] It's also driven by demographic shifts, including increased migration and urbanization, that are straining our aging infrastructure and beleaguered institutions.[19]

The chronic scarcity and dysfunction this convergence of factors produces often leads to frustration with "the system"—a demoralizing feeling that "the government" is broken and no longer living up to its end of the bargain. Services become unreliable or unavailable, public spaces are more difficult to access and keep clean and safe, and limited resources are spread ever thinner over an increasingly complex and bewildered bureaucracy.

We certainly agree that many public institutions need to be radically modernized, even in the world's most advanced economies. As a matter of principle, all organizations need to change with the times. But tearing them to the ground is perhaps the surest way to slide back down the Hierarchy of Stability—and a danger to all businesses and citizens unprepared for the greater turbulence that would inevitably follow.

As we learned in Chapter 3, the capacity of public institutions to engender trust and trade between strangers is the greatest differentiator between advanced, emerging, and frontier economies. So any efforts to undermine their utility or authority will only destabilize economic and social conditions even further. This is particularly troublesome in years like

2024, when for the first time, more than half of humanity participated in national elections.[20]

But rather than prompting greater investment and renewal, in recent years populist politicians and their wealthy patrons have risen to power on the promise of a shrinking role for the public sector in public life. Many institutions that have taken centuries to build—election systems, health systems, and justice systems—are being weakened and undermined. Ironically, these are often the very institutions designed to engender greater trust between strangers and help countries migrate up the Hierarchy of Stability and achieve greater prosperity.

This is precisely what makes recent editions of the Edelman Trust Barometer so discouraging. Beyond collapsing trust in both public and private institutions, we now seem to be losing trust in our fellow human beings. In its 2023 survey of over 32,000 respondents across 28 countries, only 30 percent said they were willing to help someone who disagreed with their point of view if they were in need. Even fewer—just 20 percent—would want to live in the same neighborhood or work in the same company with someone who disagreed with them. This does not bode well for peaceful relations in the years ahead. If anything, these conditions seem to echo the rising social tensions experienced a century ago, which eventually dragged humanity into decades of political and economic chaos.[21]

Yet, astonishingly, despite the looming disruptions posed by advanced technologies, rising demographic pressures, and falling trust in others, the global economy has so far continued its steady ascent—roughly tripling in size since the start of the twenty-first century.[22] One could reasonably argue that this is an indication of the resilience and enduring potential of the current world order. But sustained global growth only tells part of the story. For over two decades, the growing frequency of *market failures*—recessions, panics, banking failures, currency crises, and deflation—has been mostly stabilized and contained through a prolific expansion of debt.

Starting with the dot-com bubble and 9/11, then accelerating with a full-scale rescue of the financial system in 2008, and culminating with budget-busting pandemic packages in 2020, the world economy has performed admirably, though in no small part thanks to massive stimulus programs, particularly among advanced economies.[23] Like cardiologists treating a failing heart, policymakers were quick to respond to each of these crises, shocking the economy back into action by flooding the system with fresh spending (fiscal stimulus) and cheap debt (monetary stimulus).

The short-term goal was to avoid painful recessions and collapsing asset prices. The hope was that, in the long term, life support could be withdrawn and economic growth would resume under its own momentum. Unfortunately, whenever politicians and central bankers threatened to scale back this unprecedented support, most conspicuously in the summer of 2013, capital markets had a "tantrum," economic optimism faded, and policymakers lost their resolve—or their jobs.[24]

As a result, many households, companies, and governments have become conditioned to cheap and plentiful credit, which is accumulating at the fastest pace in history. Consider that global debt expanded by US$10 trillion in the first half of 2023 alone, and by US$100 trillion over the past five years—even faster than the growth of the overall economy. As of this writing, it is now at a staggering US$300 trillion and climbing.[25]

So far, policymakers have managed to avoid a reprise of the Great Depression. But no system can rely on stimulus indefinitely without triggering adverse consequences. As the burden of paying back debt shifts from one generation to the next, it can become a divisive issue centered around intergenerational justice. That's less of an issue when economies are growing quickly, as they were during the second half of the twentieth century. Rising productivity enables future generations to shoulder a larger tax burden, facilitating the repayment of debts accumulated by their parents. However, when growth is slowing as it has been in recent decades, and borrowing continues at a breakneck pace,[26] it forces difficult fiscal tradeoffs that politicians have so far been unwilling to make—such as raising taxes, reducing spending, or defaulting on debt. Instead, like many households and businesses, they have relied on an extended era of ultra-low rates and easy access to credit to mask these growing structural risks.

With rates finally returning to the more historical levels last seen right before the Global Financial Crisis, policymakers won't be able to "kick the can down the road" for much longer. For instance, in 2023, the US government paid nearly US$700 billion in interest—roughly US$2 billion a day—and for the first time, the same as it spends on defense and

Medicare. Meanwhile, among emerging and frontier economies, there have been more sovereign debt defaults in the past three years than over the previous two decades, and, according to the World Bank, 60 percent of low-income countries are currently at "high risk of debt distress."[27]

The historian Niall Ferguson recently argued that the stakes in play for the United States and other advanced economies couldn't be higher: "Any great power that spends more on debt service . . . than on defense will not stay great for very long."[28] An American debt default may be highly unlikely, because the government can simply print more money to pay off its obligations. But the alternatives to default—higher inflation, slower growth, and budget cuts—all point toward lower living standards and tougher business conditions for many years to come.

To be clear, debt on its own isn't inherently dangerous. After all, moneylending is perhaps the world's second-oldest profession, and borrowing its second-oldest vice.[29] In fact, without mechanisms to redistribute capital

Global Debt Levels at All-Time Highs

Increased borrowing can support growth but generates greater economic volatility

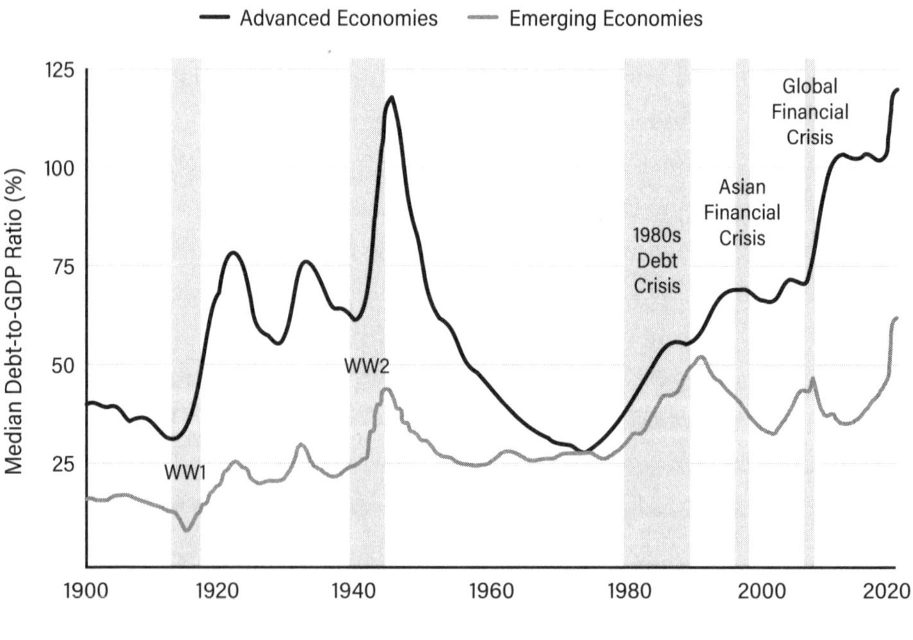

Source: IMF Global Debt Database, *Financial Times*

between savers and borrowers, modern civilization as we know it would be impossible. Debt has been used for thousands of years to finance critical infrastructure and investments—and more recently to help counterbalance the natural boom and bust of the business cycle—all of which provide proven benefits to societies over the long run.[30] However, when an increasing share of debt is being used to fuel the shorter-term impulses of households (e.g., buy now, pay later), businesses (e.g., leveraged buyouts), and countries (e.g., myopic industrial policies), it makes it more difficult to pay back these loans in the future.[31] Until business leaders and policymakers wake up to this sobering reality, by choice or by force, greater turbulence in financial markets and the broader economy is likely to follow.[32]

The last of the "big five" megatrends we all need to factor into our strategic and risk planning is the impact of a *changing climate*. From rising seas to scalding heatwaves to devastating droughts and fatal floods, the effects of a changing climate are inescapable. But let's be perfectly clear: whatever comes next, Planet Earth will survive. It's humanity that is most at risk.

Whether we attribute recent environmental patterns to human activities, or believe that the planet is simply progressing through a natural phase of transition, one thing is certain—extreme weather events are accelerating in frequency and impact, and they can no longer be ignored.

In decades past, our leaders could be forgiven for this short-sightedness. While observational trends in weather were growing more ominous by the year, scientists struggled to model out the complexity of the Earth's many interactive systems. They also struggled to explain this dynamic web of interactivity to lay audiences and policymakers. Meanwhile, business leaders remained captive to the narrow interests of owners—historically focused more on value than values. Since bottom lines weren't dramatically affected by a changing climate, strategic plans and investments rarely took these distant and slow-moving threats into consideration.

However, in recent years, scientists and businesses have amassed a much deeper and more sophisticated understanding of how climate systems have been evolving. Accelerating advances in computer hardware (such as next-gen graphics cards) and software (deep learning neural networks) have helped scientists make exponential advances in modeling how climate systems work and how they're likely to change in the future.[33]

Climate Change Is Inevitable

Rising surface temperatures in recent decades are destined to continue

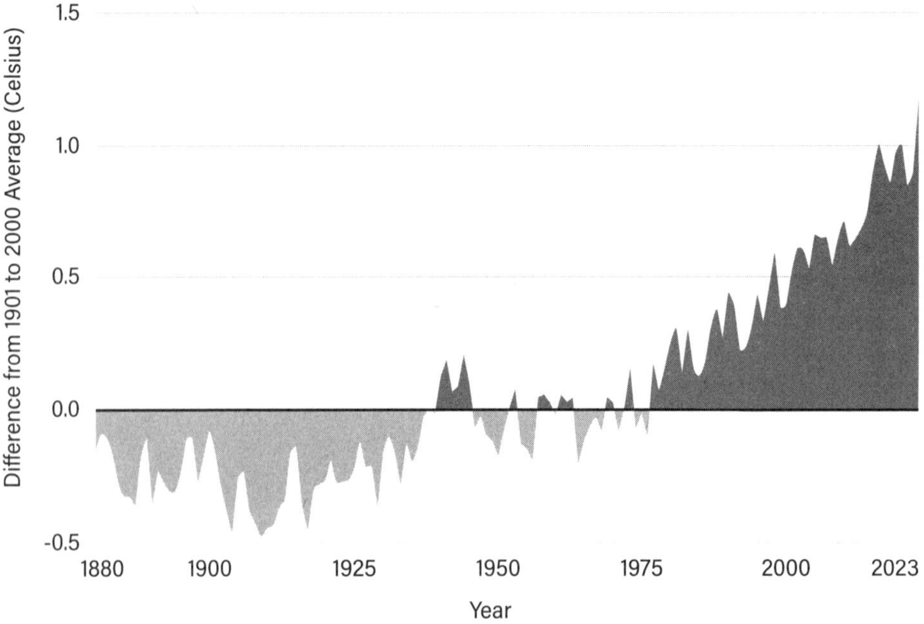

Source: NASA Land-Ocean Temperature Index

These new models will also help scientists more accurately predict the effects of weather patterns on natural disasters, biodiversity, and even human populations and economies.

That said, we don't need the world's most powerful supercomputers to identify certain obvious trends. All of us can look at the global warming chart (see "Climate Change Is Inevitable") and recognize the basic upward slope that coincides with the rise of the first advanced economies in the early twentieth century. We can debate whether that's coincidental or causal. What we can't dispute is that the weather is getting more extreme by the year, and that the "Great Acceleration" is causing significant economic damage across the entire Hierarchy of Stability.

On average, Americans now experience extreme weather events with damages above US$1 billion once every three weeks. In the 1980s, when adjusted for inflation, it was once every four months.[34] In Latin America, the worst droughts in seventy years have restricted traffic through

Extreme Weather Events Are Becoming More Frequent and Costly

Total economic damage is becoming difficult to ignore

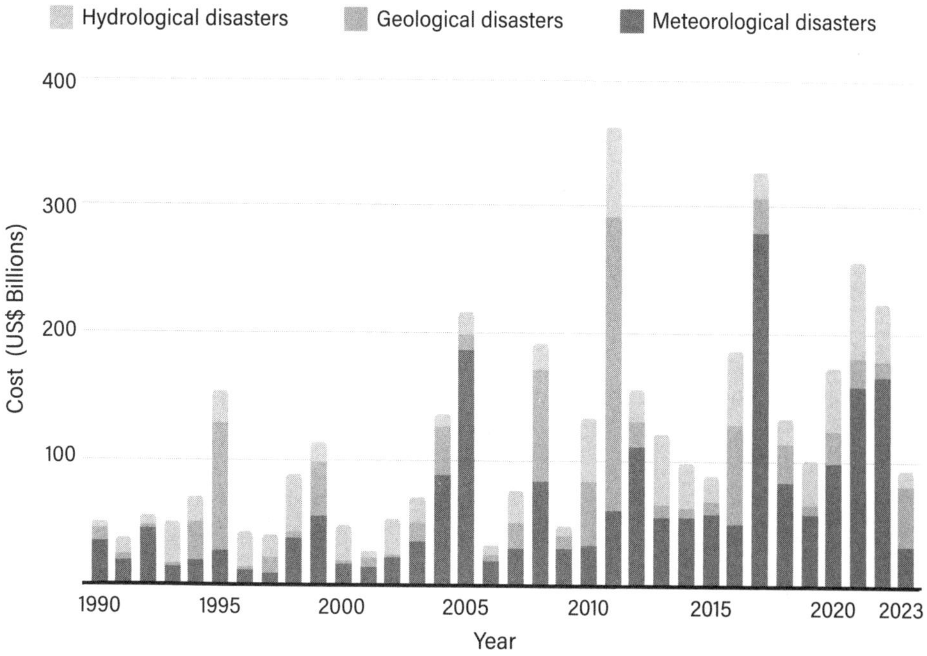

Source: Our World in Data, World Bank

the Panama Canal by over 50 percent, increasing costs and uncertainty in global supply chains.[35] In Africa, growing threats such as floods, hordes of locusts, and droughts are causing so much food insecurity, population displacement, and stress on water resources that economists now expect a 15 percent hit to African GDP by 2050.[36] In Asia and beyond, rising sea levels threaten over US$14 trillion in fixed assets.[37] And the list goes on.

Advanced economies may have more resources available to absorb the impacts of these ominous trends, but so far they have struggled to deploy them coherently or substantially. Meanwhile, climate change seems destined to affect emerging and frontier economies disproportionately, both because of their geography and owing to short-sighted leadership.

Yet there is a silver lining. The epic scale and scope of these potential damages creates a large and truly global community with vested interests in finding structural solutions. From real estate directly exposed to nature's wrath, to insurance companies and pension investors with rising portfolio risk, to climate technologists and impact capitalists looking to build the future one innovation at a time, there are more ways than ever to profit from managing and mitigating the gray rhino of climate change.[38]

Surprisingly, the business community has been slow to recognize these immense commercial opportunities. But as the frequency of disruptive climate events accelerates in the years ahead—as with each of the other big five forces—investing in stability will become a strategic imperative for organizations everywhere.

To us, the logic is both simple and obvious—there's a reason a herd of rhinos is called a "crash." What we find so remarkable, given that logic, is how few organizations seem adequately prepared for the coming storm.

AN ENTERPRISE FOR ALL SEASONS

Consider that in 2023, as the world was emerging from a pandemic, geopolitical tensions were nearing Cold War heights, and natural disasters were devastating countries across the planet, McKinsey surveyed more than 2,500 global business leaders operating in nine of the most advanced economies. Even under these menacing conditions, only half of the leaders surveyed believed that their companies were well braced for external shocks.[39] As the research cautioned, "Organizations with little to no experience with agility or adaptability can end up in a double bind: unmotivated to prepare for crises during periods of calm *and* unable to change course and respond quickly when disruption occurs."[40]

Careful readers of this book will not be surprised that so many organizations were caught flat-footed. As we've argued, business conditions in advanced economies have been so good for so long that many leaders have either forgotten—or were never trained—to prepare for and manage through turbulent times.

Meanwhile, further down the Hierarchy of Stability, leaders intuitively understand that a singular focus on profitability is not the most reliable path to enduring success. Higher-risk environments are certainly correlated with higher returns, but not for all competitors. In practice, those statistics are driven by a few big winners offset by a long tail of losers.

So investments in stability, as part of a systematic approach to managing risk, become table stakes both for survival and success.

As a general rule, in the face of danger the last thing we should do is bury our heads in the sand. "It's a classic bias in human thinking," the macroeconomist Nouriel Roubini has argued. "Most of us never want to imagine the worst. We are optimists by nature."[41] This hopeful perspective is an important driver of entrepreneurial activity and risk-taking, particularly under stable conditions.

But as we're all learning, in the New Age of Uncertainty, one-hundred-year storms are becoming seasonal events, even among advanced economies. Leaders will need to plan for more of the rare and unpredictable black swan events, such as 9/11 and the Global Financial Crisis, while also bracing for charging rhinos. This is all in addition to conventional continuity risks, like succession and competition. In short, we'll need to prepare our enterprises to thrive in all seasons.

If you're lucky, you've picked up this book during a bountiful spring or summer, in the fairest of weather, and you're busy making hay while the sun is shining. Under these favorable conditions, think of the insights we've presented throughout the book as an early warning system—like moving to Canada in July and first learning about cold-weather gear like base layers and "toques."

If you're reading it during an autumn transition, as the days get shorter and the nights grow colder, we hope it serves as a pragmatic reminder to keep the firewood piled high. For those who have reached for this book in the darkest depths of winter—during an extended period of scarcity and adversity—we hope the strategies and cases will not only stimulate some innovative problem solving, but also provide a ray of hope that spring will someday return, and that the human creativity and ingenuity that got us into this mess in the first place can also get us out of it.

In short, to thrive in all seasons, we need to anticipate and plan for periodic change. We must prepare our businesses, our ownership, our families, and ourselves to navigate with confidence through both fair and stormy weather. In these complex and ever-changing environments, we need to aim not for perfection, but for progress. We hope the many cases featured throughout the book have provided ample inspiration for you to embrace this frontier mindset, and demonstrated how these concepts can work in practice. Below we'll share a few final suggestions on where to get started.

PREPARING YOUR BUSINESS

Let's begin with the business subsystem—the economic lifeblood of a family enterprise. Throughout the book, we've proposed a model of resilience where crises are considered endemic. As their frequency increases and their impacts grow in the years ahead, managing operational risks should become the opposite of "whack-a-mole." Knowing this, leaders of enduring enterprises must be skilled at scanning their horizons. They get curious about what lies beyond the frontiers of the known and familiar.

Those who thrive under these conditions have learned to metabolize uncertainty and take valuable lessons from others. As you think about a business issue you're currently wrestling with, recall the Carvajals in Colombia, the Baalbakis in Syria, the Tatas in India, and the Lees in South Korea. Now imagine what you might do under analogous circumstances. Their stories are now your stories—part of your strategic inventory—and we encourage you to use them to stress-test your assumptions.

Not all leaders are blessed with grace under fire, but with practice and discipline, we can all get better at making decisions in turbulent conditions. One simple exercise proposed by Nobel laureate Daniel Kahneman is to conduct a "pre-mortem," which helps leadership teams proactively identify potential pitfalls before committing to a course of action. It is specifically designed to help you detect blind spots, uncover biases, test assumptions, and understand the knowledge gaps that might otherwise go unnoticed during traditional strategic planning.[42]

Such simulations are how armies prepare for war, and how astronauts prepare for space—among the most complex, expensive, and death-defying enterprises of all time. Teams test and refine their responses to a battery of adverse scenarios until their performance under pressure is perfected. That way, if any issues emerge during their missions, when lives are at stake, teams aren't improvising on the fly. Whether they're in a foxhole fighting under heavy fire, or in a space capsule trouble-shooting a critical malfunction, these teams can improvise, like an experienced jazz band, in harmonious and synergistic ways.[43]

Few leaders will ever face the same level of existential risk as officers and astronauts on active missions, or have as much time or money to plan for every contingency. But, as with battlefields and space flight, the best business simulations involve a series of disorienting dilemmas that challenge leaders to solve problems they haven't ever faced before. They test leaders both intellectually and emotionally—making sure they can keep a cool head when everyone around them is losing theirs.[44] They also challenge us to problem-solve together—since these moments will inevitably require collective action. Like runners training at high altitude, when teams simulate life in high-risk scenarios they get better at navigating uncertainty with confidence.

If you're willing to engage in this kind of preemptive training, then whenever the next hurricane, headline, or hot war catches you by surprise, you'll at least have one notch already on your belt, and will be able to respond faster than those who have not prepared at all. That response time, it turns out, is one of the best predictors of long-term performance in good times and bad.

In a 2020 paper, researchers at the Boston Consulting Group studied the link between organizational resilience and performance. Based on 1,800 American companies operating between 1995 and 2020, they concluded that resilience in unfavorable periods accounts for roughly 30 percent of long-term outperformance. In other words, long-term success was driven both by how well companies responded to shocks and how well they chased profits. Moreover, the researchers found that the speed and success of the initial response accounted for 63 percent of this outperformance.[45]

Yet, faced with the dilemma of balancing efficiency or resilience, many leaders still choose profitability over pliability. The management scholar and former business school dean Roger Martin framed the dangers of such a lopsided approach this way: "Pursuit of all resilience and no efficiency is as problematic as pursuit of efficiency with no resilience. The only difference is in the nature of the death."[46]

Enduring Enterprises Perform Better on Three Fronts

Absorbing shocks, accelerating recovery, and "bouncing back better"

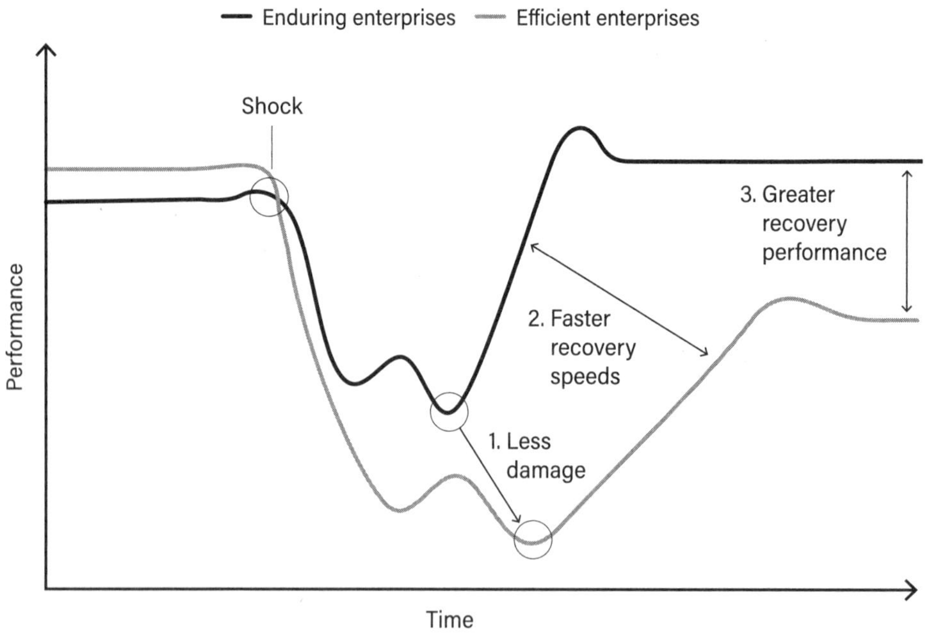

Source: Adapted from BCG Henderson Institute

Knowing when to go on the offense and when to play defense is both art and science. Striking the right balance, and adjusting over time as conditions change, requires a form of leadership that is not often found in advanced economies, but that is typified by each of the cases from emerging and frontier economies that we've featured throughout the book.

Winston Churchill is perhaps the quintessential political illustration of the lesson that leading successfully through conflict requires a fundamentally different skill set and temperament than leading through peace. This basic idea was the premise behind the contingency theory of leadership, pioneered in the 1960s by the Austrian scholar Fred Fiedler, and subsequently refined by the psychologists Victor Vroom, Philip Yetton, and Arthur Jago, among others.[47]

The model posits that effective leadership requires congruence between a leader's innate style and the prevailing situation. Successful leaders learn to read their circumstances and adopt the behaviors needed depending on such factors as the time they have to respond, the extent to which they have the information needed to make the right decision, and the degree to which the decision requires the buy-in of subordinates in order to be successfully implemented. Others take a more radical approach, and argue that rather than forcing someone to change their approach to suit a new context, we should instead change the leader altogether—elevating Churchills when conditions call for bold action, and replacing them with Clement Attlees during times of peace and prosperity.[48] Whether we focus on changing the style or the leader, the consensus is that fitting the skills of a leader to the prevailing conditions matters hugely.

As the author G. Michael Hopf has poetically observed, "Hard times create strong men, strong men create good times, good times create weak men, and weak men create hard times."[49] The most resilient and effective leaders we know have a unique capacity to respond to hard times. They demonstrate what our friend and colleague Dr. Chris Robichaud at the Harvard Kennedy School calls "existential leadership"—effectively navigating periods of extreme uncertainty when lives and livelihoods are on the line.

This sustained situational vigilance doesn't come naturally to all leaders, in all organizations, in all seasons. It's also less alluring than the flavor of leadership taught in most Western business schools, and it is particularly rare among organizations at the peak of the Hierarchy of Stability. Unless we operate in a naturally defensive or safety-conscious industry, instilling a greater sense of preparedness and urgency can often feel like taking the punch bowl away from our teams in the middle of a party.

But while changing seasons are inevitable in the years to come, comfort and complacency remain common impediments. Often the best that leaders can do in these moments is to disappoint people at a pace they can tolerate, knowing that it is the only viable path to building an enduring enterprise.

PREPARING YOUR OWNERS

So far we've devoted most of our attention to crisis management, rather than crisis governance. In our experience, this lopsided focus is quite common among executives, boards, and even academics.[50] However, preparing owners to govern effectively during periods of greater uncertainty poses a unique set of challenges. When one's business model and legacy are both under threat, good governance becomes even more essential for survival and success.

As a result, enduring enterprises invest heavily in *educating family shareholders* about what they own, why they own it, and how it's governed. These are essential ingredients for building long-term commitment among a diverse community of family members. A client once observed that when owners inherit shares in a family enterprise, those shares don't come with a "user manual." These owners must be trained to understand what the business does, starting with the products and services it offers and how they are designed, produced, and delivered. They must also be educated about the values, purpose, and vision that together make up the company's ownership philosophy.[51] In frontier economies, especially, it is critical for owners to understand the organization's risk and crisis management protocols, and to trust the teams that will steward the enterprise through recurring cycles of feast and famine.

In many ways, family owners serve as the institutional memory of an enterprise. Sharing the origin stories of how the business was started and the trials that founders had to endure can inoculate later generations against hubris and complacency. The notion that even great wealth can be lost is a strong signal that the enterprise—and the family's fortune—should never be taken for granted.

The distributed wisdom and experience of owners is particularly valuable in volatile environments, when strategic dilemmas and value trade-offs will challenge the skill and resolve of even the most effective decision-makers. A family's deep purpose, shared vision, and core values can provide stability and clarity during periods of rapid change.

Enduring enterprises embrace the ongoing education of their family owners as an integral component of their continuity strategy. They hold regular family meetings and organize structured conversations about the family's past practices and current operations. They preview strategic plans and future scenarios that will shape the mission and performance of the organization in the years and decades to come. In short, they find ways to transfer a culture of effective leadership, stewardship, and entrepreneurship across generations.

Particularly in recent years, this objective has required families to consider a more nuanced definition of engagement—one that goes beyond the preconceived expectation that children will follow their parents dutifully into the family business.[52] There are, in fact, four distinct ways in which family owners can engage with their shared enterprise—but while three of these are highly valuable, one of them is not:

1. They can be *operating owners*—directly involved with the management of the enterprise. These owners guide strategy and lead operations with "boots on the ground" on a daily basis. This role has historically been the most common, and it can help to streamline decision-making, though it doesn't always produce the best outcomes for individuals or the system. This is particularly true when there is a mismatch between the desires and skills of family members and the strategic needs of the enterprise.
2. They can be *governing owners*—actively involved in strategic planning and decision-making fora such as boards, family councils, family offices, and family foundations, though only at a governance level. This role is an excellent way of tapping human capital for those who are either not interested in or not available for daily operational engagement, but who can still add considerable value to oversight and decision-making at the highest levels of the enterprise.
3. They can be *engaged owners* who are neither in governance nor management, but stay connected with the enterprise both emotionally and economically. They participate in all collective activities, answer emails and messages from the family and the business, arrive prepared for meetings, ask great questions of leaders, and generally support the unity and commitment of the family.
4. Finally, they can also be *investing owners*—mostly focused on dividends and valuations, but otherwise emotionally detached from the enterprise. For those in this camp, the family business is just like any other asset in their portfolio, subject to the same raw calculus of risk and return. These owners often

resist family engagement, and they are the ones most likely to agitate for selling their shares, particularly during crises when resources are most scarce.

Over time, as families and their businesses grow in complexity and diversity, there tends to be a gradual migration away from operating roles among family members. Governance roles become a natural way of keeping particularly talented owners engaged without requiring them to dedicate their entire careers to the family enterprise. Similarly, nurturing a diverse community of engaged owners through sustained investments in learning and socialization becomes a strategic imperative.

In short, as we enter the New Age of Uncertainty, keeping a sizable quorum of owners in the first three of these categories is essential, both for continuity and for resilience. If too many owners drift away from the enterprise and become mere investors, many of the strategic advantages of being a family company become diluted. Thriving across the ever-changing seasons is hard enough without structural misalignments among owners around long-term vision, core values, liquidity policies, and so on.

Enduring enterprises also deploy *adaptive governance* structures to buttress their resilience. They frequently adjust their sense-making and decision-making to match their new circumstances—even if it feels awkward and unfamiliar at first. Some owners who aren't forced to build a board—by regulators, partners, or lenders—often dismiss or discount this strategic resource. But as we discovered during the 2020 pandemic, boards and their leadership teams become the nerve centers through which all critical business information and decision-making flows during a crisis—both downwardly into an organization, and upwardly to its owners.

During a crisis, leaders throughout the system need to huddle more closely and frequently to improve their speed and agility. Like penguins in the winter, governance systems often grow much closer during a crisis before expanding once again as conditions improve in the proverbial spring.

To be clear, there is no permanent solution for effective decision-making. As a business's context evolves, so, too, must its decision-making systems. But in times of abundance, there's much less pressure to change. Some families, particularly in advanced economies, can get a decade or more from their governance system before it begins to malfunction. Others aren't so lucky, learning the hard way that good governance is a moving target. Large groups debating complex, abstract problems are tolerable when the world is stable. But as a situation slides down the Hierarchy of Stability, business leaders need to move decisively. This kind of response typically requires smaller, more nimble teams that can meet frequently and share information openly and rapidly.

Perhaps the most daunting question owners face during these moments is whether they have a shared *commitment to continuity* or are ready to exit the business altogether. After all, there's no point adapting your governance if there is no shared commitment to a collaborative future.[53] As we approach the largest generational wealth transfer in history, answers to this question will have systems-level implications for operating companies, investment portfolios, and philanthropic foundations around the world for decades to come. They will also deeply impact the families themselves, because their lives and livelihoods are often inextricably linked to the fortunes of the business.

PREPARING YOUR FAMILY

Talk to the members of any enterprising family that has succeeded in emerging and frontier markets, and you will hear many anecdotes of how they have overcome adversity countless times throughout their history. One of our favorites was shared by a founder who took his five children on a fishing trip to a beautiful but remote island in the Gulf of Mexico. The day after they arrived and set up their camp, the weather turned and a furious storm rolled in, with hurricane-force winds. Realizing that the barren island offered no shelter, the father looked for the biggest tree he could spot and tethered himself and the children to it. After a terrifying night, they returned home the next day, traumatized but unharmed. The image of the children and their father tied to a tree in an unrelenting storm left an indelible impression, and remains part of the family's lore three generations later. It has become a lesson on the importance of familial interdependence in the face of adversity.

According to Dr. Froma Walsh, one of the leading authorities on family resilience, such *family belief systems* are a cornerstone in collective well-being. She argues that "we cope with crisis and prolonged adversity by making meaning of our experience: linking it to our social world, to our cultural and spiritual beliefs, to our multigenerational past, and to our hopes and dreams for the future."[54]

Yet, in the fog of war, natural disaster, or economic turmoil, families often neglect to articulate and share a common narrative. The purpose of what they are doing and why it matters recedes to the background. This omission weakens their ability to "make meaning" out of their shared experience, and inadvertently compromises the family's resilience. Importantly, according to Walsh, the most productive of these narratives stress a relational view of resilience, rather than one of self-reliance and rugged individualism. To evoke Rudyard Kipling in *The Jungle Book*, this further reinforces the strategic logic of modularity and symbiosis—that "the strength of the Pack is the Wolf, and the strength of the Wolf is the Pack."

Such narratives help to contextualize adversity, framing it as a common threat that the family can tackle if it can effectively harness collaboration and demonstrate grit. They provide hope and a sense of control over the family's shared destiny—feelings that otherwise can be elusive in these environments.[55] In the absence of these guiding principles, the external stresses that families naturally experience can easily aggravate internal conflicts.

When we worked with a family at the peak of the civil war in El Salvador, we observed this dynamic in action firsthand. As these conflicts inevitably bubbled up, it was useful for us to remind the family members that they were operating in an extremely fluid and hostile environment. After a while it dawned on them that their internal conflicts were a direct byproduct of their external environment. As one of them commented, "We fight with each other because, in this volatile situation, family is the one thing we can control." Redirecting anxiety into more constructive efforts—such as investing in the stabilizing strategies—first requires acknowledging that the source of stress and internal conflict is at least partly external.

But even shared stories and open communication can only help so much. Recognizing these limits, many families build in time for *collective "shore leave"*—strategic investments to get away from the front lines and decompress in more stable environments. This unique form of seasonal migration allows family members to recharge their emotional batteries—essential for sustaining collective resilience over the long term.

Practically all of the successful families we know in emerging and frontier economies have secondary homes in more stable jurisdictions such as New York, Miami, Dubai, London, or Singapore. These cities offer them the unique opportunity to spend time away from the pressures of the frontiers, in blissful anonymity, engaged in precisely the type of joyful play and connection that Walsh highlighted as essential for nurturing greater individual and collective resilience.

Then, at some point, these family members must inevitably return to the front lines. When they do, the grim realities of landing back home are difficult to ignore. Feelings of anxiety and personal insecurity quickly return. Many who live and work further down on the Hierarchy of Stability have been victims of kidnappings, break-ins, and personal assaults. They often live in family compounds or walled communities protected by their own private security teams. Some families have described this experience to us as living in a gilded cage, evoking Rousseau's warning when he said that "tranquility is found also in dungeons; but is that enough to make them desirable places to live?"[56]

The emotional bonds that hold extended familial networks together are often frayed by these sustained stressors, and any relational fissures lurking beneath the surface during times of abundance are quickly exposed under pressure. In these moments, the psychological boundaries between individual family members can begin to dissolve, producing more psychological enmeshment, reactivity, and intensity, which can easily strain even the healthiest relationships.[57]

For instance, it isn't uncommon for those in management to gradually resent being the only "boots on the ground," raising their families in conflict zones, while those not directly involved live comfortably away from danger, but still reap the benefits.[58] This point is especially challenging for younger family members, who are trying to forge their own identities in the world, but are forced to do so under the menacing context of chronic uncertainty.[59]

Consequently, it is imperative for family leaders to invest in building connections across each of these divides. Holding meetings to educate family members about the business, organizing site tours and internships, hosting fireside chats with key executives, engaging in collective philanthropic activities, investing in the continuous development of family members capable of participating responsibly on boards, councils, and assemblies that make up the governance system of their enterprises—these activities can all foster a greater sense of emotional connection and trust.

But such proactive efforts rarely happen without intention. People often wrongly assume that successful families hold themselves together automatically—the "all you need is love" theory of governance. But while love always helps, nothing could be further from the truth. Instead, they develop leaders who take personal responsibility for doing whatever the family needs to hold itself together. And what the family needs increases dramatically the larger the family grows—for instance, greater investments to sustain a shared identity, to buttress and reinforce family values and norms, and to foster a sense of togetherness. In that sense, we all have the families we deserve.

PREPARING YOURSELF

Many leaders fail to prioritize self-care even in the best of times, despite ample evidence of its many benefits. But during a crisis, when judgment and decision-making can literally become a matter of survival, having the strength and resources to endure extended periods of stress is essential. Under these conditions, leaders need to follow the advice they receive every time they board a commercial airplane. In the event of a sudden decompression, they need to first put on their own oxygen masks before helping others.

We are often so focused on plowing through our daily task lists and taking care of others that we neglect our own well-being. When leading large and complex enterprises through periods of transformational change, this can easily lead to exhaustion, burnout, and poor decision-making. Regular exercise, sufficient sleep, good nutrition, and mindfulness can all help you maintain a clear head and a healthy body. In turn, this sends an important signal throughout the enterprise that the system is in good hands.

In a timely article in November 2023, with hot wars raging in Ukraine and Gaza, cold wars brewing in Taiwan and Korea, and media wars confusing and distracting citizens everywhere, author David Brooks reminded his readers that the crust of civilization has always been thin, and that "breakdowns into barbarism are the historical norm."[60] In these moments, Brooks encourages us to resist becoming overwhelmed or desensitized, as countless generations have in the past.

Instead, we need to be clear-eyed about the potential for chaos and disorder in human affairs while remaining hopeful that our leaders and communities will leverage their better angels, and negotiate a path toward greater peace and prosperity. Greek poets understood this dichotomy well thousands of years ago. As Brooks pointed out, it may have been the original inspiration for the development of theatrical tragedies (to keep us vigilant) and comedies (to keep us optimistic).

The capacity to find strength in adversity, and to bring humor and perspective to our darkest moments, is a common characteristic among successful leaders. One Mexican entrepreneur we know well is the poster child for this type of resilient personality. His family business has been directly threatened over the years by the criminal syndicates dominating political and economic affairs along the US-Mexico border. In his various campaigns to bring greater safety and stability to thousands of workers and customers, he has at times become the target of the cartel's bullying. One unforgettable morning, he arrived at work and discovered a cooler filled with the severed heads of local police officers. This particular leader was able to shrug off the danger—joking with us that "at least they were delivered on ice."

Not everyone is wired to handle uncertainty with such resolve. Even those who do are often subconsciously affected by the chronic stress it entails, despite their best efforts to ignore the wolves howling at the door. To avoid being overwhelmed in these challenging moments, it's crucial for all of us to develop productive coping mechanisms. If we do, we'll at least be braced for impact the next time crisis darkens our doorstep.

THE END OF THE BEGINNING

We began the book by making the case that we should never take stability for granted, even among the most advanced economies. This stability stems from centuries of accumulated investment in key institutions, infrastructures, and markets, which freed citizens and businesses from many of the worries and concerns that have plagued human societies for millennia.

However, the hopeful spring that prevailed after World War II—and that accelerated into a bountiful summer after the Cold War—has recently given way to an autumn of escalating turbulence.[61] Hard infrastructure, such as roads and power systems, and soft infrastructure, including schools and justice systems, are increasingly under threat from new technologies, shifting populations, eroding trust, escalating debt, and a tempestuous climate. Meanwhile, the stability of markets for capital, goods, talent, and information have all been undermined by short-sighted governments and gangsters, leaving them more vulnerable to manipulation and dysfunction.

To be clear, this book isn't intended to be a demoralizing reminder of all that's broken in the world. In fact, our goal was just the opposite—to break through our pervasive denial about these risks and find new ways to thrive both in adversity and prosperity for generations to come. These insights can help you navigate the future with conviction, knowing that others have conquered similar challenges on the road to leading some of the most iconic and enduring enterprises on the planet. Their stories of survival and success can vaccinate you against despair.

Whenever you're feeling discouraged or disoriented, we hope you'll take some inspiration from each of them: the enlightened stewardship of the Carvajal family, the remarkable endurance of Kongō Gumi, the ingenious differentiation of the Añaños family, the systemic modularity of the Zamil Group, the symbiotic successes and challenges of Samsung, the redundant infrastructures of Le Plaza Hotel, the migratory agility of the Baalbaki family, the strategic simplification of Grupo Arcor, and the pioneering diversity of the Tata tribe. These stories of endurance are obviously unique to their families, their geographical locations, and the times in which they lived and made major decisions. But they reinforce a broader approach to thriving in the toughest conditions, which can be emulated by leaders everywhere: *Treat crises as inescapable, pursue continuity with intention, and focus on both growth and resilience.*

Those born and raised in frontier economies are less likely than those in advanced economies to be phased by rolling blackouts, broken bridges, or even severed heads. These enduring enterprises are built for black swans and gray rhinos—in addition to all of the typical risks that any business faces on the path to multigenerational success. Some take a more strategic and proactive approach—preparing for whatever life might throw at them. Others are more tactical and reactive—navigating crises based on instinct and experience. In both cases, their investments in stability can be scaled up or down as conditions warrant, providing inspiration for how to cope with minor disturbances and traumatic shocks.

The lucky few who find themselves moving up the Hierarchy of Stability during a polycrisis will quickly discover that public institutions and infrastructures become more reliable, and greater trust in strangers becomes possible—though competition also becomes more fierce. Investments in stability are still valuable, but the marginal returns diminish when roads are straighter and safer and when capital becomes cheaper and more abundant.[62]

Building the Enduring Enterprise

Bringing it all together

Proactive Planning		**Adaptive Response**		**Enhanced Recovery**		
Anticipating and responding more quickly to threats	+	Limiting the damage from threats when they arise	+	Resuming operations quickly and pursuing growth as crisis subsides	=	**The Enduring Enterprise**
Managing risk strategically with the FERM framework		Navigating crises effectively with the seven Stabilizing Strategies		Leveraging the Hierarchy of Stability to orient and inspire		

In contrast, those skidding down the hierarchy—by far the majority of countries worldwide—will quickly discover how dangerous it can be to take their current level of stability for granted. On-demand power, food, water, and climate allow the average citizen to live with a level of comfort that once eluded kings. But when the modular foundations of globalization begin to break down—as they did during the COVID-19 pandemic—trust quickly evaporates, alliances fragment, trade slows, infrastructure fails, and social tensions rise. The lower we slip down the Hierarchy of Stability, the more precious each small step toward resilience becomes.

This shift represents a new strategic mindset: building businesses that can navigate the ever-changing landscape, not just chase the next shiny new trend. As owners and operators start embracing this new logic and outperforming their growth-obsessed peers, a fascinating trend will emerge. Business leaders everywhere will increasingly trade in their current high priests of efficiency and growth—the likes of Elon Musk and Jeff Bezos—for enduring enterprises like Carvajal, Baalbaki, and Zamil, who have learned to thrive in all seasons. By studying their stories and applying their timeless wisdom, we can all be better equipped to face the many new dangers and opportunities that lie ahead.

KEY INSIGHTS

- Five disruptive megatrends, all decades in the making, are currently converging and are likely to threaten stability at all levels on the Hierarchy of Stability in the years ahead.
- These megatrends include *disruptive technologies* such as artificial intelligence; *demographic shifts*, including aging populations and labor migration; rising *social tensions* caused by an erosion of trust in governments, businesses, media, and other institutions; *market failures* that threaten the financial stability of nations, companies, and households; and a *changing climate* where the frequency of natural disasters and the damage they cause is becoming more dramatic every year.
- These five "gray rhinos" are not inevitable disasters, but rather predictable challenges that can be navigated successfully with adequate foresight and preparation.

- Businesses and families that proactively consider these trends in the context of their organizational designs and strategic planning will be better positioned to weather the coming storms.
- Regardless of the season in which we currently find ourselves—a bountiful summer or a grinding winter—building an enduring enterprise requires planning for change, fostering a culture of adaptability, and nurturing the long-term health of our businesses, our ownership, our families, and ourselves.
- How to prepare your *business*:
  - Treat crises as endemic: Don't be lulled into a false sense of security by current stability—proactive planning for disruptions is essential.
  - Stress-test your assumptions: Conduct simulations and pre-mortems to expose weaknesses in your plans and decision-making processes.
  - Balance growth and resilience: Don't prioritize short-term gains over long-term survival.
  - Stay vigilant: Study trends and learn from the experiences of others who thrive in adversity, especially those in frontier economies.
  - Develop leadership for all seasons: Different leadership styles are needed for different situations—be prepared to adapt your leadership approach as conditions change.
- How to prepare your *owners*:
  - Focus on education: Owners need to understand their business and their values and have a shared vision for building an enduring enterprise.
  - Invest in engagement: Family members can be involved in different ways—not everyone needs to work in the business to add value, but all owners need a strong emotional connection to the enterprise to sustain their unity and commitment.
  - Embrace dynamic governance: As business and environmental conditions evolve, governance structures need to be adjusted to ensure effective decision-making,

particularly as we shift up and down the Hierarchy of Stability.

- How to prepare your *family*:
  - Build a common narrative: A shared understanding of the family's history and values strengthens resilience during difficult times.
  - Communicate openly: Honest communication helps families navigate challenging moments and avoid internal conflicts.
  - Invest in "shore leave": Planned breaks from stressful environments allow families to recharge and maintain emotional resilience.
  - Bridge divides: Create opportunities for family members across generations and locations to sustain connection and trust.
- How to prepare *yourself*:
  - Prioritize self-care: Leaders need to be healthy and resilient to take care of others and make sound decisions during crises.
  - Maintain your objectivity: Acknowledge the challenges but don't become overwhelmed, and remain open to external support.
- As the post–World War II era of relative stability gives way to a period of greater turmoil, infrastructure, markets, and trust are increasingly under threat.
- But this isn't doomsday: Despite the many challenges that lie ahead, we want this book to empower leaders, not demoralize them!
- Remember that in turbulent times, resilience is more valuable than growth, so leaders simply need to find new strategies and heroes.
- Those who seek to build and sustain an enduring enterprise now have a new playbook, one that is still being written by families in some of the world's most complicated operating environments.

ACKNOWLEDGMENTS

This book is the product of ten years of work. Lots has happened in those years as life has continued to unfold at its wonderfully unforgiving pace: children and grandchildren were born, our firm expanded globally and transitioned to a new generation of partners, wonderful new colleagues joined and dear ones retired. Work on this study proceeded intermittently—one conversation at a time, sometimes at airports and on flights to and from client assignments; during Thanksgivings and summer holidays when we brought our families together; at professional conferences and university programs when we teamed up to teach; on field trips specifically designed to gather data; and, of course, before, during, and after our firm's quarterly meetings, when we debriefed about the myriad dilemmas facing enterprising families around the world and documented what we were learning. While it is certainly true that writing is a lonely business, developing, validating, and writing these ideas together made all the difference. It also made the work more interesting and fun.

But, as our client families have taught us, no meaningful endeavor is ever the result of individual actors working alone. There is always a relational context of family, friends, and colleagues without whose support the quality of our insights would be diminished and our work outright impaired.

We both have the good fortune to have enormously generous and supportive wives, Nathalie DeCiantis and Margarita Rodriguez-Lansberg. They challenged our ideas throughout and encouraged us to plow forward when the going got tough and the challenge of ever finishing this book seemed insurmountable. Most importantly, they created the space necessary for writing. The time away from them and from our children (Oskar, Zara, Daniel, Nella, Simon Emilio, Elise, Anny, and Gabriel) and granddaughters (Michelle, Claudia, and Dario) is the biggest sacrifice we make as authors. We must be doubly thankful to them, since it is our concern for the world that they will be inheriting that provided the impetus for us to write this book in the first place. They are our greatest source of hope, inspiration, renewal, and fun. Additionally, we are immensely grateful to our parents, whose hard work, diverse ethnicities, and entrepreneurial exploits laid the foundations for our understanding of these global phenomena. One of the places where our generational differences show is that Ivan's parents passed away many years ago, while Devin's remain an integral part of his family. Frank and Leila's unwavering support and love have been constant throughout his life, and are the source of his confidence and resilience.

We are also deeply grateful to all the families featured in the book. While a few of the cases are derived primarily from publicly available information (e.g., AJE, Samsung, Arcor, and Tata), members of some of the featured families enthusiastically shared their stories with us directly and gave us feedback (e.g., Carvajal, Zamil, Le Plaza, Baalbaki). We selected them not just because they are archetypal examples of the strategies that engender resilience to uncertain and volatile environments, but also because we are convinced that much of what they practice can be useful to enterprising families and corporate leaders everywhere.

But it is undoubtedly the hundreds of our client families that have taught us the most. It is our privilege to know them and to be "in the room" where they discuss the fundamental dilemmas they face, their aspirations and concerns about the future, and the challenges associated with governance and continuity. Their commitment to their families and to their enterprises is an enormous source of inspiration to us.

We are also indebted to our students and to those families that have participated in executive programs we have led at Northwestern's Kellogg School of Management and at Harvard and other educational institutions, such as Monterrey TEC, IESE, ESADE, IMD, INCAE, and ESE, to mention a few.

Between the two of us, we have been exposed to thousands of business families over the course of over twenty-five years of teaching and research. Their stories provide an important bedrock of lived experience from which our understanding stems.

Finally, we would like to wholeheartedly thank many of our colleagues who directly supported our work in multiple ways. We are grateful to Daniel Lansberg, a gifted intellect and networker (and also Ivan's son and Devin's roommate at Harvard), for bringing the two of us together and for launching what has turned out to be a deeply fulfilling intergenerational collaboration, without which this book would have never happened.

John Ward at Kellogg was Ivan's teaching partner for over twenty years. He was an early supporter of our ideas for the book and instrumental in helping us secure seed funding to cover our fieldwork. We are indebted to the Tanoto Foundation for providing that funding at a critical launching phase of this study.

Morio Nishikawa and the Family Business Advisors Association (FBAA) were instrumental in giving us access to the legendary business families in Japan. We are extremely grateful for the time they devoted to us during our visits to their country and for their generous sharing of insights on the continuity of these enduring enterprises.

Our partners and colleagues at Lansberg Gersick Advisors (LGA) have also been extraordinarily supportive of our work on this book. Kelin Gersick, Katherine Grady, and Dimitris Valatsas carefully read and gave us hugely insightful feedback on earlier versions of this manuscript. Issa Dababneh, our team's gifted graphic designer, helped us enormously with the tables, charts, and figures we use throughout the book. The members of our administrative team at LGA, Arleen Valente, Gabriel Hernandez, and Cindy Lark, have always been ready to support our work—our heartfelt thanks to them all.

Lastly, we are grateful for the support of the editorial team at PublicAffairs, especially Clive Priddle, Anupama Roy-Chaudhury, and Michelle Welsh-Horst. Clive and Anu's careful read of the manuscript tightened and sharpened the text. More importantly, they believed in the potential impact of our ideas from the start. We also want to thank Kathy Streckfus and David Hayes, whose keen eyes for grammatical and narrative detail ensured that our ideas were captured in a way that was accessible to the broadest possible audience.

We are deeply indebted to them all. Their support has been invaluable. We hope you enjoy the product of this truly collaborative effort.

APPENDIX 1

STRATEGIC ISOTOPES IN ACTION

For those eager for more examples and guidance on how the seven strategies can be deployed across the three phases of a crisis, this appendix has been developed just for you.

Leveraging the concept of isotopes introduced in Chapter 12, we present twenty-one discrete variations of the seven stabilizing strategies. Below they are listed in chronological order—for instance, Migration-1, Migration-2, Migration-3. If you're specifically looking for inspiration on how to navigate the middle phase of a crisis, simply reference all entries marked with a 2—such as Redundancy-2, Simplification-2, and Diversity-2. We hope this breakdown will provide you with the inspiration and the courage to begin experimenting within your own organizations.

Migration

- **Migration-1:** The first order of business for leaders facing an imminent crisis is answering the following question: Should we stay or should we go? As we learned in Chapter 9, reading the winds of change and then making an informed strategic choice will inevitably become a seminal event in the evolution of the enterprise. Analyzing this "fight or flight" decision with a clear head—factoring in business, ownership, and family considerations, and including multiple stakeholders in the process—can help leaders build consensus around a plan that balances legacy and opportunity, plus familial and financial security. The Baalbaki family in Syria and the Saeed family in

Yemen chose different paths, yet both today are leading thriving international enterprises from the safety of new and distant shores. The geographic distribution of a family's activities and assets is always a choice, in good times and bad. Just make sure your key decision-makers fully explore all of their options and scenarios before deciding to pivot or persevere. Remember: the goal is first to arrive, then to survive and thrive.

- **Migration-2:** If you made the initial decision to stay put until conditions improved, as you enter Phase 2 the option to leave is still on the table. For companies already operating in multiple jurisdictions, some essential services can safely be migrated to more stable environments (e.g., where security or infrastructure is more reliable). Regardless, the start of Phase 2 is an ideal moment for another "pivot or persevere" discussion with your senior leadership team. The Carvajal case provided many examples of migrating assets laterally between environments in order to adjust to shifting regulatory requirements (in the case of its Peruvian operations) or to capitalize on strategic opportunities (in the case of its Puerto Rican expansion). What distinguishes Migration-2 from Migration-1 is that it's often more challenging to leave, and more difficult to assimilate once you arrive.
- **Migration-3:** Whenever resource scarcity turns into resource abundance, and conditions begin to stabilize, it attracts a commercial feeding frenzy. In these moments, leaders need to decide whether their future lies in operating in this more stable environment or in a lateral migration to another market a few notches further down on the Hierarchy of Stability. Either location can be prosperous, but they require different mixes of the seven strategies and different tolerance for risk. Those that were merely crisis "tourists" will be grateful for a return to normalcy and reactivate a high-growth mindset. Those that have "gone native" and embraced the chaos will likely look for other contexts where they can continue to ride the waves of turbulence to their advantage—like the many enterprising families who prefer to operate exclusively in frontier economies.

Simplification

- **Simplification-1:** If the decision in Phase 1 was to persevere, leaders next need to immediately shift their focus to identifying and protecting their key assets, processes, and relationships. For those, such as Grupo Arcor and Carvajal, who have been through countless crises before, this exercise will be second nature. They will already have some sense of how to scale back their overhead substantially without compromising their most vital commercial activities, and how to alter their product portfolio in response to the emergent challenges faced by customers and suppliers. For others, the early stages of a crisis will expose unknown vulnerabilities and existential risks. In these moments, remember that sometimes it's necessary to cut off the hand in order to save the arm—as Ford proactively demonstrated in the years leading up to the Global Financial Crisis.
- **Simplification-2:** In this phase of a crisis, many organizations have already cut back their operations "to the bone"—perhaps even more than might have been needed, out of an abundance of prudence and caution. This is the moment to reassess budgetary constraints and opportunities, now that the core functions of the enterprise have been stabilized. Recall that Arcor was one of the few confectionery companies to survive the initial 2001 economic shock, and that it quickly went on the offensive after it was clear that it had sufficient resources to ride out the storm. During this phase, those who are slow to adapt to the initial shock are faced with a series of tough decisions about engaging in layoffs and reducing executive compensation, suspending dividends, divesting struggling legacy assets, and renegotiating contracts and partnerships. The strategic challenge for these leaders is to make the short-term sacrifices the crisis demands (prioritizing Horizon One activities) without compromising the long-term viability of the enterprise (selectively investing in Horizon Two projects and dusting off Horizon Three moonshots). At IBM, this endeavor involved reducing its workforce by over 100,000 employees and radically streamlining its product portfolio. Without these

draconian cost cuts, it may not have come out of the 1990s in a position to compete in the more dynamic technological ecosystem that emerged in the early twenty-first century.

- **Simplification-3:** During this phase, greater leadership bandwidth and capital investment can begin to redirect from Horizon One necessities toward Horizon Two opportunities and Horizon Three aspirations. These moments are less about stabilizing the core and more about growing from it. Consider how the German family-run conglomerate Siemens AG streamlined operations following the 2008 financial crisis, focusing on health care, energy, and infrastructure, which they believed would flourish in the future regardless of the economic conditions. Phase 3 is also an ideal time to document lessons from navigating the crisis experience—particularly reviewing which systems were most essential to preserve and protect, and thinking about what to do again or avoid the next time uncertainty spikes. Creating a "Crisis Playbook" isn't a guaranteed vaccination against any future trauma, but it does encourage ongoing attention to the health of these essential activities. Consider that enterprising families that survived the Asian financial crisis of 1997 were much better prepared a decade later for the Global Financial Crisis than many of their Western peers. Similarly, those businesses (and countries) that endured the SARS epidemic in 2003 were better prepared for the COVID-19 pandemic decades later. As every good Scout knows, it's always best to "be prepared."

Redundancy

- **Redundancy-1:** Once an enterprise's core activities have been identified, it's vital that leaders secure additional resources to reinforce these mission-critical systems. What makes that challenging during the first phase in a crisis is that most competitors are simultaneously looking to procure these same key resources. Two assets in particular are vital during these precious early moments: the quality of existing relationships and the speed of decision-making. Few companies in advanced economies have the foresight to build redundancy so directly into their operating models, but those like Le Plaza in Haiti and HSA in Yemen are naturally well-prepared to ride out the approaching storm. In short, during Phase 1, redundancy is available almost exclusively to those who have already invested in both belts and suspenders. It's one of the reasons we believe all leaders should embrace a mindset of "productive paranoia," as Jim Collins describes in his book *Great by Choice*. This is especially valuable for those who get lulled into a false sense of security by the relative stability of their current circumstances. If nothing else, increasing cash reserves is table stakes for any enterprise that plans to survive a coming storm. Just be careful if you borrow to build up this reserve, since financial conditions and banking relationships are often strained during a crisis. As many have observed, bankers can be "fair weather friends," inclined to lend you their umbrella when the sun is shining, but ask for it back the minute it begins to rain.

- **Redundancy-2:** Leaders who were diligent about keeping backup reserves and resources for a rainy day are typically rewarded with outperformance when risk is still spiking. The challenge of riding out the storm is one of strategic provisioning—ensuring that continued investments in redundant infrastructures keep resources available when we need them most, particularly while the risk of crisis aftershocks remains high. Recall the experience of Mexico's Cemex, where the Zambrano family has systematically planned for volatility, investing in a diffuse logistics and distribution network that has proven reliable over decades in even the most remote and hard-to-reach areas.
- **Redundancy-3:** These are the moments to finally wind down the most aggressive procurement policies and backup systems, though leaders should be careful not to fall back into a false sense of security. Documenting which redundancy protocols were most and least effective, and whether these shifted over

time, will help leaders determine minimum thresholds for liquidity, maximum thresholds for debt, and how these variables ought to evolve over time to ensure that resources are available "just in case" conditions suddenly worsen without notice. Having too much redundancy built into your enterprise is far less dangerous than having too little, particularly as conditions normalize. However, keeping surplus inventory or cash on hand puts pressure on operating margins, so this strategy should be used more surgically and tactically until dark clouds form on the horizon once again.

Symbiosis

- **Symbiosis-1:** Drawing stability and support from powerful external stakeholders can cut both ways during the early stages of a crisis. During a sudden regime change, for example, political affiliations may become massive liabilities. Similarly, if business success is highly dependent on communities directly targeted by the crisis (for instance, frequent travelers at the onset of a pandemic), the stabilizing benefits of their loyalty and support will naturally be eroded. As a result, leaders should consider a *stakeholder mapping* exercise—surveying the power brokers within their ecosystem for opportunities and vulnerabilities that may result from more turbulent conditions. In advanced economies, national governments and financial institutions are often the key pillars of stability during the early phases of a crisis. In emerging economies, where the mandate of federal authorities is often less influential, regional and municipal authorities, other well-capitalized family enterprises, and the communities themselves collectively underpin macroeconomic and social stability. Consider how Tata Steel mobilized its employees and neighbors so effectively in response to the threat of expropriation in the 1980s. In frontier economies, where public institutions are weak and ineffective, multilateral agencies such as the United

Nations, the World Bank, and Amnesty International can also become powerful partners and patrons, particularly when domestic governments are directly affected by a crisis. In all three contexts, moving quickly to identify, prioritize, and nurture these partnerships is critical for securing access to vital information, materials, and financial capital.

- **Symbiosis-2:** While consumers and competitors are still adjusting to protracted adversity, leaders need to manage their community stakeholders carefully. As we saw with Arcor in Argentina, whenever customers are struggling, revenues are at risk. Demonstrating genuine care for those most affected by the crisis—through outreach, philanthropy, and product innovation—isn't just good community citizenship, it's also good business. Similarly, those with powerful political patrons are often most vulnerable at the start of Phase 2. Governments that successfully handle an initial shock may need to reassess their resources and relationships, as budgets are likely to be strained. If politicians failed the early tests of the crisis and were widely criticized for their response, regime change is more likely. Both scenarios should be actively discussed among decision-making teams. For those with no such relationships, this could be a good moment to begin building these connections—particularly in the face of a situation that will continue to strain organizational resources for months or even years to come.
- **Symbiosis-3:** Perhaps the greatest risk during this phase is an overreliance on political relations—particularly if regime change is what is prompting the regression to the mean. In these moments, it's critical for leaders to reassess the health of their connections to political and financial power brokers as well as to their communities of customers and employees. The shifting economic and political climate will shape the power and wealth of these key stakeholders. Don't take a page from South Korea's *chaebol* and wait until a public backlash to adjust your allegiances. Also, expect that demands for

transparency will increase under stable conditions, so any privileged relationships may come under scrutiny more easily than they did during the crisis—when such transgressions were either ignored or tolerated, given broader crisis management responsibilities.

Diversity

- **Diversity-1:** The earliest phase of a crisis is not typically the ideal time to be deploying capital on expansion or acquisition. But it is often the moment when your past efforts to diversify assets and talent will yield the greatest stabilizing benefits. Consider Tata's experience with the heavy-handed industrial policy that emerged after India's independence. The nationalization of Tata Airlines in 1953 was certainly a heavy blow to the group's operating portfolio and global ambitions, but the shock was absorbed by the group's other diverse activities—from steel and chemicals to textiles and tea—which helped sustain its operations and performance. Additionally, as we learned in Chapter 11, "cognitively diverse" groups are more effective at navigating uncertainty, so when conditions suddenly worsen and a clear path forward seems elusive, ensuring that your crisis management team represents a broad array of perspectives about the business, its stakeholders, and the crisis itself will lead to better decision-making outcomes.
- **Diversity-2:** Once the dust settles after an initial shock, certain companies and even entire industries will have been caught in the crosshairs, while others will manage to keep their heads above water, and still others will be unexpected beneficiaries. We like the analogy of sinking, swimming, and surfing to distinguish between these disparate outcomes. Those that are sinking and unlikely to survive become natural targets, while those that are surfing are often flush with cash and become natural acquirers. In these moments, it's critical that those growing by

acquisition consider not only the feasibility of the business during a crisis, but how it might perform when conditions normalize, and also whether correlated or uncorrelated diversity would be more advantageous. Recall how Tata's leaders navigated decades of restrictive industrial policy by strategically entering new sectors less heavily regulated by the government, minimizing the risks associated with punitive policy changes. For instance, by expanding into IT and consulting services in 1968, the group leveraged new opportunities that were less constrained by the regulatory pressures affecting their steel and automotive divisions.

- **Diversity-3:** When conditions finally begin to stabilize, the benefits of a diverse portfolio typically diminish as efficiency and profitability return. Particularly in advanced economies, where institutional stabilizers are strongest and most established, a reversion to the mean often indicates that competitive markets will once again reward a greater focus on price and performance. Incumbents who have endured the traumas of a crisis are often best positioned for success when it recedes—as Tata was during and after the Great Depression. This phase also presents a natural opportunity to leverage domestic stability by seeking expansion into adjacent markets, where competition may be less battle-hardened or incumbents less ready to risk capital for growth. It is no coincidence that Tata's global acquisition spree began shortly after India's restrictive industrial policy was loosened in the early 1990s, with the acquisition of NatSteel, Jaguar, and Tetley, among many others. During Phase 3, as the crisis fades and the war for top talent heats up, successful leaders may consider whether to continue in their current roles or begin new chapters in their professional development. This naturally drives up the cost of labor and makes it harder to recruit, so first movers who are quick to identify, attract, and retain talent will have a natural competitive advantage.

Modularity

- **Modularity-1:** As we explored in Chapter 6, flexible manufacturing systems naturally outperform during the initial phases of a crisis, since their modular designs are built to ensure that the failure of a single part doesn't cause the entire system to collapse. From Zamil's Total Building Solutions to IKEA's modular home furnishings, utilizing interoperable parts and platforms provides a natural competitive advantage whenever procurement and manufacturing conditions worsen. Additionally, for organizations with existing links to external partners—which are often larger and better resourced—Phase 1 is an ideal moment to leverage these modular relationships to access scarce resources and insights. Larger multinationals, especially those that have operated globally for decades, have endured traumatic events before, and have much to teach about initial crisis response. These strategic partners can come in handy both as a crisis grinds on and once conditions eventually improve. The COVID-19 pandemic also provided ample evidence that the quality of our strategic partnerships is a major factor when crisis conditions first arise—playing a role in everything from procuring materials to sharing information to accessing capital. Weaker relationships buckle under the pressure, while stronger ones provide distinct advantages that help both parties adapt to the initial shock of a crisis. This is particularly true among the familial networks so pervasive in developing countries.
- **Modularity-2:** During the second phase, it will already be clear which of these relationships and partnerships are robust and which ones are fragile. Pruning unhealthy relationships and strengthening healthy ones is an excellent way to ensure that the benefits of modularity continue to generate both stability and opportunity. At Baalbaki, recall that family members' close ties to Linde helped them to eventually resurrect their joint venture partnership. This allowed both companies to capitalize on growing demand for white goods in the Middle East

at a time when many emerging and frontier economies were investing in electrification, consumers were rapidly adopting these new household technologies, and foreign imports were still largely constrained.

- **Modularity-3:** When conditions eventually normalize, international partnerships are likely to be among the first to respond to the changing context, given that often these partners are sophisticated Western multinationals. These global enterprises have the resources to begin preparing for a return to the "next normal" months or even years in advance, so shifting back into stability plays naturally into their strengths. McDonald's, Caterpillar, General Motors, and Exxon may scale back their R&D activities during a recession, but they never shut them down entirely. As a result, their international partners will continue to have access to cutting-edge products and ideas unavailable to competitors. Phase 3 is also a natural moment to finish pruning relationships and leaving networks that proved to be unhealthy during the crisis, and to celebrate and expand those that were most stabilizing and productive.

Differentiation

- **Differentiation-1:** Deploying any of the strategies above can help to provide stability and is more about protecting the downside than chasing the upside. However, whenever markets begin to break down, a range of new entrepreneurial opportunities inevitably emerges. Like the Añaños family in Peru during the Shining Path uprising, many enterprising families capitalized on the first few months of the COVID-19 pandemic, leveraging their assets and relationships to fill gaps in broken supply chains. Ensuring that leadership teams are on the lookout for these opportunities can provide a silver lining to any emerging crisis.
- **Differentiation-2:** Once markets plateau at peak uncertainty, and new production and consumption patterns settle

into a volatile but predictable rhythm, existing markets will be thinned out by failing competitors, and new niches will inevitably emerge that aren't being serviced by the remaining incumbents. For instance, during the second phase of the pandemic, artisanal mask manufacturers, ghost kitchens, e-learning platforms, and content creators sprang up to service those trapped at home or on the front lines of essential services. Those who are able to move swiftly can become very big fish very quickly. Consider that AJE's most explosive era of early growth took place during the sustained disruption of the Shining Path insurrection, since no competitors were as well adapted to navigating these conditions quite like the Añaños family and their legions of loyal customers and distribution partners.

- **Differentiation-3:** Whenever environmental conditions shift, and resource availability transitions from abundance to scarcity and back again, niche providers can often be reexposed to the rigors of pure competition. As these specialized markets become more crowded, leaders often focus on sustaining market dominance, since first-mover (or last-one-standing) advantages provide a natural defense against fresh competition. Consequently, differentiation in Phase 3 often involves doubling down on the company's unique value proposition—products, brands, channels, and processes—making them even more distinctive and less easily replicable. For the AJE Group, this phase corresponds to the era in Peru when the ongoing threat of the Shining Path's rebellion had been contained. The company was finally able to set its sights on the capital city before eventually taking on the world.

For those interested, we are currently developing a quick reference guide for how to deploy these isotopes under specific scenarios, such as terrorist attacks, mass labor strikes, devastating hurricanes, fraudulent elections, hyperinflation, and so forth. We have shared our early hypotheses throughout the book, but need more time and data to incubate them adequately. The result will be akin to a Gallup StrengthsFinder assessment, but for organizational endurance. Like a pilot's checklist, it will help to ensure that leaders are diagnosing conditions appropriately, and not just relying on strategies that may have worked well for them in the past but are no longer feasible. To learn more or contribute to the research, please feel free to reach out! In the meantime, the table "Considerations for Deploying the Seven Stabilizing Strategies" provides some initial guidance.

Considerations for Deploying the Seven Stabilizing Strategies

Strategy	Strengths	Weaknesses	Requirements for Success
Differentiation	Natural protection against competition	When the barrier evaporates...	Circumstantial chaos, protectionist industrial policies
Modularity	Flexibility and scalability	Lack of absolute control	Clear protocols, partnership interface
Symbiosis	Ability to mooch strength from other stakeholders	Dependency, vulnerability to regime change	Skill in managing political and community relations
Redundancy	Resilience of key systems, speed	Incremental cost and complexity	Preemption and dynamic optimization
Migration	Ability to tap greater resource availability	Leaving behind assets and straddling multiple contexts	Ability to know when to leave, where to go, how to survive the journey, and how best to assimilate
Simplification	Survival, efficiency, resources focused on essential functions	Fragility, over-simplifying stunts future growth potential	Ability to identify essential services, death by a thousand cuts
Diversity	Natural hedge against idiosyncratic risk, better problem solving	Increased complexity, vulnerability to systemic risks	Dynamic portfolio management, effective multi-level governance
All Seven	Increased stability in unstable environments	Prolonged dependence, which can hamper adaptability	Judgment in getting the dosage right, balancing strategies, timing, dynamic adjustment

Additional Questions for Reflection for Leadership Teams at the Onset of a Crisis

STRATEGIC QUESTIONS

- ☐ What is the core issue causing the disruption in the market?
- ☐ How does this disruption affect our unique value proposition?
- ☐ What are the immediate and potential long-term effects of this disruption on our business model?
- ☐ What are the strengths that we can leverage during this time?
- ☐ How flexible is our current strategy, and how can we adapt it to respond more dynamically to market changes?

CUSTOMER-CENTRIC QUESTIONS

- ☐ How have our customers' needs and behaviors changed as a result of the disruption?
- ☐ What new needs have emerged that we can address?
- ☐ Are there any segments of our customer base that are more affected than others?
- ☐ How can we maintain a strong relationship with our customers during this turbulent time?
- ☐ What feedback are we receiving from our customers, and how can we incorporate this feedback swiftly into our strategy?

OPERATIONAL QUESTIONS

- ☐ What operational constraints are we facing, and how might we alleviate them?
- ☐ How can we ensure the continuity of our supply chains?
- ☐ What resources do we need to secure immediately to maintain operations?
- ☐ Are there opportunities to streamline our operations and reduce waste?
- ☐ What contingencies do we have in place, and what new contingencies might we establish?

FINANCIAL QUESTIONS

- ☐ What is our current financial health, and how can we maintain it?
- ☐ How can we manage cash flow more efficiently during this time?
- ☐ Are there new revenue streams we can explore to mitigate the effects of the disruption?
- ☐ What cost-saving measures can we implement without compromising our business values?
- ☐ What financial support or partnerships can we leverage?

INNOVATION AND GROWTH

- ☐ What opportunities does this disruption present for innovation?
- ☐ How can we encourage and foster innovation within our team?
- ☐ Are there emerging markets or trends we can capitalize on or migrate into?
- ☐ What skills and knowledge do we need to acquire to navigate this disruption successfully?
- ☐ What partnerships or collaborations can we explore to strengthen our market position?

TEAM AND CULTURE

- ☐ How can we foster a culture of agility and adaptability to support asset redeployment?
- ☐ What training and development programs can we institute to prepare our team for change?
- ☐ How will we communicate the changes to our team to foster buy-in and engagement?
- ☐ Can we create cross-functional teams to leverage diverse skill sets and perspectives in the redeployment process?

APPENDIX 2

PSYCHOLOGY OF RISK

Assessing Risk Appetite

For those interested in gaining a better understanding of the distribution of risk appetite within their own family enterprise, there are two general ways to gather this information. The first involves asking the question directly: "In general, how would you describe your risk appetite?" Respondents are provided with a range of options from low to high and asked to pick the one that best describes them. This approach may require a basic definition and some context setting, but it has the benefit of directly addressing the object of study. It is also the most common approach, and the one that Oxford Risk used to produce the normally distributed histogram shown in Chapter 13.

When we survey clients and students, we often frame the range of options as follows:

1. I am very cautious and avoid risk as much as possible.
2. I am somewhat cautious but willing to live with some level of risk.
3. I am willing to accept greater risk provided there is adequate research to inform my choices.
4. I am a natural risk-taker and will typically follow my instincts.

Consider how you would personally answer the question. Are you a natural risk-seeker, or more naturally risk-avoidant? If you were to find yourself in a casino, would you skip the gaming floor and instead catch a show or some fine dining? Or are you inclined to head straight for the roulette table and wager a king's ransom on a single spin of the wheel? Now consider your parents, your partner, and your children. Consider your senior executives, your frontline employees, your customers, and your joint venture partners. Each of these key stakeholders will be inclined to answer this question differently. We can also ask these same stakeholders about the seven stabilizing strategies. Which ones has the family utilized in the past? Which ones do you feel are most likely to work best to mitigate particular risks? These distributions should become critical inputs into how we make decisions and plan for the future.

Additionally, recognizing the innate biases involved in any descriptive self-assessment, we also suggest asking the same basic question about risk appetite *indirectly*, inspired by the pioneering work of Daniel Kahneman and Amos Tversky.[1] It involves what behavioral scientists call "revealed preferences," or how our intrinsic risk appetite is manifested in the way we respond to a carefully designed scenario, rather than simply asking directly how we feel about risk. For instance, we can ask, "Given the best and worst case scenarios presented by the four options below, which would you prefer?" Rather than a simple gradient from low to high, this indirect approach lays out several options that resemble lower- and higher-risk scenarios and allows for quantitative comparisons. Below is a simplified example:

1. Best case: US$200K gain. Worst case: US$0 loss.
2. Best case: US$800K gain. Worst case: US$200K loss.
3. Best case: US$2.4M gain. Worst case: US$800K loss.
4. Best case: US$4.8M gain. Worst case: US$2.4M loss.

Each of us will be drawn to one of these scenarios over the others based on our intrinsic risk appetite, just as we would if we were asked directly. What makes the indirect method both more interesting and more informative is that it tests our risk appetite through a practical scenario rather than asking us abstractly to render a self-judgment.

Measuring Risk Appetite Among Owners: Approach #1

Ask directly...

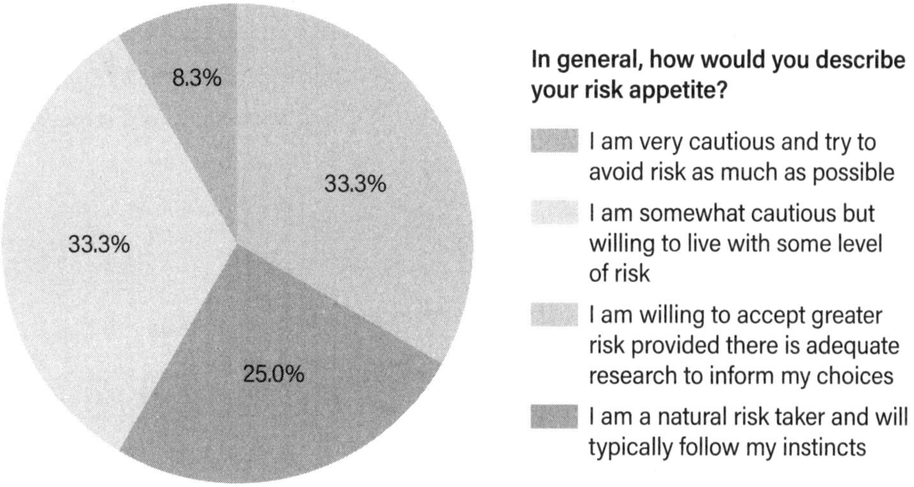

Measuring Risk Appetite Among Owners: Approach #2

Ask directly...

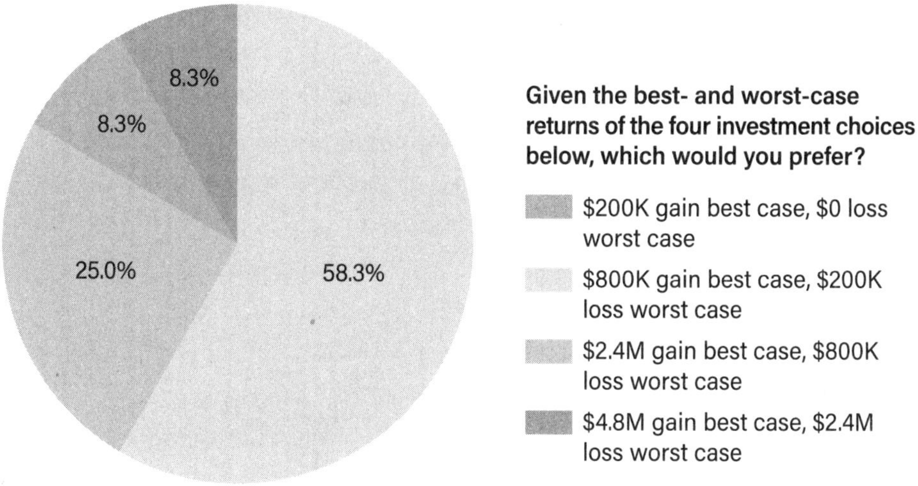

Wherever possible, we prefer to survey stakeholders using both approaches, since they often produce slightly different outcomes. This by itself provides a great vector into a conversation about how little we understand our individual and collective risk appetites, and how thinking about these differences can help us determine how to chart a path forward that reflects these cognitive realities.

To generate a more systemic or 360-degree perspective, you could also ask key stakeholders how they might categorize other stakeholders (top executives, board members, trustees, partners, and owners) based on the following four descriptors:

1. Extremely prudent
2. Conservative
3. Moderately risk-prone
4. High risk-taking

This is often a very revealing exercise in terms of how we perceive the risk appetites of ourselves and others. Together, these approaches provide leaders with key inputs for calibrating risk across the enterprise.

Assessing Risk Capacity

As with risk appetite, leaders can survey their stakeholders to better understand their individual capacity to bear each risk, as well as the system's collective capacity to absorb and respond. Ideally input is sought directly from owners—since ultimately it is their capital that is at risk. For instance, you could ask each owner about the capacity to bear risk based on the following categorical statements, ranked from "Completely true" to "Completely false":

- You have sufficient resources to support you and your family for the rest of your life.
- You have sufficient liquidity to support your current lifestyle.
- If you lost 10 percent of your wealth today, your current lifestyle would not be impacted.
- If you lost 25 percent of your wealth today, your current lifestyle would not be impacted.
- If you lost 50 percent of your wealth today, your current lifestyle would not be impacted.

- If you lost 75 percent of your wealth today, your current lifestyle would not be impacted.

This exercise can provide an even more granular view of the individual risk capacity of owners and how any differences shape their aspirations for the enterprise. At a minimum, we recommend that business leaders survey owners with the following two questions (for instance, on a scale of 1–10):

1. How important is liquidity to you personally? (i.e., do you need regular distributions from the business to support your current lifestyle, or do you have sufficient resources outside of the family enterprise?)
2. How is your lifestyle affected by the distribution of capital from the family enterprise? (i.e., does the business sustain your current lifestyle, or is it simply the "frosting on the cake"?)

Measuring Risk Capacity: Approach #1

How important is liquidity to you personally?

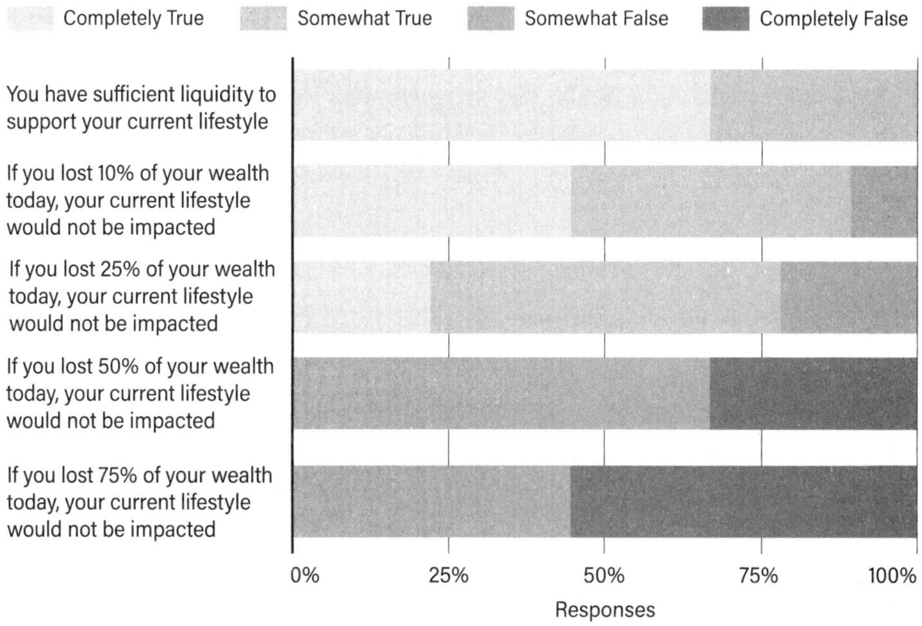

Measuring Risk Capacity: Approach #2

How is your lifestyle affected by the distribution of capital from the FB?

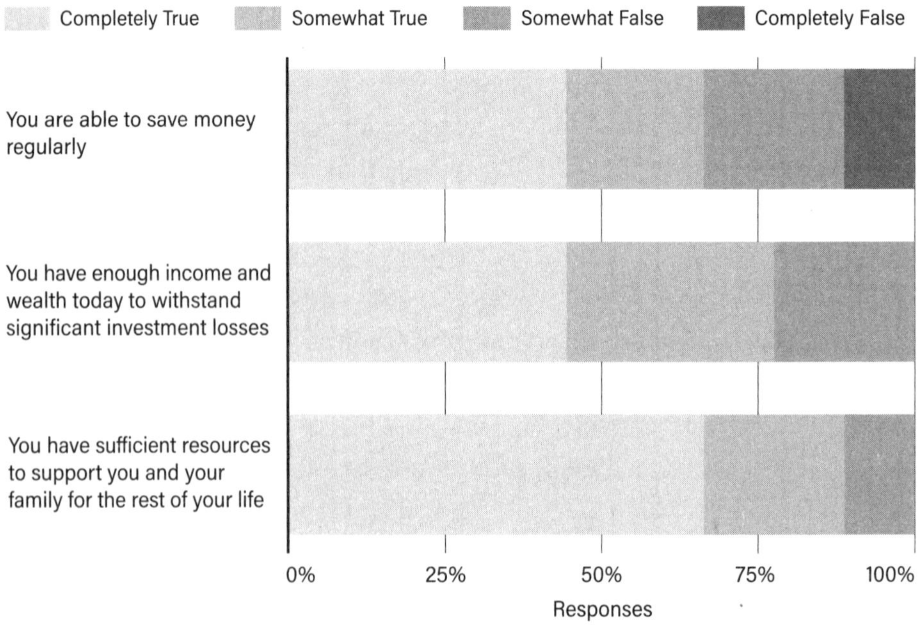

This simple questionnaire will render results like those shown above (see "Measuring Risk Capacity"), providing leaders with guidance on one of the most critical variables affecting an enterprise's long-term prospects—how much capital should be returned to shareholders relative to how much should be reinvested in the business—both in the pursuit of growth and in the management of risk.

NOTES

PART 1: THE NEW AGE OF UNCERTAINTY

1. The term "resilience" has been interpreted in a variety of ways in the organizational, familial, and psychological literature. We embrace the definition used by Trenton A. Williams and his colleagues: "The process by which an actor (i.e., individual, organization, or community [we would add *family*]) builds and uses its capability endowments to interact with the environment in a way that positively adjusts and maintains functioning prior to, during, and following adversity." See Trenton A. Williams, Daniel A. Gruber, Kathleen M. Sutcliffe, Dean A. Shepherd, and Eric Yanfei Zhao, "Organizational Response to Adversity: Fusing Crisis Management and Resilience Research Streams," *Academy of Management Annals* 11, no. 2 (2017): 742.

2. Simon S. Montefiore, *A Family History of Humanity* (New York: Knopf, 2023).

3. Among advanced economies, there is a growing body of research indicating that the average lifespan of corporations is shrinking, from half a century in the 1960s to less than twenty years in 2024, and it's still dropping precipitously.

4. For an excellent review of the literature on resilience in family companies, see Yasin Yilmaz, Sebastian Raetze, Julia De Groote, and Nadine Kammerlander, "Resilience in Family Businesses: A Systematic Literature Review," *Family Business Review* 37, no. 1 (2024): 60–88.

5. Nearly 2,500 years ago, the Greek general Thucydides, inspired by his frontline experience on both sides of the Peloponnesian War, wrote vividly about the causes and consequences of conflict. Similarly, Sun Tzu's *Art of War*, inspired by the fragmented power struggles of China's Spring and Autumn Period (770–221 BCE), was an attempt to manage and mitigate further conflict.

CHAPTER 1: INTRODUCING THE FRONTIERS OF CAPITALISM

1. Confucius believed that the family was the basic unit of society and that the proper conduct of family relations was the basis of all other human relations. Smith observed that individuals naturally care for their own well-being and that of their families and close friends through affectionate principles, which also extend to the well-being of their communities and country. Fukuyama argued that the family was the origin of social capital, or the trust and cooperation that bind people together in a society. He claimed that the family was the first and most important institution teaching people how to behave in a group, and that it was the source of loyalty, reciprocity, and obligation. He also argued

that the family was the basis of political order, and that the decline of the family in the West was the cause of social disorder and moral decay. See Francis Fukuyama, *The Origins of Political Order* (New York: Farrar, Straus and Giroux, 2011).

2. In his provocative book *Debt: The First 5,000 Years*, the anthropologist David Graeber argues that for most of human history, such credit was typically based on barter and reserved exclusively for people we knew—evoking its Latin roots as "a loan or a thing entrusted to another." In contrast, virtually all modern businesses rely on financial innovations such as currencies and bank loans. Rather than relying on trust in individuals, they require trust in the integrity of a broader financial system. This is particularly true in advanced economies. As Graeber writes, "If one owes a favor, or one's life, to another human being, it is owed to that person specifically. But if one owes forty thousand dollars at 12-percent interest, it doesn't really matter who the creditor is; neither does either of the two parties have to think much about what the other party needs, wants, is capable of doing—as they certainly would if what was owed was a favor, or respect, or gratitude. If you end up having to abandon your home and wander in other provinces, if your daughter ends up in a mining camp or working as a prostitute, well, that's unfortunate, but incidental to the creditor. Money is money, and a deal's a deal." See David Graeber, *Debt: The First 5,000 Years*, updated and expanded ed. (Brooklyn, NY: Melville House, 2014).

3. One of the most influential models of this theory of development was proposed in 1960 by W. W. Rostow, who identified five stages of growth that all countries must pass through: (1) traditional society, where the economy is based on agriculture and subsistence; (2) preconditions to take-off, where the society develops manufacturing and trade; (3) take-off, where industrialization and rapid growth occur; (4) drive to maturity, where the economy diversifies and technology improves; and (5) age of high mass consumption, where the society enjoys a high standard of living and consumerism. See Walt Rostow, *The Stages of Economic Growth: A Non-Communist Manifesto*, 3rd ed. (Cambridge: Cambridge University Press, 1991).

4. Kenneth J. Arrow, "Gifts and Exchanges," *Philosophy and Public Affairs* 1, no. 4 (1972): 357.

5. And boy have they flourished. World GDP increased a hundredfold between 1960 and 2024, from roughly US$1 trillion to over US$100 trillion, as a growing share of humans were drawn into the global marketplace. On the surface, it appears that the benefits have been mostly inclusive, with world GDP per capita increasing from US$457 to US$12,647 over that same period—despite the population swelling from 3 billion to 8 billion. However, as many economists and activists have argued in recent years, the gains of this commercial revolution have been unevenly distributed, and countries where trust is highest have been the prime beneficiaries. World Bank Open Data, https://data.worldbank.org.

6. Daron Acemoglu and James A. Robinson, *Why Nations Fail: The Origins of Power, Prosperity, and Poverty* (New York: Crown, 2012), 75. Acemoglu and Robinson argue that "even the poorest citizens of the United States have incomes and access to health care, education, public services, and economic and social opportunities that are far superior to those available to the vast mass of people living in sub-Saharan Africa, South Asia, and Central America" (p. 428).

7. Quoted in *Governance and the Law*, World Development Report (Washington, DC: World Bank, 2017), n.p.

8. See Creating Emerging Markets, Harvard Business School, www.hbs.edu/creating-emerging-markets/Pages/default.aspx.

9. In particular, they conceptualized "reputation" as consisting of prominence, perceived quality, and resilience and developed a process model that illustrates how reputation can facilitate survival in ways that persist over time.

10. Cheng Gao, Tiona Zuzul, Geoffrey Jones, and Tarun Khanna, "Overcoming Institutional Voids: A Reputation-Based View of Long-Run Survival," *Strategic Management Journal* 38, no. 11 (2017): 2147–2167.

11. See Rafael La Porta, Florencio Lopez-de-Silanes, and Andrei Shleifer, "Corporate Ownership Around the World," *Journal of Finance* 54, no. 2 (1999): 471–517; Margarita Tsoutsoura, "Family Firms and Management Practices," *Oxford Review of Economic Policy* 37, no. 2 (2021): 323–334. See also Danny Miller and Isabelle Le Brenton-Miller, *Managing for the Long Run: Lessons in Competitive Advantage from Great Family Businesses* (Boston, MA: Harvard Business School Press, 2005).

12. To be clear, such expanded familial influence isn't without its challenges. David Graeber, Francis Fukuyama, and other institutional scholars have demonstrated how dynastic families can inhibit the development of inclusive institutions and limit the distribution of wealth. Consequently, we view family governance as both a feature and a bug in modern capitalism—powerfully shaping the governance of some of the world's most essential institutions, often for the better, but occasionally for the worse.

13. August Krogh, "The Progress of Physiology," *American Journal of Physiology* 90, no. 2 (1929): 247.

14. Ross Pomeroy, "Strange Life Forms Create an 'Alien' Ecosystem in an Abandoned Uranium Mine," Big Think, February 3, 2023, https://bigthink.com/life/strange-life-uranium-mine.

15. Biologist Tom Brock is credited for coining the term "extremophiles" and for launching the new field of scientific research on microorganisms that thrive in the harshest conditions on our planet.

16. Andreas Weber, *The Biology of Wonder: Aliveness, Feeling and the Metamorphosis of Science* (Gabriola Island, BC, Canada: New Society Publishers, 2016), 28.

17. James Conca, "How Extremophile Bacteria Living in Nuclear Reactors Might Help Us Make Vaccines," *Forbes*, July 21, 2020, www.forbes.com/sites/jamesconca/2020/07/21/if-extremophile-bacteria-can-live-in-nuclear-reactors-maybe-they-can-help-us-make-vaccines/?sh=976f8a876193.

18. See "Overview," Santa Fe Institute, www.santafe.edu/engage/support, accessed April 18, 2024.

19. One famous example at the turn of the twentieth century was the study to determine the optimal weight of a coal shovel (spoiler alert: it's 21.5 pounds!), calculated with precision by the grandfather of management science, Fredrick Winslow Taylor. In fact, many of the business challenges that emerged during the Industrial Revolution were Mount Fuji problems. These were naturally easier to solve than many other types of questions because they dealt with the world of physical labor—such as how many workers on how many shifts it would take to maximize unit output.

20. This term was popularized in Kimberly Kay Hoang's book *Spiderweb Capitalism: How Global Elites Exploit Frontier Markets* (Princeton, NJ: Princeton University Press, 2022) to describe situations that are both ethically ambiguous and commercially lucrative.

21. The empirical literature on the resilience of family companies strongly supports the view that a long-term orientation and family core values are key drivers of resilience. See Yasin Yilmaz, Sebastian Raetze, Julia De Groote, and Nadine Kammerlander,

"Resilience in Family Businesses: A Systematic Literature Review," *Family Business Review* 37, no. 1 (2024): 60–88, for an exhaustive review of this research.

22. This is despite significant barriers and costs in starting a business, including "dealing with construction permits, getting electricity, registering property, getting credit, protecting minority investors, paying taxes, trading across borders, enforcing contracts, and resolving insolvency." World Bank, *Doing Business 2020: Comparing Business Regulation in 190 Economies* (Washington, DC: World Bank, 2020), https://documents1.worldbank.org/curated/en/688761571934946384/pdf/Doing-Business-2020-Comparing-Business-Regulation-in-190-Economies.pdf, 17.

23. Moisés Naím, *Illicit: How Smugglers, Traffickers, and Copycats Are Hijacking the Global Economy* (New York: Doubleday, 2005).

24. David Remnick, "A. G. Sulzberger on the Battles Within and Against the New York Times," New Yorker, June 10, 2023, www.newyorker.com/culture/the-new-yorker-interview/a-g-sulzberger-on-the-battles-within-and-against-the-new-york-times.

CHAPTER 2: NAVIGATING THE HIERARCHY OF STABILITY

1. Hunter S. Thompson, "Security," *The Spectator*, 1955, reprinted in *Proud Highway: Saga of a Desperate Southern Gentleman, 1955–1967*, vol. 1 of *The Fear and Loathing Letters*, edited by Douglas Brinkley (New York: Random House, 2012), 4–5.

2. The "everything bubble" refers to the inflated valuations of almost every asset class, from stocks and bonds to real estate and cryptocurrencies. Fueled by record-breaking levels of debt and unprecedented monetary easing by central banks around the world, the everything bubble has defied the conventional wisdom of economics and created a disconnect between asset prices and economic fundamentals that is virtually unprecedented in modern economic history.

3. World Economic Forum, *The Global Risks Report 2018*, 13th ed. (Geneva: World Economic Forum, 2018), www3.weforum.org/docs/WEF_GRR18_Report.pdf, 6.

4. Yale sociologist Charles Perrow alerted the world long ago about the risks inherent to "tightly coupled" complex organizations in which risks cannot be accurately assessed and failures are inevitable. See Charles Perrow, *Normal Accidents: Living with High-Risk Technologies* (Princeton, NJ: Princeton University Press, 2005).

5. Sasha Maslov, "Running a Business Under the Shadow of War," *New York Times*, February 12, 2022, www.nytimes.com/2022/02/12/business/ukraine-business-economy.html.

6. Hunter S. Thompson, *Hey Rube: Blood Sport, the Bush Doctrine, and the Downward Spiral of Dumbness. Modern History from the Sports Desk* (New York: Simon and Schuster, 2004), 124.

7. Frank Knight, *Risk, Uncertainty, and Profit* (Boston: Houghton Mifflin, 1921).

8. Frederick Funston and Stephen Wagner captured a modern version of these frontier conditions in their textbook *Surviving and Thriving in Uncertainty: Creating the Risk Intelligent Enterprise* (Hoboken, NJ: John Wiley and Sons, 2010): "What if forecasts are unreliable, probabilities offer little guidance, and the unexpected occurs much more often than we assume? Turbulence is difficult (some would argue impossible) to predictively model, volatility is inevitable, and interactions are complex and tightly coupled. These three conditions generate high uncertainty and often huge and sudden losses for the unprepared. They also limit the value of conventional wisdom, especially in uncertain and turbulent times" (p. 24).

9. Two Israeli psychologists, Amos Tversky and Daniel Kahneman, were among the first to conduct groundbreaking research on the cognitive biases that influence decision-making under conditions of uncertainty. Their early theories were influenced by a number of factors, including their own experiences living in a region that for millennia has been a hotbed of conflict. In the wake of the Six-Day War in 1967, during which both men served actively in the army, they found that many Israelis were struggling to make sense of the existential risk that lurked beyond the frontiers of their constantly shifting sovereign borders.

Their Nobel Prize–winning breakthrough came a few years later with the publication of a 1974 paper outlining a series of experiments that demonstrated how people often rely on heuristics, or mental shortcuts, when making decisions, leading to biases and errors in judgment. For example, they found that people tended to overestimate the probability of rare events when they were more easily recalled—as the Six-Day War between Israel and its Arab neighbors clearly would have been at the time—leading to what they called the "availability heuristic." This phenomenon powerfully affects our judgment, because our decisions are disproportionately influenced by recent and vivid events relative to more objective or historical information. See Amos Tversky and Daniel Kahneman, "Judgment Under Uncertainty: Heuristics and Biases. Biases in Judgments Reveal Some Heuristics of Thinking Under Uncertainty," *Science* 185, no. 4157 (1974): 1124–1131.

10. Such systematic uncertainty can lead to panic and contagion in the financial system, as investors lose confidence in the absence of reliable statistical guidance, then rush to sell assets or withdraw deposits. These moments can then trigger a vicious cycle of falling asset prices, rising defaults, and tightening credit conditions, which spill over into the real economy and cause bank runs, recessions, or even depressions. This was precisely the case during the 2008–2009 Global Financial Crisis, the US savings and loan crisis of the 1980s, the Great Depression during the 1930s, and many other panics and crashes littered throughout modern financial history.

11. In his September 12, 1962, speech at Rice University, Kennedy said, "We choose to go to the moon. We choose to go to the moon in this decade and do the other things, not because they are easy, but because they are hard. Because that goal will serve to organize and measure the best of our energies and skills. Because that challenge is one that we are willing to accept, one we are unwilling to postpone, and one which we intend to win."

12. Quoted at "Top 500 Hunter S. Thompson Quotes (2024 Update)," Quotefancy, https://quotefancy.com/hunter-s-thompson-quotes.

13. "Seneca," New World Encyclopedia, www.newworldencyclopedia.org/entry/Seneca.

14. According to the International Monetary Fund's World Economic Outlook Database, the average annual growth rate of real GDP per capita for advanced economies was 1.6 percent from 2000 to 2020, and it is projected to be 1.4 percent from 2021 to 2026. For emerging economies, the average annual growth rate was 4.5 percent from 2000 to 2020 and is projected to be 3.9 percent from 2021 to 2026. For frontier economies, the average annual growth rate was 3.8 percent from 2000 to 2020 and is projected to be 3.6 percent from 2021 to 2026. International Monetary Fund, World Economic Outlook Database: Groups and Aggregates Information, April 2023, www.imf.org/en/Publications/WEO/weo-database/2023/April/groups-and-aggregates.

15. Hugh Courtney, *20/20 Foresight: Crafting Strategy in an Uncertain World* (Boston: Harvard Business School Press, 2001), 4.

16. Courtney, *20/20 Foresight*.

17. Hugh Courtney, Jane Kirkland, and Patrick Viguerie, "Strategy Under Uncertainty," *Harvard Business Review*, November–December 1997, https://hbr.org/1997/11/strategy-under-uncertainty.

18. Courtney et al., "Strategy Under Uncertainty."

19. The model follows the general concept behind psychologist Abraham Maslow's groundbreaking Hierarchy of Needs. The graphic captures a few key characteristics that differentiate the privileged peak from the base of the pyramid in modern capitalism.

20. "Life should not be a journey to the grave with the intention of arriving safely in a pretty and well preserved body," Thompson purportedly wrote, "but rather to skid in broadside in a cloud of smoke, thoroughly used up, totally worn out, and loudly proclaiming 'Wow! What a Ride!'" The source of the quotation, however, is not certain. See "Quote Origin: Life Is Not a Journey to the Grave with the Intention of Arriving Safely," Quote Investigator, June 26, 2023, https://quoteinvestigator.com/2023/06/26/safe-journey.

CHAPTER 3: UNDERSTANDING THE ORIGINS OF STABILITY

1. By far the youngest member of this centenarian club was Suntory, founded in 1899 and known around the world today for producing award-winning whiskeys and spirits. Next youngest was Toraya, the official supplier of traditional Japanese sweets to the Royal Court since 1635. Middle of the pack was Sumitomo, a Japanese *zaibatsu* (literally "financial clique") founded in 1615 as a bookshop in Kyoto before developing into an industrial and financial powerhouse. Second eldest was Kikkoman, manufacturers of the world's favorite soy sauce since 1603, and saviors of their community from famine countless times over the centuries.

2. The principles even encouraged innovative business strategies such as organizing skilled craftsmen into interchangeable workgroups, or *kumi*, that competed to do the best work, ensuring a constant commitment to quality for which the company was renowned. It also encouraged family leaders to always "submit the cheapest and most honest estimate" to help sustain key customer relationships across generations.

3. The ancient temple builder still operates as a subsidiary of Takamatsu, but it lost its independence and identity as a family business. Masakazu Kongō stepped down from his role as president after the acquisition. However, in a fascinating testament to the enduring power of tradition, on the first and fifteenth days of every month, over 120 Kongō carpenters and other employees still gather for a small prayer ceremony in remembrance of Prince Shōtoku to thank him for his patronage over 1,400 years ago.

4. Thomas Hobbes, *Leviathan*, chap. 13.

5. For instance, physical infrastructure (such as roads and aqueducts), and social infrastructure (enforceable rules and markets).

6. Max Weber, *Economy and Society: An Outline on Interpretive Sociology*, 3 vols., trans. Ephraim Fischoff, ed. Guenther Roth and Claus Wittich (New York: Bedminster Press, 1968).

7. This system ultimately evolved into the earliest private banks, run by powerful dynastic banking families such as the Medicis and later the Rothschilds. In this way, banking shares its origins with casinos, brokerages, unions, and other commercial intermediaries—by taking a percentage off the top as a fee for providing the public utility of access to capital, and therefore generating profits regardless of whether customers made or lost wealth.

8. Consider that before the Dutch launched this new corporate entity, monarchs were among the few commercial speculators who could deploy the amount of capital needed to sail large fleets of ships halfway around the world. Accepting these royal commissions was far from a guaranteed path to riches. Beyond the typical risks of pirates and storms that have plagued seaborne trade for millennia, monarchs could nullify contracts and execute partners with the wave of the hand or the stroke of a pen. As a result, partnering with the crown was extremely risky business—even for Columbus and Magellan.

9. Interestingly, it was precisely around this time that the terms "risk" and "investment" first began to appear in the written English record. Risk made the jump from Romance languages into English via the Middle French *risque* and the Old Italian *riscare*. Both terms referenced "danger" or "running into danger," and were initially used by sailors, merchants, and bankers to describe common hazards of the sea such as rocks, storms, and pirates. Similarly, the term "investing" comes from the Latin word *investire*, which means "to clothe" or "to surround." In medieval Latin, it also acquired the meaning of "to give (someone) the legal right or power to do something or to own land or property."

10. John Maynard Keynes, *The Economic Consequences of the Peace* (New York: Harcourt, Brace, and Howe, 1920), chap. 2.

11. FDR also worked hard to establish new stabilizing institutions in the domain of international affairs. They included the inauguration of the World Bank, the International Monetary Fund, the World Trade Organization, and the United Nations, which FDR and others hoped would bring greater peace and predictability to the innate anarchy of global political and economic affairs. Together, these institutions helped to instill greater trust not only in millions of our fellow citizens, but increasingly to billions of unknown citizens in faraway lands.

12. Take inflation—a common macroeconomic destabilizer that has been dormant for over forty years. When prices become untethered from inflation targets, it affects our basic economic intuition in profound ways. Those who have lived through periods of hyperinflation know this form of commercial vertigo well—grocery shopping on the way to work in the morning because it is materially cheaper than on the way home that same evening.

13. When this happens, it typically foreshadows what demographers William Strauss and Neil Howe call a "fourth turning." In their provocative book *The Fourth Turning: An American Prophecy* (New York: Broadway Books, 1997), they argued that the history of Western civilization follows a recurring pattern of four "turnings" that play out over the course of a typical human lifetime—a sequence of sociological evolution, revolution, and renewal that has occurred in many countries and empires throughout history.

14. "The Two Mexicos," *The Economist*, September 19, 2015, www.economist.com/leaders/2015/09/19/the-two-mexicos.

15. Other scholars have identified the importance of familial and extended networks in building social capital and buttressing the resilience of family enterprises. See P. C. F. Amara and A. Da Rocha, "Building Resilience During the COVID-19 Pandemic: The Journey of a Small Entrepreneurial Family Firm in Brazil," *Journal of Family Business Management* 13, no. 1 (2023): 210–225; I. Mzid, "Family Capital and Organizational Resilience of Family Firms in Tunisia," in *Family Businesses in the Arab World*, ed. S. Basly, 41–61 (Cham, Switzerland: Springer, 2017); Isabelle Le Breton-Miller and Danny Miller, "Family Businesses Under COVID-19: Inspiring Models—Sometimes," *Journal of Family Business Strategy* 13, no. 2 (2022): 100452.

16. See Ecclesiastes 11:1.

17. The availability of cheap labor in these markets also makes it possible for families, even those with relatively modest means, to find people who can assist with many of the chores, such as child rearing and cleaning and cooking. See Agarwala (2016), Das (2018), and Yeoh et al. (2009). In many entrepreneurial families, these hired helpers become adopted members of the family. Over time, if the family succeeds with building a successful business, they, too, benefit, not just by making an income but also by gaining access to housing and education. It is not unusual for these individuals to be on the payroll of the business and receive health insurance and other benefits.

18. Other scholars have documented the critical role that owner-managers and founding entrepreneurs play in generating family enterprise resilience. See Sydney Finkelstein and Donald C. Hambrick, "Top Management-Team Tenure and Organizational Outcomes: The Moderating Role of Managerial Discretion," *Administrative Science Quarterly* 35, no. 3 (1990): 484–503. See also Gabriele Santoro, Antonio Messeni-Petruzzelli, and Manlio Del Giudice, "Searching for Resilience: The Impact of Employee-Level and Entrepreneur-Level Resilience on Firm Performance in Small Family Firms," *Small Business Economics* 57, no. 1 (2021): 455–471; Tony Wall and Lawrence Bellamy, "Redressing Small Firm Resilience: Exploring Owner-Manager Resources for Resilience," *International Journal of Organizational Analysis* 27, no. 2 (2019): 269–288.

19. Consider the case of a Middle Eastern founder born into a household of modest means. He taught himself English and became a translator for the royal family, and eventually for the country's king, at precisely the moment in history when important deals with foreign multinationals were being forged. Like the driver in the movie *Sabrina*, his exposure to high-level conversations taught him the language and methods of business and provided access to a world initially beyond his reach. From these humble beginnings, he built the trust and connections needed to launch and lead a global industrial and investment powerhouse that today represents many foreign brands and manages assets around the world.

20. See Rosa Nelly Trevinyo-Rodriguez and Miguel Ángel Gallo, eds., *The Power of Inclusion in Family Business* (Bingley, UK: Emerald Publishing, 2022).

21. Edgar Schein, "The Role of the Founder in Creating Organization Culture," *Organization Dynamics* 12, no. 1 (1983): 13–28.

22. This self-reinforcing learning cycle that is conducive to enhancing the resilience of family enterprises has also been observed by other scholars. See, for example, Yasin Yilmaz, Sebastian Raetze, Julia De Groote, and Nadine Kammerlander, "Resilience in Family Businesses: A Systematic Literature Review," *Family Business Review* 37, no. 1 (2024): 60–88.

23. See Ivan Lansberg, *Succeeding Generations: Realizing the Dream of Families in Business* (Boston: Harvard Business School Press, 1999), 129–140.

24. See Lansberg, *Succeeding Generations*, 140–148.

25. Under these conditions, internal stability is often restored through the typical ways in which families seek the compliance of dissident members—withholding affection, explicit scolding from senior members, family gossip, or exclusion from family gatherings. These are all signs of disapproval meant to ensure that a rapidly growing family observes and respects a general set of rules and norms designed to hold the system together in the face of a turbulent external context.

CHAPTER 4: INVESTING IN STABILITY

1. For instance, the cost of coffee jumped from 50 pesos in 1990 to 1,500 pesos in 1999, a thirtyfold increase, while the price of a loaf of bread increased fortyfold and a gallon of gasoline sixteenfold.

2. For instance, since the late 1950s Carvajal had been the leading printer and publisher of phone books and yellow pages throughout much of Latin America. In those days phone books were critical sources of information—the vehicle for holding social and commercial networks together, and through which advertisers paid to disseminate information about their products and services. The Carvajals dominated this market for about fifty years from Mexico to Argentina—that is, until Google and Facebook disrupted these lucrative businesses virtually overnight. At the same time, advanced color printing and low-cost scanning turned a high-margin specialized business into a home office commodity, threatening another major business line and further challenging Carvajal to reinvent itself. In response, the company's agile family leaders migrated their strategic center of gravity away from specialized printing and into the burgeoning market for specialized packaging just as online shopping was beginning to take off.

3. "'Crossing the River by Feeling the Stones,'" interview with W. Brian Arthur by Rick Tetzeli, *McKinsey Quarterly*, August 1, 2023, www.mckinsey.com/capabilities/risk-and-resilience/our-insights/crossing-the-river-by-feeling-the-stones.

PART 2: STABILIZING STRATEGIES IN ACTION

1. As the Prussian general Carl von Clausewitz elegantly put it, "War is not merely a political act, but also a real political instrument, a continuation of political commerce, a carrying out of the same by other means." He understood that states interact dynamically and continuously, so it should come as no surprise that friction along their frontiers will occasionally erupt into conflict and chaos.

2. Ryan Stanton, "Business Leaders Overestimate Preparedness for Disruption: PwC Global Crisis and Resilience Survey," PwC, April 6, 2023, www.pwc.com/gx/en/news-room/press-releases/2023/pwc-global-crisis-and-resilience-survey.html.

3. For management scholars, "absorptive capacity" refers to the timely choice and effective deployment of any strategy that gives family enterprises significant long-term strategic advantages. See Joshua J. Daspit, Rebecca G. Long, and Allison W. Pearson, "How Familiness Affects Innovation Outcomes via Absorptive Capacity: A Dynamic Capability Perspective of the Family Firm," *Journal of Family Business Strategy* 10, no. 2 (2019): 133–143.

CHAPTER 5: DIFFERENTIATION

1. Ben Bland and Andres Schipani, "Peruvian Upstart AJE Takes on Coke and Pepsi in Asia," CNBC, July 23, 2014, www.cnbc.com/2014/07/23/peruvian-upstart-aje-takes-on-coke-and-pepsi-in-asia.html.

2. Piero Morosini, *Seven Keys to Imagination: Creating the Future by Imagining the Unthinkable and Delivering It* (Singapore: Marshall Cavendish, 2010), 45–46.

3. Christopher J. Robertson, Anthony van der Hoek, and Rhonda Kallman, "Kola Real's Low-Cost International Expansion Strategy," *Thunderbird International Business Review* 50, no. 1 (2008): 59–74.

4. "Fighting Cola with Kola," AJE Group, accessed on May 30, 2020, https://businessinvestorguide.com/company-profile/aje-group-fighting-cola-with-kola.

5. As is typical of enterprising families operating in underserved communities, their social contract also extended beyond the company and into broader philanthropic activities, in this case via the Eduardo and Mirtha Añaños Foundation. Launched in 2003, its principal mission is to share the entrepreneurial skills, values, and philosophy of hard work that has led AJE to achieve its incredible success. From funding meals for thousands of disadvantaged schoolchildren to rescuing communities from natural disasters and sponsoring the creation and growth of microenterprises across Peru and around the world, the AJE Group is a shining example of how to "create shared value"—a concept first defined by the legendary Harvard professor Michael Porter, and that we'll explore in greater detail in Chapter 7 on "Symbiosis."

6. "Soft Drinks—Worldwide," Statista, accessed May 30, 2024, www.statista.com/outlook/cmo/non-alcoholic-drinks/soft-drinks/worldwide.

7. Such adaptive radiation occurs naturally whenever vacancies emerge within an ecological niche. The Galapagos Islands—occupying a secluded habitat more than 1,200 kilometers from the Ecuadorian mainland—provide the quintessential example. They have produced so much differentiation that we're still discovering new species nearly 200 years after Darwin first set foot on their volcanic shores.

8. Such Darwinian insights have long been used to conceptualize family dynamics and personality development. If, for example, parents value academic excellence, firstborns will pick up on that and generally do better at school. According to Frank J. Sulloway, firstborns are, in fact, overrepresented as academics and overachievers. Frank J. Sulloway, *Born to Rebel: Birth Order, Family Dynamics, and Creative Lives* (New York: Pantheon Books, 1996), chap. 4.

9. Efosa Ojomo, "The Necessity of Market Creating Innovations," Christensen Institute, accessed May 30, 2024, www.christenseninstitute.org/blog/the-necessity-of-market-creating-innovations.

10. "Tata Nano," Wikipedia, accessed May 30, 2024, https://en.wikipedia.org/wiki/Tata_Nano.

11. Navi Radjou, Jaideep C. Prabhu, and Simone Ahuja, *Jugaad Innovation: Think Frugal, Be Flexible, Generate Breakthrough Growth* (San Francisco: Jossey-Bass, 2012).

12. "From Jugaad to Justice: Endemic Corruption and the Possibility of an Indian Spring," Knowledge at Wharton, University of Pennsylvania, https://knowledge.wharton.upenn.edu/article/jugaad-justice-endemic-corruption-possibility-indian-spring.

13. Dan Senor and Saul Singer, *Start-Up Nation: The Story of Israel's Economic Miracle* (Toronto: McClelland and Stewart, 2011).

14. "About Henokiens," International Association of Bicentenary Family Companies, www.henokiens.com/content.php?id=4&lg=en.

15. Malcolm Gladwell, "How David Beats Goliath," *New Yorker*, May 4, 2009, www.newyorker.com/magazine/2009/05/11/how-david-beats-goliath.

CHAPTER 6: MODULARITY

1. Drawn from private interviews; transcripts from the Creating Emerging Markets project at Harvard Business School (www.hbs.edu/creating-emerging-markets/Pages/default.aspx); and Christina R. Wing, Suraj Srinivasan, and Esel Çekin, "Family

Matters: Governance at the Zamil Group," HBS Case Collection, Harvard Business School, August 2019, www.hbs.edu/faculty/Pages/item.aspx?num=56494.

2. It was uncommon at the time for daughters to travel abroad on their own—a practice still pervasive in the country, though less so in recent years, particularly among more progressive families such as Zamil.

3. In a testament to the enduring value of this modular arrangement, five of the brothers were living together while at university in Los Angeles, ensuring that they were "not just brothers, [but] also good friends." Wing et al., "Family Matters."

4. IKEA financial reports, available at www.inter.ikea.com/en/performance/download-financial-reports.

5. Consider the paradox of the Ship of Theseus, first proposed by Plutarch in the first century AD. Every year, Athenians would commemorate their founder-king's heroic rescue of the youth of Athens from the Minotaur by sailing his ship on a pilgrimage to the island of Delos. Over hundreds of years, the parts of Theseus's ship would naturally need to be replaced as they decayed, leaving Plutarch to wonder whether the modern vessel was even the same ship anymore, or simply a mirror or ghost of the original. Beyond the question's natural intrigue—which has perplexed the giants of philosophy for centuries—it demonstrates one of the benefits of modular construction that even the ancients were quick to realize. When resources are scarce, designing structures to simplify maintenance and upkeep is far superior to disposal and replacement.

6. Wing et al., "Family Matters."

7. One of the earliest public institutions that attempted to fill this void was the International Telegraph Union. Founded in 1865 near the end of the American Civil War, its express purpose was to encourage the development of new telegraphic networks between countries, which many believed would transform the way information was shared around the world. Prior to the first submarine cables crossing the Atlantic in the 1850s, news took weeks to cross the ocean by boat. Now consider how much you would pay to receive critical information today that would otherwise arrive next week.

However, to leverage this massive transformational potential, the nascent industry needed to align around a set of common manufacturing specifications, such as for wire gauges; communications standards, such as Morse Code; and commercial terms, as for tariffs. Only once these new protocols were established could telegraph networks connect and scale more rapidly. This early success provided a modular playbook for the governance of all subsequent communications technologies, including telephones and radio, along with railways, power grids, and other infrastructure networks. Each of these helped to bring greater stability and productivity to businesses and citizens for generations to come.

The protocols that govern these modular systems are perhaps their most defining feature. For instance, without a common width for rail gauges, transportation networks in Europe and Asia still require massive transfer stations that limit their interoperability. Similarly, when electrical grids differ across countries—from the shapes of outlets to the underlying voltage—this naturally limits compatibility with foreign products and technologies, inhibiting consumer choice and market competition.

8. The role that social (and relational) capital plays in the resilience of family enterprises is a recurring theme in the family business literature. See, for example, Michele Stasa and Ondřej Machek, "Social Capital in the Family Business Literature: A Systematic Review and Future Research Agenda," *Family Business Review* 35, no. 4 (2022): 415–441;

Ali Azouz, Nicolas Antheaume, and Brigitte Charles-Pauvers, "Looking at the Sky: An Ethnographic Study of How Religiosity Influences Family Business Resilience," *Family Business Review* 35, no. 2 (2022): 184–208; Raj V. Mahto, Orlando Llanos-Contreras, and Melany Hebles, "Post-Disaster Recovery for Family Firms: The Role of Owner Motivations, Firm Resources, and Dynamic Capabilities," *Journal of Business Research* 145 (2023): 117–129.

9. The ability to function both independently and interdependently as circumstances change offers a significant adaptive advantage to enterprising families during economic downturns, political upheavals, or natural disasters. For example, being able to tap cousins and extended in-laws as potential investors in new ventures, or as employees in critical roles requiring higher degrees of trust, enhances organizational flexibility and access to human capital. These familial connections also heighten the psychological pressure on individuals to comply with the norms prevalent in the network. Those who break norms and violate trust can incur high personal costs, so the integrity of the system is naturally calibrated.

In times of need or in pursuit of opportunities, family networks can also serve as a form of social collateral, since individuals are more likely to repay loans to those with whom they have a personal relationship. This is a fundamental principle of modern microfinance, the transformational approach to economic development pioneered by the Bangladeshi economist and Nobel Prize winner Mohammad Yunus at Grameen Bank decades ago.

10. In Turkey, the related concept of *torpil* is associated with the intervention of powerful private and government officials who can help facilitate desired outcomes, often obtaining services or helping relatives in need.

11. Nature's intricate web of life exemplifies modularity: How could a complex ecosystem sustain even brief periods of stability if its components were not working in some form of dynamic equilibrium? A familiar example is the hive of the honeybee, studied and admired since antiquity for its modular construction. Darwin once described the honeycomb as a masterpiece of architecture that is "absolutely perfect in economizing labor and wax." Charles Darwin, *On the Origin of Species by Means of Natural Selection* (New York: D. Appleton, 1872), 224. Similarly, Canada geese have evolved a remarkable modular behavior—the "flying V" formation—to optimize the efficiency of their annual migratory journey between the United States and Canada. Researchers have estimated that this modular formation improves the flock's flight range and endurance by nearly 50 percent.

CHAPTER 7: SYMBIOSIS

1. Youngjin Yoo and Kyungmook Kim, "How Samsung Became a Design Powerhouse," *Harvard Business Review*, September 2015, https://hbr.org/2015/09/how-samsung-became-a-design-powerhouse.

2. "Revenue of Leading Affiliates of Samsung Group as Percentage of Gross Domestic Product (GDP) in South Korea from 2017 to 2022," Statista, www.statista.com/statistics/1314374/south-korea-samsung-groups-revenue-as-a-share-of-gdp.

3. Devin DeCiantis and Ivan Lansberg, "A Little Nut Rage Is Good: How an Infamous Incident and Its Fallout May Finally Change South Korea's Relationship to Its Family-Run Conglomerates," *The Atlantic*, March 13, 2015, www.theatlantic.com/international/archive/2015/03/a-little-nut-rage-is-good/387787.

4. "Dr. Manu Chandaria, Chair and CEO, Comcraft Group (Steel and Aluminum)," Creating Emerging Markets, Harvard Business School, Interviews, www.hbs.edu/creating-emerging-markets/interviews/Pages/profile.aspx?profile=mchandaria.

5. Christopher Marlowe, *Doctor Faustus*, Chorus 1, lines 20–22, Owl Eyes, www.owleyes.org/text/faustus/read/chorus-1.

6. Marlowe, *Doctor Faustus*, Scene 1, lines 53–54, Owl Eyes, www.owleyes.org/text/faustus/read/scene-1.

7. Some have suggested that the play was also a cautionary tale for modernizing Europe about the risks of sacrificing religion on the altar of science and progress.

8. Think of the relationship between a clownfish and an anemone, beautifully dramatized in the Pixar classic *Finding Nemo*. Over millions of years, clownfish have evolved to live safely among the stinging tentacles of sea anemones, providing them with shelter from predators and a safe place to lay eggs. In exchange, clownfish help the anemones by cleaning their tentacles from parasites and debris, defending them from small predators, and providing them with fertilizer in the form of waste.

9. A fascinating case of parasitism in nature is the cuckoo bird, which lays its eggs in the nests of other birds such as warblers, sparrows, and robins. Young cuckoo chicks hatch before their hosts, pushing out the eggs of their step siblings, at which point the host parents feed and raise the cuckoo chicks as their own.

10. William Hamilton's theory of kin selection hypothesizes that organisms will behave altruistically toward close relatives in proportion to their shared genes. He predicted that full siblings would tend to compete for scarce resources "whenever the benefits of doing so are more than twice the costs, because it takes two sibs to equal the genetic material that is shared with the self," as Frank J. Sulloway put it. See Sulloway, "Why Siblings are Like Darwin's Finches: Birth Order, Sibling Competition, and Adaptive Divergence Within the Family," in *The Evolution of Personality and Individual Differences*, ed. David M. Buss and Patricia H. Hawley, 86–120 (Oxford: Oxford University Press, 2011), 90.

11. For example, according to Frank Sulloway, who also wrote the best-selling book *Born to Rebel: Birth Order, Family Dynamics, and Creative Lives* (New York: Pantheon, 1996), firstborn children tend to identify with their parents and win favor with them by helping with the upbringing of their younger siblings, or helping with household or business chores, and, more generally, by becoming surrogate parents of the later born. When lead siblings or cousins pursue their interests at the expense of their peers rather than in a more mutualistic manner, in which hierarchical differences are viewed as benefiting the interests of all, familial collaboration breaks down, and the resilience and adaptability of the family is invariably undermined.

12. See Gideon Lasco, "Did Margaret Mead Think a Healed Femur Was the Earliest Sign of Civilization?," Sapiens, June 16, 2022, www.sapiens.org/culture/margaret-mead-femur.

13. Adam Smith, *An Inquiry into the Nature and Causes of the Wealth of Nations*, vol. 1, ed. Edwin Cannan (London: Methuen, 1904), chap. 1.

14. Michael E. Porter and Mark R. Kramer, "Strategy and Society: The Link Between Competitive Advantage and Corporate Social Responsibility," *Harvard Business Review* 84 (2006): 78–85.

15. Chavez quickly purged the military and national oil company of dissidents, increasing his control over the judiciary and the media, and launched a series of radical reforms to redistribute wealth and power to his supporters.

16. Joseph Luparello, "Life Shakers: From Criminal to Class Acts, Santa Teresa Rum Transforms the Lives of Inmates in the San Antonio Prison," *Chilled Magazine* 16, no. 4 (2023): 30–31.

17. "Alan Greenspan vs. Naomi Klein on the Iraq War, Bush's Tax Cuts, Economic Populism, Crony Capitalism and More," transcript of video, Democracy Now, September 24, 2007, www.democracynow.org/2007/9/24/alan_greenspan_vs_naomi_klein_on. Greenspan's observation is similar to one by Alfredo Carvajal, who said, "There is always corruption. Sometimes more, sometimes less. But corruption is part of normal life. You just have to navigate with the hope that there are also ethical people. And that they will prefer you because you are trustworthy."

18. Paying for power is so pervasive in Chinese society that in 2012 the country's official Mandarin dictionary added the word *maiguan*—"to buy a government promotion." In his award-winning book *Age of Ambition: Chasing Fortune, Truth, and Faith in the New China* (New York: Farrar, Straus and Giroux, 2014), author Evan Osnos describes a small town in Inner Mongolia where the post of chief planner was sold for US$103,000, and party secretary was on sale for US$101,000: "It followed a certain logic: in weak democracies, people paid their way into office by buying votes; in a state where there were no votes to buy, you paid the people who doled out the jobs. Even the military was riddled with patronage; commanders received a string of payments from a pyramid of loyal officers beneath them. A one-star general could reportedly expect to receive ten million dollars in gifts and business deals; a four-star commander stood to earn at least fifty million" (p. 252).

19. Reyhan Harmanci, "The Adani Group's $100 Billion Loss, Explained," Bloomberg, February 9, 2023, www.bloomberg.com/news/newsletters/2023-02-09/adani-group-s-100-billion-loss-and-hindenburg-claims-explained.

20. The *Financial Times* quoted public policy professor Rohit Chandra from the Indian Institute of Technology Delhi as saying, "Is India going to move towards the east Asian model or the Russian model? So far the tendency looks towards the latter [more] than the former." Stephanie Findlay and Hudson Lockett, "'Modi's Rockefeller': Gautam Adani and the Concentration of Power in India," *Financial Times*, November 12, 2020, www.ft.com/content/474706d6-1243-4f1e-b365-891d4c5d528b.

21. "How to Run a Business in a Dangerous and Disorderly World," *The Economist*, July 27, 2023, www.economist.com/leaders/2023/07/27/how-to-run-a-business-in-a-dangerous-and-disorderly-world.

22. Quoted by Morgan Sloan, "José Ortega y Gasset (1883–1955)," Philosophy Now, 2020, https://philosophynow.org/issues/141/Jose_Ortega_y_Gasset_1883-1955.

23. This choice often involves articulating clear values that authentically represent the identity and fundamental priorities of the owners. It means committing to these values publicly as well as implementing internal controls, along with instituting monitoring mechanisms such as auditing systems for tracking bribery attempts. Such companies may also participate in industry-wide initiatives and advocacy campaigns, sharing best practices around doing business with integrity and advocating for legal and regulatory reforms.

24. See David de Jong, *Nazi Billionaires: The Dark History of Germany's Wealthiest Dynasties* (New York: HarperCollins, 2022), for a fuller account of how, in the absence of external stabilizers, seemingly "honorable" business families can descend down the

ethical slippery slope one choice at a time, and before they know it find themselves in bed with the most nefarious elements in their societies.

CHAPTER 8: REDUNDANCY

1. Tragically, in addition to dysfunctional politics, Haiti also suffers from systematic deforestation—which anthropologist Jared Diamond has cited as a major cause of the country's developmental paralysis. Today, roughly 98 percent of Haiti's original forest cover is gone. Once-fertile lands are now unproductive wastelands, and the dry, loose soil is more susceptible than ever to floods and landslides.

2. Agnès Pierre-Louis, "Opinion: How Is Haiti? 10 Years After a Catastrophic Earthquake," January 12, 2020, www.essence.com/feature/haiti-earthquake-10-years.

3. "Haiti's Le Plaza: More Than Just a Hotel," TravPR.com, September 5, 2018, https://travpr.com/pr-74368-haitis-le-plaza-more-than.html.

4. Armies have long understood the value of secure and stable supply lines. The role of the quartermaster was designed expressly for this purpose. It may be less exciting or adrenaline-inducing than platoon leader or commander, but the effective management of food and equipment has been instrumental in driving military success for millennia. Some historians describe combat logistics as "the sinews of war"—the critical connective tissue without which any army's muscle and bone are useless. Although redundancy is studied diligently at West Point, Sandhurst, and Bundeswehr, it's easy to understand why it gets such little attention in broader society, particularly within advanced economies.

5. "'Keep 'em Rolling': 82 Days on the Red Ball Express," National WWII Museum, New Orleans, February 1, 2021, www.nationalww2museum.org/war/articles/red-ball-express.

6. Pankaj Ghemawat, "CEMEX: An Emerging Market Multinational," Strategy + Business, April 13, 2015, www.strategy-business.com/blog/CEMEX-An-Emerging-Market-Multinational.

7. Fast fashion provides a classic example of how redundancy can become a liability, particularly when consumer tastes and preferences are so fickle and prone to change. Under these conditions, maintaining excess inventory can backfire, since the costs of warehousing and obsolescence can significantly impact profitability. In response, some companies, including H&M and Zara, have shifted to just-in-time design and inventory models to minimize surpluses and maximize sell-throughs. However, it also leaves them more vulnerable when supply chains break down or some critical aspect of their operating environment is suddenly thrust into chaos.

8. Pavel Rybák, "Ekonomika ČSSR v letech padesátých a šedesátých," July 21, 2011, Britské listy, www.blisty.cz/art/59458-ekonomika-cssr-v-nbsp-letech-padesatych-a-sedesatych.html.

9. For the Fragile States Index, a project of the Fund for Peace, see https://fragilestatesindex.org.

10. Freud (as paraphrased by Erik Erikson) viewed these as "the cornerstones of our humanness." Sigmund Freud, *Civilization and Its Discontents*, trans. James Strachey (New York: W. W. Norton, 1961), 48; Erik Erikson, *Childhood and Society* (New York: W. W. Norton, 1986), both cited in C. L. Lim, ed., *The Cambridge Companion to International Arbitration* (Cambridge: Cambridge University Press, 2021), 303n23.

11. Evan Osnos, "Doomsday Prep for the Super-Rich," *New Yorker*, January 22, 2017, www.newyorker.com/magazine/2017/01/30/doomsday-prep-for-the-super-rich.

CHAPTER 9: MIGRATION

1. The coup was orchestrated by a coalition of military officers who were members or sympathizers of the Ba'ath Party, a regional movement that prioritized Arab nationalism, socialism, and secularism. As the cold war was heating up, the Soviets seized the opportunity to develop another ally within the "third world," extolling the virtues of central planning to Syria's new leaders.

2. "Resilience of the Family Business: The Baalbaki Group of Syria," *Tharawat Magazine*, July 1, 2013, www.tharawat-magazine.com/crisis-risk-thinking/family-business-baalbaki-group-syria.

3. Among the most epic examples from nature is the multigenerational relay race of *Danaus plexippus*. Each year, millions of monarch butterflies make the journey of nearly 5,000 kilometers (3,000 miles) from Canada to Mexico. Much like the human "snowbirds" who vacation in Florida and Arizona over the winter, these intrepid butterflies make their way south to the oyamel fir forests, high atop the Sierra Madre Mountains, a more hospitable and resource-rich climate to ride out the colder months. However, unlike migratory humans, over the course of an annual pilgrimage the butterfly population will cycle through three to five generations. To put that in perspective, the members of the colony arriving back in Canada in the spring are completing a journey their great-great-great-grandparents started the autumn before.

4. "Refugee Data Finder," United Nations High Commissioner for Refugees, www.unhcr.org/refugee-statistics, accessed on May 20, 2024.

5. In our experience, the internal dynamics of enterprising families also generate their own set of push and pull vectors that typically determine who within the family ultimately migrates. These internal pushes often result from the children's need to differentiate from one another. While firstborn children are the most likely to stay close to home (and to the family business), if migration pressures build, later-born children are more likely to seek out new territories. The pulls often come from the family's entrepreneurial ambition to grow the enterprise and demonstrate its capacity to conquer new lands. The fuel for this can, and often does, come from rivalries among siblings or cousins—in which those who migrate do so to show that they can outperform those who stay behind, even in new territories where the family is yet unknown.

6. The antidotes to this tendency are: (1) regularly "updating" and asking oneself, "Knowing what I know *now*, would I still invest in this course of action?" and (2) drawing firm guidelines (or "bright red lines"), ideally a priori, that trigger an exit from the failing path.

7. Eric Ries, *The Lean Startup: How Today's Entrepreneurs Use Continuous Innovation to Create Radically Successful Businesses* (New York: Crown, 2011), 172–173.

8. Ries, *Lean Startup*, 27, 8.

9. Downstream ventures can also provide opportunities for smart multinationals to innovate. For instance, the McDonald's "Happy Meal" was actually invented by Yolanda de Cofino, a franchisee in Guatemala.

10. David Barstow, "Wal-Mart Hushed Up a Vast Mexican Bribery Case," *New York Times*, April 21, 2012, www.nytimes.com/2012/04/22/business/at-wal-mart-in-mexico-a-bribe-inquiry-silenced.html.

11. Nandita Bose, "Walmart to Pay $282 Million to Settle Seven-Year Global Corruption Probe," Reuters, June 20, 2019.

12. “Climate Change–Induced Sea-Level Rise Direct Threat to Millions Around World, Secretary-General Tells Security Council,” United Nations, Meetings Coverage and Press Releases, February 14, 2023, https://press.un.org/en/2023/sc15199.doc.htm; “Rising Sea Levels Could Cost the World $14 Trillion a Year by 2100,” National Oceanography Centre, July 4, 2018, https://noc.ac.uk/news/rising-sea-levels-could-cost-world-14-trillion-year-2100.

CHAPTER 10: SIMPLIFICATION

1. Pankaj Ghemawat, Michael G. Rukstad, and Jenny Illes, “Arcor: Global Strategy and Local Turbulence,” Harvard Business School Case 704-427, November 13, 2003 (rev. November 2005).

2. “Luis Alejandro Pagani, CEO, Grupo Arcor (Food Production),” Creating Emerging Markets, Harvard Business School, Interviews, www.hbs.edu/creating-emerging-markets/interviews/Pages/profile.aspx?profile=lalejandropagani.

3. Ghemawat et al., “Arcor.”

4. “Información financiera,” Arcor, www.arcor.com/ar/informacion-financiera.

5. Laura Gozzi, “Argentina Inflation Soars Past 100% Mark,” BBC, March 14, 2023, www.bbc.com/news/world-latin-america-64960385.

6. Damián Kantor, “Ranking Merco 2022: Entrevista Luis Pagani,” Arcor, accessed May 31, 2024, www.arcor.com/ar/institucional/ranking-merco-2022-entrevista-luis-pagani.

7. Christopher Turbill and Lisa Stojanovski, “Torpor Reduces Predation Risk by Compensating for the Energetic Cost of Antipredator Foraging Behaviours,” *Proceedings of the Royal Society B: Biological Sciences* 285, no. 1893 (2018): 20182370.

8. “Discover Our Roots,” Brown-Forman, www.brown-forman.com/history-timeline.

9. Mehrdad Baghai, Stephen Coley, and David White, *The Alchemy of Growth: Practical Insights for Building the Enduring Enterprise* (Reading, MA: Perseus Books, 1999).

10. William Ford Jr. shed the CEO role and brought in Alan Mulally in 2006. During this time, the Ford family's commitment to its legacy helped to stabilize the company's response to the financial challenges it faced. Even though the family owns a small stake (roughly 2 percent), it still controls the company through a dual stock mechanism that ensures continued control (with 40 percent of the votes). As a result, during the Global Financial Crisis in 2008 and 2009, while its competitors were negotiating government bailouts, Ford was able to increase its market share, return to profitability, and fix its deeply leveraged balance sheet.

11. Bill Vlasic, “Choosing Its Own Path, Ford Stayed Independent,” *New York Times*, April 8, 2009, www.nytimes.com/2009/04/09/business/09ford.html.

12. Scot J. Paltrow and Jonathan Weber, “$8-Billion Loss Posted by IBM; More Layoffs Set,” *Los Angeles Times*, July 28, 1993, www.latimes.com/archives/la-xpm-1993-07-28-mn-17823-story.html.

13. James C. Collins and Morten T. Hansen, *Great by Choice: Uncertainty, Chaos, and Luck. Why Some Thrive Despite Them All* (New York: HarperCollins, 2011), chap. 6.

14. Recent fuselage issues with several of Boeing's 737 line have exposed the potential vulnerabilities of *over*simplification—one we'll address in Chapter 11 on diversity.

15. Franklin also helped to establish the Union Fire Company in Philadelphia in 1736—a precursor to the modern-day public fire department. In addition, his concern for preemptive solutions prompted his invention of the first safe indoor fireplace—known

as the Franklin stove—which was lined with metal to prevent fires from spreading, and included an inverted siphon to draw smoke up the baffle and safely out of the house.

CHAPTER 11: DIVERSITY

1. "Through The Mill," Tata Group, accessed May 31, 2024, www.tata.com/newsroom/through-the-mill.

2. "Blazing a Trail," Tata, accessed May 31, 2024, www.tata.com/newsroom/titan-diversity-blazing-a-trail.

3. See "1905–2000: A Century of Philanthropic Initiatives," Tata Trusts, accessed May 31, 2024, www.tatatrusts.org/about-tatatrusts/our-history.

4. "J. R. D. Tata," Wikipedia, accessed May 31, 2024, https://en.wikipedia.org/wiki/J._R._D._Tata.

5. "Tata Group Business Overview," Tata, accessed May 31, 2024, www.tata.com/business/overview.

6. Even a century and a half of success—and a diversified and resilient portfolio—doesn't inoculate against the common threats all families face, particularly during the passing of the baton between generations. Consider that in 2016, Ratan Tata fired his protégé and chosen successor, Cyrus Mistry, the first non-Tata to lead the company in its history, over a disagreement about the company's strategic vision. The allegations and counter-allegations—which included fraud investigations by the Indian government—are complex and imbued with an emotional energy that some family businesses can naturally evoke.

7. By the fifth century BCE, two-field crop rotation was already common in China—with one field being planted each year while the other remained fallow. Around the same time, the Greeks were experimenting with crop rotation on their larger estates. This practice gained additional structure under the Romans. Cato the Elder, in *De Agri Cultura* (On Agriculture, 160 BCE), and Pliny the Elder, in his classic *Naturalis Historia* (Natural History, 77 CE), documented their understanding of how soil conditions and organized farm operations could expand agricultural productivity. By the ninth century AD, it was common practice throughout medieval Europe to divide land into three parts: a field for winter crops, a field for summer crops, and a field left fallow to regain fertility. This system significantly enhanced productivity by allowing two-thirds of the land to be cultivated each year instead of just half the land. It also increased overall nutritional output—with the spring crops, mostly legumes, helping to improve the general health of northern European populations.

8. For an excellent summary of humanity's long history of illogical speculation, see John Kenneth Galbraith, *A Short History of Financial Euphoria* (New York: Penguin, 1994).

9. Harry Markowitz, "Portfolio Selection," *Journal of Finance* 7, no. 1 (1952): 77–91.

10. See Katherine W. Phillips, "How Diversity Makes Us Smarter," *Scientific American*, October 1, 2014, www.scientificamerican.com/article/how-diversity-makes-us-smarter.

11. Emma Hinchliffe, "Women Run More Than 10% of Fortune 500 Companies for the First Time," Society for Human Resource Management (SHRM), Executive Network, January 30, 2023, www.shrm.org/executive-network/insights/women-run-10-fortune-500-companies-first-time; "In 2023, Women CEOs Finally Outnumbered CEOs Named John," *CEO Magazine*, March 8, 2024, www.theceomagazine.com/business/management-leadership/countrics-with-the-most-female-ceos. The exact figures are 10.6 percent and 5.4 percent. Leading the pack is Norway, with 13.4 percent.

12. See Anna Marks, Karen Bowman, Kevin Tracey, and Karen Edelman, "Executive Summary: Gender Parity on Boards Will Be Elusive Without Greater Focus and Action," Deloitte, 2023, www2.deloitte.com/us/en/insights/topics/leadership/women-in-the-boardroom.html. The exact figure was 23.3 percent in 2023.

13. Neus Feliu and Ivan Lansberg, "Women in Family Enterprise: Understanding the Unique Ownership Challenges of Daughters in Business Families," in *The Power of Inclusion in Family Business*, ed. Rosa Nelly Trevinyo-Rodríguez and Miguel Ángel Gallo (Bingley, UK: Emerald Publishing, 2022).

14. PwC, "Family Business Survey 2023," www.pwc.com/us/en/services/trust-solutions/private-company-services/library/family-business-survey.html.

15. McKinsey & Company, "Why Diversity Matters" (2015); Boston Consulting Group, "How Diverse Leadership Teams Boost Innovation" (2018); Nielsen, "From Consumers to Creators: The Digital Lives of Black Consumers" (2018); *Harvard Business Review*, "Diverse Teams Feel Less Comfortable—and That's Why They Perform Better" (2016); *Harvard Business Review*, "How and Where Diversity Drives Financial Performance" (2017); Deloitte, "The Diversity and Inclusion Revolution: Eight Powerful Truths" (2018).

16. Diogenes Laërtius, *Lives of the Eminent Philosophers*, Loeb Classical Library (Cambridge, MA: Harvard University Press, 1925), Book 5, chap. 1, p. 463, online at University of Chicago, https://penelope.uchicago.edu/Thayer/E/Roman/Texts/Diogenes_Laertius/Lives_of_the_Eminent_Philosophers/5/Aristotle*.html.

17. While humans continue to debate the value of diversity, the evidence from nature is abundantly clear. Diverse plant communities better withstand drought, disease, and herbivory and support higher levels of pollination, nutrient cycling, and carbon sequestration. Diverse animal populations reduce the risk of "inbreeding depression" and increase the potential for healthy adaptation. Diverse forests adapt better to climate change, show greater resistance to biotic threats, and bounce back faster from forest fires. Diversity ensures that the ecosystem as a whole is more resilient to environmental changes and can recover quickly from catastrophic collapse. This logic has obvious analogues to operational and investment portfolios, which are susceptible to a variety of internal and external pressures.

18. J. N. Tata to Dorab Tata, 1902, quoted at Tata Steel, *Corporate Sustainability Report (2003–04)*, www.tatasteel.com/files/csr-2003-04/page_03.htm.

19. Jens Kengelbach, Hady Farag, Bernhard Schwetzler, and Christin Rudolph, "Invest Wisely, Divest Strategically: Tapping the Power of Diversity to Raise Valuations," Boston Consulting Group, April 22, 2014, www.bcg.com/publications/2014/divestitures-invest-wisely-divest-strategically-tapping-power-diversity-raise-valuations.

20. In the past few years, some of the largest conglomerates in history have elected to break up into smaller operating entities, including 220-year-old DowDuPont, 138-year-old Johnson and Johnson, 132-year-old General Electric, and 118-year-old Kellogg. Samantha Delouya, "A 220-Year-Old American Corporate Powerhouse Is Breaking Up," CNN, May 23, 2024, www.cnn.com/2024/05/22/business/dupont-de-nemours-company-split/index.html.

PART 3: NURTURING A FRONTIER MINDSET

1. Maxim Sytch and Dagny Dukach, "Leading a Business in Ukraine During the War," *Harvard Business Review*, February 24, 2023, https://hbr.org/2023/02/leading-a-business-in-ukraine-during-the-war.

2. Sytch and Dukach, "Leading a Business in Ukraine During the War."

3. Marcel Proust, *Le Temps retrouvé* (*Time Regained*, 1926), trans. C. K. Scott-Moncrieff and S. Hudson, rev. T. Kilmartin, cited from Susan Ratcliffe, ed., *Oxford Essential Quotations*, 6th ed. (Oxford: Oxford University Press, 2018), at Oxford Reference, www.oxfordreference.com/display/10.1093/acref/9780191866692.001.0001/q-oro-ed6-00008648.

CHAPTER 12: NAVIGATING CRISES WITH CONFIDENCE

1. Crisis is a universal phenomenon, though it manifests in varying degrees across the Hierarchy of Stability. Financial downturns, leadership scandals, technological innovations, pandemics, terrorist attacks, cybersecurity breaches, or any number of other destabilizing shocks can knock an organization off balance no matter where it is in the world. Yet those at the peak and those at the base can expect some predictable differences. For instance, the frequency and intensity of crises naturally increase in emerging and frontier economies, given fewer external stabilizers. Additionally, some types of crises, such as narco terrorism, hyperinflation, and social unrest, are much more common at the base, though they are certainly not exclusively at the base.

2. The original quote was probably "Everybody has plans until they get hit for the first time," which is what Tyson said to a reporter in August 1987. See "Everybody Has Plans Until They Get Hit for the First Time," Quote Investigator, August 25, 2021, https://quoteinvestigator.com/2021/08/25/plans-hit.

3. Quoted at "Top 500 Jim Rohn Quotes (2024 Update)," Quotefancy, https://quotefancy.com/jim-rohn-quotes.

4. Winston Churchill, Speech at the Lord Mayor's Day Luncheon, November 10, 1942.

5. Devin DeCiantis, "Building Resilience into Your Family Business," *Harvard Business Review*, September 28, 2022, https://hbr.org/2022/09/building-resilience-into-your-family-business.

6. Devin DeCiantis and Ivan Lansberg, "What Family Businesses Need to Adapt to a Crisis," *Harvard Business Review*, May 7, 2020, https://hbr.org/2020/05/what-family-businesses-need-to-adapt-to-a-crisis.

7. Suntory in Japan provides another fascinating example. As the company was emerging from the devastation and disruption of World War II, it was committed to rebuilding, in particular growing its whiskey sales to Western consumers. Starting with the delivery of a case of their finest spirits to senior US military officials, the company was about to embark on an exciting new phase of international expansion in the "new normal" that emerged in the wake of the war.

8. When designing these retreats, consider carefully who is invited to participate. Some families prefer to involve only senior leaders—executives, board members, and large shareholders—which is totally understandable given that these individuals are the ones with the best understanding of the enterprise's strategic context. However, such conversations often touch on organizational purpose, core values, and opportunities for transformative change—all factors that connect deeply to the owners' vision for the future of their enterprise. In our experience, enterprising families who cast a wider net and engage a broader array of their members in these fundamental discussions are better able to navigate the regression to the mean, since the next generation will need to live with the consequences of these actions for much longer than those currently in power.

9. Quoted in Motley Fool, "A Look at Warren Buffett's Annual Letter," Nasdaq, March 11, 2017, www.nasdaq.com/articles/look-warren-buffetts-annual-letter-2017-03-11.

10. Mohammad R. Mhawish, "Life in Gaza Is a Series of Calculations: How Much Water Do You Really Need?," *The Economist*, October 23, 2023, www.economist.com/1843/2023/10/23/life-in-gaza-is-a-series-of-calculations-how-much-water-do-you-really-need.

11. Some of this can be explained by the fact that their businesses and their lives are dominated by chronic uncertainty—so the amount of change necessary to adapt to the new conditions is relatively limited. Doing business in Baghdad always requires having redundancy built explicitly into resource planning, and diversity built directly into any business model. So the key challenge at the outset of a crisis is more about incremental versus transformational change.

12. One of the key takeaways from Shakespeare's *King Lear* is that planning for your death—at least during Elizabethan times—was the height of arrogance and hubris, since these decisions were the exclusive domain of the supernatural.

CHAPTER 13: MANAGING RISK IN AN AGE OF UNCERTAINTY

1. "Tsunamis in Japan," World Data, www.worlddata.info/asia/japan/tsunamis.php, accessed April 29, 2024.

2. Before the Fukushima meltdown, Japan's Nuclear Regulation Authority had never considered the prohibition or decommissioning of the country's fifty-four coastal reactors, since they were heavily dependent on seawater to power their cooling systems. Since World War II, given its lack of a domestic oil industry and dwindling reserves of coal, the country has relied heavily on civilian nuclear power to fuel its economic growth.

3. Martin Fackler, "Tsunami Warnings, Written in Stone," *New York Times*, April 20, 2011, www.nytimes.com/2011/04/21/world/asia/21stones.html.

4. Danny Lewis, "These Century-Old Stone 'Tsunami Stones' Dot Japan's Coastline," *Smithsonian Magazine*, August 31, 2015, www.smithsonianmag.com/smart-news/century-old-warnings-against-tsunamis-dot-japans-coastline-180956448.

5. "Thinking Ahead with YGL Michele Wucker," YouTube, posted by "yglvoices," April 5, 2013, www.youtube.com/watch?v=wlngQdxduKw. See also Michele Wucker, *The Gray Rhino: How to Recognize and Act on the Obvious Dangers We Ignore* (New York: St. Martin's Press, 2016).

6. Particularly in advanced economies, it's easy for leaders to be lulled into a false sense of security when they haven't experienced these risks directly within their lifetime. In contrast, businesses that have recently faced currency depreciations, military coups, or natural disasters are naturally more inclined to engage in preventive behaviors, just like families that have recently been traumatized by a motorcycle accident, lung cancer, or a kidnapping.

7. Many of the enterprise risk management (ERM) frameworks currently in use were inspired by the financial services industry and their regulatory response to the Global Financial Crisis. As a result, there is a strong focus on operations and compliance within isolated "silos of risk"—particularly around financial variables such as credit quality, liquidity, and capital adequacy. However, these tools lack a systematic or holistic view of the enterprise.

8. See "How the Economic Machine Works by Ray Dalio," YouTube, posted by "Principles of Ray Dalio," September 22, 2013, www.youtube.com/watch?v=PHe0bXAIuk0.

9. Chauncey Starr, "Social Benefit Versus Technological Risk," *Science*, n.s., 165, no. 3899 (1969): 1232–1238.

10. At the same time, enterprising families can develop a distorted sense of how much control they have over their destinies. Their success can easily breed hubris and a false sense of confidence, which can dampen their willingness to adequately plan.

11. In recent years, a variety of "risk maps" have been painstakingly developed by large insurance companies, investment managers, multilateral agencies (e.g., the International Monetary Fund), and think tanks (e.g., the World Economic Forum). These annual reports are filled with beautiful charts and powerful warnings about everything that could go terribly, horribly wrong with the global economy in any given year. For those like us who are fascinated by the topic of risk and uncertainty, they provide rich data for reflection. However, they fail to achieve their full potential for two principal reasons: (1) they're too convoluted for the average non-technical reader; and (2) they don't do a great job of actually predicting key risks. For instance, in the 2020 edition of the World Economic Forum's Global Risk Report, pandemics didn't even make the top ten. Or earlier, in the 2007 report, while "Asset Price Collapse" was highlighted as a top risk, cascading bank failures and global recession were nowhere to be found. This follows a typical pattern in the risk management industry, echoing President Dwight D. Eisenhower's prescient warning that "plans are worthless, but planning is everything." See World Economic Forum, "The Global Risks Report 2020," January 2020, www.weforum.org/publications/the-global-risks-report-2020; World Economic Forum, "Global Risks 2007: A Global Risk Network Report," January 2007, www3.weforum.org/docs/WEF_Global_Risks_Report_2007.pdf; Dwight D. Eisenhower, "Remarks at the National Defense Executive Reserve Conference," November 14, 1947, American Presidency Project, University of California, Santa Barbara, www.presidency.ucsb.edu/documents/remarks-the-national-defense-executive-reserve-conference.

12. Kelin E. Gersick, John A. Davis, Marion McCollom Hampton, and Ivan Lansberg, *Generation to Generation: Life Cycles of the Family Business* (Boston: Harvard Business School Press, 1997).

13. When helping families map out the three concentric circles of risk, we are often reminded of a famous paper written by Charles Schultze, then director of the economic studies program at the Brookings Institution and former chair of the Council of Economic Advisors under President Jimmy Carter. Schultze was advocating for fiscal balance, if not outright constraint. In an essay for the Brookings Institution, he argued that it wasn't the "wolf at the door" (i.e., imminent economic crisis), but rather the "termites in the walls" (i.e., long-term economic stagnation), that should motivate us to pursue fiscal prudence. Charles Schultze, "Of Wolves, Termites, and Pussycats: Or, Why We Should Worry About the Budget Deficit," *Brookings Review* 7, no. 3 (1989): 26–33.

14. The stabilizing strategies can be effective here as well. For instance, symbiosis is an obvious way to manage political risks (think Samsung), diversity a natural antidote to asset concentration (think Tata), and modularity an antidote to succession challenges (think Zamil). Importantly, when left unattended, these risks often become the unforced errors of continuity planning—as in Kongō Gumi's demoralizing collapse under the weight of excessive leverage, after forty successful generations of family stewardship.

15. Generally speaking, those who operate in frontier economies are more tolerant of risk than those in advanced economies out of necessity, since many of the risks are more prevalent in them. Recall how Hunter S. Thompson criticized advanced societies for their tedious stability. Of course, there are plenty of ways to take on additional risk in affluent societies—from complex financial products and entrepreneurial startups to casinos and

heli-skiing. But clearly those living and leading in New York, London, and Berlin have a broader spectrum of choice with respect to how much risk they want in their lives. Living in an advanced economy allows them to set the dial with greater agency and intention.

16. Instead, we found that most related research focuses on the aggregated behaviors of individuals—what some who study behavioral finance describe as our "animal spirits." This term was originally coined by John Maynard Keynes in 1936 to describe the emotions and instincts that guide human behavior in economic decisions. These emotions and instincts ultimately can affect the aggregate confidence of consumers and investors, leading to decisions that can drive economic cycles. But nearly a century later, these early ideas have produced few breakthroughs in our understanding of how groups of related stakeholders can make better decisions about risk *together*. John Maynard Keynes, *The General Theory of Employment, Interest and Money* (New York: Harcourt, Brace, 1936).

17. For instance, in family companies founders and operators are often more confident in their capacity to manage risk than family shareholders not in management, who are less directly involved. Similarly, those with a steady income or with a large nest egg outside the business may be more inclined to take on additional risk than those whose livelihoods depend exclusively on the success of a shared enterprise, or who have been traumatized by past losses or crises.

18. In emerging and frontier economies, the distribution may be skewed a little to the right. In advanced economies, it often skews further to the left. But the shape of the bell curve is remarkably universal.

19. In our work with families, we often develop a simple age distribution table that allows them to estimate how many next-gen members of the family are likely to enter their college years simultaneously (requiring that more liquidity be made available), or how many seniors might be entering their retirement years (again requiring more liquidity), or how fast the business will need to grow if the family aspires to replicate a similar level of lifestyle expenditures across generations.

20. In our experience, achieving this strategic alignment is impossible without actively engaging all key stakeholders in conversations about the future. This naturally requires conversations about opportunities to pursue and threats to be managed.

21. Think of governance as a risk management exercise in anticipating generic risks and designing mechanisms for effective oversight. Employment policies are an excellent example of a governance tool for managing the common risk of nepotism. Similarly, a dividend policy is a tool for managing the risk of shareholder disputes over liquidity. While such policies are critical, their effectiveness hinges on the ability to have useful governance forums to oversee their implementation. So policies and agreements are necessary, but on their own insufficient, to manage these risks.

CHAPTER 14: BUILDING AN ENDURING ENTERPRISE

1. Additionally, as we learned in Chapter 6, the open infrastructure and common protocols that enabled telegraph networks to grow so exponentially also laid the groundwork for all future communications infrastructure—including technologies such as the telephone and the internet, which would redefine information sharing on a global scale.

2. Jake Rossen, "'Please Tell Me Your Problem': Remembering ELIZA, the Pioneering '60s Chatbot," Mental Floss, February 14, 2023, www.mentalfloss.com/posts/eliza-chatbot-history.

3. The first successful conquest was the defeat of world chess champion Garry Kasparov by IBM's Deep Blue in 1997. Then, over a decade later, IBM's Watson easily beat two of *Jeopardy*'s greatest champions, Ken Jennings and Brad Rutter, over a three-day tournament in 2011. In 2016, DeepMind's AlphaGo defeated world champion Lee Sedol in Go—notable because at the time Go was considered to be a game beyond the capacity of computer mastery.

4. Orianna Rosa Royle, "Bill Gates Teases the Possibility of a 3-Day Work Week Where 'Machines Can Make All the Food and Stuff,'" *Fortune*, November 23, 2023, finance.yahoo.com/news/bill-gates-teases-possibility-3-121847610.html. For additional context on the military applications and implications of AI, see Jeremy Hsu, "AI Chatbots Tend to Choose Violence and Nuclear Strikes in Wargames," *New Scientist*, February 2, 2024, www.newscientist.com/article/2415488-ai-chatbots-tend-to-choose-violence-and-nuclear-strikes-in-wargames; Noah Bressner, "Pentagon Stares Down 'Drone Swarm' Threat," Axios, March 15, 2024, www.axios.com/2024/03/15/drone-swarms-ai-military-war; and Amy J. Nelson and Gerald L. Epstein, "The PLA's Strategic Support Force and AI Innovation," Brookings Institution, December 23, 2022, www.brookings.edu/articles/the-plas-strategic-support-force-and-ai-innovation-china-military-tech.

5. See Yuval Noah Harari, *Homo Deus: A Brief History of Tomorrow* (New York: HarperCollins, 2017).

6. Bryce Quillin, "Changing Global Demographics: The Certain Future," OpenMind BBVA, October 14, 2019, www.bbvaopenmind.com/en/economy/global-economy/changing-global-demographics-the-certain-future.

7. Lynda Gratton and Andrew Scott, *The 100 Year Life: Living and Working in an Age of Longevity* (London: Bloomsbury, 2016).

8. *Akiya* is a term in Japanese that literally translates to "empty house." It refers to the phenomenon of abandoned homes, particularly in rural areas of Japan, where the population is shrinking most quickly. In the coming years, it's expected that Japan will have around 11 million *akiya* homes, and by 2038, nearly one-third of Japan's homes could be vacant. See Natsuno Otahara, "Overseas Interest Rises for Japan's Abundance of Vacant Homes," *Asahi Shimbun*, January 25, 2024, www.asahi.com/ajw/articles/15112746.

9. Zoe Caplan, "U.S. Older Population Grew from 2010 to 2020 at Fastest Rate Since 1880 to 1890," US Census Bureau, May 25, 2023, www.census.gov/library/stories/2023/05/2020-census-united-states-older-population-grew.html.

10. China presents perhaps the biggest systemic risk, given the immense size of its population, its critical role in global supply chains, and the lingering effects of the country's half-century experiment with a "one-child policy." Other countries with low fertility rates, such as Taiwan and South Korea, will be close behind.

11. Josh Funk, "Charlie Munger, Warren Buffet's Longtime Sidekick at Berkshire Hathaway, Dies at 99," *Time*, November 28, 2023, https://time.com/6340572/charlie-munger-death-obituary.

12. James B. Stewart and Rachel Abrams, *Unscripted: The Epic Battle for a Media Empire and the Redstone Family Legacy* (New York: Penguin, 2023).

13. Krishnadev Calamur, "What Did the Arab Spring Cost? One Estimate Says $800 Billion," Parallels, NPR, October 12, 2013, www.npr.org/sections/parallels/2013/10/12/232128320/what-did-the-arab-spring-cost-one-estimate-says-800-billion.

14. The United Nations estimated in 2020 that 300 million migrants were living in a country other than their motherland. Roughly 50 million had settled in the United

States, and another 16 million in Germany, where numbers have quadrupled since 1970. Interactive World Migration Report 2022, United Nations International Organization for Migration (IOM), 2021, worldmigrationreport.iom.int/wmr-2022-interactive.

15. Donald Trump's bombastic campaign to build a wall along America's southern border provides a natural illustration of the broader dilemma. Political pageantry, opportunism, and overt racism aside, at its heart the border fence is about protecting domestic jobs.

16. Georg Simmel, "The Sociology of Secrecy and of Secret Societies," *American Journal of Sociology* 11 (1906): 450.

17. See "2024 Edelman Trust Barometer," Edelman, accessed June 1, 2024, www.edelman.com/trust/2024/trust-barometer.

18. Jonathan Haidt, "The Smartphone Kids Are Not All Right," *The Atlantic*, March 21, 2024, www.theatlantic.com/podcasts/archive/2024/03/smartphone-anxious-generation-mental-health/677817.

19. Consider that in business, a growing population of customers is typically a blessing, generating greater opportunity, impact, and profit. But for public institutions, particularly in large cities where many immigrants are forced to settle, greater demand is often a curse. When constituents are growing faster than infrastructure, you are destined to disappoint.

20. This includes many of the world's largest and most fragile democracies, where authoritarian leaders seem destined to make significant inroads—most notably the United States, but also India, Indonesia, Mexico, South Africa, Taiwan, Venezuela, and Britain. In many ways, as of the time of this writing, the future of liberal democracy is hanging in the balance. See Enda Curran and Alan Crawford, "Brace for Elections: 40 Countries Are Voting in 2024," Bloomberg, October 31, 2023, www.bloomberg.com/news/articles/2023-11-01/brace-for-elections-40-countries-are-voting-in-2024.

21. "2023 Edelman Trust Barometer: Global Report," Edelman Trust Barometer, 2023, www.edelman.com/sites/g/files/aatuss191/files/2023-03/2023%20Edelman%20Trust%20Barometer%20Global%20Report%20FINAL.pdf; Isobel Finkel, "The World Risks Sliding into a New Global War," Bloomberg, December 1, 2023, www.bloomberg.com/news/newsletters/2023-12-01/the-world-risks-sliding-into-a-new-global-war.

22. "World GDP 1960–2024," Macro Trends, accessed June 1, 2024, www.macrotrends.net/global-metrics/countries/WLD/world/gdp-gross-domestic-product.

23. Eswar Prasad and Isaac Sorkin, "Assessing the G-20 Stimulus Plans: A Deeper Look," Brookings Institution, March 5, 2009, www.brookings.edu/articles/assessing-the-g-20-stimulus-plans-a-deeper-look.

24. Christopher J. Neely, "Lessons from the Taper Tantrum," *Economic Synopses*, no. 2 (2014), https://research.stlouisfed.org/publications/economic-synopses/2014/01/28/lessons-from-the-taper-tantrum.

25. "Global Debt Is at $307 Trillion. Why Does It Matter?," World Economic Forum, December 21, 2023, www.weforum.org/agenda/2023/12/what-is-global-debt-why-high.

26. M. Ayhan Kose and Franziska Ohnsorge, "Global Economy's Speed Limit Set to Fall to Three-Decade Low," World Bank, April 19, 2023, www.worldbank.org/en/news/press-release/2023/03/27/global-economy-s-speed-limit-set-to-fall-to-three-decade-low.

27. International Debt Report 2023, World Bank, December 2023, www.worldbank.org/en/programs/debt-statistics/idr/products.

28. Ferguson continued, "True of Hapsburg Spain, true of *ancien régime* France, true of the Ottoman Empire, true of the British Empire, this law is about to be put to the

test by the US beginning this very year, when (according to the CBO) net interest outlays will be 3.1% of GDP, defense spending 3.0%." Niall Ferguson, "The Second Cold War Is Escalating Faster Than the First," Bloomberg, April 20, 2024, www.bloomberg.com/opinion/articles/2024-04-21/china-russia-iran-axis-is-bad-news-for-trump-and-gop-isolationists.

29. Nearly 4,000 years ago, the Babylonian king Hammurabi declared four separate "debt jubilees"—or the canceling of all debts—at moments when excessive lending and borrowing threatened the peace and stability of his empire. See John Bringardner, "A Robin Hood for the Debt Crisis?," *New Yorker*, November 26, 2013, www.newyorker.com/business/currency/a-robin-hood-for-the-debt-crisis. Also Merryn Somerset Webb, "Sound the Trumpet! Debt Jubilees Have Arrived," *Financial Times*, May 29, 2020, www.ft.com/content/fb2c1718-a193-11ea-94c2-0526869b56b0.

30. Hedge fund titan Ray Dalio highlighted this dynamic in his recent macroeconomic research, arguing that "money and credit are stimulative when they're given out and depressing when they have to be paid back. That's what normally makes money, credit, and economic growth so cyclical." See Ray Dalio, "Where We Are in the Big Cycle of Money, Credit, Debt, and Economic Activity and the Changing Value of Money," LinkedIn, February 15, 2022, www.linkedin.com/pulse/where-we-big-cycle-money-credit-debt-economic-activity-ray-dalio.

31. It is precisely this additional escalation of volatility that we need to track closely. History warns us that when unsustainable debt burdens are coupled with economic shocks or policy disruptions, they have an alarming tendency to spread into wider financial contagions and severe recessions. In a famous speech from 1955, a former chairman of the Federal Reserve, William McChesney Martin, warned specifically about an excessive reliance on debt-fueled stimulus. "If we fail to apply the brakes sufficiently and in time, of course, we shall go over the cliff. If businessmen, bankers, your contemporaries in the business and financial world, stay on the sidelines, concerned only with making profits, letting the Government bear all of the responsibility and the burden of guidance of the economy, we shall surely fail," he said. "Those who have the task of making such policy don't expect you to applaud. The Federal Reserve, as one writer put it, after the recent increase in the discount rate, is in the position of the chaperone who has ordered the punch bowl removed just when the party was really warming up." William McChesney Martin Jr., "Address Before the New York Group of the Investment Bankers Association of America," Fraser, October 19, 1955, www.fraser.stlouisfed.org/title/statements-speeches-william-mcchesney-martin-jr-448/address-new-york-group-investment-bankers-association-america-7800.

32. "Making Debt Work for Development and Macroeconomic Stability," International Monetary Fund, April 26, 2022, www.imf.org/en/Publications/Policy-Papers/Issues/2022/04/26/Making-Debt-Work-For-Development-and-Macroeconomic-Stability-517258.

33. Consider the Earth-2 supercomputer (E-2)—a bleeding-edge initiative by NVIDIA, maker of the world's most sophisticated AI processors. The company's goal is to use this system to create a digital twin of the Earth, then make it available to scientists to model out complex cause-and-effect relationships in planetary systems that would have been impossible to even contemplate a few short years ago. Jensen Huang, "NVIDIA to Build Earth-2 Supercomputer to See Our Future," *NVIDIA Blog*, November 12, 2021, https://blogs.nvidia.com/blog/earth-2-supercomputer.

34. Amrith Ramkumar, "Climate Change's $150 Billion Hit to the U.S. Economy," *Wall Street Journal*, November 14, 2023, www.wsj.com/science/environment/climate-change-us-economy-c9fbda96.

35. "Severe Drought Is Constraining the Panama Canal," *The Economist*, November 23, 2023, www.economist.com/the-americas/2023/11/23/severe-drought-is-constraining-the-panama-canal.

36. "Climate Change Is an Increasing Threat to Africa," United Nations Framework Convention on Climate Change (UNFCCC), October 27, 2020, https://unfccc.int/news/climate-change-is-an-increasing-threat-to-africa.

37. Ebru Kirezci, Ian R. Young, Roshanka Ranasinghe, Sanne Muis, Robert J. Nicholls, Daniel Lincke, and Jochen Hinkel, "Projections of Global-Scale Extreme Sea Levels and Resulting Episodic Coastal Flooding over the 21st Century," *Scientific Reports* 10, Article no. 11629 (2020), www.nature.com/articles/s41598-020-67736-6.

38. The McKinsey Global Institute has estimated that US$143 trillion in investment will be needed worldwide to support decarbonization and electrification efforts. That represents roughly US$9 trillion to US$12 trillion in annual investments by 2030. These massive economic incentives have become a new gold rush for companies and countries around the world. "Playing Offense to Create Value in the Net-Zero Transition," *McKinsey Quarterly*, April 13, 2022, www.mckinsey.com/capabilities/sustainability/our-insights/playing-offense-to-create-value-in-the-net-zero-transition.

39. Interestingly, those who felt they *were* well prepared generated 50 percent higher total shareholder returns than their peers, based on their performance during the 2020–2021 pandemic recovery.

40. McKinsey and Company, "The State of Organizations 2023," 2023, www.mckinsey.com/~/media/mckinsey/business%20functions/people%20and%20organizational%20performance/our%20insights/the%20state%20of%20organizations%202023/the-state-of-organizations-2023.pdf, 11.

41. Nouriel Roubini, *Megathreats: Ten Dangerous Trends That Imperil Our Future, and How to Survive Them* (New York: Little Brown, 2022).

42. Decision-makers are asked to imagine two potential future outcomes of a given course of action: one an extraordinary success and the other a catastrophic failure. The group then splits into two teams, one to explore each of these two outcomes, and ultimately reconvenes to share and integrate their conclusions. Discussing these possibilities, first separately and then together, encourages more critical thinking and contingency planning, ultimately leading to more informed and well-rounded decisions. See Daniel Kahneman and Gary Klein, "Strategic Decisions: When Can You Trust Your Gut?," McKinsey and Company, March 1, 2010, www.mckinsey.com/capabilities/strategy-and-corporate-finance/our-insights/strategic-decisions-when-can-you-trust-your-gut.

43. "Nobel Laureate Daniel Kahneman—Premortem to Eliminate Thinking Biases," YouTube, posted by Imaginarium, December 29, 2014, www.youtube.com/watch?v=MzTNMalfyhM. See also Daniel Kahneman, *Thinking, Fast and Slow* (New York: Farrar, Straus and Giroux, 2011); Gary Klein, "Performing a Project Premortem," *Harvard Business Review* 85, no. 9 (2007): 18–19.

44. Rudyard Kipling, "If—," in *A Choice of Kipling's Verse* (New York: Charles Scribner's Sons, 1943) (paraphrase).

45. Martin Reeves, Saumeet Nanda, Kevin Whitaker, and Edzard Wesselink, "Becoming an All-Weather Company," Boston Consulting Group, September 9, 2020, www.bcg.com/publications/2020/how-to-become-an-all-weather-resilient-company.

46. Roger L. Martin, *When More Is Not Better: Overcoming America's Obsession with Economic Efficiency* (Cambridge, MA: Harvard Business Review Press, 2020).

47. See Fred Edward Fiedler, *A Contingency Model of Leadership Effectiveness* (Urbana: Group Effectiveness Research Laboratory, University of Illinois, 1963); Victor H. Vroom and Philip W. Yetton, *Leadership and Decision Making* (Pittsburgh: University of Pittsburgh Press, 1973); Victor H. Vroom and Arthur G. Jago, *The New Leadership: Managing Participation in Organizations* (Englewood Cliffs, NJ: Prentice Hall, 1988).

48. The theory also suggests that effective leaders learn to read their circumstances and adopt the behaviors needed depending on such factors as the time they have to respond, the extent to which they have the information needed to make the right decision, and the degree to which the decision requires the buy-in of subordinates in order to be successfully implemented.

49. G. Michael Hopf, *Those Who Remain* (self-pub., 2016). Interestingly, this also speaks to the problems that succeeding generations have with nepotism, and growing up in abundance and wealth.

50. Devin DeCiantis and Ivan Lansberg, "What Family Businesses Need to Adapt to a Crisis," *Harvard Business Review*, May 7, 2020, https://hbr.org/2020/05/what-family-businesses-need-to-adapt-to-a-crisis.

51. Ivan Lansberg and Kelin Gersick, "Educating Family Business Owners: The Fundamental Intervention," *Academy of Management Learning and Education* 14, no. 3 (2015): 400–413.

52. Craig E. Aronoff and John L. Ward, *Family Business Ownership: How to Be an Effective Shareholder* (New York: Palgrave Macmillan, 2016). See also Wendy Sage-Hayward, Gaia Marchisio, and Barbara Dartt, *Own It! How to Develop a Family Enterprise Owner's Mindset at Every Age* (New York: Palgrave Macmillan, 2022).

53. For families (or individual members) choosing to trade their legacy assets for a fresh entrepreneurial start, the results are decidedly mixed. While some family owners are successful at redeploying their inheritance and building substantial new enterprises, rarely do we see these inherited businesses match the scale and success of those who stay committed to the continuity of the original enterprise. Of course, this still requires thoughtful stewardship and learning to govern effectively.

54. Froma Walsh, *Strengthening Family Resilience*, 3rd ed. (New York: Guilford Press, 2016), 39.

55. One family we worked with in Indonesia hired a children's writer and illustrator to create an ongoing series of books documenting the family's legacy. The grandmother gets the books printed and shares them with her grandchildren. The stories are themed around specific anecdotes, depicting how the family responded to a wide array of challenges that tested their fundamental values—such as hard work, humility, filial piety, gratitude, and collaboration—and provides an accessible source of inspiration whenever uncertainty spikes and adversity looms.

56. Jean-Jacques Rousseau, *The Social Contract and Discourses*, trans. and ed. G. D. H. Cole (London: J. M. Dent and Sons, 1923), chap. 4.

57. Ivan Lansberg and Edith Perrow, "Understanding and Working with Leading Family Businesses in Latin America," *Family Business Review* 4, no. 2 (1981): 127–147.

58. This problem is most pronounced when a portion of the family lives abroad, and sending dividends overseas compromises resources needed to protect and expand the business at home. Expats are often quick to counter that it is their capital at risk, and that returns ought to be commensurate with these risks. In the absence of effective governance, these well-documented "agency" tensions often simmer below the surface, and they can easily boil over into outright conflict.

59. This chronic struggle between "I and we" often sparks its own conflicts, especially as children reach their adolescent years. Some refuse to follow the rules around personal safety and actively evade bodyguards. Others misbehave in school, or stay out late, violating curfews. Still others may post information about the family that compromises privacy and exposes the family to additional security risks.

60. David Brooks, "How to Stay Sane in Brutalizing Times," *New York Times*, November 2, 2023, www.nytimes.com/2023/11/02/opinion/sunday/resilience-bad-news-coping.html.

61. Paul Poast, "Not a World War but a World at War," *Atlantic*, November 17, 2023, www.theatlantic.com/international/archive/2023/11/conflicts-around-the-world-peak/676029.

62. As the UAE's minister of the economy, Abdulla bin Touq al Marri, shared during a meeting in May 2024 with potential global investors in New York City, "When we pitch the UAE, we pitch openness, we pitch stability, we pitch visionary leadership. Stability is a key part, given that we are in the eye of the storm. It has been stable for the last 50 years, and will be stable for the next 200 years." Abdulla bin Touq al Marri, interview with Liz Hoffman, Semafor, 2024, www.semafor.com/newsletter/05/23/2024/uae-economy-minister-pitches-western-investors-on-stability.

APPENDIX 2: PSYCHOLOGY OF RISK

1. Amos Tversky and Daniel Kahneman, "The Psychology of Preferences," *Scientific American* 246, no. 1 (1982): 160–173.

INDEX

Page numbers followed by (fig.) and (table) refer to figures and tables, respectively.

Credit: Courtesy of the author

Devin DeCiantis is the managing partner at Lansberg Gersick Advisors (LGA), a trusted advisory and educational partner to the world's leading family enterprises. Raised in Toronto, Canada, he holds a master's degree from the Harvard Kennedy School with a focus in finance and economics, as well as a bachelor's in business administration from York University. He has worked with private- and public-sector leaders throughout the Americas, Europe, the Middle East, and Asia and has taught about family enterprise at Harvard University, Yale University, and the Kellogg School of Management at Northwestern University. His writing has also been featured in *Harvard Business Review*, *The Atlantic*, and *The Walrus*.

Credit: Courtesy of the author

Ivan Lansberg is the co-founder at LGA, where he advises complex family enterprises worldwide. Over the last four decades, he has made significant contributions to the understanding of family business governance and succession. He was one of the founders of the Family Firm Institute (FFI) and the first editor of its professional journal, *Family Business Review*.

After receiving bachelor's, master's, and doctoral degrees from Columbia University, Lansberg taught at the Columbia Graduate School of Business. He became a professor of organizational behavior at the Yale School of Organization and Management for seven years before going into consulting. His books *Succeeding Generations* and *Generation to Generation* were both published by Harvard Business School Press and have been widely praised as landmark works.

Lansberg is a frequent speaker at family business programs organized by universities and industry groups. He is on the faculty of the Kellogg School of Management.

PublicAffairs is a publishing house founded in 1997. It is a tribute to the standards, values, and flair of three persons who have served as mentors to countless reporters, writers, editors, and book people of all kinds, including me.

I. F. Stone, proprietor of *I. F. Stone's Weekly*, combined a commitment to the First Amendment with entrepreneurial zeal and reporting skill and became one of the great independent journalists in American history. At the age of eighty, Izzy published *The Trial of Socrates*, which was a national bestseller. He wrote the book after he taught himself ancient Greek.

Benjamin C. Bradlee was for nearly thirty years the charismatic editorial leader of *The Washington Post*. It was Ben who gave the *Post* the range and courage to pursue such historic issues as Watergate. He supported his reporters with a tenacity that made them fearless and it is no accident that so many became authors of influential, best-selling books.

Robert L. Bernstein, the chief executive of Random House for more than a quarter century, guided one of the nation's premier publishing houses. Bob was personally responsible for many books of political dissent and argument that challenged tyranny around the globe. He is also the founder and longtime chair of Human Rights Watch, one of the most respected human rights organizations in the world.

• • •

For fifty years, the banner of Public Affairs Press was carried by its owner Morris B. Schnapper, who published Gandhi, Nasser, Toynbee, Truman, and about 1,500 other authors. In 1983, Schnapper was described by *The Washington Post* as "a redoubtable gadfly." His legacy will endure in the books to come.

Peter Osnos, *Founder*